Books by the Same Author

- Business Ethics & Managerial Values
- Management of Change & OD
- New Compensation Management
- Business Ethics and Corporate Governance
- Training and Development
- International HRM
- Managing Cultural Diversity
- Constructive Industrial Relations and Labour Laws
- International Practices in Industrial Relations
- HRM: Competitive Advantage
- Performance Management
- Non-profit Organisations
- Team Leadership
- Strategic Human Resource Management

Forthcoming

- New Horizons in Management
- Managing Organisation Behaviour
- Winning Teams

MANAGEMENT OF NON-PROFIT ORGANISATIONS

TOWARDS PROFESSIONALLY MANAGING OF SOCIETIES AND A HANDBOOK FOR GOVERNANCE OF VOLUNTARY AGENCIES

S.K. BHATIA
Director
Human Resource Management Foundation, New Delhi
and
Senior Faculty,
Business Management Institutes

Formerly:
- Director (Personnel), Oil India Ltd.
- Director (Pers. and PR), Mekaster Group Co's.
- Add. General Manager (Pers. and Admn.) Bharat Heavy Electricals India Ltd.

Foreword by

DR. (PROF.) M. ADHIKARY
Director
New Delhi Institute of Management
Former Dean, FMS, University of Delhi

DEEP & DEEP PUBLICATIONS PVT. LTD.
F-159, Rajouri Garden, New Delhi-110027

MANAGEMENT OF NON-PROFIT ORGANISATIONS

TOWARDS PROFESSIONALLY MANAGING OF SOCIETIES

ISBN 978-81-8450-010-3

Typeset by S.S. COMPOSERS,
3190, Mohindra Park, Shakur Basti, Delhi-110034.

Printed in India at NEW ELEGANT PRINTERS,
A-38/2, Maya Puri, Phase-I, New Delhi-110064.

Published by DEEP & DEEP PUBLICATIONS PVT. LTD.,
F-159, Rajouri Garden, New Delhi-110027.
Phones: 25435369, 25440916
E-mail: ddpbooks@yahoo.co.in • deep98@del3.vsnl.net.in
Sales Showroom:
2/13, Ansari Road, Daryaganj, New Delhi-110002 • Telefax: 23245122

Dedicated to my wife

KUSUM

for her infinite patience,

understanding and inspiration

Contents

PART VI

ENVIRONMENT CONTEXT

PART VII

ANNEXURES

Foreword

In recent days, there is an enormous growth of non-profit organisations, such as—welfare societies, charities, private foundations, etc., all over the world. They are gaining importance as all aim to add to the quality of life of selected segments of society. Non-profit organisations perform a pivotal role in economic growth and development of the community. Their role in education (schools, training, research, consultation, national resources conservation) and community services (health services, social services, recreation, libraries, arts) are instrumental in supplying capital and critical input for certain community populations. Non-profit organisations (NPOs) contribute to the community by stimulating employment, income and social output and also developing a better skilled manpower service.

NPOs are now in position to get better contributions from donors either in India or NRI's abroad, and through NPOs ties with leading commercial organisations. All Non-profit organisations are human 'change agents', as their product is a changed human being.

Another lot of organisations, the NGOs in India are wide spectrum of organisations which may be non-governmental, quasi or semi-government, voluntary or non-voluntary, non-profit or profit-oriented bodies, with legal status and registered under special Acts (like section 25 of Companies Act, 1956, Societies Registration Act, or Indian Trusts Acts, etc.). However, of late the process of commercialization of social institutions has set in. Some of these voluntary organisations are being misused as a medium of diverting public money for personal gains in the disguise of charity, gaining publicity, attaining high status, etc. Because of certain reasons and sad experiences, people are losing faith in these institutions and hesitate in giving donations to them. NGOs should wake up to conscience and work with full devotion for the objectives of the society. This requires self-introspection. Certain changes which NPOs and NGOs need to make can include:

(i) Keeping their expenditure on their salary, conveyance, overhead to be at bare minimum such that money meant for public benefit should be used most judiciously,

(ii) Playing an active role in removing various social evils from our society—they can make protests against any unjust or unlawful practice.

(iii) As today there is stronger emphasis on "doing well" while "doing good", all voluntary organisations also need management practices all the more, because they do not have a conventional "bottom line". NPOs to make certain changes in their operations such as remain focused on achieving mission and objectives, introduce better planning process for their project implementation, apply latest concepts and techniques of managerial **marketing** and financial controls. Another area of management to be considered is performance control and feed-back which can help in improving the implementation of projects. It is also necessary to devise a new criterion for performance evaluation of NPOs as it is not judged by the yardstick of profits.

(iv) Another critical aspect requiring attention is style of leadership prevailing in NPOs seems to be marked by centralized power and decision-making with lack of adequate information sharing and delegation. This calls for a change in culture of transparency, communication networking, team-working and maintaining ethical standards in organisational and personal values. Thus, adoption of various management practices can enable NPOs to optimize the utilization of their resources; and that infact is the theme of this book.

My congratulations to Mr. S.K. Bhatia on his thoughtful endeavour and contribution on the subject of 'Management of the Non-profit Organisations', a subject which is fast growing in welfare state. The book has a very comprehensive coverage, and I am sure, that it will serve as a concise guide on wide range of concepts that are relevant in the context of non-profit organisations. I have no doubts that as a pioneering Indian book on the subject it will be very useful to students, teachers and practicing managers in non-profit organisations.

DR. (PROF.) M. ADHIKARY
Director
New Delhi Institute of Management
Former Dean, FMS, University of Delhi

Preface

The non-profit organisations are central in our Indian society as they are engaged in all major social tasks and are supplementing governmental programmes. There are various forms of non-profit institutions, e.g. NGOs, charitable trusts, social setups, etc.

Non-profit institutions are human change agents. Their product is a changed human being (Peter F. Drucker). Their "product" is a cured patient, a child that learns, developed young men or women into a self-respecting adult, and a changed human life altogether.

Non-profit institutions need management all the more because they do not have a conventional "bottom line". They need to learn how to use management as their tool so that they can concentrate on their mission and objectives. With this in view, this book contains different role for leadership and innovative concepts in management for success of non-profit institutions. There is 'management boom' in non-profit institutions.

The objective of this book is to share introduction to the concept of non-profit organisations. It addresses the key areas of functioning for non-profit organisations, from clarifying the concept of non-profit organisation and to pursue the mission and then to manage such type of organisation.

In nutshell purpose of this volume is to:

- Elaborate the importance and formation of non-profit organisation.
- Pursuing the mission.
- Managing the organisation.
- Controlling and evaluating the performance of NPO.

Requirements of Good Governance of NPO

(i) It requires a vision and mission.
(ii) Result orientation.
(iii) Increasing the accountability, transparency in all processes which means having an efficient transparent and open system.
(iv) Decentralised organisation operation.
(v) From a control orientation to community empowerment.

Coverage of this book

1. Understanding non-profit organisation

(i) What are non-profit organisations, some special categories, why are the NPOs different, non-profit operations of commercial organisation, the dilemma of non-profit organisation, applicability of management practices, limitations of known management practices.
(ii) Defining mission statement, criteria for objectives, and long-term planning for non-profit organisations, the need for planning of measurable targets.
(iii) Defining the need and the beneficiary.
(iv) Marketing for welfare organisation's need of marketing activities and its significance to non-profit organisation.

2. Pursuing the mission

(i) Market research, why non-profit organisations need market research.
(ii) Test marketing, the practice and its rationale, pricing the service as a testing device.
(iii) Public relations/external communications programmes.
(iv) Client feedback and follow-up for non-profit organisations.
(v) Basic measurement criteria such as results, measurement of activity, human development indicators, and other considerations.

3. Managing the organisation

(a) Hiring and retaining staff, problems of staffing in NPO, sources of manpower in NPO.
(b) Human relations management, i.e. interacting with groups of people, employee relations, succession planning, formal appraisal and counselling, interactions with other groups.
(c) A perpetual quest for donations, donor base and support networks.
(d) Understanding differences in finance function in a commercial organisation and finance function in a non-profit organisation. Sources of funds, outflow of funds, understanding financial statements and types of financial statements.
(e) Different types of costing practices for management purposes, i.e. standard costs, cost of capital employed, differential costs.
(f) Various types of budgets, budgetary controls, performance controls of NPO, appraisal and counselling programmes.

There are hardly few books on 'managing the non-profit organisations'. This volume covers comprehensively various concepts in management of non-profit institutions. I hope readers, students, faculties as well as employees and leaders will find a knowledgeable resource for improving effectiveness of their non-profit institutions.

New Delhi

S.K. BHATIA

Acknowledgements

Text books for educational purpose are a team project. While my name is on the cover of this book, literally, it is combined contribution of the writings of so many scholars and authors from whose distinguished works, ideas and valuable contributions have enabled me in completion of this book. As far as possible, I have tried to include their names and publication in each chapter and list of references. Every effort has been made to gratefully acknowledge them, but if any have been inadvertently overlooked, I crave their indulgence. I shall make necessary arrangement to acknowledge at the first opportunity.

Some articles were collected from various sources—newspapers, seminars, magazines and text books, during long years of service and used as teaching material. Unfortunately, these sources were not noted and it is impractical to offer acknowledgements. I express my thanks to those who contributed anonymously to this book.

I am immensely grateful to Prof. Late Peter F. Drucker, who is known world over as "The Dean" of the business and management philosophers. I have quoted few extracts from his book titled "Managing Non-profit Organisation", 1990 by Harper Collins Publishers for having clear understanding and appreciation of this subject. My thanks.

I am immensely grateful to my son, Neeraj and daughter-in-law Pulkit, in USA, who not only arranged my study visit to USA, but also helped in arranging the literature on the subject, from various sources. Company of little Arunika and playful Arjun made my study tour more lively and interesting. I thank my wife for her unfailing support and encouragement throughout this project.

I am grateful to Dr. M. Adhikary, Former Director, New Delhi Institute of Management and Dean, FMS, University of Delhi for writing a brilliant and learned foreword for this book.

Finally and most important my daughter's family Namita, her husband Atul, loving children Malvika and Geetka in UK for learning, inspiration and joy.

I thank Deep & Deep Publications Pvt. Ltd. for managing the book into its final form.

New Delhi

S.K. BHATIA

PART I

NON-PROFIT ORGANISATIONS: PERSPECTIVES

CHAPTER

1

Introduction: Role and Significance of Non-profit Organisations (NPOs)

1. NPOs: A THIRD SECTOR

Non-profit organisations (NPOs)/Non-government Organisations (NGOs) have emerged as one of largest sector after government and private organisations. Now NPOs/NGOs sector is known as third sector. It is growing fast. NPOs are also very large sector aboard particularly in United States of America.

Peter Drucker, the world's most influential management thinker, a guru, an international legend, a business icon, has termed Non-profit organisations as 'Third Industry'. We quote his views:

> "I have been saying that the organisation is not limited to the business world. I have been trying to show of the so-called "Third Industry," made of non-profit organisations and public service, as incubators of independence and diversity, as keepers of values and a source of leadership in civil society."
>
> "The understanding that the growth areas of 20th century in developed countries were linked to the business world. There were others : governments, liberal professions, health, education, areas where good management is dramatically lacking. The most promising area in the 21st century will be the non-profit social industry."

2. CHARACTERISTICS OF NPOs

Non-profit organisations are voluntary, organised by citizens on a local, national or international level. Some *important features* are that: (a) they are supposed to be independent from government, (b) their organisations are *not meant for profit*, (c) they are expected to be *"value-based"*, and (d) are set-up to *serve public/social purpose*. In fact they aim to *add quality of life* of selected segments of society and are *"human change agents"* as termed by Peter F. Drucker. Their governance structure must *preclude self-interest* and *private financial gain*. They have *great flexibility* in operations. They are involved in *numerous activities*.

3. LARGE PRESTIGIOUS SECTOR

Some statistical data about NGOs in India for 2002-03 is mentioned to appreciate their largeness:

(i) Number of NGOs 1.2 million.
(ii) Amount of foreign contribution received: Rs. 5047 crores.
(iii) Large amount is received from Ministry of Home Affairs and donor countries such as USA, Germany, UK and Ford Foundation, UN organisations, etc.
(iv) Largest amount spent by NGOs is for establishment expenses (Rs. 674 crores) which tops the list, followed by rural development (Rs. 487 crores) and construction and maintenance of schools and colleges (Rs. 275 crores).
(v) Employment figure is 19.4 million in NGOs as compared to nearly 20 million in government—central, state and local bodies.

The enormous size of this voluntary sector can further be imagined. In USA about fifty percent of adult people volunteer their time to NPOs. These organisations range from large universities with assets in billions of dollars to small volunteer, community-based units.

In India, also, so called charitable foundations or trusts are the country's richest source of financial assets : Mission leaders such as bishops, swamis, maulanas, monks are touring world over for expansion of their following, etc. Similarly, presidents/chair-persons of voluntary social bodies are enjoying enormous social prestige and fame. They have in away become vote-banks for politicians.

4. SOME DEFICIENCIES

It is alleged that some financial resources of Non-government Organisations in clandestine way, are finding their way in wrong hands, who have even acquired capabilities to not only subvert or over-throw political stability of governments, but have shaken the ego and image of world super-powers. Several NGOs are known to be front organisations for militant groups.

The NGOs are active in pointing out the deficiencies in the functioning of the government, be they on human rights or wild life preservation or child labour. However, NGOs have apparently no transparency, no accountability and answerability of annual accounts, unlike to share-holders or audits in private organisations and in government to Auditor General of India and Parliament, etc. As mentioned by one writer, NGOs are virtually money-making machines for their owners. In fact, setting-up an NGO has become a profession for most people. A lot of money is coming for NGOs and accountability is just in name, Home Ministry black listed 824 NGOs in six states in North-East Region in 2003.

5. NEED FOR GOOD GOVERNANCE

Since NGOs are growing manifold and to attract donations from within the country and abroad, the issue of their accountability becomes important. It is equally vital that these voluntary organisations are managed more professionally; a proposal to modify some provisions of the law for NGOs is under consideration. This modification may cover various aspects such as registration of NGOs after every five years, banks to record sources of contributions received by them, etc.

6. AIM OF BOOK

The purpose of this book titled "Management of Non-profit Organisations" is to highlight need for application of management concepts to improve utilisation of their resources and emerge as growing entity. These management concepts are such as : mission statement, planning process, organised marketing, public relations for credibility, staffing, financial and controlling systems, etc This volume covers all these and many more areas shared in easily understandable simple language. The book will serve the need of NGOs, NPOs and other various type societies e.g. of charitable trusts, environment protection, hospitals, clubs, educational and social set-ups. It will enable them to become more effective, repose trust in donors and increase their contribution to the welfare of specific beneficiaries.

Box

Bring Shine to NGOs, says PM

"Improving the quality of manpower in government programmes is a major challenge facing us today. An equally important challenge is to improve the quality of management of the non-government sector," said Prime Minister Manmohan Singh in Mumbai on Saturday

The PM was speaking at the 66th annual convocation of the Tata Institute of Social Sciences (TISS). Delivering the convocation address, Singh said a convocation is an extremely important day in the life of a student. "You stand today at a new threshold in your life. Here, in this great institution, you have imbibed the values and skills needed to deal with the world outside," he said.

"Some of you may have trained to enter the organised sector of our economy while others may aim to work with non-governmental organisations. These may be two very different worlds. But I do believe they are united by their commitment to improve the lives and livelihoods of our people." Singh expressed hope that institutions like TISS could send forth into society motivated and hard working young men and women who can improve the human resources element of government's national programmes. He called for long-term and synergistic partnership between the government, civil society and the corporate sector to improve the efficiency of public service and delivery systems.

CHAPTER

2

Understanding Non-profit Organisations

Non-profit organisations play an important role in the community in USA. Natural Resources Conservation Service (NRCS) and The Conservation Partnership often collaborate with these non-governmental organisations. It benefits everyone if we are able to work together to better our communities and improve our natural resources. Non-profit organisation structure is much different from the government. An understanding of how non-profit organisations are structured and how they operate is necessary in order to facilitate effective partnerships and cooperations in the community.

In this chapter on non-profit organisation, we have covered some aspects as under:

1. What is an organisation?
2. Why organisations are necessary?
3. What are non-profit organisations (NPOs)?
4. Characteristics of NPO.
5. Challenges which NPO must address.
6. Broad groups of NPOs.
7. NPOs position in USA.
8. Formation of NPO under laws in India.
9. Categories of NPOs.
10. How are NPO's structured.
11. Points to consider when dealing with NPOs.

1. WHAT IS AN ORGANISATION?

- Organisation is a consciously *coordinated social unit, composed of people,* that functions on *continuous basis,* to achieve a common goal (goals).

- To put it in other words, organisation is a planned unit, deliberately structured for attaining specific goals, or
- Organisation is seen as *groups of people, working together*, for common goals.
- Organisations can be for profit purpose such as—production, commercial service, etc. or for non-profit social purpose, welfare, charitable, etc.

2. WHY ORGANISATIONS ARE NECESSARY?

(i) Organisations are necessary element of civilised life. As individuals we cannot do so well, organisations *enables us to achieve goals.*

(ii) Organisations *preserve knowledge* between past, present and future generations. They add to our knowledge by developing new and more efficient ways of doing things.

(iii) Organisations *provide careers* to employees, livelihood, personal satisfaction, self-fulfilment.

(iv) Performance of organisation is key factor (Peter Drucker).

(v) Organisations add to quality of life of selected segments of society.

3. WHAT ARE NON-PROFIT ORGANISATIONS (NPOs)?

Definition

The term non-profit organisations (NPOs) refers to those *legally constituted, non-governmental entities* incorporated under law as *charitable or not-for-profit corporations*, that have been set-up to *serve public purpose* and are tax *exempt according to income tax laws.*

- NPO organisations are *private sector* organisations with *public purposes*. This combination gives them great flexibility in their operations.
  NPOs have grown enormously all over the world during last 50 years. All NPOs are aiming to add to *quality of life* of selected segments of society. According to Peter F. Drucker, all NPOs are 'human change agents', because their product is a changed human being. NPOs serve basic needs. NPOs in India have set-up public 'toilets' and are managed by them. They have focus on social responsibilities, etc.
- In developing countries, NPOs have few volunteers in contrast to western world. Non-profit organisations provide a central *role in economic growth*. Their role in education (schools, research, training, consultation) and community services (health services, social services, recreation, libraries, arts) are instrumental in supplying access to capital for certain community populations. Non-profits affect and *contribute to the community by stimulating* employment, income, creating a more skilled work force and introducing new technology. Chamber of Commerce and tourism councils are examples of non-profit organisations whose missions promote economic growth.

4. CHARACTERISTICS OF NPO

Some salient features of NPOs are as under:

(i) They must have a *public service* mission.

(ii) They must be organised as a *not-for-profit* or charitable corporation.

(iii) Their governance structure must *preclude self-interest* and private financial gain.
(iv) They must be *exempt from paying income tax*.
(v) They must possess the *special legal status* that stipulates gifts made to them are tax deductible.
(vi) Sometimes they are called *foundations or endowments* that have large equity funds.

However, we may note that, NPO do not include these three categories of organisations:

(a) Enterprises set-up to make profit, but are not doing so.
(b) Organisations governed by collection of people to *serve some public good, but not granted any special* corporate status by state authorities.
(c) Organisations that are registered as non-profit but do not have public purpose (i.e. trade associations, labour unions, country clubs, etc.).

5. A NON-PROFIT ORGANISATION MUST ADDRESS THESE CHALLENGES FOR RESPONSIBLE GOVERNANCE

(i) Articulating its *'mission'* clearly.
(ii) Engaging in 'planning with *eye on risk and benefits*' of every proposal relating to organisation mission.
(iii) Identifying its *'constituency' and involving* them in NPO's operation.
(iv) To ensure the organisation remains needed and wanted by *reviewing the mission*.
(v) According to Halal's 1996 model, *stakeholders of NPOs* are:
- Suppliers,
- Customers,
- Owners,
- Governors/Trustees,
- Staff (including management), and
- External influences, such as society, government.

Note: NPO does have not shareholders. But it should have auditors, and have own Income Tax Pan Number (PAN) in India.

(vi) Governance, *organisational accountability*, financial reporting and long-range planning are very *different in non-profit organisations*, whose details are laid in state laws.

The above challenges provide a basic framework for responsible governance and management in NPOs.

6. BROAD GROUPS OF NPOs

Some broad groups of NPOs are as under:

(a) First, addressing *social or economic issues*, such as handicapped, educational institutions., etc.
(b) Second, private funding institutions such as USAID (United States Aid Agency) for international development.

(c) Third, organisations' concerned with adding to the welfare of their own members. Cooperatives such as Kaira Milk Producers' Cooperative in Gujarat.

(d) Some *special groups* are such as Sisters of Charity of Mother Teresa. They derive commitment and dedication from religious sources. Some are for destitude women, mentally handicapped or orphanages, etc.

There are NPOs of commercial organisation's which make profit by setting special foundations for science, arts, education, etc.

7. NPOs POSITION IN UNITED STATES OF AMERICA (USA)

In USA, NPOs range from large universities with assets in billions of dollars to small volunteer, community-based organisations.

- They present about 5% of all institutions and own 2% of nation's assets. Their contribution to the nation's quality of life is incalculable.
- They contribute to nation's economy and employ over 15 million people.
- In USA about 50% of adult population volunteer their time to NPOs.

8. FORMATION OF NPOs UNDER LAWS IN INDIA

One can start a NPO just by getting together with some friends to form a self-help group. It can have a separate legal organisation in order to:

(a) Own its property and its own bank account,

(b) To give it a continuity as an organisation, and

(c) Project yourself personally for operations of the non-profit organisation.

Incorporation of NPO's under Various Laws

- So one has to *incorporate* NPO by filing of *articles* of incorporation under the *State Societies Registration Act.*
- NPO has to get registered as a *charitable* trust with the Commission of Income Tax and get registration number under Section 12A(a) of the Income Tax Act, 1961.
- This will enable *tax exempt* non-profit status that could receive tax deductible donation.
- NPO forbids the distribution of profits to owners.
- NPO may be for serving charitable, religious, scientific or educational purposes so as to provide service to public.
- NPOs can operate in other sort of business and receive income from sales and other forms of activity including donations and grants. NPOs can employ staff and can enter into contracts of all sorts, etc.
- Union Home Ministry's permission number under Foreign Contributions (Regulations) Act, 1976 is required to accept donations from abroad.

9. CATEGORIES OF NON-PROFIT ORGANISATIONS (NPOs)

Categories of NPOs are:

(i) *Health services*—such as hospitals, preventive health care programmes for alcoholics, aids, public health care, smokenders, malnutrition, stress services, counselling centres such as Sanjeevani Nirmal Hirdaya.
(ii) *Education/Research*—universities for promotion of arts, research institutions, library, museum, zoo, girl scout, plans to check teenage pregnancy, etc.
(iii) *Religion*—churches, temples, mosques, gurudwaras, etc.
(iv) *Social services*—child care centres, old-age homes, charitable institutions, orphanages, handicapped homes, civil rights, population control, help-age care, CRY, UNCEF, etc.
(v) *Civic and fraternal services*—sports, Red Cross, environmental protection, state park, toll road, country club, pollution control, energy conservation, recycling wastes, pets care, salvation army, wild life, gardens, etc.
(vi) Other's such as public broadcasting, campaign for improved T.V. viewing, YMCA, YWCA, forest fires, consumer cooperatives, craft society, etc.

10. HOW ARE NPOs STRUCTURED?

Non-profit organisations have a board of trustees that includes officers. Depending on the size of a group, they may also have committees and an executive director.

Board of Trustees

This group, also referred to as board of directors or council, govern non-profit organisations. Generally, the board consists of volunteers. They have six major responsibilities:

1. Determine mission and set policies from year to year.
2. Institute economic agendas and boundaries including *budgets and financial* discipline.
3. Appoint, assess, and if necessary, terminate the appointment of the *chief executive.*
4. Secure and maintain *ties with the community.*
5. Provide monies for the activities of the organisation through *contributions and fund-raising.*
6. Guarantee that the vision and mission of the organisation's charter and the law are being followed.

Committees

When a non-profit organisation reaches considerable size and complexity, the board usually finds that it is difficult to carry out all of its responsibilities efficiently. They will then divide into smaller committees that will allow for a detailed analysis of specific areas such as fund-raising, planning, budgeting or programmes. The full board then discusses these analyses and make any recommendations by the committees. Some common committees in non-profits are the executive, financial, development, fund-raising, and planning committees. Other committees in selected organisations might focus on interest areas such as forestry, conservation, agricultural land resources, and land use. Still other committees focus on specific projects such as for organising legislature tour, annual meeting, or field day.

Chief Executives

Chief executives may have the title of executive director, or executive vice-president or president. The chief executive acts as a facilitator and consensus builder. He or she will mediate and engage in board-centered leadership, along with managing and implementing the board's ideas, policies and decisions. With the approval of the board, the executive will hire, recruit and supervise staff and volunteers. Chief executive will clarify job descriptions and procedures as well as establishing networks with other non-profit organisations, government agencies and local businesses. These networks enable partnerships and cooperation in the community. Conflict resolution among the board, staff and the public are also primary responsibilities of the chief executive.

11. POINTS TO CONSIDER WHEN DEALING WITH NON-PROFIT ORGANISATIONS

- Non-profit organisations depend upon a *constant flow of resources,* including funding. Financial support usually comes from member dues and programme services, private gifts, contributions, and fund raising activities. Non-profits can also get grants and receive state and central funds. (See Box 1)
- Many organisations *plan their priorities, issues and projects* a year in advance. So that adequate resources might be available for providing the group. At other times, organisations are able to respond rapidly.
- It is important to *research the organisation before visiting them* or meeting with one of their leaders. They are guided by policies and plans. Policies focus on critical issues and give a general guide to action. Non-profit organisations reflect their philosophy, values, limits and conduct. It is helpful to know in advance of a meeting what issues you might share in common and which issues might result in a conflict of interest. Most groups at the local, state, and national levels have Web sites.
- Incorporated non-profit organisations *have by-laws.* This document outlines the rules governing the group and can have legal ramifications. The board ensures that its by-laws are written and reviewed regularly.
- In the private sector, non-profit organisations are referred to as non-profit organisations. They do not use the term "NGO", an abbreviation for non-governmental agencies, that is commonly used by government agencies in India.
- Non-profit organisations can be referred by the *identity of their beneficiaries.* Typically, they respond to a need in the community. It is that need that translates into their mission and purpose as an organisation.
- A number of organisations also support *environmental and conservation initiatives.* For example, conservation is one of six primary interest areas of the General Federation of Women's Clubs, who have local affiliates throughout the United States. Non-profits benefit others by educating, setting professional standards, developing and disseminating information to the public, ensuring representation of private interests, exercising and supporting political choice and organizing volunteer efforts. They enrich the lives of people in the community.

Box I

'Tsunami Funds in Terror Hands'

Tsunami donations post-December 2004 may have been diverted to terror modules across the world believes US terrorism experts.

Professor Jimmy Gurule, former assistant attorney general of the United States and an expert on terrorist funding network, says the US government had identified around 48 charities, which directly or indirectly fund terrorist organisations.

"Some percentage of the multi-billion dollars donated by the international community towards tsunami rehabilitation were diverted to terror groups like Al-Qaeda," Gurulé said. While US Treasury and state departments are currently looking into the matter, some money might also have made its way to terror outfit Lashkar-e-Tayyeba (LeT), which was behind the series blast on Mumbai local trains, he said.

Gurulé, who was also Under Secretary for Enforcement, US Treasury Department from 2001 to 2003, said that his government has come out with a guideline in September, meant for the international community, suggesting the charities, which are genuine in their efforts and also the necessary checks and balances on how to donate money.

In Saudi Arabia alone, some of these organisations collected as zakaat or religious donation around US $10 billion and $1 billion. "Around one to four per cent of these funds are diverted for purposes of terror Saudi-based International Islamic Relief Organisation is one such organisation with offices in 20 countries and it has been found that the organisation has close ties with Al-Qaeda," he pointed out.

Gurulé further said that another efficient system of funding terror outfits is through hawala, largely practiced in the sub-continent. "The system is used to transfer money globally without any bounds and a legal system needs to be put into place to prevent this from happening. Although the system of verification of new customers by banks has been put into place, financial organisations need to be more aware.

Gurulé, a professor of criminal law at University of Notre Dame, US, is at present in trip to India, meeting policy-makers in New Delhi, Mumbai and Pune to discuss financing of terrorism.

CHAPTER

3

Some Fallacies about Non-profit Organisations

Non-profit organisations are so common and taken for granted that they are almost invisible to the casual observer. As a group they are called foundations, associations, not-for-profits, or tax-exempts. Some more familiar names include the Salvation Army, the Ford Foundation, New York. "Non-profit organisations are considered to be those businesses that do not directly seek to financially enrich members, management, or associations. Typically they promote education, health care, religion, or other benevolent goals." In the United States, an organisation such as a non-profit hospital must satisfy specific internal revenue service criteria to maintain its tax-exempt status. Other nations have similar constraints on striving to make a profit. Non-profit organisations with benevolent rather than financial goals.

HAVE IMPACT ON SOCIETY

Non-profit organisations are an immense community, national, and international resource. Consider, for example, the size and scope of America's non-profits:

> With $ 1 trillion in assets and an annual turnover of $500 billion, non-profits now account for 6% of the nation's gross domestic product and employ 7 million people, or 1 out of every 18 members of the labour force.

Although volunteers are the backbone of most non-profit organisations, the managerial employment opportunities within the non-profit sector are considerable. Since 1970, the non-profit sector has outgrown the U.S. economy by a ratio of four to one.

FALLACIES ABOUT NON-PROFIT ORGANISATIONS

The general public embraces some mistaken notions about non-profit organisations. The net result is a restricted and usually negative perspective preventing aspiring managers from considering a career in the non-profit sector. Here are some common fallacies about non-profit organisations that need to be addressed.

(i) Fallacy 1: Managing a Non-profit Organisation is Nothing Like Managing a Business

Management guru Peter Drucker recently struck down this particular fallacy as follows:

> . . . . newspaper or television reporters who interview me are always amazed to "learn that I am working with non-profit institutions. "What can you do for them?" They ask me or help them with fund-raising?" And when I answer, "No, we work together on their mission, their leadership, their management", the reporter usually says, "but that's business management, isn't it?"
>
> But the "non-profit" institutions themselves know that they need management all the more because they do not have a conventional "bottom line." They know that they need to learn *how to use management* as their tool lest they be overwhelmed by it. They know they need management so that they can concentrate on their mission. Indeed, there is a "management boom" going on among the non-profit institutions, large and small.

(ii) Fallacy 2: Rewards are Scarce in Non-profit Organisation

Because most people associate non-profit organisations with volunteers, they erroneously conclude that no one gets paid. John W. Rowe, president of New York's Mount Sinai Medical Center, you would be surprised to hear that bit of news. Rowe's 1993 salary of $ 799,492 made him the highest-paid non-profit executive in the United States. In fact, a 1993 salary survey of America's largest 250 non-profits found 300 executives earning more than $ 200,000 a year. For their part, the non-profit executives claim that the demands of these jobs require highly skilled managers who must be compensated fairly.

Volunteers are also richly compensated for their services. Although their rewards are not monetary or tangible, there are intrinsic payoffs stemming from the satisfaction of helping others.

(iii) Fallacy: People do Volunteer Work because they have extra time on hands

Volunteers come from virtually every walk of life, rich and poor, young and old are the lifeblood of non-profit organisations. Volunteers collect donations, trend to the sick, feed and shelter the homeless, protect animals and the environment, and comfort the elderly. It is a common yet mistaken notion to assume that most of this volunteer activity is carried out by people with lots of free time. Most volunteers are busy, fully employed members of the community. Their donated time is precious. Thus, non-profit managers are challenged not to waste busy volunteers' time. Sound management practices—including participative goal setting, adequate training, coaching and feedback, TQM, performance appraisal, and positive reinforcement—are especially important when managing volunteers.

Reference

Robert Kreitner, Management, AITBS Publishers and Distributors, Delhi-51.

CHAPTER

4

Trends and Challenges of Non-profit Organisations

Some developments, problems and challenges being faced by NPOs are covered as under:

1. Developments and problems in functioning of NGOs.
2. Challenges of NGOs in new millennium.

I. SOME DEVELOPMENTS AND PROBLEMS IN FUNCTIONING OF NPOs

(a) *Non-profit and business organisation collaboration*: In these complex times, no organisation can succeed on its own. Thus, non-profits and business organisations are embracing collaboration for mutual benefits as there is an increasing concern about sustaining non-profit organisation.

Non-profits are partnering with business to further their missions, develop resources, strengthen programmes to arrive in competitive world. One source of *larger contribution* is business corporations.

Likewise commercial companies are discovering that *alliances generate significant* rewards, i.e. increasing customer preferences, improving employee recruitment and morale, promoting brand identity, strengthening corporate culture, building goodwill, and testing innovations.

One of the three factors motivates corporation to give the gifts:

(i) The gift will *influence public opinion* about the corporation. To impress upon the public that they care about community, the environment, the needy or some special cause. For example, oil companies, cigarette companies or companies that manufacture war machinery have used corporates giving gifts as a means to counteract a specific public image problem. Some companies do give gifts to maintain an edge over their competitors by *projecting an image of strength*, generosity, power through charity.

(ii) The gift will *benefit employees* as a way to enhance loyalty and positive feeling among employees. Some examples are such as daycare centres for little children of employees, or introducing cash matching programmes for employee contributions or to give to colonies where their employees live.

(iii) Gift will *assist in marketing efforts* such a giving free samples as a marketing device or a tea vending machine to management institute and in this process company also gets credit for a charitable contribution as well.

(b) There is *diminishing distinction* between non-profit organisations and market-driven profit-oriented concerns. Such as hospitals have been purchased by profit-making business is one indication of the trend.

(c) There is a perceived *crisis in leadership* development and nurturing in NPOs. They are not training future leaders to take care of management of NPOs.

(d) NPOs have certain *system of traditions*, social mores that cannot be ignored in their practices.

(e) NPOs have also more *bureaucratic interference and corruption* which has developed in post-independence era.

(f) NPOs were earlier guided by concept of "trusteeship of wealth by those who control (propagated by Shri M.K. Gandhi and Shri Aurobindo). But now conditions are deteriorating.

(g) There is *absence of long-term planning and establishing of measurable targets* in NPOs of all fields of operation, be health care (such as eradication of AIDS, leprosy, polio, TB, etc.), education (removal of illiteracy, universal education to all children, etc.) or orphanages or care of destitute or retarded persons. If NPOs proceed on clearly defined goals which are time bound, then NPO's performance can be measured and can prove effective organisations.

(h) Similarly difficulty of NPOs is of *laying a clearcut mission.* As in case of business organisations mission can be clear as serving the shareholder or fair return, etc. It is clear in the minds of employees that they are furthering interests of shareholders.

(i) NPO's activities relate to *social problems* and need careful study as to compulsions and actual steps to be taken to correct needs of victims. It is like commercial organisations where rational marketing approach works, i.e. defining the need, the product, the beneficiary and reaching the potential beneficiary constitute the essence of marketing.

NPOs have to understand what really *victim or client need and wants* to be done. Solutions to problems cannot be found by outsiders. It amounts to wrong formulation of problem and getting wrong solutions. The outcome is misdirection of time, effort and other resources, thus wastage of resources. For examples, rehabilitation of sex workers (prostitutes) by returning them to their families has yielded disastrous results unless we train them for new trade and help women to establish themselves. Trend is now towards encouraging self-help plans among members.

Other example can be abolishing child labour. But it has to be recognised that there are certain skills involving manual dexterity which can be better acquired as a child. There are many activities where whole family used to participate. It may require to develop optimum solutions to meet the essential needs of the child without generating new problems. Social problems need careful solutions.

2. CHALLENGES OF NGOs IN NEW MILLENNIUM

As NGOs are not functioning well. So some of the challenges of 21st century for NGOs are:

(i) *Need of honest and dedicated persons to run the NGOs*: The persons associated with NGOs today rather than service-oriented are interested in making money out of NGOs. These persons have made it a whole time profession to manipulate the money for their own benefits. They lack the *qualities of leadership* to perform following functions:
- Understand and direct change,
- Work with his team and lead in the field so as to be accessable to the people he leads,
- To find creative solutions,
- To delegate for motivation of followers,
- To create work culture, and
- To manage one's feeling and emotions.

(ii) To practice ethical values in their activities so as to avoid becoming suspicious in the eyes of the people.

(iii) Need of transparency in functioning of NGOs to create confidence. Avoiding wastage, bogus organisations, etc. (See also Box 1)

Box I

Centre Blacklists NGOs

The centre has blacklisted over 3,000 NGOs in the country, including many in Tripura, on account of allegations of financial irregularities and lapse in security. Consequently, the Tripura government has been directed to monitor role of all NGOs in the state.

Sources said the Centre has blacklisted 3,416 NGOs across the country, of these, 69 are based in Tripura. They added that misappropriation of funds from different ministries and foreign funding were responsible for the crackdown.

Besides Tripura, other north-eastern states also figure in the list. The centre has hitherto been floppy in recognising and helping NGOs in the north-east. Thus racketeers find it easy to manipulate government funds.

On the other hand, several NGOs have been linked to militant outfits and foreign organisations. "Numerous organisations receive funds from foreign firms in the name of running welfare activities," a senior police official said.

What further prompted the Centre into action were the complaints from individuals, state governments and intelligence agencies with regard to financial discrepancies and national security. Action against errant NGOs was contemplated after through investigations. Henceforth, blacklisted organisations will not be accorded any assistance, financial or otherwise.

SYED SAJJAD ALI, Agartala, August 25, 2005, *Hindustan Times*, New Delhi.

(iv) Need of injecting vitality in voluntary organisations. So that they process their proposals, timely, complete with requisite information and coordination in NGO. To have a system of evaluation and proper staffing procedures.

(v) NGOs to have participation with people rather than concentrating for government/ donors for grants.

(vi) Lack of proper personnel policy.

(vii) Foreign funds mostly for religious purposes destabilize the secular structure of our country.

(viii) The performance of non-profit organisation is covered behind a veil of secrecy, that is lifted only when disasters occur.

(ix) Problem of ineffective organisation's is they do not accomplish their social missions, e.g. non-profit hospital dumps medically unstable patient who cannot afford to pay.

(x) Individuals who control tax-exempt organisations get excessive benefits for themselves. Managers and employees abuse their authority for own benefits.

(xi) Some organisations take excessive risks, e.g. when Orange County's Treasurer (in USA) borrowed high money to invest in speculative securities.

(xii) NPOs lack competition that would force efficiency.

(xiii) NPOs lack barometer of their success. Alternative measures of performance are hard to find (other than profits).

(xiv) Do not articulate a clear public service mission.

(xv) Some NPOs in India (who are exempt from tax) have enormous resources say amounting to Rupees one hundred billion.

(xvi) Improvements in system of formation and functioning of NGO can be:

- Registration of NGOs after verifying the credentials of the persons associated with NGO.
- Association of beneficiaries in running of NGOs.
- Provision of special audit in case of any doubt of misappropriation.
- Appointment of auditors in consultation with sponsoring organisation.

Box 2

Requirements for a Successful Not-for-Profit Organisation

(i) Credibility

This is key. Janaagraha gained credibility in a number of ways. We are completely transparent in our intent and goals and we freely share all of our research, intellectual property, tools and data. We have completely funded the initiative ourselves, taken criticism from the government, NGOs, and citizens and remained standing and committed to creating change. Most importantly, our approach is not to point out problems and 'expose' the government, but a solution-oriented one. Rather than mirroring the state of affairs (which is common knowledge), we are concerned about changing the reflection, as partners.

(ii) Strategic goals

A great heart is a necessary but insufficient condition. It is important that we measure ourselves periodically against stated goals and objectives. The key difference between not-for-profit organisations and private institutions is that we are not required to have any measurements or indications of performance. And performance indicators are equally critical in the development arena.

(iii) Leadership spread

This is critical for scale. We found it very difficult initially to find people who had the same kind of skills, leadership, financial flexibility and passion for the work we were doing. That is slowly changing. We relied heavily on volunteer energy even for key positions. We have now decided that there are some support areas that require consistency and order, which can come predictably through well-paid, permanent staff. Additionally, we are now ready to put in place a strong governance board and advisory board that will guide the organisation and support its development at critical moments.

(iv) Professionalism and scientific thought

While Janaagraha is often considered 'too structured' in its approach, this is one of our greatest assets as rigour is required even in social development organisations. We design strong training processes and tools to blend grass-roots experience with intellectual frameworks.

(v) Volunteer management

We are in the business of changing mindsets of empowerment and we begin with our volunteers, especially in India where we do not have a culture of volunteerism. Volunteer energy keeps the organisation from stagnating and keeps us constantly challenged. At the same time managing volunteers is a serious responsibility—we must ensure that they find their time enriching and their energies are well utilised. This is still a significant area of challenge for Janaagraha.

(vi) An open approach

Whether it is communication tools, using innovations and latest thinking in branding and community communications, or technology as a means to facilitate wider deliberation, Janaagraha has had no mental barriers in adapting from private sector practices wherever it addressed a felt need.

(vii) Transcending barriers

In a public space of reform, the most important quality of an organisation and its leadership is to constantly find common ground, look at the viewpoints or others, and reach out to everybody, regardless of differences in ideology, class, religion, caste, profession and gender. Working in a space like this becomes a personal journey; rich in self-awareness and improvement.

(viii) Janaagraha's successes

(a) Janaagraha's successes can be bracketed into three areas—the tangible successes, grass-roots efforts and advocacy. In the tangible area, our Ward Works campaign got citizens neighbourhoods, particularly with the budget for the improvement of infrastructure in their area. Taking the corporate approach to launch the 'participative democracy' campaign, we conducted a series of workshops and we used four popular personalities in our advertisement to get people involved in the transformation of their city. The response was unbelievable, despite the pessimistic prognostications about the apathy of citizens and corporators. At the end of the campaign, 65 wards responded and over 5000 citizens came forward to be trained. We had well planned structures to engage the citizens and at the end of the exercise, 22 wards had their priorities listed in the budget for the first time, which accounted for Rs. 11 crores out of the budgeted Rs. 50 crores.

(b) At the grass roots level, we have three initiatives. We have the modelled after the gram sabhas, with citizens coming together at the local level and interacting with their government as partners and we are working towards the institutionalising of citizen participation. In order to create the culture of volunteerism, we take a lot of young people into our programmes. Bala Janaagraha is a programme for school children which attempts to create societal values in children: of community, ownership and participation.

(c) Under advocacy, our initiatives include participation in the National Urban Reformation (NURM) project. The three critical clauses that we have sought to detail and include as part of the core of the reforms are: disclosure, citizen participation and integration of various service providers and arms of the government. We have created a number of development and planning tools for citizens to understand how the government functions and how we can actually participate in those processes.

(d) *Challenges*: Janaagraha completes four years of existence in December 2005. When it began, Janaagraha was an idea and not an institution. One of our challenges was to strengthen an idea. In the space that we work in, we have to accept a certain lack of control—on the commitment of the citizens, the mindset of the government and the calibre of our volunteers. We have been challenged on all three fronts.

Our decision-making process is open, transparent and participatory and there is no explicit organisational hierarchy. Our structure breeds ownership and provides flexibility, and we have blended the concept of a 'movement' with professionalism.

CHAPTER

5

Formation and Management of a Society

Following aspects regarding formation and management of a society under the Societies Registration Act, 1860 are covered in this chapter:

1. Why need for legal society?
2. What is a society?
3. Who can form society?
4. Difference between registered and unregistered societies.
5. Difference between society and company.
6. Formation of a society.
7. Taxation exemption.

1. WHY NEED FOR LEGAL SOCIETY?

There is need for legal entity which could own, possess and manage the funds and assets for achievement of charitable objects.

2. WHAT IS SOCIETY?

Society is an association of persons (generally incorporated) united together by mutual consent to deliberate, determine and act jointly for some common purpose. (The Societies Registration Act, 1860).

3. WHO CAN FORM SOCIETY?

Society can be formed by following reasons:

(a) Individuals, minimum seven or more persons,
(b) Foreigners,
(c) Limited companies,
(d) Registered society.

(b)–(d): According to Memorandum of Association of proposed society.

Note: Minors are not eligible.

4. DIFFERENCE BETWEEN REGISTERED AND UNREGISTERED SOCIETIES

An unregistered society has no legal status and thus cannot sue or be sued. In case of registered society the procedure is as under:

1. Properties belonging to society (registered under the Act) are vested in the governing body of society.
2. Suit can be filed by or against a registered society.
3. If any judgement is obtained against an office-bearer of society, this cannot be enforced against office-bearer, but can be enforced against property of the society alone.

Note: Various state governments have expanded these provisions in the Act.

5. DIFFERENCE BETWEEN SOCIETY AND COMPANY

For non-profit purposes (charitable) registration can also be obtained also under Section 26 of the Companies Act, 1956.

Features	*Society under Societies Registration Act, 1860*	*Companies under The Companies Act, 1956*
• Objects	Charitable, literary, scientific, etc.	Can have Non-profit activities
• Procedure	Simple and easy	Complicated
• Management	Easy and simple	Laborious, rigid, time-consuming (provisions to be complied)
• Name	Selection of name not difficult	Approval of name to be obtained from registrar
• Penalties	Very easy	More stringent
• Legal entity	Legal entity with certain limitations	A legal entity

6. FORMATION OF A SOCIETY

6.1 Purposes for which society can be formed: (under the Societies Registration Act, 1860)

(i) Grant of charitable assistance—for poverty, education, religion, etc.
(ii) Creation of military orphan funds.
(iii) Promotion of science, literature, arts, diffusion of knowledge (useful). Political education, libraries, public museum, painting galleries, designs, etc.

6.2 Memorandum of Association (MOA)

Memorandum of Association is the charter of a society. It is a document depicting and describing the objects of its existence and its operation.

6.3 Format of MOA (Memorandum of Association) to contain:

(i) *Name of the society,*
(ii) *Place* of its office,
(iii) The objects for which society is established,
(iv) Names, addresses and occupations of *governing body* members and president to whom management of affairs is entrusted,
(v) Names, addresses, signatures (witnessed) of *seven or more persons* subscribing to MOA (on prescribed format), and
(vi) *Rules and regulations* of the society are framed to guide the members of the governing body and its internal management such as conditions for admission of members, payment of subscription, appointment and removal of governing body, notice for meetings quorum for transactions in meetings, etc.

6.4 Registration of Society

- Socety to file required documents with Registrar of Societies along with registration fee Rs. 50.
- The Registrar shall after satisfaction with compliances of provisions of the Act and correctness of documents, will issue certificate of registration.
- It then gives the society a legal entity status. Members become bound and must confine its activities given in its MOA.
- In case of non-registration the governing body members have alone a legal status and society has no legal status.

6.5 Members

Members of the society have duties and responsibilities as under:

- A person can be admitted as member according to rules and payment of subscription. No one can claim admission as a matter of right.
- *Member's rights*: These rights include to receive notices, to vote, to receive copies of by-laws of society.
- Member is liable to be sued for recovery of damage to property or arrears of subscription by the society. In brief, society can proceed against member for recovery of penalty imposed on member as a result of breach caused by him.

6.6 Working and Management of Society

- *Governing Body*: Activities of society are managed by the governing body. Members of governing body are chosen (elected) from members. At times, government may appoint a nominee in public interest.
- Members of governing body are trustees of the property of society. Property rests with the governing body. Members of governing body collectively have to comply with provisions such as documents to sent the registrar, maintaining accounts, managing funds for attaining objects of society.

- Every society is required to hold *general meeting* at a time. Society has to prepare statement in model forms, and get the *auditing* of accounts by independent person. The office-bearers of society or person authorised by governing body can sue or defend on behalf of society.

6.7 Alteration/Amendment of Memorandum of Association and Rules of Society

- Registrar may agree to change of name and rules of society as proposed by governing body.
- Governing body may *apply* for amalgamation of society with any other society.
- The members of society by 3/5th majority may apply for dissolution of a society.
- Court may dissolve a society on an application made by district magistrate showing that activities of society constitute a public nuisance or opposed to public policy.
- Members of society cannot receive any property which remains surplus after payment of debts and liabilities. Member by 3/5th majority can give surplus to some other society.
- An inspector so appointed may investigate into affairs and management of society.
- The registrar can get and seize books and records/funds/property of the society.
- The registrar is the authority who supervises the activities and functions of societies. The registrar is public servant.

7. TAXATION

Under Sec. 11(1), property under the trust religious, public or charitable societies are *exempt from tax*, but societies having *private trusts* (where benefits go to contributors) *are not exempt from tax*.

- *Charitable purpose* includes relief of poor, education, medical relief and advancement of general public utility. Religious purpose includes advancement, support or propagation of religion.
- Society (associations registered with Central Government) may receive foreign contributions and have to maintain accounts, which may be audited by Chartered Accountant (CA). Failing this, it leads to punishment as an offence.

CHAPTER

6

Non-government Organisations (NGOs)

In this chapter we shall cover various aspects on NGOs:

1. Meaning and characteristics of an NGO.
2. Role of NGO.
3. Difference between voluntary organisation and NGO.
4. Formation of NGO under different laws:
   (a) As a charitable trust.
   (b) As a society under the Societies Registration Act, 1860.
   (c) As a company (under Sec. 25) of the Companies Act, 1956.
5. Management of NGOs:
   (a) Mission statement.
   (b) Planning.
   (c) Organising.
   (d) Controlling.

1. MEANING AND CHARACTERISTICS

(a) Meaning

Non-government organisations are groups and institutions that have primarily humanitarian or cooperative rather than commercial objectives. They are private agencies in industrial countries that support international development; indigenous groups organised regionally or nationally; and member-groups in villages. NGOs include charitable and religious associations that mobilize private funds for development, distribute food and family planning services and promote community organisation. They also include independent cooperatives, community associations, water-user societies, women's groups. Citizen Groups that raise awareness and influence policy are also NGOs.

(b) Characteristics of an NGO

- An NGO is a non-profit making, voluntary, service-oriented/development-oriented organisation, either for the benefit of members (a grass-roots organisation) or of other members of the population (an agency).
- It is an organisation of private individuals who believe in certain basic social principles and who structure their activities to bring about development to communities they are servicing.
- It is a social development organisation assisting in empowerment of people.
- An organisation or group of people working with specific objectives and aims to fulfil tasks that are oriented to bring about desirable change in a given community or area or situation.
- An organisation committed to the root causes of the problems trying to better the quality of life especially for the poor, the oppressed, the marginalized in urban and rural areas.
- Organisations established by and for the community with or without little intervention from the government; they are not only a charity organisation, but work on socio-economic-cultural activities.
- NGOs are also traditionally known as:
  - o Voluntary Organisations (VOs),
  - o Voluntary Agencies (VAs),
  - o Voluntary Development Organisations (VDOs), and
  - o Non-governmental Development Organisations (NGOs).

2. ROLE OF NGO

Indian Constitution has enunciated welfare state as one of the Directive Principles of State Policy and essentially the society and social organisations also have a role to play in providing basic needs and amenities to and addressing the problems of the weaker sections (women and children). Government has identified, considering the social pattern of living and needs of citizens, schemes in which NGOs and voluntary organisations can participate. These are broadly:

- Age Care
- Agriculture
- Animal Welfare
- Art and Craft
- Children
- Cities and Urban
- Culture and Heritage
- Disability
- Education
- Environment
- Health
- Human Resource
- Rural Development

- Science and Technology
- Tribal People
- Waste Management
- Welfare
- Women Development
- Other Social and Cultural Activities

NGOs provide expert analysis in the field; serve as early warning agents and help monitor and implement international agreements. NGOs also help raise public awareness of issues, play a major role in advancing UN goals and objectives and contribute essential information at UN sponsored events. NGOs advocate many of the causes of concern to the United Nations, volunteer resources and execute and oversee development projects.

3. DIFFERENCE BETWEEN VOLUNTARY ORGANISATIONS (VOs) AND NGOs

Although the terms VOs and NGOs are used interchangeably, however, they differ widely in their objectives, methodology, style of functioning, motives, legal status, socio-political orientation, ideological affinity, economic strength, etc.

(i) *Voluntary organisations* are opposite to business, cooperative and trade associations. Voluntary organisations or agencies are essentially non-profit and non-partisan organisations. They are largely independent of the government and are characterised primarily by humanitarian or cooperative rather than profit-making objectives. The quintessence of VOs is voluntarism and the spirit of voluntarism stems from varied sources such as e.g., love of humanity, charity, welfare of the needy and destitute, etc. VOs are controlled and administered by an association of citizens rather than any influence from the government.

(ii) *NGO*: The term NGO, has acquired wide acceptance internationally. The United Nations nomenclature of an NGO refers to any international organisation not established by inter-governmental agreement including which accept members designated by governmental authorities, provided that such membership does not interfere with the organisation's free expression of views. NGOs are different from the market induced organisations and other organisations of the State. They are formalised organisations beyond the market and the State, receiving their resources partly from voluntary contributions of the society. The term NGO in India has been use to denote a wide-spectrum of organisations which may be non-governmental, quasi or semi-governmental, voluntary or non-voluntary, partisan or non-partisan, formal or informal, non-profit or profit-oriented bodies, with a legal status and registered under special Acts (like Companies Act, Societies Registration Act, etc.). To be eligible for funding from various agencies, it should have legal status (i.e. a legal personality). —(Handbook for NGOs, A Nabhi Publication)

4. FORMATION OF NGO AND DIFFERENT LAWS

Basically a Non-governmental Organisation (NGO) is perceived to be an association of persons or a body of individuals. Such body with a definite name and objective may be a registered one or unregistered one. But when such body seeks external funding for carrying out its philanthropic or other social objectives, the funding agencies (either international or national) will definitely look for some legal character for such organisation. Legal character is acquired only after registration incorporation of the association of persons under any of the applicable laws.

An association of persons with non-profit motive may be registered under any of the following Indian Acts:

(a) As a Charitable Trust.
(b) As a Society under the Societies Registration Act.
(c) As a licenced company under section 26 of the Companies Act, 1956.

(a) Formation of an NGO as a Trust

The Indian Trusts Act (section 3) defines "trust" as an obligation annexed to the ownership of property, and arising out of a confidence reposed in and accepted by the owner or declared and accepted by him for the benefit of another, or of another and the owner. According to Section 7 of the Indian Trust Act, a trust may be created: (a) every person competent to contract, and (b) by or on behalf of a minor.

While Hindus generally create charitable and/or religious endowments, Muslims create wakfs for the same purpose. In both cases, some property is dedicated to public utility such as, tanks, wells, gifts of food, dharamsalas, schools, places for supplying drinking water, relief for sick and poor, etc. An institution is founded and somebody is entrusted with the duty of performing the acts.

(b) Formation of an NGO as a Society

An NGO may be formed as a society. A society may be defined as a company or an association of persons (generally unincorporated) united together by mutual consent to deliberate, determine and act jointly for same common purpose.

As per the Societies Registration Act, 1860 (see Annexure 2.VI), a society be formed by minimum seven (or more) persons, eligible to enter into a contract, any of the following purposes:

(i) Grant of charitable assistance;
(ii) Creation of military orphan funds; and
(iii) Promotion of science, literature or the fine arts; instruction and diffusion of useful knowledge, diffusion of political education, foundation or maintenance of libraries or reading rooms for general use of the members or the public, public museums and galleries of paintings and other works of art, collections of natural history, mechanical and philosophical inventions, instruments or designs.

Besides, the State Governments are empowered to add more objects to the above list.

The chief advantage of forming a society are that it gives a corporate appearance to the organisation, and provides greater flexibility as it is easier to amend the memorandum and bye-laws of the society than in case of a trust, terms of which strictly manifested in the trust deed. However, formation of a society requires more procedural formalities than in case of a trust.

(c) Formation of an NGO as a Company Licensed under Section 25 of the Companies Act

Under Section 25 of the Companies Act, 1956, an association formed or to be formed:

(a) for the purposes of promoting commerce, art, science, religion, charity or any other useful object,
(b) with intention to apply its profits or other income for promoting its objects, and
(c) which prohibits payment of any dividend to its members, is permitted to be incorporated without addition of the word "Limited" or "Private Limited".

5. MANAGEMENT OF NGO

Management Principles

Management principles in relation to profit-oriented organisations are equally applicable to non-profit organisations as well. Peter F. Drucker has stated that non-profit organisations themselves know that they need management all the more, because they do not have a conventional 'bottom line'.

(a) Objectives or Mission Statement

Formulating of a mission statement identifies the sections of the society whom the organisation envisages to serve. Without defined objectives, the efforts or activities of an organisation remain directionless. Objectives are essential for laying down targets and measuring performance of an organisation.

Formulation of objectives is based upon and requires—(i) identifying a problem, (ii) finding probable solutions to it, (iii) measures to be taken or product to be distributed/marketed, and (iv) beneficiaries to be rescued from the problem.

(b) Planning

Non-profit organisations are largely occupied in handling the immediate problem before them and they look for the other problem or other area where the problem exists only after the one before them has been deal with. Voluntary organisations, usually undertake at the most two to three projects at a time. Besides, the various aspects of a project, viz. preparing a plan, making strategies, fund raising, persuading volunteers, training volunteers and actual implementation of the project are generally carried out one by one and not simultaneously as in case of commercial concerns.

For long-term plans, large amounts of grants are required from government or corporate houses for NGOs.

Planning as a management practice is found in NGOs funded by government or sponsored by big corporate houses only, since government/corporate funds are sanctioned only for a well designed project proposal after proper appraisal and is followed by consistent review.

For successful implementation of any project/activity, thoughtful and considerate planning is very essential. In NGOs, planning may involve the following:

(i) Designing project to achieve the targets,
(ii) Making a plan of activity for the project,
(iii) Designing strategies for implementation of the project, and

(iv) Identifying the requirements of man, machines, material and money. These shall helpful in preparing a convincing project proposal.

(c) Organising

For NGOs actual implementation of project some areas to be organised are:

(i) Marketing

For NGOs 'marketing' the service/product is equally significant. `Marketing' here refers to availment of the service/product offered by NGO by the targeted beneficiary group. It is important to create awareness about the service, the reason why it is being provided, its advantage to the beneficiary and the society in general and the price at which it is available. Besides, it is equally important to create a 'desire' to consume the service/product, so as to make the project successful.

(ii) Staffing

NGOs generally depend on the services of social workers but many a times, they have also to hire staff. Staffing involves, identifying the jobs for which paid staff is required and the essential qualifications of the staff suitable for it, providing proper training to them as they have to work in a much different atmosphere while rendering their service and creating amenable work environment for the staff.

(iii) Financing

It is important that funds are received/raised in adequate and appropriate quantum at each stage so that neither the project gets stuck up for want of funds nor there is any excess lying unutilised. In non-commercial concerns, optimum utilization of funds is all the more important.

While small to medium NGOs mainly depend for finance on private contributions, public donations, sale proceeds of items produced by them, charity shows, etc., larger NGOs are financed mainly by government/corporate grants.

Proper financing also involves investment of surplus available funds, for optimum utilisation and generating more resources by way of interest/dividend or capital gains for future use. Besides, while making investment it is important that funds be invested in specified forms of deposits so as not to loose the income-tax exemption for the NGO.

(iv) Project Implementation

After organising the necessary resources for a project, the next stage is its implementation. For proper execution, every project is reckoned as a venture.

(d) Controlling

The ultimate objective of NGO is to improve the life of the targetted group of beneficiaries to the extent of minimising the hardship being faced by them. All efforts of planning and organising have to be directed and regulated towards achieving this objective, which requires controlling at all stages.

The essence of controlling is to ensure that all available resources are being utilized for productive purposes at an optimum level and rate. Controls are exercised to ensure that the plan is being executed and if it has to be modified, it is being done rationally.

Whenever some natural disaster occurs and NGOs come there to provide relief to workers, they have to face several types of problems like—thugs/mafias ask for their cut, opposition and resistance from the bureaucracy, politicians being more concerned of taking political advantage of the situation.

In normal circumstances also, NGO workers have to face the wrath of the police and the underworld.

NGOs should therefore take into consideration all anticipated opposition and sign measures for combating it.

(i) Feedback

One main measure of controlling is the feedback. NGOs should develop easy questionnaires soliciting comments of the beneficiaries on the quality of service being provided, what it lacks and suggested measures to improve it. Such feedback is an important tool of information which helps in further improving upon the project.

(ii) Budget

Budget is an important aspect of control system.

Operations Budget: An operations budget consists of:

(i) Revenues or income,
(ii) Expenses or expenditure,
(iii) Quantitative measures of output, and
(iv) Explanations and notes.

Budget is used as a control device by matching revenue and expenses for the concerned department against the budget projections. A periodic evaluation of performance, preferably every month, is necessary to ensure that the performance is in line with the projections; major deviations on either side need to be probed and corrective measures be taken or the budget projections be revised, if required.

(iii) Performance Control

While budget control refers to comparing output with planned projections, performance control refers to comparing actual output with optimum output that can be obtained with total available resources. For example, in case of a hospital number of beds for inpatients can be compared with patient usage over a period (i.e. number of patients × average inpatient time). Similarly in relation to outpatient department, the performance can be measured by patient to doctor ratio.

Box I

A.P.J. Abdul Kalam asks NGOs to Innovate

Suggesting that the term Non-governmental Organisation bore negative connotations given how much work is being achieved in the nation with their help. President A.P.J. Abdul Kalam suggested on Monday that it was time to start referring to them as "societal transformers".

Inaugurating the National Summit of Rural NGOs here the President indicated that he favoured innovation in adopting plans for growth in rural areas and said employment generation was the foundation for sustainable development in villages.

"Repeating what we are doing for several decades with more of the same may not be the way to proceed further. We need innovation and transparent performance in our action," he said and asserted that there was, however, a need to make NGOs and village authorities more accountable and transparent.

Making 12 suggestions, the President asked the Government to double grants-in-aid to Centre for Advancement of People's Action and Rural Technology (CAPART) to Rs. 10,000 crore annually and maintain continuity in Management structure of rural development bodies for at least five years, irrespective of regime change.

Citing the successful experiments at Rashtrapati Bhawan, Kalam said, "this is the first home of the country, we thought, it will be more appropriate to use the land for societal missions."

He said two herbal farms were created on an unutilized land in the premises. The first was used for assisting farmers on how to add value by learning how to extract, store and market their products while the second was for the visually challenged where they could feel, smell and learn about various plants through the Braille boards.

Kalam said along with a spiritual garden and a nutritional garden, a cultivated Jatropha curcus, the bio-fuel plant, was created to educate farmers about increasing their earning capacity by utilising the features of the plant. He also asked NGOs to direct their energies towards least developed regions like Bihar, eastern Uttar Pradesh and the North-Eastern states.

—HT Correspondent, New Delhi, April 25, 2006

CHAPTER

7

Non-government Organisations (NGOs) and Government Policy

In this chapter, following aspects relating to government policy on NGOs are covered:

1. Definition of NGO.
2. Background.
3. Features of an NGO.
4. Two groups of voluntary organisations.
5. Merits and demerits of NGOs.
6. Levels of operation.
7. Orientation of NGOs.
8. Government policy and state cooperation with NGOs in tax exemptions.

Non-government organisations (NGOs) are also called voluntary agencies or non-profit organisations.

I. DEFINITION

- NGO is a non-profit-making, voluntary, service-oriented/development-oriented organisation, either for the benefit of members (a grass-roots organisation) or of other members of the population (an agency).
- It is an organisation of private individuals who believe in certain basic social principles and who structure their activities to bring about development to communities that they are servicing.
- It is social development organisation assisting in empowerment of people. It is independent of any external control. It is flexible and democratic in its operation. They have a long history of active involvement in the promotion of human welfare and well-being.

2. BACKGROUND

Voluntary agencies are functioning in almost all the countries of the world. In some countries, voluntary services have played an important role in stimulating and initiating the development of social services while in other countries they have given leadership in promoting the establishment and progressive extension of Government responsibilities. In some countries these agencies carry the major responsibilities and may provide the only social services available to the people. For example, the voluntary services in India have played a significant role as the problems are so large that it is not possible for the Government alone to tackle it.

3. FEATURES OF AN NGO

Voluntary organisations have certain features and characteristics which distinguish them from other organisations. Following are the few features of a voluntary organisation:

(i) It is *registered under an appropriate Act* to give a corporate status to a group of individuals, so that they get a legal personality, and an individual liability may give place to group liability.
(ii) It has an administrative structure, and a duly *constituted managing/executive committee.*
(iii) It has *definite aims and objects* and programmes in fulfilment of these.
(iv) It is an organisation initiated and *governed by its own members* on democratic principles without any external control

These features can be summarised:

- Voluntary spirit,
- Hard work and dedication to welfare,
- Flexibility in operation,
- Sharply, selflessness and non-profit,
- Self-reliance,
- Close to community it serves and accountable. Solves their socio-economic problems and accepted by the community,
- Democratic managing committee, and
- Registered under an appropriate Act to get legal corporate status.

4. TWO GROUPS OF VOLUNTARY ORGANISATIONS

Voluntary Organisation falls in two groups, viz.,

1. Non-profit and Non-partisam Organisations

Non-profit and non-partisam organisations are those voluntary organisations which have legal entity. It should have broad-based objectives serving the social and economic needs of the community as a whole and mainly the weaker sections. It should not work for profit but on "no profit and no loss bases." Its activities should be open to all citizens of

India irrespective of religion, caste, creed, sex or race. It should have the necessary flexibility, professional competence and organisational skills to implement programmes.

Its office-bearers and organisational skills help in implementing programmes. Its office-bearers should not be elected members of any political party. It declares that it adopt constitutional and non-violent means for development. It is constituted on the basis of secular and democratic concepts and methods of functioning.

2. Conventional Voluntary Organisations

As pointed out earlier, Conventional Voluntary Organisations are those which have their own constitution, elected office-bearers with defined division of responsibility of the office-bearers, etc.

J.B. Singh classified them:

(1) Charity

Giving food, clothing, medicine, alms, in cash and in kind, land, building, etc.

(2) Welfare

Providing facilities for education, health, drinking water, roads, communication, etc.

(3) Relief

Responding to call of duties during natural calamities like floods, drought, earthquakes, and man-made calamities like refugee influx, ravages of war, etc.

(4) Rehabilitation

Continuing and follow-up of the work in areas struck by calamities and starting activities that are durable in nature.

(5) Services

Building up infrastructure in depressed backward areas.

(6) Development of socio-economic environment around human beings.

(7) Development of Human Beings

Conscious raising, awakening, raising conscience, organizing, recording of priorities to suit social justice: redeeming the past and opening doors for opportunities to the oppressed and the exploited.

Various NGOs cover the following areas:

- awareness programmes,
- marketing,
- training for employment,
- education,
- environmental protection,
- survey and research,
- agriculture and related programmes,
- networking and consultancy,

- information technology,
- distribution of funds,
- housing,
- working for social justice,
- offering legal advice,
- organising mother and child care programmes,
- protecting the interests of consumers,
- organising value-based education sessions,
- working for prohibition, and
- assisting in housing.

5. MERITS AND DEMERITS OF NGOs ARE AS UNDER

Merits

- They have the ability to experiment freely with innovative approaches and, if necessary, to take risks.
- They are flexible in adapting to local situations and responding to local needs and therefore able to develop integrated projects, as well as sectoral projects.
- They enjoy good rapport with people and can render micro-assistance to very poor people as they can identify those who are most in need and tailor assistance to their needs.
- They have the ability to communicate at all levels, from the neighbourhood to the top levels of government.
- They are able to recruit both experts and highly motivated staff with fewer restrictions than the government.

Demerits

- Paternalistic attitudes restrict the degree of participation in programme/project design.
- Restricted/constrained ways of approach to a problem or area.
- Reduced replicability of an idea, due to non-representativeness of the project or selected area, relatively small project coverage, dependence on outside financial resources, etc.
- Territorial possessiveness of an area or project reduces cooperation between agencies, seen as threatening or competitive.

6. LEVELS OF OPERATION OF NGOs

NGOs may be operating at local (city-wide), national and international levels.

(a) *City-wide Organisation* include organisations such as the Rotary or Lion's Club, chambers of commerce and industry, coalitions of business, ethnic or educational groups and associations of community organisations. Some exist for other purposes, and become involved in helping the poor as one of many activities, while others are created for the specific purpose of helping the poor.

(b) *National NGOs* include organisations such as the Red Cross, YMCAs/YWCAs, professional organisations, etc. Some of these have state and cuts branches and assist local NGOs.

(c) *International NGOs* range from secular agencies such as Redda Barna and Save the Children Organisations, OXFAM, CARE, Ford and Rockefeller Foundations to religiously motivated groups. Their activities vary from mainly funding local NGOs, institutions and projects, to implementing the projects themselves.

7. ORIENTATION OF NGOs

NGOs activities or areas of operation can be understood from their orientation:

- *Charitable Orientation* often involves a top-down paternalistic effort with little participation by the "beneficiaries." It includes NGOs with activities directed toward meeting the needs of the poor-distribution of food, clothing or medicine; provision of housing, transport, schools, etc. Such NGOs may also undertaken relief activities during a natural or man-made disaster.
- *Service Orientation* includes NGOs with activities such as the provision of health, family planning or education service in which the programme is designed by the NGO and people are expected to participate in its implementation and in receiving the service.
- *Participatory Orientation* is characterized by self-help projects where local people are involved particularly in the implementation of project by contributing cash, tools, land, materials, labour, etc. In the classical community development project, participation begins with the need definition and continues into the planning and implementation stages. Cooperation often have a participatory orientation.
- *Empowering Orientation* is where the aim is to help poor people develop a clearer understanding of the social, political and economic factors affecting their lives, and to strengthen their awareness of their own potential power to control their lives. Sometimes, these groups develop spontaneously around a problem or an issue, at other times outside workers from NGOs play a facilitating role in their development. In any case, there is maximum involvement of the people with NGOs acting as facilitators.

8. GOVERNMENT POLICY AND STATE COOPERATION WITH NGOs IN TAX EXEMPTIONS

India is a big country, where government efforts alone may not be able to meet the social needs of its large population and hence involvement of voluntary organisations is not only welcome but essential and desirable.

Since the beginning of the First Plan there has been a co-operative venture between the State and NGOs. The Planners in India have all along emphasised the role of voluntary agencies and have recognised the services rendered by them. The First Plan said: "A major responsibility for organising activities in different fields of Social Welfare like the welfare of women and children, social education, community organisation, etc. falls naturally on NGOs. These private agencies have long been working in their own humble way and without adequate aid for the achievement of their objectives with their own leadership, organisation and resources. Any plan for social and economic regeneration should take into account the services rendered by these agencies and the State should give them the maximum co-operation in strengthening their effort. Public Cooperation through Voluntary Social Service Organisations is capable of yielding valuable results in channellising private efforts for the promotion of social welfare."

Third Five Year Plan has also stated that: "Properly organised voluntary effort may go far towards augmenting the facilities available to the community for helping the weakest and the most needy to a somewhat better life. The wherewithal for this has to come from the time, energy and other resources of millions of people for whom voluntary organisations can find constructive channels suited to the varying conditions in the country. It is through the quiet influence of voluntary workers steadily engaged in acts of selfless service that the voice of reason can prevail."

Consequently there has been development by government, non-government or industry for welfare of society. There has been an enormous increase in their number over the country during the last 30 years, though the extent of increase varies from state to state and region to region. They registered a five-fold increase—from 1939 agencies in 1953, their number had gone up to 8052 in 1980. Presently, it is estimated that there are several lakh of NGOs working in the country in different fields of charity and human welfare.

On closer examination it becomes evident that the distribution of voluntary organisations (in terms of percentage to the total) in different States and Union Territories continues to be very uneven particularly in view of their size and population.

In small city of Chandigarh, there are several thousands of NGOs working in the fields of education, health, housing, slums, environment, children, women, old-age, etc.

In Seventh Five Year Plan, greater stress has been laid for the involvement of Voluntary Organisations/NGOs in the implementation of development programmes. More specifically, the voluntary organisations are asked to perform the role in the following directions. These continue in future plans as well:

(a) To supplement government efforts so as to offer the rural people: choices and alternatives;
(b) To be the eyes and ears of the people at village level;
(c) To set an example; it should be possible for the voluntary organisations to adopt simple, innovative, flexible and inexpensive means with its limited resources to reach a larger number with less overheads and with greater community participation;
(d) To activate the delivery system and to make it effective at the village level to respond to the felt needs of the poorest of the poor;
(e) To disseminate information;
(f) To make communities as self-reliant as possible;
(g) To show how village support and inadequate resources could be used as well as how human resources, rural skills and local knowledge grossly unutilised at present could be used for their own development;
(h) To domestify technology and bring it in simpler forms to the rural poor;
(i) To train a cadre of grass-root workers who believe in professionalising volunteerism;
(j) To mobilize financial resources from within the community with a view to making communities stand at their own feet; and

(k) To mobilise and organise the poor and generate awareness to demand quality services and impose a community system of accountability on the performance of village level government functionaries.

Income-tax Act, 1961

As originally defined in Section 2(15) of the Income-tax Act, 1961—"charitable purpose" includes relief of the poor, education, medical relief, and the advancement of any other object of general public utility not involving the carrying on of any activity for profit. It may be noted that the last ten restrictive words, "not involving the carrying on of any activity for profit", which were absent under the 1922 Act, were originally added under the 1961 Act and now they stand omitted from 1st April, 1984 by the Finance Act, 1983.

It is to be noted that the definition of the expression "charitable purpose" in Clause (15) of section 2 is of great importance in view of its vital link with the substantive provisions of Sections 11 and 12, whereby income from property held for charitable or religious purposes and the income as voluntary contributions of trusts or institutions created wholly for charitable or religious purposes are wholly exempt from income-tax. Such exemption is, however, subject to the fulfilment of the conditions as laid down in sections 12A and 13 and also subject to the provisions of Sections 60 to 63 of the IT Act, 1961. Section 12A, which is effective from 1.4.1973, lays down the conditions as to registration of charitable or religious trusts or institutions with the Chief Commissioner/Commissioner of Income Tax, and Section 13 provides that the exemption provisions of Sections 11 and 12 shall not apply in certain cases specified therein. Chapter V containing, amongst others, the provisions of Sections 60 to 63, deals with "Income of other persons, included in assessee's total income."

Emerging Role of Non-government Organisations (NGOs)

In this chapter we have discussed following aspects as role of NGOs:

1. NGO's commitment towards social change.
2. NGOs are social change organisations.
3. Corporate social responsibility of business organisations.
4. Forms in which the partnership between NGOs and business can take.
5. Changes NGOs need to make in their operations to help in corporate social responsibility.

1. NGO's COMMITMENT TOWARDS SOCIAL CHANGE

India is one of the major countries involved in the issues of development. Societies in India are constantly faced with pressures for social transformation and change. As a part of this society, individuals who are considered as actors are inspired by commitment to do something for the society, for their fellow human beings or others. This social commitment is universal in a given society and it exists in various forms.

Government and Non-governmental organisations carry out initiatives and attempt to realize the social commitment towards a meaningful social change. While governmental and non-governmental organisations need to bring together their special talents and resources, a third party—the private sector—should also be brought into this relationship. The private sector, being the dominant engine of growth, needs to deliver "economic development and social opportunity" to ensure social justice and equality to achieve the long lasting dream of social harmony and stability. A business corporation committed to economic development, has to establish its creditability with partners, citizens, public sector, government and NGOs. Companies may facilitate goal achievement towards development and poverty eradication and thereby help to enable rapid growth of industries with local competency and mobilize all sections of the society.

2. NGOs ARE SOCIAL CHANGE ORGANISATIONS

Social enterprises, NGOs being a major part of it, address a gap in the relationship between people and government. These organisations outside of government either provide a way to influence government for or against legislation or offer individuals a platform for community-oriented activism on a particular cause or interest.

In a wider platform the functions of the NGOs can be expanded and the coverage includes:

- Delivery of services,
- Conduct of research and introduction of innovations,
- Development of human resources, and
- Wider lobbying on many issues of concern for the improvement of society.

Aided by advances in information and communications technology, NGOs have helped to focus attention on the social and environmental externalities of business activity and would continue doing so in the future. Multinational brands have been acutely susceptible to pressure from activists and from NGOs who have challenged—a company's labour, environmental or human rights record.

3. CORPORATE SOCIAL RESPONSIBILITY (CSR) OF BUSINESS ORGANISATIONS AND NGOs SERVICES

Corporate social responsibility implies continuing commitment by business to behave ethically and contribute to economic development while improving the quality of life of the workforce and their families as well as of the local community and society at large. One of the reasons for this heavy shift toward embracing social responsibility can be attributed to globalization and pressure from stakeholders to ensure that companies' practices do not negatively impact the environment and society.

Being socially responsible not only increases the social acceptability of the products but also enhances the company's image and branding. This community involvement has made companies realize that in order for them to remain competitive and ensure sustainability, they must address the needs of their shareholders in their business. This can be cited with an example of the Tatas. There is a difference between making money for oneself and creating wealth for others. This is the story of a house that has created wealth for a nation—a story struggle, adventure and achievement.

The house of Tata is unique among Indian industrial houses in that 63 per cent of the capital of the parent firm, Tata Sons Limited, is held by Tata (Philanthropic) Trusts endowed by Sir Dorabji Tata and Sir Ratan Tata, the two sons of Jamsetji Tata, and named after them. These trusts have sponsored and promoted a number of public institutions of national interest, including hospitals, educational and research centres and scientific and cultural establishments. The Tata Group has promoted art and culture through the National Centre for the Performing Arts and Marg Publications.

The group has so had a long and fruitful relationship with sports. This relationship has given the nation many stars and will continue to do so in the future. It is hardly surprising, therefore, that the Tata group is still a household name.

Corporates need to grasp quickly their social responsibilities rejecting their sole idea of profit maximization to the exclusion of all else. However, the non-governmental organisations being a major force in driving the society for a transformation and change, lend their services for community empowerment and thus can be referred to as social change organisations.

Integration of CSR is an essential business process. NGO's services can include: Development of CSR policy and guidelines; Training/sensitizing company staff on social developmental issues; Identifying the company's key stakeholders and designing processes for their management; Identifying reliable and effective partners and managing these relationships; Institution of a system of CSR performance management, evaluation and reporting; Social Auditing; Benchmarking a company's social responsibility programmes to ensure consistency; and the others.

As the competition is becoming very stringent on the global front, business corporations are slowly understanding and recognizing the value of stakeholders. Thus the shift is conspicuously directed towards community well-being rural continuum and thinking about basics to grow big. In days to come this will provide a bigger platform for NGOs as lead liaisoning agents.

There are some organisations that tend to look beyond the corporate enterprise and would like to drive businesses by marrying them into social realities. *Beyond Business* is one among those organisations that focuses on how corporates and NGOs could work together and learn from each other. It emphasizes the need for corporates to tune themselves and go beyond the market. And it says that there are strategic advantages that can be derived from bonding with communities.

4. FORMS IN WHICH THE PARTNERSHIP BETWEEN NGOs AND BUSINESS CAN TAKE

The process of commercialisation of social institutions has set in. Charitable trusts, welfare bodies, voluntary agencies and NGOs, are being misused as a medium of diverting public money for personal gains. It is not only the funds and services of these institutions which are being misused for personal benefit in disguise of charity, but these are also being maneovered for gaining publicity, developing contacts with influential persons, attaining high status, getting a berth in elected bodies like Panchayat, Assembly or Parliament and even position in the Government. For this reason, people are losing faith in these institutions and they generally hesitate in giving donations to them. This has made the people more self-centred and the sentiment of public benefit or charity is getting blurred day-by-day.

Well, it is still not very late. The NGOs should wake up their conscience and work for the society with full devotion to their objectives. The trustees and executive members of these institutions should endeavour that the benefits of their effort reach the needy persons while keeping their self-interest at bay. Expenditure on their own conveyance, administration, salary, overheads, honorarium, etc. should be kept at bare minimum and money meant for public benefit should be used most judiciously.

NGOs can also play an effective role in removing various social evils from our society. They should never forget to make protests against any unjust or unhealthy or unlawful practice. An individual's voice is generally and quite easily subdued. But when a group of individuals raise an alarm it can transform into a movement or even revolution. However, they should not turn violent and should make protests in peaceful manner only, such as:

(i) NGOs should write letter to the editor of various newspapers, to bring any wrong thing in the notice of concerned authorities.
(ii) By distributing pamphlets NGOs can highlight the problem and their activities in that regard and gather public support.
(iii) NGOs can highlight upon various social evils and the various problems emanating therefrom, such as dowry, 'sati', drugs, alcohol consumption, AIDS, etc. by organising street shows.
(iv) Social problems, which concern the masses, can be highlighted through advertisements or news items and interviews in print and electronic media.
(v) NGOs may even take recourse to legal action or file PIL (Public Interest Litigation) before the court, if the gravity of the problem so demands.

NGOs can increase the impact of their work by helping companies to put their work and programmes into action by various ways: (i) NGOs by increasing credibility of the company in the eyes of stakeholders, (ii) NGOs promote products and services of the company by directly reaching and communicate, (iii) Companies can top into NGO net-works for development issues to gain access to socially and environmentally progressive markets. NGOs can prove themselves as substitutes for media advertising in a broader sense. NGOs have to play an active role in establishing fair and equitable society. Otherwise, there will be a social revolution.

5. CHANGES NGOs NEED TO MAKE IN THEIR OPERATIONS TO HELP IN CORPORATE SOCIAL RESPONSIBILITY

Vision and Objectives

NGOs should remain true to their vision and clearly focused on achieving outcomes relevant to their objectives. They should maintain ethical organisational and personal values, standards and conditions of service. They should define their governance by specifying the roles and responsibilities of staff and members.

Accountability

NGOs need to be accountable not only to those who funded them, but also to the people they serve. They should also be accountable to their members, and to their own staff. Accountability is not always easy. Often pressures from donors and governments make NGOs emphasize accountability to those bodies, to the neglect of others.

Appropriate HRD Systems

As organisations move from small to large and dynamic entities, they need a number of HRD systems to manage the people, convince the people, and also for the word-of-mouth advertising. Counselling and training for growth and development of people is also considered as an area of challenge for the HRD systems. If the NGO concerned has a set of efficient employees with good communication skills, then these employees can act agents to carry out direct selling.

Leadership Style

More commonly prevailing style of leadership in NGOs seems to be marked by centralized power and decision-making with lack of adequate information-sharing, delegation, consultation or real participation from the staff. There is also an absence of second-line leadership and the organisation becoming dependent upon one person whose authority goes unquestioned. This calls for organisational renewal processes and creating a culture of transparency, empowerment, freedom, flexibility and creativity.

Communication and Teamwork

The NGOs must know what audiences they want to reach and what responses they want to get. They must encode their messages so that the target audience can decode them. Effective communication hence is very much essential during both encoding and decoding the sales message. In short, the higher the degree of communication, so also will be the product sales of the company.

Box I

NGOs: To whom are they Accountable

The activities of non-governmental organisations have grown manifold and, hence, the issue of their accountability becomes important. This in no way minimises their importance or questions their functioning. NGOs can create a self-regulatory body, to which they can be accountable and they can co-opt eminent citizens in this body, says R. Vaidyanathan.

One of the largest members of India Uninc is the NGO (non-governmental organisation) sector or what is known as the third sector (after government and private) in academic circles. An NGO is any voluntary, non-profit, citizens' group which is organised on a local, national or international level. They could be registered as a society, trust or Section 25—companies though some cooperatives also claim this label.

Two Important criteria are that they are supposed to be Independent from government and they are organisations not meant for making profit. They are also expected to be "value based".

(a) Type of Activities

The type of activities they are involved in is mind-boggling (Table 1). It indicates that the range of concerns of the third sector, which is as large as that of the sovereign state. The list is indicative and not exhaustive and it reveals the range of activities in which the third sector is involved.

(b) Forms of NGOs

The NGOs are involved in different type of activities and, correspondingly, the type of organisation could differ as Indicated in Table 2.

The funding for these NGOs could be domestic or international. The international flow of funds is regulated by the Foreign Contributions Regulation Act (ECRA Act) of the Centre.

(c) Number of Registered NGOs and Money Received

Table 3 provides the trends in the number of registered associations and amount of money received under the Act. It is taken from the records of the Ministry of Home Affairs as presented by them. As is the case with many government statistics, the latest year for which data is available is 2002-03.

(d) States Receiving Amounts from Centre

The report of the Home Ministry also provides other information on the States receiving largest amount and purpose pertaining to 2002-03.

It suggests that important States/Union Territories are Delhi (Rs. 881 crore), followed by Tamil Nadu (Rs. 775 crore) and Andhra Pradesh (Rs. 630 crore). The US leads in the list of donor countries (Rs. 1,680 crore) followed by Germany (Rs. 715 crore) and the UK (Rs. 685 crore).

The leading donor agencies are Ford Foundation US (Rs. 121 crore), World Vision International (Rs. 90 crore) and Foundation Vincent E Ferer Spain (Rs. 79 crore). The largest recipients are World Vision of India, Tamil Nadu (Rs. 98 crore) followed by the Rural Development Trust, Andhra Pradesh (Rs. 85 crore).

(e) Expenses

The interesting information is on the purpose of the donations. Establishment expenses (Rs. 67 crore) tops the list followed by rural development (Rs. 487 crore) and construction and maintenance of schools and colleges (Rs. 275 crore).

(f) States with Largest NGOs

Maharashtra, Tamil Nadu, West Bengal, Gujarat and Andhra Pradesh are some of the States with large number of NGOs. It is curious to note that the poorest States such as Bihar, Uttar Pradesh, and so on, do not have as many numbers.

(g) Numbers Employed

The number of persons employed in NGOs is not separately available. One estimate by PRIA (Society for Participatory Research in Asia) Research published by Indianngos.com, indicates the figure at 19.4 million with West Bengal (1.52), Tamil Nadu (1.49) and Delhi (1.03) leading the pack.

These imply that the total number of government employee at nearly 20 million (Central, State and local bodies) and the number employed by NGOs are comparable.

By definition, NGO activity is voluntary and, hence, one expects that the overheads of the organisations are lean. In financial parlance, the fixed cost is expected to be relatively very small. Contrary to this belief, we find that the Establishment Expenses are the major reasons for receiving donations from abroad. In other words, the NGOs are perhaps becoming like top-heavy Government Departments wherein substantial portion of developmental expenses are spent on salary wages and other expenses such as telephone, travel—the domestic and international.

Another important aspect is the funding and functioning of NGOs who get funds from domestic sources. Unfortunately, we do not have a full picture of the financing (sources and uses of funds) of the entire spectrum of the NGOs.

The NGOs are active in pointing out the deficiencies in the functioning of the Government, be they on human rights or wild life preservation or child labour. It is also important that the activities of the NGOs are transparent, particularly from the point of view of their sources and uses of funds.

Since the Companies Act does not cove them, it is not required of them to file annual report with the Registrar of Companies. They are not part of the Government and, hence, the Comptroller and Auditor General of India do not audit their accounts. For instance, this writer has tried unsuccessfully for nearly three years to get the annual report, including annual accounts of three leading NGOs of this country, which are often featured in newspapers and TV channels.

Their activities have grown manifold and, hence, the issue of accountability becomes important. This in no way minimises their importance nor questions their functioning.

One can argue that they are accountable to their donors but it is not like a corporate situation where the company is accountable to its share-holder They have larger impact on our civil society and hence their role is more than that of giving details to their donors. Particularly in our civil society, which places importance on voluntary efforts and appreciates it, the responsibility much more.

To start with, they can publish their annual reports, including accounts, in their Web sites on a regular basis. It would also facilitate domestic individual donors to decide regarding providing funds to them based on their effectiveness measured by overheads.

We are not suggesting that a Central regulatory organisation be created with a large number of retired bureaucrats occupying posts and demanding quarterly statements from the NGOs.

We would rather have NGOs create a self-regulatory body, which is a creature of their own and to which they are accountable. They can co-opt citizens in this body. This becomes important since it is perceived of the NGOs are engaging in religios conversions in a rather aggressive fashion and some others are using the NGO banner for blackmailing well functioning corporate and government entities.

Of course, the nature and dimensions of such activities may be relatively small as of today but it would be prudent to be proactive and generate credible self-regulating of the third sector.

It would not be appropriate to suggest that everything is fine with every NGO in the country. Numbers are growing, causes are getting enlarged and funding particularly from abroad is increasing.

Hence, perhaps, the time has come for them to be more transparent and enhance disclosure practices to be like Caesar's wife. And transparency and regulation, and full disclosure are the things, which they demand from corporates and the Government. Hence, is it too much to expect the same from them.

TABLE 1

Types of Activities of NGOs

- Age Care
- Agriculture
- Animal Welfare
- Art and Craft
- Children
- Cities
- Community Development
- Transformations
- Disability
- Disaster Management
- Education
- Environment
- Health
- HIV/AIDS
- Housing and Slums
- Micro Finance
- Population
- Poverty
- Rural
- Culture and Heritage
- Tribals
- Waste Management
- Water
- Women
- Others

Source: Indianngos.com

TABLE 2

Typical Forms of NGOs

Item Type of NGOs

1. **Advocacy**: These NGOs advocate or campaign on issues or caused. They do implement programmes/projects, PETA advocates the cause of ethical treatment of animals.
2. **Consultancy/research organisations**: They work on social and developmental research and consultancy.
3. **Training/capacity-building organisations**: Training is called capacity-building by NGOs and some NGOs work on capacity-building of other NGOs.
4. **Networking organisations**: They provide network for other NGOs in specific fields. AVARD work on networking NGOs in rural development.
5. **Mother NGOs**: These are recipients of funds as well as givers. They have a work focus but instead of implmenting projects they identify projects and monitor, revaluate and build capacities of other participating NGOs. CRY is one example.
6. **Grass-roots organisation**: They directly work with the community. In a sense all Mahila Mandals tall in this category.
7. **City-based organisations**: They restrict their focus to cities. AGNI in Mumbai could be an example.

8. **National organisations**: They have a national presence: CRY, Concam India, etc.
9. **International organisations**: They are part of an international NGOs. Like mother NGOs, they receive and disburse. CARE and Oxfam could be examples.
10. **Self-Help Groups**: They are formed by beneficiary communities. Typically women form these groups of ten plus members. In rural Andhra Pradesh and Tamil Nadu they are increasing in numbers. They are funded even by commercial bank for productive activities in a sense they are not typical NGOs.
11. **Religious NGOs**: Region-based organisations, many affiliated to international church groups.

Source: indianngos.com

TABLE 3

Number of Associations and Amount of Money Received

	Association Registered under the Act (End March)	*Amount of Foreign Contributions Received (Rs. Crores)*
1993-94	15039	1865
1998-99	19834	3402
1999-00	21244	3924
2000-01	22924	4535
2001-02	24563	4872
2002-03	26404	5047

Source: http:/mha.nic, in/fcra/annual/summary/2002-03.

The author is Professor of Finance and Control, Indian Institute of Management, Bangalore, and can contacted at vaidya@iimb.ernet.in. The views are personal and do not reflect that of his organisation).

Box 2

New Civic Engagement by NGOs

Activism is no longer confined to conference halls. It is spilling into the streets and is reaching out to legislators and bureaucrats in the form of advocacy. With the *jholawalas* getting into high-power advisory committees, the politics of protest is moving into the main-stream of India's policy circles. Civil society is armed with effective tools of intervention like RTI and modern means of communication.

The new campaigns mobilise public opinion through awareness drives and channel public anger into meaningful engagement with policy-makers. Given below are some snap-shots of their impact:

RTI

After intense lobbying from civil society groups, the government enacted the law last year.

Rural Employment

After campaigns by NGOs, the Centre implemented the NREG scheme to provide employment to one member of every rural household for 100 days.

Mid-day Meal

The Supreme Court in 2001 responded to a PIL by PUCL and directed the government to provide mid-day meal to every child in primary schools.

Clean Air

In 2001 the Supreme Court in response to a PIL, directed all commercial vehicles in Delhi to switch to CNG.

WORLD VIEW

- 22% websites in the world are controlled by advocacy groups.
- 5,000 websites give tips on how to organise protests.
- 30,000 online petitions are registered at petitition-online.com every day.
- 10 million people protested on February 15, 2003 in 600 cities—the largest global protest ever—against US invasion of Iraq.
- 1.5 million people took part in May Day demonstrations this year in the US for Immigrant Rights—the largest single day protest in US history.

Source: *H.T.*, Sept. 2006.

Box 3

Public Pressure for Change

One of yawning gaps in governance is the lack of meaningful citizen-government interface from one election to another. But the growth of organised voluntary activity is enabling concerned citizens to channelise private initiative to meet public goals.

Indian democracy is moving to another level, with its citizens demanding their own space in an increasingly DIY (do-it-yourself) world. Two impulses have contributed to this change: one is the failure of the government to deliver on its promises and the other is its inability to meet its development goals in certain spheres. It is here that civil society groups have stepped in to enhance the democratic potential of the state, leading to new and innovative models of citizen participation.

Governance is becoming more inclusive through public-private partnerships (PPP), NGO activism and certain institutional arrangements through which civil society groups can influence government policy. According to Action Aid, within days of the December 2004 tsunami, in Tamil Nadu alone, about 3 lakh people had been accommodated in relief camps organised by a joint government-civil society initiative and by the end of October 2005, about 65,438 families from 461 villages through 29 partner NGOs and 7 community-based organisations had been reached.

Tools of Empowerment

- PIL
- RTI Act
- Public hearings
- E-governance
- Panchayati Raj
- Community policing

NGOs can generate public pressure for change through innovative means like report cards, which have been used by the Public Affairs Centre (PAC) in Bangalore. The Mazdoor Kisan Shakti Sangathan (MKSS) in Rajasthan has used *jan sunwais* or public hearings for improved local-level accountability.

Public protest is increasingly being used as a tool for advocacy, and many grass-roots campaigns have grown into full-fledged social movements. The demand for right to information was first raised in the panchayats by the MKSS, before it became broad-based. Now, a year after RTI came into force, there exist a number of success stories across the country—from a rickshaw puller in Bihar successfully getting a house, to villagers in Karnataka invoking RTI for improved quality of foodgrains.

Many in the corporate world are also going beyond mere tokens of social responsibility. For example, the Azim Premji Foundation, in partnership with the Karnataka government's Sarva Shiksha Abhiyan, is aiding primary schools in 3700 villages in seven districts, contributing to a marked improvement in results. Under another successful PPP, Kisan call centres have been delivering extension services to farmers in the local language since 2004.

There has been a rise in e-governance initiatives in many Indian states. One such model, Karnataka's Bhoomi programme for computerising land records, has resulted in a steep decline in the level of corruption, with Andhra Pradesh and Chhattisgarh emulating the model.

Direct management of water resources by water users' associations in parts of India is a good example of citizens directly partaking in governance. The government's Swajaldhara scheme is a participatory, demand-driven rural water supply scheme with partial cost sharing and full operation and maintenance costs by the local community.

As the next story shows, the creative use of new technology networks is helping empower citizens to self-organise outside the ambit of government and traditional media.

PART II

MANAGING OF NPOs

CHAPTER

9

Management and Organisation of NPO

Like commercial business organisations, non-profit organisations more need application of management concepts to improve utilisation of its resources and be a viable entity (Peter F. Drucker). These management concepts are: (a) Mission statement, (b) Planning process, (c) Organising marketing, staffing, financing, controlling, etc. We have covered some concepts in Chapter 4. Some aspects are discussed in this chapter while others are dealt with in subsequent chapters.

(i) Organisation structure of NPO.
(ii) Some functional bodies/policies.
(iii) Planning process.
(iv) The evaluation process.
(v) Ethics in NPO.

(I) ORGANISATION STRUCTURE OF NPO

A typical organisation structure for a non-profit organisation is given in Figure 1.

(II) SOME FUNCTIONAL BODIES/POLICIES

Some functional aspects are mentioned below:

(a) Board of Trustees

They are individuals from the community and may not receive monetary compensation for serving on the board. Responsibilities of the trustees are:

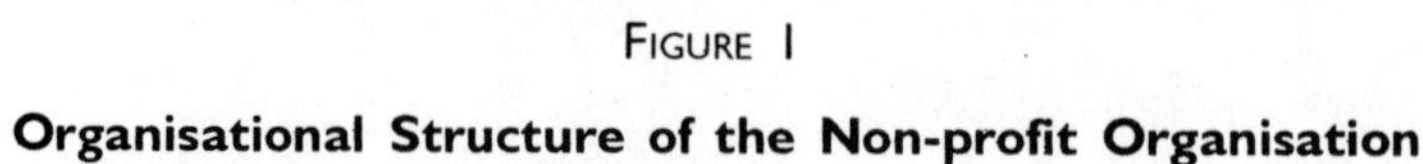

FIGURE I

Organisational Structure of the Non-profit Organisation

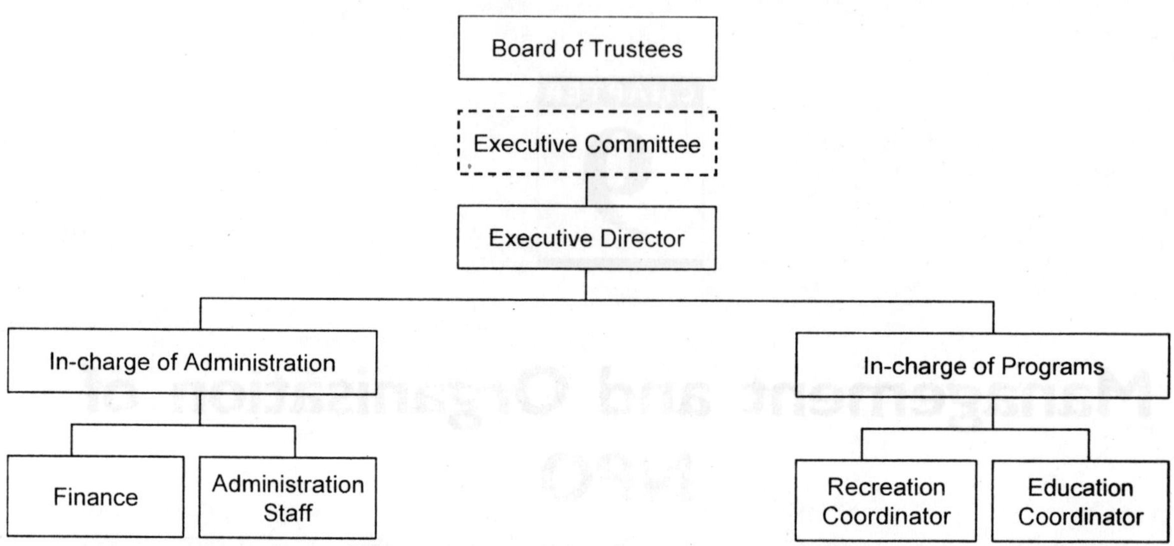

- To determine *organisation mission* and *set policies* for its operation,
- To *set overall* programme yearly and long range,
- To set *budgets and financial* controls,
- To select and evaluate appointment of executive director,
- To develop *communication link to the community* promoting work of the non-profit organisation, and
- To establish *policies that protect NPO* from misuse of funds and establish controls.

Important as it is to understand what the duties of trustees include, it is equally important to understand what they do not include. Trustees should not:

- Engage in the day-to-day operation of the organisation.
- Hire staff other than the chief executive.
- Make detailed programmatic decisions without consulting staff.

(b) Executive Director

He is appointed by the board and is to provide *strategy direction*, guidance and controls of the board. He looks after *forward planning* and implementation of its policies and programmes to achieve their mission. NPOs usually strive to keep costs of administration low in proportion to costs to run programmes.

Fund raising can be main job of the NPOs executive director. He has to balance his time between raising money and programmes. Executive director has to devote adequate time, to planning, particularly strategic realistic plans.

(c) Policy Management

Some policies to be formulated are:

- NPO has a values statement that is revised regularly.
- The mission statement is reviewed by the board of trustees at least every two years.
- The constitution and by-laws are reviewed by the board.
- The board sets annual goals for NPO.
- Board controls the signing authority for NPO.
- The non-profit organisation has a strategic plan.
- A *strong culture of accountability* is necessary for effective governance. Every individual should be responsible for a specific task otherwise it leads to corruption, delays, diffused decision-making, poor service, etc.

(d) Financial Management

Some financial policies to be take care are:

- NPO has annual budget and plan for achieving it,
- Financial statements are presented to the board quarterly,
- NPO has an annual independent audit,
- The cost of fund raising has not to exceed 25% of funds raised,
- At least 75% of expenses are directed to charitable objects of the organisation,
- Every programme is to be evaluated, service users are involved in evaluations.

Box I

Responsibilities of Trustees

(i) Hiring and Working with the Chief Executive

The character of almost every non-profit organisation is set in large measure by its chief executive. This is because the chief executive not only speaks for the organisation publicly but he also hires the staff that deals on a day-to-day basis with the organisation's constituency. Thus, the public's impression of the organisation is very much in the chief executive's hands. Consequently, the selection of this person is a very great responsibility. In selecting the chief executive the following rules should be followed:

- Trustees should agree on what their expectations are. They should decide what kind of person they are looking for and what special qualifications the person should possess before they look at a single resume.
- Trustees should document what the job entails. There should be a clear job description that lists both general responsibilities and specific tasks.
- In talking to serious candidates, trustees should be honest about organisational problems. They should not pretend things are fine when they are not. If there are financial problems, staff problems, or even trustee problems, there is nothing to gain in the long-run by hiding them.

- Trustees should be clear about how the chief executive's performance is going to be evaluated. If there is a formal review process, it should be described. If there is not, the person should be told what criteria will be used to determine how successfully he is doing the job.
- In many cases, trustees may wish to utilize the professional experience, expertise, and contacts of an executive search firm. Although there may be substantial costs involved, the trustees may decide that such an investment is worthwhile in order to find and select the best person for the job.

(ii) Evaluation

Regular evaluation of a chief executive is also an important responsibility of the trustees. It is an excellent way to foster good communication about perceived successes, failures, and expectations for the future. Evaluation should take place at least once a year, at some time immediately prior to the negotiation over salary for the upcoming year.

Trustees should never feel guilty about initiating a process of evaluation that may lead to termination. Those who resist doing so are not exercising their responsibility to the organisation they are serving.

(iii) The Performance

This review is a convenient first opportunity to alert the chief executive that the trustees are dissatisfied with his performance. The more specific the criticisms at this stage, the easier it will be for the board president to communicate them and to develop a procedure whereby the executive is given some time to try to improve job performance.

(iv) Developing a Good Working Relationship

The relationship between the board and the staff of a non-profit organisation is critical to its successful operation. Much of the tone of that relationship is set by the chief executive and the board president When these two individuals work well together, many Potential problems between staff and board can be averted.

(III) WHAT IS A PLANNING PROCESS?

Planning is an ongoing process involving several steps that are listed below:

Step 1: Set parameters and boundaries.
Step 2: Identify limiting conditions.
Step 3: Change limiting conditions where possible.
Step 4: Design a plan of action.
Step 5: Carry out the action plan.
Step 6: Evaluate what you have done.
Step 7: Repeat what you have done.

There are two patterns of planning process as under:

(i) Linear Planning Model
(ii) Integrated planning model

These are explained below:

(i) Linear Planning Model

FIGURE 2

Linear Planning

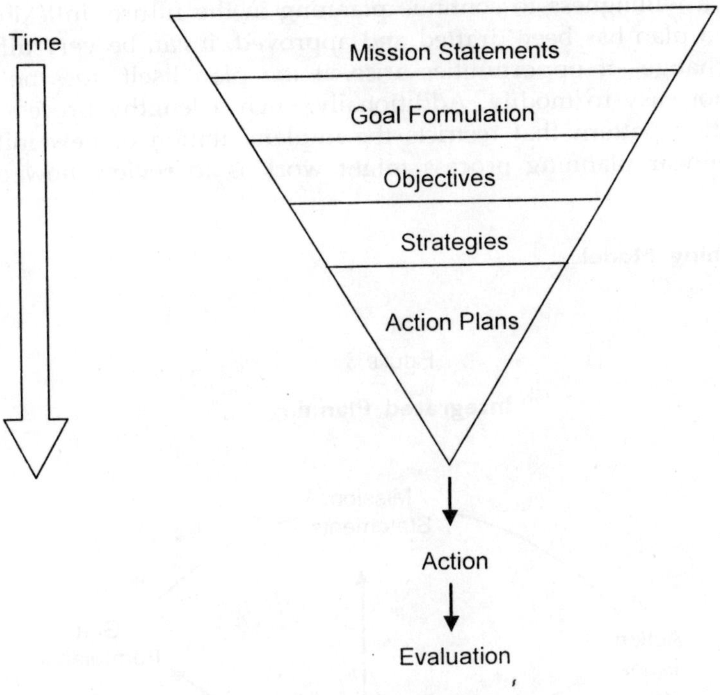

Linear planning proceeds by a process of condensation ad distillation following the steps outlined earlier in the chapter. It considers a whole range of options at each level of planning (mission, goals, objectives, and strategies) and in each case eliminates all but the very few that appear most reasonable and sensible. The linear planning model is best described visually by a triangle, as shown in Figure 2. The triangle, a visual metaphor for linear planning over time, reveals two special characteristics of this approach to planning. First, it shows how linear planning always proceeds from a process of broad mission and goal formulation to the more narrow and specific process of writing action plans, and second, it shows how linear planning tends to slough off many options and narrow down to a very few.

Linear planning has advantages and disadvantages. The principal advantage is its comprehensiveness. When a non-profit organisation wants to look at itself in a systematic way, evaluating and speculating about its future in a wide variety of areas, the linear approach works well. Similarly, when the organisation undertakes a controversial, risky, or expensive new project, or significantly changes its mission, it can prove to the world at large that the new direction has not been undertaken lightly, that many people have been consulted, and that many options have been considered. Another advantage is that a linear planning process often generates a formal public document that provides the framework for actions and protects the organisation from pressures to consider other approaches.

Unfortunately, the very comprehensiveness of linear planning is one of its major disadvantages. It is often a slow and frustrating process. Many organisations spend months drafting mission statements, begin to tackle goals, and simply give up in exhaustion without a plan and without a willingness to continue planning in the future. Inflexibility is a second disadvantage. Once a plan has been drafted and approved, it can be very difficult to change. Should conditions change—if opportunities arise, if the plan itself does not seem to be on track—the plan is not easy to modify. Additionally, such a lengthy process often places an organisation in holding pattern that restricts the implementation of new initiatives. A good way to see how a linear planning process might work is to review how one organisation managed the task.

(ii) Integrated Planning Model

FIGURE 3

Integrated Planning

An integrated planning model is best *represented visually by a circle* that resembles a wheel with spokes (Figure 3). The planning coordinator sits at the center of the wheel collecting information from and communicating it to the wheel's perimeter via the spokes. At the perimeter, various people are working on specific tasks. These tasks are already familiar to us—one group may be evaluating current activities, another might be reviewing statements of purpose, a third might be surveying the organisation's membership to formulate new goals for the future, a fourth might be talking to potential funders, a fifth might be working on budgets relating to specific action plans, and so forth. In some cases, one group or even one individual might take on several of these tasks. In order for the wheel to turn—representing the organisation's forward progress in planning the planning coordination process must take place at the center. This involves three types of activity; collecting information from the planning groups at the wheel's perimeter, communicating relevant information back to these groups, and ultimately fitting all the pieces of information into a coherent plan.

Integrated planning is by its very nature an *ongoing process*. List the wheel that serves as the visual metaphor for the process, it has no beginning point and no end point and is continually moving. For this reason, *integrated planning tends to emphasize the process of planning*.

(i) *This is one of its advantages over linear planning*. Unlike linear planning, an integrated process enables an organisation to be immediately responsive to change, opportunity, and setbacks. It does not have to begin the process of planning all over again in order to respond to a sudden change in the funding environment, political reversals, or in staffing and governance that could lead to new opportunities and activities. Rather, when changes occur, goals can be reformulated and action plans can be drafted all at the same time. It is the role of the planning coordinator (or planning committee) to see that all of these tasks are completed that there is adequate communication flow, and that the results of the various components of planning dovetail to make a coherent whole.

(ii) *A second advantage of integrated planning is that it encourages the board, staff, and constituency to remain involved in the process in an ongoing way*. In linear planning, people often have only one or two opportunities in each decade to take a fundamental look at missions and goals. They tend to spend a lot of time being careful to "get it right" and then the discussion is dropped. In integrated planning, the process drives itself forward continually and the discussion of mission, goals, objectives, and strategies is repeatedly revisited. Furthermore, a discussion of strategies does not wait for the discussion of mission to be completed, because there is no such thing as closure on that discussion. What does happen is that a continually evolving plan is drafted and updated. Because the plan can always be revised as the planning process moves forward and because the various planning components fit together, no air of finality hangs over the draft passed along. It is true that there is rarely a comprehensive planning document as in linear planning. However, there are working policies adopted by the board periodically, goal statements—(reviewed at least annually), as well as objectives, strategies, and specific activity schedules to guide the actions of the staff.

(iii) *A third advantage of integrated planning is that it tends to move more quickly toward action*. Linear planning models, as we have seen, are slow because they assume that distillation is the essence of planning and that in any planning decision, every reasonable alternative should be considered. Although this does lead to informed choices in planning, those choices may be a long time in coming. In the work they do and the way in which they do it justifies their special position. Tax deductibility of gifts and tax exemptions are two of the most important of these benefits, but there are many others. If the differences between non-profit and commercial enterprises to shrink, then the rationale for preserving those benefits will diminish as well. In the end, these benefits are too valuable to lose.

(iv) The Valuation Process

It is appropriate to explain the evaluation process. No non-profit organisation is governed or managed perfectly and most have serious shortcomings in several areas. The ones that are most successful are able to get the board and staff to commit to a process for evaluating problems and making thing better. This is done by taking a few important steps:

1. Accurately diagnosing the organisation's current situation and identifying areas in which there are opportunities for positive change.
2. Separating the problems into those that need immediate attention and those that might be dealt with later.
3. Building board and staff consensus so that the identified problems can be dealt with honestly, forthrightly, and in a timely manner.
4. Developing a realistic, affordable, multi-year schedule for implementing change.
5. Continuing the diagnostic, evaluation, and self-improvement process year after year.

Assessing Strengths, Weaknesses, Problems and Opportunities

The diagnosis of an organisation's current strengths, weaknesses, problems, and opportunities involves making assessments in several areas and evaluating the organisation from several points of view. The process involves asking questions about how well the organisation measures up to a pre-defined ideal.

Mission, Image, and Case for Support

A. Mission

A strong organisation is one whose purpose is relevant to current needs of the community it serves and to the requirements of a broad and well-defined constituency.

- Is the mission statement up-to-date or out-of-date (i.e., how closely does it actually conform to what the organisation seems to be about)? How might the mission statement be reworded so that it is more reflective of the organisation's purpose?
- Is the mission itself still relevant to the needs of those served (i.e., is there a compelling reason for the organisation to exist)? Can this be demonstrated in a concrete way that would convince a skeptic? Should the mission be broadened or changed in some way to become more relevant to contemporary needs?
- Who is being served (i.e., who are the clients)? Is this constituency sufficiently diverse or is it too narrowly focused on a small group? If the constituency should be broadened, what concrete steps might be taken to accomplish this?

B. Image

The organisation should be well known and well respected in its community and among its constituency.

- Does the organisation's name mean anything to people in the community? How familiar are people with its activities? Are there people who should know about the organisation but don't? How can the organisation's profile be raised?
- What is the organisation reputation? Is it well respected? Is there any old history or controversy that plagues its image? How can this be taken care of?

C. Case for Support

The organisation should present a compelling case for support both to its clients and to its contributors?

- How convincing is the organisation's pitch to its users and its funders? Are the services, activities, and programmes of the organisation described in a way that will entice full participation?
- How clearly and simply are the financial needs of the organisation outlined?

(V) ETHICS IN NON-PROFIT ORGANISATIONS

We shall cover following areas:

(a) Some ethical aspects in NPOs.
(b) Need for social survey to get objective facts.
(c) Ethical aspects in social survey.

(a) Ethical Aspects in NPOs

- Ethics is *essential for all managers*—business profit organisations and non-profit organisations. Managers without ethics are like a human body without blood vessels.
- NPOs are to follow certain criteria in discharging *social responsibilities,* e.g. environmental issues, follow certain standards, establish codes of conduct, etc.
- NPOs are to build a *values-driven organisation,* i.e. articulate their values, publicize them, repeat them. Values require to be kept up-to-date so that promote NPOs vision to all the stakeholders.
- Further, it is essential to *incorporate the values into all decision processes* at all levels of NPO. *Non-financial* values have great importance as to fund raising there should be absolute transparency, total honesty with contributors so that none gives to a cause of objection.
- While campaigning against *immorality of business,* how much thought do manager's in *NPO give in their own conduct*?
- How ethically robust are NPOs *employment policies*?
- How *honest is advertising/publicity*?
- Do managers *use exaggeration* either in campaigning or fund raising?

(b) Social Survey for Objective Facts

Commonsense is undependable. Objective research often shows that commonsense ideas are highly limited or false so there is need to find objective findings through social survey.

In social survey methods or steps are as under:

(i) Selecting a topic to be studied.
(ii) Defining the problem to narrow the topic.
(iii) Defining the literature, i.e. to know existing knowledge.
(iv) Formulation of hypothesis.
(v) Choosing a research method such as drafting of interview questionnaire, population to be studied, i.e. numbers, etc.
(vi) Conducting a pilot study and finalising a questionnaire. Training of interviewers is important.
(vii) Collecting the data through various sources such as:
   - Survey,
   - Participants observation,
   - Document and records,
   - Secret measures, and
   - Experiment, i.e. identifying experimental group and control group.
(viii) Processing data and analysing the results.
(ix) Sharing the results or preparing a report.

(c) Ethics (Morality) in Social Research or Survey

Some ethical requirements for social researcher are:

- Honesty, truth and *keeping confidentiality of information.*
- *Falsification of results* not to be done. *Do not misrepresent* or distort data. Project the anonymity of people to avoid embarrassing.
- Free from researcher's own values. (See Box 2)

Box 2

Laczniak's Fourteen Ethical Propositions

- Ethical conflicts and choices are interent in NPOs decision-making.
- Proper ethical behaviour exists on a plane above the law. The law merely specifies the lowest common denominator of acceptable behaviour.
- There is no single satisfactory standard of ethical action agreeable to everyone that a manager can use to make specific operational decisions.
- Managers should be familiar with a wide variety of ethical standards.
- Consensus regarding what constitutes proper ethical behaviour in a decision-making situation in diminishes as the level of analysis proceeds from abstract to specific.
- The moral tone of an organisation is set by top management.
- The lower the organisational level of a manager, the greater the perceived pressure to act unethically.

- Individual managers perceive themselves as more ethical than their colleagues.
- Effective codes of ethics should contain meaningful and clearly stated provisions, along with enforced sanctions for non-compliance.
- Employees must have a non-punitive, fail-safe mechanism for reporting ethical abuses in the organisation.
- Every organisation should appoint a top-level manager to be responsible for acting as an ethical advocate in the organisation.

Source: G. Laczniak, "Business Ethics: A Manager's Primer," Business, Georgia Stafe University (January-March, 1983): 23-29, Quoted in Fred R. David, *op. cit.*, p. 23.

CHAPTER

10

Strategic Management in Non-profit Organisations

In this chapter the following aspects regarding applicability of strategic management in non-profit organisations are discussed:

(a) Applicability of strategic management in NPO.
(b) Difference between NPO and profit organisation.
(c) Sources of revenues is most important factor of distinction.
(d, e) Strategic management concepts and tasks of strategic management for organisation direction.
(f, g, h) Vision, mission, objectives and goals.
(i) Strategy formulation and implementation.
(j) Strategy evaluation and control.
(k) Steps to control constraints.

(A) APPLICABILITY OF STRATEGIC MANAGEMENT IN NPO

The basic concepts of strategic management are applicable to profit and non-profit organisations. All organisations formulate the *objectives, strategies and tactics*. In fact, they analyse the environments—internal and external, formulate strategies, analyse and select the appropriate strategies. However, there are distinct differences between profit and non-profit organisations.

(B) DIFFERENCE BETWEEN NPO AND PROFIT ORGANISATION

Non-profit organisations can be basically classified into groups, viz.: (i) private non-profit organisations, and (ii) public non-profit organisations. Significant differences among profit organisations and non-profit private organisations are in Figure 1.

FIGURE 1

Differences between Profit and Non-profit/Private Organisations

	Profit Organisations	*Non-profit/Private Organisations*
Ownership	Private	Private
Funding	Sales revenue	Membership fee, contribute from public and/or private sources, sale of products or services
Formation	Single proprietorship, partnership, corporation	Floated by members
Activities	Production and/or marketing of goods and/or services	Educational, charitable, social service, health service, foundation, cultural, religious, and recreational
Objective (main)	Profit maximization	Service maximization

Though the public organisations like central government, state governments and local governments are also included under non-profit organisations, *typically* the term non-profit includes private non-profit organisations such as hospitals, private universities, private colleges and recreational societies, etc. Public utilities like transportation corporation, water supply corporations, dairy corporations are in a grey area somewhere between profit and non-profit organisations. Non-profit organisations assumes importance as the society, particularly, low-income people depend on these organisations. Further, they provide services which cannot be provided by the profit-making organisations.

(C) SOURCES OF REVENUE IS MOST IMPORTANT FACTOR OF DISTINCTION

The *sources of revenue* is one of the important factors which differentiates the profit organisations and non-profit organisations. The profit organisations mainly depend upon the revenue of sales of goods and/or services. Their sources of income is the customer who buys and uses the product and/or service, and who pays for it when received. Profit results when the revenue is more than the costs of producing and distributing the product. Profit is the main measure of the corporation's effectiveness.

The non-profit organisations depends on *membership dues, assessments,* donations, funding from sponsor agencies, subscriptions to the periodicals published by the organisations. Thus, revenue for these organisations comes from a variety of sources.

(D) STRATEGIC CONCEPTS IN NON-PROFIT ORGANISATIONS

Various issues of strategic management concerning to non-profit organisations include: formulation of *mission, goals* and *objectives, environmental analysis, strategy formulation* and *implementation and strategic control.*

Strategy formulation process reviews the internal environmental conditions and external environmental conditions with a view to analyse the strengths, weaknesses, opportunities and threats of the firm, develop the alternative strategies and select the best strategy. Strategy formulation policy helps to obtain information from the environment deciding and redeciding an organisational vision, mission, objectives and goals as shown in Figure 2.

FIGURE 2

Organisational Direction Process

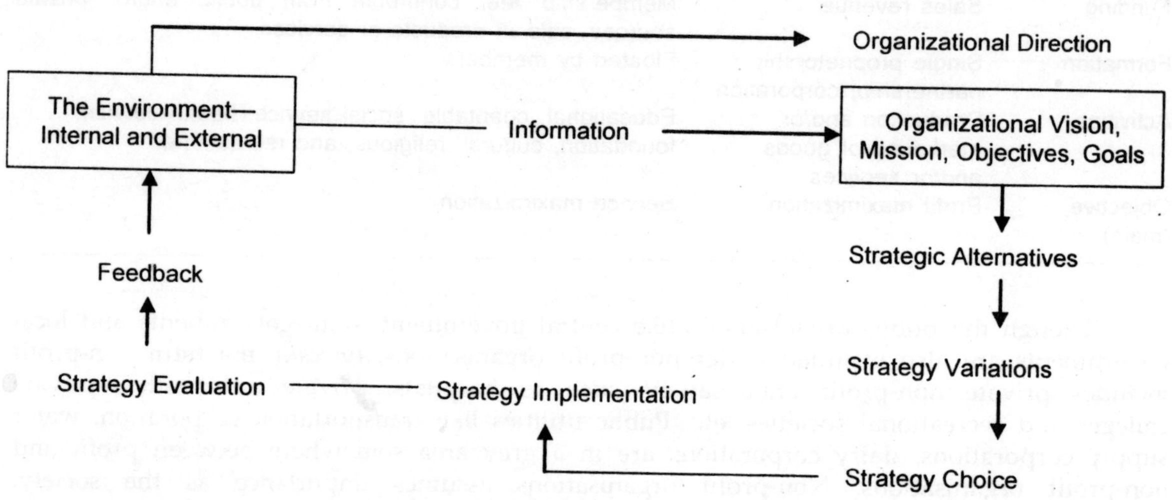

(E) FIVE TASKS OF STRATEGIC MANAGEMENT

Strategic management consists of five tasks in establishing organisational direction. (Also see Box 1)

(i) Articulating a vision of organisation's future where the organisation needs to be leading.
(ii) Translating that vision into a mission that defines the organisation's purpose.
(iii) Converting the mission into performance objectives, (sometimes objectives are converted into plans and policies.)
(iv) Detailing each objective into specific goals.
(v) Formulating strategies and tactics to achieve the goals.

(F) VISION

Vision and mission statements are powerful shapers of effective corporate cultures for many organisations. These statements present the values, philosophies and aspirations, that guide organisational action. In fact, they motivate and inspire the current and future employees of the organisation.

An organisational vision is the answer to the question: "What do we want to create?" Shared visions in organisations, "create sense of commonality that permeates the organisation and gives coherence to diverse activities." The corporate vision has the potential power to focus the collective energy of insiders and to give outsiders a better idea of what an organisation really is.

FIGURE 3

Organisational Direction

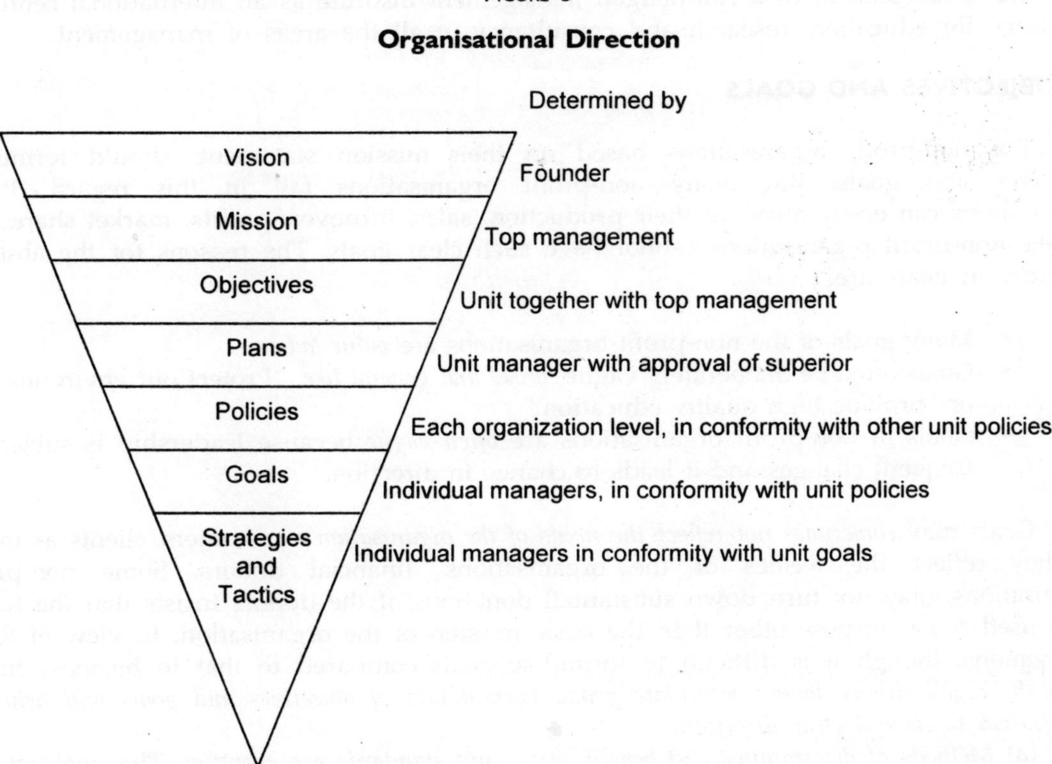

Vision is developed through sharing across an organisation

Famous stories of successful visions involve visions that have been widely shared across entire organisations. Of course, an individual leader, often a founder has a powerful impact on the others. The leaders by working hard convince others in NPO.

(G) MISSION

Formulation of well defined mission is important to non-profit organisations to have a clear direction. In fact, the major non-profit organisations formulate mission. According to Peter F. Drucker, "the best non-profits devote a great deal of thought to defining their organisation's mission.

The non-profit organisations while formulating the mission should consider the vision and ask questions like: What is our business? Or what are our activities? Who is the customer? Or who are our clients? What does our customer (or client) consider the value?

As an example, the mission statement of one non-profit medical institute is:

Our mission shall be the promotion of human knowledge within the field of the basic sciences (principally in the field of medical research and medical education) and the effective application thereof for the benefit of mankind."

The mission statement of a management educational institute is:

The establishment of a full-fledged management institute as an international centre of excellence for education, research and consultancy in all the areas of management.

(H) OBJECTIVES AND GOALS

The non-profit organisations based on their mission statement, should formulate objectives and goals. But many non-profit organisations fail in this regard. Profit organisations can easily measure their production, sales, turnover, profits, market share, etc. But the non-profit organisations cannot have such clear goals. The reasons for the absence of clarity in goals are:

- Many goals of the non-profit organisations are *value-laden*.
- Goals often be deliberately vague, *broad and general like*. "Protect our environment," or "provide high quality education."
- Goals in non-profit organisations are *often vague* because leadership is subject to frequent changes and it leads to change in direction.

Goals may *sometimes not reflect the needs of the organisation's* customers/clients as much as they reflect the wishes of the organisations' financial donors. Some non-profit organisations, may not turn down substantial donations, if the donors insists that the funds to be used for a purpose other than the basic mission of the organisation. In view of these observations, though it is difficult to formulate goals compared to that in business firms, *non-profit organisations should formulate goals. Formulation of objectives and goals will help the organisation to have a clear direction.*

(a) *Methods of determining cost-benefit ratios and standards are essential*. The goals of the non-profit *health organisation include*:

(i) Community services like health, educational and environmental protection.
(ii) A centre for prevention of ill health, community problems.
(iii) Education for the community regarding health, sanitation, cleanliness, consumerism, etc.
(iv) Training and education of volunteers who will carry out the mission of the organisation like instructors, medical practitioners, religious priests, etc.
(v) Providing facilities for physicians, teachers, etc.

(b) *Determining the goals of a temple or church is equally* perplexing. The goal to provide: (i) worship facilities, (ii) religious education, (iii) evangelical effort, (iv) missionary effort, (v) opportunities for members to fulfil social and psychological needs, (vi) fund raising charitable organisations, (vii) contribution to the identification and solution of societal problems, (viii) contribution to the development of educational and health facilities like Sri Satya Sai Central Trust, and (ix) revival of the ruined temples like Tirumala Tirupati Devasthanams.

(c) Figure 4 shows the objectives and goals of a management institute.

FIGURE 4

Objectives and Goals of a Management Institute

Objectives

To pursue the stated mission, the Institute strives to achieve the following objectives:

(i) To train young students, add the value, develop their competency and inculcate professionalism among them in order to prepare appropriate managers and entrepreneurs for Eritrean economy.
(ii) To undertake research studies with a view to provide inputs to the policy-makers of the Government and business.
(iii) To organise management development and training programmes with a view to equip practicing managers with latest skills and techniques of management profession.
(iv) To organise seminars and conferences in order to disseminate the advanced managerial knowledge to the practicing managers.
(v) To provide consultancy services with a view to solve the managerial and operational problems of Eritrean business.
(vi) To undertake any related activities to pursue the mission.

Strategies

To achieve the above mentioned objectives, the following strategies are formulated:

(i) Strengthening teaching facilities like curriculum revision, preparation of qualitative course material and teaching aids.
(ii) Human resource development. It includes the development of junior staff through Ph.D., programmes of linkage Universities.
(iii) Support the library in process of procurement of books and journals.
(iv) Secondment of senior faculty.

Goals

Our goals during 1997-98 Academic Year are:

(i) Educate the students towards their M.B.A., degree with conceptual, practical skills and knowledge.
(ii) Modify the curriculum incorporating the courses relevant to Eritrean business.
(iii) Carry out the research studies in the areas of:
- Human Resource Management, and
- International Marketing.

(iv) Provide Tutorial classes for the government officers who are pursuing Certificate Course in Management of the Open University, UK.
(v) Provide consultancy services.
(vi) Organisation of National and International Seminars and Conferences.
(vii) Conduct Management Development and Training Programmes.

(I) STRATEGY FORMULATION AND IMPLEMENTATION

Strategy formulation is more or less the same in non-profit organisations compared to that of profit organisations. In general, most of the organisations attempt to satisfy specific social needs. The strategies of non-profit organisations *complement* the strategies and services of governmental agencies. For example, the strategies of Ministry of Health, Government of India and the non-profit health organisation strategies are more or less similar. They include: providing medical and health facilities to the people, development of hospitals and health clinics, development of doctors and para-medical personnel, etc.

(J) STRATEGY EVALUATION AND CONTROL

Strategy evaluation and control is rather very difficult as the objectives and goals are unclear. For example, the efficiency of hospitals can be measured in a number of ways. The standards are also not effective unless the goals are clearly stated. The control is more difficult, when goals are not clear or when goals are conflicting.

However, the strategies of non-profit organisations may be evaluated in one aspect. The approach to evaluation in the absence of quantifiable objectives, is being cost-aware and concentrating upon making the operation efficient i.e., to achieve the same output with less input. However, if the organisation does not have objectives/goals, the importance of a budget-based organisation is determined by the size of its staff and the size of its budget.

(K) STEPS TO CONTROL THE CONSTRAINTS

The non-profit organisation can deal with the complications arising from the constraints to some extent through the following measures:

(i) Selection of a Dynamic and Forceful Leader

He should be influential to make the others tc accept his decisions. The leader can formulate appropriate mission, objectives and goals and raise to approach that the decisions are pushed from top to the down. Therefore, the lower level managers should adapt the approaches of 'play it safe,' 'await the guidance', etc.

(ii) Develop a Mystique

The non-profit organisation can be integrated toward efficient goal accomplishment by developing a 'mystique' that dominates the enterprise and attracts the likely sponsors. The shared value about the important mission by the employees and sponsors can serve to motivate unusually high performance and client satisfaction. Once established, the mystique sets the character and values to decision-makers and others are expected to follow.

(iii) Generate Rules and Regulations

The non-profit organisations suffer from the absence of objectives and goals and concentrating on the sponsors rather than clients. Hence, the top management should formulate rules and regulations so that the employees will pay enough attention towards the clients.

(iv) Appointment of a Strong Board

Appointment of a strong board of trustees will help the organisation in funds raising, formulation of mission and objectives. Then the employees can concentrate on the clients. The board can concentrate on strategic issues as well as on the operational issues like hiring, directing and developing the budget.

(v) Establishment of Performance-based Budget

Establishment of performance-based budgets is the fifth approach in dealing with complications of non-profit organisations. This approach is to institute an information system that ties measurable objective to budget line items. One such system is planning, programming and budgeting system. It includes five steps:

- Specify objectives as clearly as possible in quantitative measurable terms.
- Analyse the actual output of the non-profit organisation in terms of the stated objectives.
- Measure the cost of the particular programme.
- Analyse alternatives and search for those that have the greatest effectiveness in achieving the objectives.
- Establish the process in a systematic way so that it continues to occur over time.

Box I

Need for Strategic Management in NPO

Social services departments are striving to come to terms with fundamental changes in their external environment. Some of these changes mirror the management revolution in the private sector, inspired by the now familiar ideas of excellent service to *customers, cost effectiveness, leadership and enterprise*. This has meant a change in the nature of public services in general and relationship between central and local governments in the past decade. Local authorities had now to learn to adapt to the introduction of radical principles of restraint on local government spending, the new community charge, competition in providing services, privatization and consumerism. Social services were subject to these changes too, and were forced to look at the provision of services very differently. The ideas of *joint planning* and collaboration with other agencies began to develop. Social services departments are now emerging, like many other local departments and local councils themselves, with a new and predominantly 'enabling role', no longer the sole or even the main provider of services. More traditional methods of management based on a reactive, *ad-hoc* approach, with autonomous decision-making by social work professionals, are no longer sufficient to cope with this speed of change in the environment. Management experts suggest that in this situation organisations require a strategic management approach. Social services departments are no exception.

Concept of Strategic Management

Strategic management is associated with the setting, planning and meeting of the primary goals of the organisation. It requires the formulation of strategies to cope with a wide range of variables. It should enabled departments to abandon the familiar role of passive victim at the mercy of conflicting pressures, uncertain political and economic climates and other competing organisations. It requires a clear vision of the future and of the future goals of the organisation and a willingness to take risks. At a more concrete level, strategic management depends on flexible structures, a different management style and a new range of organisational processes. These include strategic, medium-term, planning functions based on research and analysis, with effective budgetary control systems and performance monitoring.

The key to the understanding of the strategic management approach is the way in which organisations manage the external environment in which they operate. The introductory section indicates two broad categories of environment, one that concentrates on the other organisations with which the local organisation transacts and another that emphasises macro-level forces, such as the economic climate or

FIGURE 5

Strategic Management Model of Norman Tutt and his Co-authors

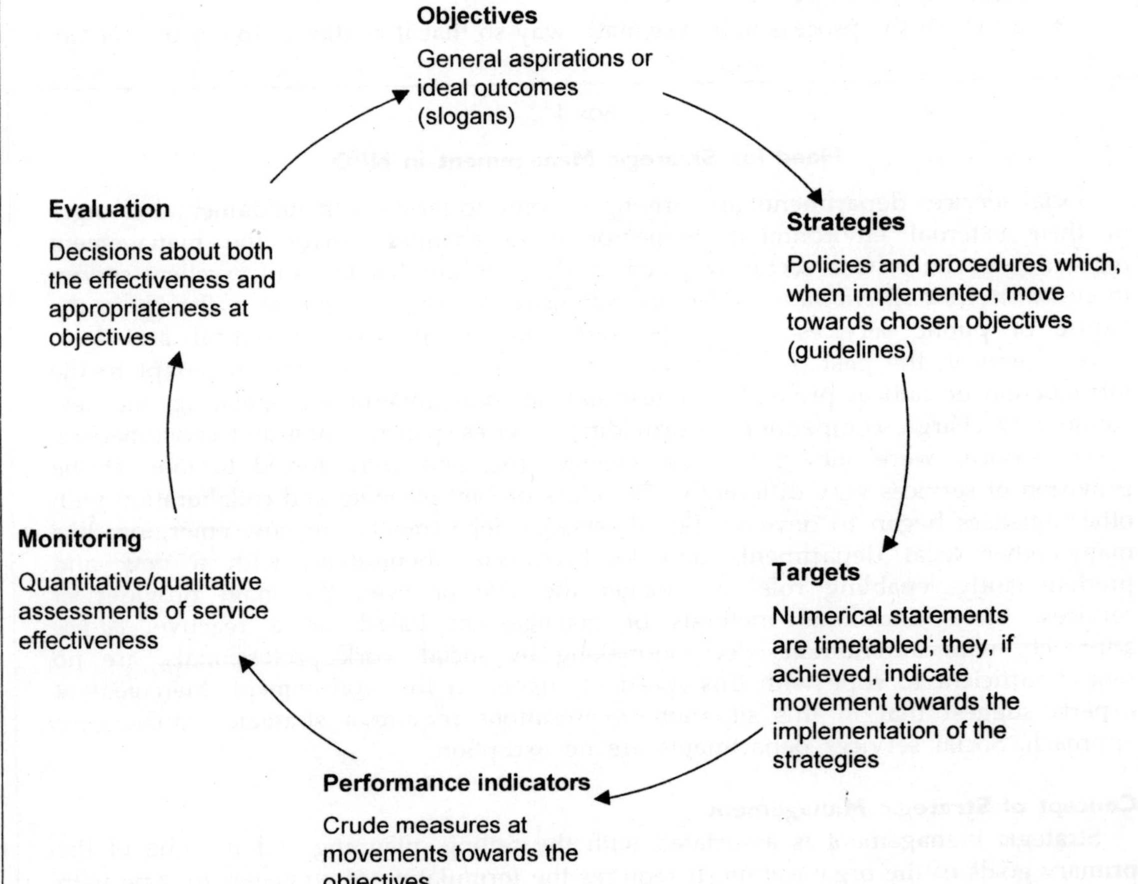

demography. How the public services manage this environment will vary from the methods used by other types of organisation. Social services are obliged to provide services within an imposed statutory framework and meet their legal responsibilities. Social services departments must, therefore, concentrate on controlling or influencing the other institutions active within their environment, but also forecasting and responding to the macro-level variables. Social services departments cannot operate or develop without reference to central government, including the Social Services Inspectorate. At a local level, social services departments work within a long established local government framework of committees, elected members, annual budgets and other municipal departments. Also at a local level, these departments interact with other statutory bodies, particularly local health authorities, the police and courts at a planning and operational level. The voluntary organisations, non-profit agencies and private companies, which together make up the non-statutory sector, are now poised to become more significant figures in the external environment.

Consideration of variables and complex pattern of relationships in the external environment and the extent to which they can be managed, controlled, influenced or predicted forms the basis of this contribution on strategic management in social services.

Key stages in a strategic management cycle (Figure 5) include defining objectives, devising strategies, setting targets, monitoring progress, evaluation and back again to redefining objectives.

In social work parlance, it is important that departments move away from their helpless victim role, seize the initiative and take full responsibility for their future development. In this analogy strategic management then becomes akin to social work. This has the power to turn the client's (or department's) view of the future into a reality by setting a series of achievable goals and then keeping the client on course for independence, prosperity or success.

Box 2

Points on Planning

1. *Planning involves defining the organisation's goals, establishing an overall strategy* for achieving those goals, and developing a comprehensive set of plans to integrate and coordinate organisational work. It's concerned with both the ends (what's to be done) and the means (how it's to be done).

2. *Managers plan for four reasons*: planning gives direction by establishing coordinated efforts, planning reduces the impact of change, planning minimizes wasted time and resources and redundancy, and planning sets the standards used in controlling.

3. *Goals—desired outcomes for individuals, groups, or an entire organisation*—are often called the foundation of planning because they provide the direction for all management decisions and form the criterion against which actual work accomplishments are measured.

4. *Strategic plans cover an extensive time period, cover broad issues, and include the formulation of objectives.* Operational plans cover shorter time periods, focus on specifics, and assume that objectives are already known. Long-term plans are those with a time frame beyond three years. Short-term plans are those covering one year or less. Specific plans are clearly defined and leave no room for interpretation. Directional plans are flexible plans that set out general guidelines. A single-use plan is a one-time plan specifically designed to meet the needs of a unique situation. Standing plans are ongoing plans that provide guidance for activities performed repeatedly.

5. *Goals can be established by traditional goal setting or by management by objectives.* Traditional goal setting is an approach in which goals are set at the top organisational level and then broken down into sub-goals for each level of the organisation. Management by objectives is a management system in which specific performance goals are jointly determined by employees and their managers, progress toward accomplishing these goals is periodically reviewed, and rewards are allocated on the basis of this progress.

6. *Well-designed goals have the following characteristics*: written in terms of *outcomes* rather actions; *measurable and quantifiable*; clear as to time frame; *challenging* but attainable; written down; and communicated to all organisational members who need to know the goals.

7. Three *contingency factors that affect planning* include the level in the organisation, the degree environmental uncertainty, and the length of commitments.

8. The traditional approach to developing plans was that it was done by top-level managers who were assisted by a formal planning department. The plans developed by top managers flowed down through other organisational levels and were tailored to the particular needs of each level. Another approach to planning is to involve more organisational members in the process. Instead of plans being handed down from one level to the next, they are developed by organisational members at the different levels and in the various work units to meet their specific needs.

9. *The major criticisms of formal planning* are: (a) It may create rigidity in organisational decisions and actions; (b) plans can't be developed for a dynamic environment; (c) formal plans can't replace intuition and creativity; (d) planning focuses managers' attention on today's competition, not on tomorrow's survival; and (e) formal planning reinforces success and thereby ultimately may lead to failure.

10. *Effective planning in a dynamic environment means developing plans that are specific but flexible*; being willing to change directions if environmental conditions warrant; staying alert to environmental charges that could impact the effective implementation of plans and making changes as needed; and continuing formal planning efforts even when the environment is highly uncertain.

REFERENCES

Peter F. Drucker, "What Business can Learn from Non-profits," *Harvard Business Review*, Vol. 67, No. 4, 1989, p. 89.

Brayne, "Profiting from the Non-profits," p. 72.

The Annual Report of the Howard Hughes Medical Institute, 1989.

P.D. Harvey and J.D. Synder, "Charities Need a Bottom Line Too," *Harvard Business Review*, Vol. 65, No. 1, 1987, pp. 14-22.

David F. Hussey, "Corporate Planning for a Church," Long Range Planning, April 1974, p. 63.

W.H. Newman and H.W. Wallender III, "Managing Non-profit Enterprises," *Academy of Management Review*, January 1978, n. 26.

P.C. Nutt, "A Strategic Planning Network for Non-profit Organisations", *Strategic Management Journal*, Jan.-March 1984.

Keating, B.P. and Keating, M.O., Not for Profit, Thomas Horton and Daughters, New Jersey, 1980.

P. Subba Rao, Business Policy and Strategic Management, Himalaya Publishing House, Mumbai.

Norman Tutt, Jean Neale and William Warburton, Strategic Management in Social Service, in Hand Book of Public Services Management (edited by Charistopher Pollitt and Stephen Harrison) Blackwell Business, Oxford, OX-9, IJF, UK.

CHAPTER

11

Leadership in NPOs

Throughout history the difference between success and failure, whether in a war, a business or non-profit organisation or games has been attributed to leadership. In fact, leaders make real difference such as Tata's, Billgates, Obroi, Mother Teresa and many more.

We have covered this topic under following headings:

1. Importance of leadership.
2. Critical skills of effective managers.
3. Four leadership styles:
   (a) Transformational leadership,
   (b) Coaching,
   (c) Superleadership, and
   (d) Entrepreneurial leadership.
4. Current topics in leadership.

Managerial leadership is *hot topic* in the world due to problems faced—recession, innovative technological revolution, competitive environment. It ranks at the top in the list of development programmes in all sectors.

I. IMPORTANCE OF LEADERSHIP

It can be realised that difference between leader and manager are made now. Characteristic of the leader and manager are shown in Figure 1.

A scientist was asked what he considered to be three dangers to society. Scientist mentioned:

(i) *Nuclear* war or accident that can destroy human race,
(ii) Worldwide *epidemic*, and
(iii) Quality of *leadership*.

FIGURE I

Characteristics of the Emerging Leader *versus* Characteristics of the Manager

LEADER	MANAGER
Soul	*Mind*
Visionary	Rational
Passionate	Consultative
Creative	Persistent
Flexible	Problem-solving
Inspirational	Tough-minded
Innovative	Analytical
Courageous	Structured
Imaginative	Deliberate
Experimental	Authoritative
Independent	Stabilising

Managers with leadership qualities make the *real difference* between success and failure. Managerial leadership is important for organisation effectiveness, survival and growth.

2. SKILLS OF EFFECTIVE MANAGERS

Effective managers have following skills:

(a) Personal Skills:
 (i) Developing self-awareness,
 (ii) Maintaining stress, and
 (iii) Solving problems creatively.

(b) Interpersonal Skills:
 (iv) Communicating supportively,
 (v) Gaining power and influence,
 (vi) Motivational, and
 (vii) Managing conflict.

3. FOUR LEADERSHIP STYLES

Four leadership styles have emerged in recent years to suit these new situations: transformational leadership, coaching, "superleadership," and "entrepreneurial leadership." Each of these new styles focus as under:

(a) Transformational Leadership

Transformational leadership is leadership that inspires organisational success by profoundly affecting followers' beliefs in what an organisation should be, as well as their values, such as justice and integrity. This style of leadership creates a sense of duty within an organisation, encourages new ways of handling problems, and promotes learning for all organisation members. Transformational leadership is closely related to concepts like charismatic leadership and inspirational leadership.

Perhaps transformational leadership is receiving more attention now-a-days because of the dramatic changes that many organisations are going through and the critical importance of transformational leadership in "transforming" or changing organisations successfully.

Characteristics of Transformational Leadership are given below:

Transformational leadership leads to superior performance in organisations facing demands for renewal and change. They have following characteristics:

(i) They identify themselves as change agents.
(ii) They are courageous.
(iii) They believe in people.
(iv) They are value driven.
(v) They are lifelong learners.
(vi) They have ability to deal with complexity, ambiguity and uncertainty.
(vii) They are visionaries.
(viii) They pay attention to the concerns and developmental needs of *individual followers*. They gives individualised consideration. They gives personal attention and treat each employee individually, coaching and advises.
(ix) *Charisma*. Transformational leader provides vision and sense of mission, instills pride, gains respect and trust.
(x) *Inspiration*. They communicate high expectations, express important purposes in simple ways to achieve group goals.
(xi) *Intellectual stimulation*. They promote intelligence and careful problem-solving.
(xii) They are *more effective* than other type of leaders.

The tasks of transformational leaders perform several important tasks. First, they raise followers' awareness of organisational issues and their consequences. Organisation stand an organisation's high-priority issues and what will happen if these issues are not successfully resolved. Second, transformational leaders create a vision of what the organisation should be, build commitment to that vision throughout the organisation, and facilitate organisational changes that support the vision. In sum, transformational leadership is consistent with strategy developed through an organisation's strategic management process.

Managers of the future will continue to face the challenge of significantly changing their organisations, primarily because of the accelerating trend to position organisations to be more competitive in a global business environment.

(b) Coaching

Coaching is leadership that instructs followers on how to meet the special organisational challenges they face. Operating like an athletic coach, the coaching leader identifies inappropriate behaviour in followers and suggests how they might correct that behaviour. The increasing use of teams has elevated the importance of coaching in today's organisations. Characteristics of an effective coach are as under:

Characteristics of an Effective Coach

Trait, Attitude or Behaviour

- Empathy (putting self in other person's shoes),

- Listening skill,
- Insight into people (ability to size them up) Diplomacy and tact,
- Patience toward people,
- Concern for welfare of people,
- Minimum hostility toward people Self-confidence and emotional stability,
- Non-competitiveness with team members, and
- Enthusiasm for people.

Coaching Behaviour

A successful coaching leader is characterized by many different kinds of behaviour. Among these behaviours are the following:

Listens closely

The coaching leader tries to gather both the facts in what is said and the feelings and emotions behind what is said. Such a leader is careful to really listen and not fall into the trap of immediately rebutting statements made by followers.

Gives emotional support

The coaching leader gives followers personal encouragement. Such encouragement should constantly be aimed at motivating them to do their best to meet the high demands of successful organisations.

Shows by example what constitutes appropriate behaviour

The coaching leader shows followers, for instance, how to handle an employee problem. By demonstrating expertise, the coaching leader builds the trust and respect of followers.

(c) Superleadership

Superleadership is leading by showing others *how to lead* themselves. If superleaders *are successful,* they develop followers who are productive, work independently, and need only minimal attention from the superleader.

In essence, *superleaders teach followers* how to think on their own and act constructively and independently. They encourage people to eliminate negative thoughts and beliefs about the organisation and co-workers and to replace them with more positive and constructive beliefs. An important aspect of superleadership is building the self-confidence of followers by them that they are competent, have a significant reservoir of potential, and are capable of meeting the difficult challenges of the work situation.

The objective of superleaders is to develop followers who require very little leadership.

(d) Entrepreneurial Leadership

Entrepreneurial leadership is leadership that is based on the attitude that the leader is self-employed. Leaders of this type act as if they are playing a critical role in the organisation rather than a mostly unimportant one. In addition, they behave as if they are taking the risk of losing money but will receive the profit if one is made. They approach each mistake as if it were a significant error rather than a smaller error that will be neutralized by the normal functioning of the organisation.

Each of these four contemporary leadership styles has received notable attention in recent years. Managers should realize that these four styles are not mutually exclusive; they can be combined in various ways to generate a unique style. For example, a leader can assume both a coaching and an entrepreneurial role. Figure 2 shows the various combinations of these four leadership styles that a leader can adopt. The shaded portion of the figure represents a leader whose style comprises all four.

Characteristics of emerging leader *versus* characteristics of the manager are in Figure 1.

FIGURE I

Various Combinations of Transformational, Coaching, Superleader, and Entrepreneurial Leadership Styles

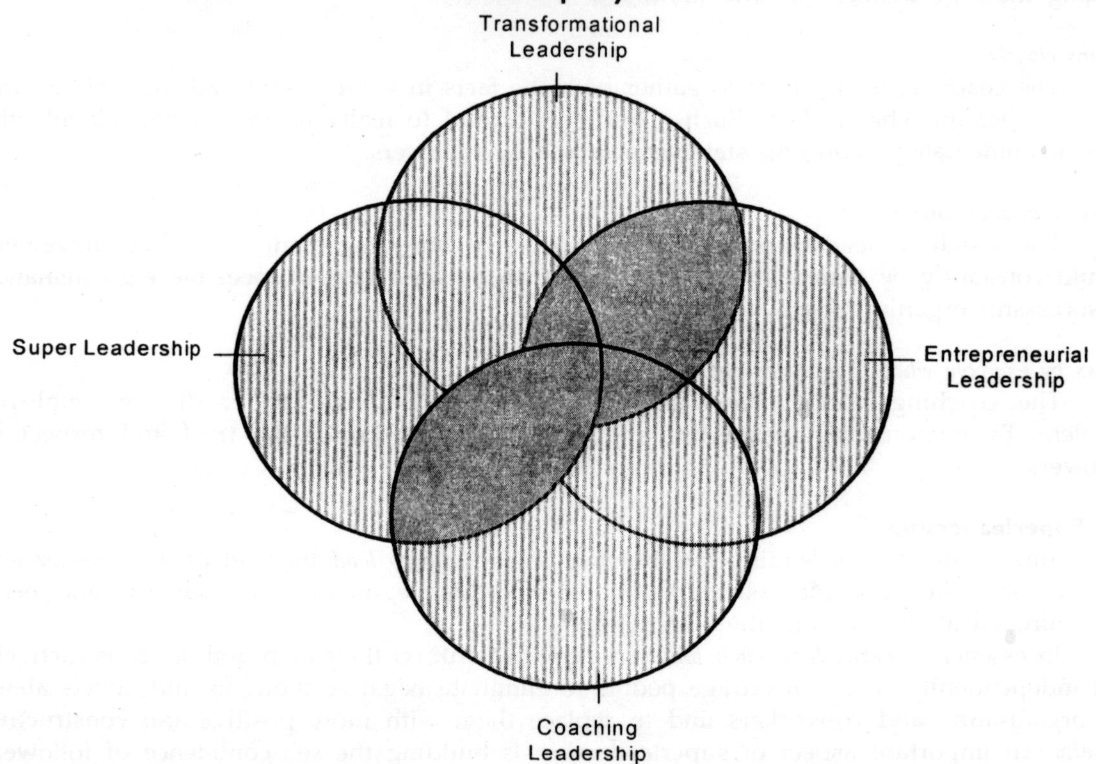

4. CURRENT TOPICS IN LEADERSHIP

Two currently popular leadership topics are leadership substitutes and women leaders. Both are mentioned under the heads "Substitutes for Leadership", "Women as Leaders," and "Ways Women Lead."

5. SUBSTITUTES FOR LEADERSHIP

Substitute leadership theory attempts to identify those situations in which the input of leader behaviour is partly or wholly canceled out by characteristics of the subordinate or the organisation. Here are some examples: A subordinate may have such high levels of ability experience, education, and internal motivation that little or no leadership is required or desired; task characteristics may be so routine that the subordinate does not require much, if any, leadership, organisational characteristics such as group cohesion and a high degree of formalization may reduce the need for leadership.

Substitute theory reminds us that—at least in some situations with some people in some organisations—things just seem to get done regardless of the quality of leadership.

Women as Leaders

In 1970, only 15 percent of all managers were women in USA. By 1989, this figure had risen to more than 40 percent. By 1995, women made up about 63 percent of the total workforce. Just imagine how many women will become leaders in their organisations.

Ways Women Lead

Women who have broken through the glass ceiling have found that there is no one mold for effective leadership. In the past, women leaders modeled their leadership styles after successful male managers. Today's women managers, however, often describe their leadership styles as transformational—getting workers to transform or subordinate their individual self-interests into group consensus directed toward a broader goal. This leadership style attributes power to such personal characteristics as *charisma, personal contacts,* and interpersonal skills rather than to the organisational structure.

Box I

For James G. Kaiser of Corning, being Employee-Centered includes a Focus on Diversity

James G. Kaiser is a senior vice-president at Corning, Inc. Kaiser is responsible for keeping the Technical Products Division competitive in the global marketplace and for masterminding the strategic planning for his division's operations. In addition, he oversees research and development for new products and is responsible for seeking business partners with whom the company can pursue joint ventures. Last, Kaiser is in charge of a series of export and sales offices in several locations.

Kaiser considers himself to be a people-oriented leader. He is an African American manager who sees his race as an asset in managing people from different cultures because it gives him a broader perspective on the differences among various types of employees. He focuses formally on cultural diversity at Corning largely through the Executive Leadership Council, a group whose mission is to offer guidance and leadership to other up-and-coming African American executives. As president of Corning's Executive Leadership Council, Kaiser provides minority executives with a network and a discussion forum that help them to understand what the achievement of excellence means within and for the African American community and how they can personally excel.

Because Kaiser is an African American leader, it could be argued that he has special insights for advising and helping minority employees to be successful leaders. For their own long-run success, however, leaders like Kaiser must be careful not to become 'specialists' who deal with only one culture, but rather 'generalists' who develop the skills to successfully manage people from many different cultures.

Box 2

Views of Management Guru

Commitment

The non-profit organisation exists to bring about a change in individuals and in society. The first thing to talk about is what missions work and what missions don't work, and how to define the mission. For the ultimate test is not the beauty of the mission statement. The ultimate test is right action.

The most common question asked me by non-profit executives is: What are the qualities of a leader? The question seems to assume that leadership is something you can learn in a charm school. But it also assumes that leadership by itself is enough, that is an end. And that's misleadership. The leader who basically focuses on himself or herself is going to mislead. The three most charismatic leaders in this century inflicted more suffering on the human race than almost any trio in history: Hitler, Stalin, and Mao. What matters is not the leader's charisma. What matters is the leader's mission? Therefore, the first job of the leader is to think through and define the mission of the institution.

A mission statement has to be operational, otherwise it's just good intentions. A mission statement has to focus on what the institution really tries to do and then do it so that everybody in the organisation can say. This is my contribution to the goal.

The task of the non-profit manager is to try to convert the organisation's mission statement into specifics. The mission may be forever—or at least as long as we can foresee.

One of our most common mistakes is to make the mission statement into a kind of hero sandwich of good intentions. It has to be simple and clear. As you add new tasks, you de-emphasize and get rid of old ones. You can only do so many things. Look at what we are trying to do in our colleges. The mission statement is confused—we are trying to do fifty different things. It won't work, and that's why the fundamentalist colleges attract so many young people. Their mission is very narrow. You and I may quarrel with it and say it's too narrow, but it's clear.

So, you need three things: opportunities; competence; and commitment. Every mission statement, believe me, has to reflect all three or it will fall down on what is its ultimate goal, its ultimate purpose and final test. It will not mobilize the human resources of the organisation for getting the right things done.

Source: Peter F. Drucker, Managing the Non-profit Organisation, Collins Business, New York.

Reference

Samul C. Certo, Modern Management, Prentice Hall India Pvt Ltd., New Delhi.

CHAPTER

12

Critical Attributes of Leadership for NPOs

In this chapter, we have discussed three aspects relating to leadership in NPOs as under:

1. Attributes of leadership.
2. Identifying, developing and recruiting leaders.
3. Nurturing leadership.

Leadership attributes generally emanating from the person holding the top staff position—the executive director (who in some cases is called the president and/or the CEO (chief executive officer). Leadership can also come from the head of the board (president or chairman) who in a non-profit organisation is almost always a different person from the staff head. In some organisations, these two individuals work together to provide team leadership.

Leadership is critical to the success of organisations of all types—private profit, non-profit, and public. Leadership cannot be defined, or that it is different things to different people, or that "if it works, it must be leadership." But none of these statements is particularly helpful. Instead, this chapter attempts to describe elements of leadership that can be found in a vast array of non-profit organisations. These attributes appear with great consistency and regularity and should be sought out in individuals and nurtured whenever possible.

1. ATTRIBUTES OF LEADERSHIP

What does one look for in a leader of a non-profit organisation? Must have four attributes: (i) vision, (ii) community engagement, (iii) aspects of organisation management, and (iv) personal attributes.

(i) Vision

- An effective leader is one who has a clear vision of the future and the organisation's place in that future. That vision must inspire people both within and outside the organisation.
- Vision means anticipating both opportunity and danger and convincing others of the importance of planning for them.
- Vision means understanding how the organisation fits within a field and a community and being able to strategies about improving upon that position.
- A leader with vision has a strong and abiding commitment to the organisation's mission that plays itself out in high-quality programmes, and an overall commitment lo excellence.

(ii) Community Engagement

- A strong leader is externally directed (at least in part) and exhibits a well-developed knowledge of the community in which the organisation is active. "Community" in this instance may be described by geography and/or is defined by the field of endeavor, such as teaching hospitals, legal aid societies, or art museums.
- A strong leader has a knowledge of constituent needs and an instinct for how to service them in a way that they will consider effective.
- Organisations with effective leaders demonstrate contextual appropriateness with their constituents. They know what constituents want, and how they want it. While this does not mean the leaders will simply do whatever their constituents ask, it does mean they will work together with them.
- The work that a leader does in the community creates substantive relationships (both individual and organisational) characterized by mutuality of purpose.
- Effective leaders are willing to engage in change relative to community life. They recognize and respect change in their communities and their work both reflects and causes change.

(iii) Aspects of Organisational Management Important to Leadership

Leadership is not the same as management but there are aspects of management that are important to leadership. For example:

- Part of a leader's management role is to *articulate the organisation's mission* and generate excitement among board and volunteers.
- An effective leader understands the importance of mission as a touchstone for organisational behaviour—staff members are reminded continually and in various ways that their jobs relate to the mission.
- A good leader can *make all staff members feel like they are part of a very special* organisation that matters and that they are critical to organisational effectiveness.
- Where effective leadership is present, there is a *commitment to mutuality between the leader and staff,* as well as between the board and the leader.
- Because a leader is skilled at overseeing all areas of management (though much of it may be delegated), the organisation is able *to respond to opportunities* in dynamic and creative ways.

- The effective leader appears to have *good instincts* about the extent of risk that is desirable for the organisational development.

(iv) Personal Attributes

Effective leaders often have a number of characteristics in common, many of which seem to come with maturity and life experience:

- Leaders exhibit a high *degree of clarity*, both personally and professionally.
- Most have a *well-articulated personal* vision (as distinct from the vision pertaining to the organisation, described earlier) and they demonstrate self-knowledge.
- Authenticity ranks high among the personal characteristic of leaders—that is, these are individuals who practice their personal values.
- As a group, effective leaders are *comfortable with change* and ambiguity. In fact, many relish identifying opportunities and *being creative agents of change.*
- Effective leaders are individuals who are engaged with the world. In spite of working long hours in many cases, they are extremely *knowledgeable about current societal issues.*
- Most effective leaders have *inquisitive creative, and agile minds.*
- All of these personal characteristics allow effective leaders to *find voice in the passion they demonstrate* for their work.

2. IDENTIFYING, DEVELOPING AND RECRUITING LEADERS

One of the major differences between business leaders and leaders in the non-profit sphere is the manner in which *they come to their positions.* In business, it is quite common to find leaders who *came up through the ranks.* They are identified as future leaders early on, receive special training (both on the job and outside of the corporation), and are trotted out and tested for their roles. Corporation invest heavily in this leadership identification and development process since so much is at stake. Effective CEOs are of extreme value to a corporation, as their often extraordinarily high compensation makes clear. Company performance and profitability depends, in many cases, on their qualities, talents, and abilities.

In *non-profit organisations*, leaders (especially staff leaders) are more often than not *recruited from the outside.* It is the exception to find organisations that have identified a leader early on, developed that individual, and planned carefully for a smooth succession. When a strong leader leaves, the organisation looks to other organisations, usually in the same field, hoping to recruit someone who seems to have the requisite experience and leadership qualities.

In non-profit organisations, the ability to *"try internal people out" is generally absent* since leaders are recruited from the outside. This puts tremendous pressure on making the right choice without the benefit of having an individual work within the organisation or the community at all.

With respect to identifying and developing leaders, the following guidelines can be of assistance:

(i) Whenever possible, evaluate the abilities of internal candidates. The identification process should begin early, well before the current leader intends to step down.

(ii) Consider the ultimate need for a new leader when hiring senior staff (below the executive director). Look for appropriate leadership potential that can be developed and tested.

(iii) Allow for on-the-job training experience and formal educational training.

(iv) When looking outside the organisation for a leader, be clear about expectations. This goes beyond a job description. Identify the leadership qualities that are most being sought.

(v) With outside candidates, be clear about the internal culture of the organisation. If a consensus-type leader is being sought, do not pursue charismatic, authority-oriented types.

(vi) Give potential leadership candidates (and their families) an opportunity to spend time on site, interacting with board and staff.

(vii) When bringing candidates from out of town, give them ample opportunity to get to know the community.

(viii) Once hired, allow for a period of adjustment. Every leader needs time to acclimate to the organisation and the community and build relationships.

(ix) Allow a new leader to put together his or her own senior team. This may or may not include people who already are in the senior slots.

(x) With respect to boards, identify any potential leader as early as possible. Give him or her an opportunity to display leadership qualities on the executive committee. Be prepared to change course if the individual identified does not live up to expectations.

3. NURTURING LEADERSHIP

How to nurture an effective leader once that person is in place. The track record of non-profit organisations has been checkered at best in this regard. However, as the value of leadership has become increasingly apparent, many are finding ways to improve. Nothing is more sobering than losing an effective leader to another organisation because he or she was taken for granted. Based on the practice of organisations that have kept their leaders by treating them well, the following seems to be a useful checklist of do's and don'ts.

- DO keep *expectations reasonable* even if the leader makes the job seem effortless.
- DO provide *adequate staff support*. Remember that being a leader often requires a freeing up from routine and internal day-to-day demands that can be done by others.
- DO NOT or assign tasks just *because the leader is good at them*—if they can be done by others, they probably should be.
- DO provide adequate compensation. Be sure that benefits are figured into the competitive compensation analysis.
- DO NOT underpay an effective incumbent leader simply because his or her salary has historically been below industry standards or has not kept up with inflation.
- DO provide *adequate time for professional networking* and field-related work not directly related to the organisation's day-to-day tasks (this can even include a specific number of days of outside consulting).

- DO NOT *assume* that days away from the office on non-organisation business are days on which leadership tasks are not getting done. In many cases, the contacts made and the field reputation developed will have a very positive impact on the organisation.
- DO provide *adequate personal* time off.
- DO NOT *assume* that there is a direct relationship between hours worked and productivity.
- DO provide time and compensation for leadership *training opportunities.*
- DO NOT *assume* that an experienced leader knows it all or does not need to recharge his or her batteries with new information.
- DO *honor and value the leader.* Appreciation and public recognition are energizing and contribute to good feelings about the organisation.
- DO NOT ever take the *leader for granted.*

Box I

Views of Management Guru on

Leadership

"We hear a great deal these days about *leadership,* and it's high time we did. But, actually, mission comes first. Non-profit institutions exist for the sake of their mission. They exist to make a difference in society and in the life of the individual. They exist for the sake of their mission, and this must never be forgotten. The first task of the leader is to make sure that *everybody sees the mission,* hears it, lives it. If you lose sight of your mission, you begin to stumble and it shows very very fast. And yet, mission needs to be thought through, needs to be changed.

We will have to look at *the mission* again and again to think through whether it needs to be refocused because demographics change, because we should abandon something that produces no results and eats up resources, because we have accomplished an objective. A good example is the school that is largely in crisis because it has achieved its original objective of getting every kind of child to go to school and stay there for years, and now we have to think through what we really do expect of the school. And this will be, in many ways, quite different from what the schoolmasters through the ages were striving for when nine out of ten kids never had the opportunity of organised schooling. Therefore, it is vitally important to start out from the outside. The organisation that starts out from the inside and then tries to find places to put its resources is going to fritter itself away. Above all, it is going to focus on yesterday. One looks to the outside for opportunity, for a need.

At the same time, the mission is always long-range. It needs short-range efforts and very often *short-range results.* And yet it starts out with a long-range objective.

We are always looking at programmes and projects with the question. Do *they produce the right results*? The leader's job is to make sure the right results are being achieved, the right things are being done.

One has the responsibility to *allocate resources,* particularly of course in organisations that depend heavily on volunteers, and heavily on donors. Leadership is accountable for results. And leadership always asks: "Are we really faithful stewards of the talents entrusted to us? The talents, the gifts of people—the talents, the gifts of money. Leadership is doing."

The next thing to do is to think through *priorities*. That's easy to say. But to act on it is hard because it always involves abandoning things that look very attractive, that people both inside and outside the organisation are pushing for. But if you don't concentrate your institution's resources, you are not going to get results. This may be the ultimate test of leadership: the ability to think through the priority decision and to make it stick.

Leadership is also example. The leader is visible; he stands for the organisation. He may be totally anonymous the moment he leaves that office and steps into his car to drive home; But inside the organisation, he or she is very visible, and this isn't just true of the small and local one, it is just as true of the big, national or worldwide one. Leaders set examples. The leaders have to live up to the expectations regarding their behaviour. No matter that the rest of the organisation doesn't do it; the leader represents not only what we are, but, above all, what we know we should be. . . . . A leader is not a private person; a leader represents. And then task yourself, as a leader, what do I do to set *standards in the organisation*? What do I do to enable the organisation to tackle new challenges, to seize new opportunities, to innovate? What do I do? Not what does the organisation do? Take action responsibility. What are my own first priorities, and what are the organisation's first priorities, what should they be? These are the action agenda. These are the things that must be done.

We are creating tomorrow's society of citizens through the non-profit service institution. And in that society, everybody is a leader, everybody is responsible, everybody acts. Everybody focuses himself or herself. Everybody raises the vision, the competence, and the performance of his or her organisation. Therefore, mission and leadership are not just things to read about, to listen to. They are things to do something about. Things that you can, and should, convert from good intentions and from knowledge into effective action, not next year, but tomorrow morning."

Source: Peter F. Drucker, Managing the Non-profit Organisation, Collins Business, New York.

Reference

Contribution gratefully acknowledged.

CHAPTER

13

Application of Marketing Approaches for Welfare Organisations

In this chapter following aspects of marketing approaches for welfare organisations are covered:

1. Welfare organisations by NPOs.
2. Application of marketing activities which will benefit NPOs.
3. Fund raising by NPOs.
4. Some practices of NPOs in fund raising. (Box 1)
5. Social marketing. (Boxes 2 and 3)
6. Views of management guru on customer. (Box 4)

1. WELFARE ORGANISATIONS BY NPOs

Educational and medical services are mostly two areas of activity run by NPOs, which tend to be *partly financed by client. But market pressure force them to charge more. Some examples* are :

(a) *Non-profit hospitals* who partly charge poor patients, they cannot afford the services.
(b) Same is the case of *professional training institutes*, e.g. medical, engineering, management charge fees which students cannot afford. NPOs have to provide acceptable quality of service at the same time.

2. APPLICATION OF MARKETING ACTIVITIES WHICH WILL BENEFIT NPOs

These aspects of marketing are important to NPOs:

(a) Marketing Survey or Research (MR)

Marketing serve is done to understand the market. Lack of relevant information can lead to failure of NPO. Market research can help to correct the problem and provide the required information in a systematic manner. Business management cannot survive if they do not cater to the actual needs of market. Similarly, NPOs can identify through market research where their prospective clients are.

However, welfare organisations are more likely to be morality, sentiment of emotion-driven and will carry on its service which is not well received by clients. Thus, study of market, segmenting it and identifying target groups whom one would want to service is necessary after this only service is to be created by NPO.

(b) Test Market Survey

NPO has to carry out a test marketing as it reduces errors of judgement. Further NPO has also to carry out pricing of service as a testing device.

(c) NPOs must also Study Points of Client Contract

In case of orphanage, NPO has to first find where they will get the orphans. Will T.V. or newspaper appeal work? It may be mentioned that one destitute home for women had set-up the home with staff in place, and then NPO started looking for clients in rural area. Thus, many practical considerations are to be taken into considerations and not to be assumed.

(d) As Part of Marketing Effort NPOs have to take Care of Public Relations and External Communications

Recipients of service must know that they have *benefited* and public to know what is being done by NPO. Public relations means relationship between the organisation and the public on a continuing basis to be carefully nurtured over the years to form a firm bond for welfare organisation. Few NPOs recognize this need for good public relations. It can also help in fund raising as public feels organisation is doing good for them. Public relations activity can identify possible sources of opposition to NPO. Some steps to build public relations are:

- *One step* is to develop a close association with leading journalists, judges in the area.
- Another is to prepare a brochure showing benefits.
- Still further, cultural shows and documentary will add to attraction of NPO.
- Keep continuing programmes of relationships building.
- A note of caution is to keep away from political parties.

(e) Client Feedback by NPOs

Getting customer feedback has become common practice in business marketing such as service organisations like hotels, airlines, banks, etc. This is important as consumers have become more conscious of their rights and ability to influence the supplier. This is also necessary as a result of interference by the consumer protection organisations, such services organisations are making a substantial investment in customer goodwill.

It is obvious that NPOs must *get feedback to ensure* that client is improving the quality of life and their suggestions are implemented. NPOs may have some limitations in getting feedback as clients are most often illiterate, who cannot answer questionnaires. However, limited feedback can be had through interviews on random selection basis and can be valuable feedback for NPOs.

3. FUNDS RAISING BY NPOs

Steps to meet a perpetual quest for donations by NPOs are given as under:

- NPOs suffer from hunger for funds as they do not generate funds from operation. They need external support. Fund raising was difficult in India, but of late some economic changes have occurred as under.
- Number of *expatriate* Indian's have increased and they send remittances to their families, who have now capacity to contribute donations.
- Raising *agricultural income of planters* and farmers as they get tax-free and other concessions.
- *Rise in donor base is being maintained* by constant contact with them, such as, alumni contributions (IITs and IIMs), identification of beneficiary with institution and get their support, patient follow up programmes after treatment with patients, etc.
- Organising of *network of ex-students of some institutes* into local groups in the locations.
- Keeping two-way communication facility with donors and institution through e-mail.
- *Recognition to donors* in form of identify cards, certificates, etc.
- Outstanding donors to be considered *as members in the governing body*—as non-voting members. (See also Box 1)

4. SOME PRACTICES OF NPO'S IN FUND RAISING (BOX I)

Box I

Some Practices of NGOs in Fund Raising

"Then there are NGOs who work on issues like mental breakdowns amongst call centre youth, among others. These are issues that affect even people from economically self-sufficient sections of society. And working with all these people does call for certain marketing acumen on the part of NGOs."

Agni of Mumbai and Janaagraha of Bangalore are two organisations that work on civic causes. While Agni has no corporate funding worth speaking about, Janaagraha is currently funded by the Ramanathan Foundation. Founded by Ramesh Ramanathan, who gave up a high-flying career with Citibank to take up civic causes, Janaagraha's purpose is to "improve the quality of life for all by improving the quality of public governance." Janaagraha has been working with Bangalore's municipal wards to develop a vision and improve governance.

In Ramanathan's words, Janaagraha has no hierarchy or structure as such, but there is a coordination office "which conceptualises, synthesises, orchestrates and, most importantly, disseminates the tools and ideas that empower citizens to effectively work with the government machinery in their areas through participation and shared responsibility. This model has worked well for Janaagraha. But as it has grown in scale and size, a more rigorous structure is being conceptualised and work is in progress on that. The NPOs is likely to see a restructured Janaagraha along the 3Ps of paradigm, promotions and practice."

But as Janaagrahas ambit of activities grows, it will also have to look at its funding. Says Ramanathan: "Janaagraha does not take any donations from outside. This model has worked fine so far but, going ahead, as the scale and depth of its activities increase, a new model is being worked out as part of the organisational restructuring exercise. That will allow for the possibility of funding specific activities within the Janaagraha scope of activities and bring greater clarity on how that funding will be channelised towards specific parts of the movement."

Taking a relook at the revenue funding model is Helpage India, which seeks to serve the old and needy. Says Mathew Cherian, chief executive of Helpage India: "Funding is going up, but not at a very fast rate. We always have a deficit budget which we have to manage. At present, our gross receipts are about Rs. 42 crore a year." Like CRY, Helpage's funding is substantially retail. "About 60 per cent of our donations comes from Indian individuals and institutional donors contribute the remaining 40 per cent. We also get some donations from corporates. But that is a very minor part." To augment the revenue streams, Cherian is planning to encourage payroll giving and start 'Helpage Charity Shops' to sell a host of products. It also generates some revenues from greeting cards.

Concern India has a funding model that relies on corporate donations substantially. There is also a separate department for production, design and sale of greeting cards. "Although these greeting cards are sold only to corporate houses, it has added some financial muscle," says Chatterjee, project director of Concern India. The total income of the foundation as on March 31, 2003, was around Rs. 2.83 crore.

As a part to market itself, the NGO offers its donor's opportunities to see where their money goes. We now have a project coordinator who works as a liaison between the NW and supported projects. Regular project visits can be made by corporates to monitor and evaluate the activities of the organisations and the NGO also sends regular project reports to donors, says Chatterjee. World Vision asks individual donors to sponsor the education of specific children and donors are encouraged to write to them. Result: greater emotional involvement between donors and beneficiaries, World Vision's two stakeholders.

Somnath Bandyopadhyaya of the Aga Khan Foundation says his organisation is encouraging its development partners to raise more of their resources themselves. The Foundation currently works with two kinds of funds. One is the internal fund, which is called the 'Imamat Fund'. Many startup projects are funded from this fund, which works as a social venture capital fund. But increasingly, the Foundation is "emphasising on enhancing the fund-raising capacities of our partners. This has started yielding rich dividends. There are some projects where our partners have been able to raise 30-40 per cent of the project cost."

NGOs also garner revenues through more traditional on-ground events. The Indian Red Cross Society, for example, hosts a regular event at Mumbai's Taj hotel where the organisation often raises as much as Rs. 15 lakh in one day. "We also slough back a part of all such proceeds by investing in various financial instruments that are available in the market," says C.J. Batliwalla, an honorary of the society. Cost control is another area of streamlining. Batliwala claims that the Society has deployed new technological processes in its blood bank to reduce the cost of operations.

Concern India hosts NGO melas and even art auctions to collect revenues and target new donors. In such events grass-roots-level NGOs market the wares and paintings produced by the communities they service.

Financial targeting is now becoming main-stream at NGOs. Says Christian of World Vision: "In terms of our local fund raising, we had targets to double our income in the next two years. Post-tsunami, I think we may double it by the end of this year itself."

Social marketing is beginning to work with a little help from natural disasters.

Source: Indian Management, March 2005.

5. SOCIAL MARKETING

Social marketing entered management parlance in the early 1970s when Philip Kotler realised that the marketing principles used to sell products to consumers could also be used to "sell ideas, attitudes and behaviours" in the social sector. Like commercial marketing, the primary focus of social marketing is on the consumer—on learning what people want and need rather than trying to persuade them to buy what the manufacturer happens to be producing.

However, along with the four P's of commercial marketing (Product, Price, Place, and Promotion), social marketing has a few more P's to it and they are: Publics, Partnership, Policy and Pursestrings. These are explained as:

Publics

This term refers to both the external and internal groups involved in a social marketing programme. External publics include the target audience, secondary audiences, policy-makers and gatekeepers, while the internal publics are those who are involved in some way with either approval or implementation of the programme.

Partnership

Social and health issues are often so complex that one agency can't make a dent by itself. The enterprise has to team up with other organisation in the community to really be effective. This involves figuring out those organisations whose goals are similar to that of the entity and then identify ways of working together.

Policy

Social marketing programmes may succeed in motivating individual behaviour change, but it is difficult to sustain unless the environment they are into supports that change. This often calls for policy changes and media advocacy programmes.

Pursestrings

Most organisations that develop social marketing programmes operate through funds provided by sources such as foundations, governmental grants or donations. Therefore, all such programmes have to address an added question: where will the entity get the money to create the programme? (See also Box 2 and Box 3)

Box 2

Steps to Social Marketing

Any social marketing plan should follow three basic steps. These are: assessment, planning and execution, says Dr. Meena Galliara of the Narsee Monjee Institute of Management Studies. NGOs planning to make themselves more effective should consider breaking these three steps into a more detailed eight steps:

Step I is situation analysis

While conducting a situation analysis, the NGO has to start by asking itself what is the social issue it is seeking to address? It could be unintended pregnancies, garbage disposal, rising stress levels in urban youth and so on. It should then get on to identifying the activities that need to be taken up (example, teen abstinence, residential gardening, etc.) to address these issues. The enterprise should also conduct a SWOT analysis in terms of resources, expertise, management support and the internal public (like employees and volunteers) that have to be addressed in such an initiative.

Step 2 is selecting the target audience

While selecting the target audience, the NGO should be able to describe the audience in terms of size, severity of the problem in the audience, psychography and behaviour. This help in understanding the primary audience and the secondary audience that should be targeted in this programme.

Step 3 is setting objectives and goals

Here, the question to be answered is: What specifically does the entity want its target audience to do as a result of this campaign or project? This differs from one stakeholder to another. If it is a donor, then the project should aim at getting increased funding; if it is the government, then it should ensure that there is no resentment from their side; if it is end-beneficiaries, then the project should get them to participate in the project. The non-profit organisation should also be able to set certain measurable goals. These include goals that identify the monetary and non-monetary costs involved in the project, campaign awareness, recall and response, and measures to map changes in the knowledge, belief and behaviour of the target audience.

Step 4 is analysing the target audience and the competition

In this phase the organisation should try and understand the behaviour of the audience, their existing knowledge and beliefs, the benefits that they perceive from this programme and the costs and barriers. Similarly, while analysing competition, the organisation has to identify some of the other competing alternative behaviours. Competition in this context is the individual himself, rather than the external world—though there could be that as well. For instance, if mothers have to get their children to polio vaccination centres, the competition could be household work, lethargy or lack of initiative displayed by these women in bringing their children to vaccination centres.

Step 5 is about developing marketing strategies

In this stage one should identify the exit and entry costs and accordingly establish pricing strategies.

Step 6 is developing a plan for evaluation and monitoring

While doing this, the organisation has to figure out which techniques and methodologies will be used to measure the effectiveness of the intervention. When will these measurements be taken? And how will the measurements be reported?

Step 7 is determining budgets and identifying funding sources

This begins with making a slew of cost calculations—costs in terms of product, distribution and communication activities, among other things. If costs exceed currently available funds, then the non-profit should also figure out additional funding sources that can be explored and the strategies required to appeal to these funders.

Step 8 is to complete the implementation plan

This calls to 2 bit of human resources management since the organisation has to get down to knowing what will be done? Who should receive the mandate? When will it be done? And for how much?

Source: Indian Management, March 2005.

Box 3

The Ten Commandments of Fund Raising

These tips, the so-called ten commandments, represent a distillation and condensation of many ideas that, together with good old common sense, make ordinary people into skilled fund raisers.

Commandment I: Remember, Only Prospectors Find Gold

A good fund-raising team spends far more time assembling lists of prospects and researching funding sources than it does actually asking for money. Knowing whom to ask is more important than knowing to ask.

Commandment 2: Be Sure that Courtship Precedes the Proposal

You would never dream of asking someone to marry you before you had a chance to get acquainted and find out whether you were compatible. In the same way, it is far preferable to ask for money after you have had a chance to get to know someone and to find out areas of compatibility between your organisation's activities and his or her approach to philanthropy.

Commandment 3: Personalize the Pitch

Every request for money should be tailored, to the extent possible, to the predilections of the giver. Obviously, it is not always practical to customize every request. Nevertheless, every different type of small giver deserves a special approach and every prospective large donor deserves a specially tailored request that takes into consideration everything you know about his or her likes and dislikes. Blanket fund raising is rarely as successful as targeted requests.

Commandment 4: Keep Long List of Donors Handy

Money rarely materializes without something to prime the pump. People who give money are conservative, and they are more likely to contribute to an operation that already has a long list of donors associated with it. Public agencies will require matching funds; corporations may wish to see substantial earned income. But in almost all cases, donors will want to see that you have other sources of cash before they join in.

Commandment 5: When Asking for Money, Assume Consent

Do you remember the last time someone tried to sell you life insurance? He or she never used the words "if you buy this policy," but rather "when you buy this policy." He or she avoided being tentative and did not give you many opportunities to say no without actually being rude. A good fund raiser should use the same approach, always assuming in all communication that the prospective donor will ultimately be making a contribution.

Commandment 6: In Written Requests, If You Can't Scan It, Can It

Most fund-raising letters and proposals are not read carefully, they are scanned. All other things being equal, those that receive the most thorough review are the ones that are most legible and easy to read at a glance. Fund-raising letters should be short with ample margins; proposals should have plenty of headings, bulleted lists, underlinings, and other scanning devices. Also, of course, brevity is the greatest of all virtues. As one funder says, "The success of proposals being funded is in inverse relation to their length and weight."

Commandment 7: Present Correct Information and Calculations

When asking for money, the individuals better get hold of a calculator and make sure their figures add up correctly. Nothing makes a poorer impression than a budget that is incorrect. It gives funders little faith in the organisation's ability to handle money if the numbers do not even look right on paper.

Commandment 8: Avoid Jargon and Communicate in Simple Language

There is nothing as nice as a clear, short sentence, composed of words of one syllable or less. A large number of adjectives and adverbs is usually the mark of a weak request. When you claim that your organisation is wonderful, the funder is unimpressed.

Commandment 9: Don't Take a No Personally

Fund raising is hard on people who are sensitive and do not like rejection, because even good fund raisers hear the word no more often than they hear the word *yes*. But after a time, the experienced fund raiser looks on a no answer to a request as a challenge—it may be no this year, but it will be yes the next time around. Persistence, after all, usually pays, specially in fund raising.

Commandment 10: No Matter How Many Times You Said Thank You, Say It Again

The secret of fund raising is not in getting the donor's first contribution, it is in getting the second and third. Developing an ongoing group of loyal supporters is essential and can only be done if just as much attention is paid to donors after they give as before. For those contributors who give large amounts of money, there should be regular correspondence updating them on the progress of the organisation's activities. For smaller donors, an occasional newsletter may be much appreciated. Mention of contributors in press materials or a special thank-you party is another way of showing your gratitude. Never take your contributors for granted and never miss an opportunity to say thanks.

6. VIEWS OF MANAGEMENT GURU ON CUSTOMER (BOX 4)

Box 4

Views of Management Guru on Customer

Strategy converts a non-profit institution's mission and objectives into performance. Despite its importance, however, many non-profits tend to slight strategy. It seems so obvious to most of them that they are satisfying a need, so clear that everybody who has that need must want the service the non-profit institution has to offer. One central problem is that too many non-profit managers confuse strategy with a selling effort. Strategy *ends* with selling efforts. It begins with knowing the market—who the customer is, who the customer should be, who the customer might be. The whole point of strategy is not to look at recipients as people who receive bounty, to whom the non-profit does good. They are customers who have to be satisfied. The non-profit institution needs a marketing strategy that integrates the customer and the mission.

An effective non-profit institution also needs strategies to improve all the time and to innovate.

And then the non-profit institution needs a strategy to build its donor base. It needs to develop a donor constituency.

All three of these strategies begin with research and research and more research. They require organised attempts to find out who the customer is, what is of value to the customer, how the customer buys. You don't start out with your product but with the end, which is a satisfied customer.

The most important person to research is the individual who *should* be the customer, the people who are believers but who have stopped going to church. Traditionally, businesses have researched their own customers and know, or try to know, as much as possible about them. But even if you have market leadership, non-customers always outnumber customers. The most important knowledge is the *potential customer*. The customer who really need the service, wants the service, but not in the way in which available today. The typical college or university, after twenty years of an enormous number of young people reaching college age, is only now accepting the fact that it has to market the college to high school counsellors, to prospective students, to their parents. Despite a sharp drop in the total number of applicants, colleges that do market effectively have more applications than they can possibly admit.

You would imagine that people would be only too eager for services aimed at helping them prevent a heart attack, or recover from it. Yes, they are, but only if the service fits them—their age, their weight. They manage their own life and their own health.

This understanding of the importance of strategy is particularly crucial to non-profit managers when it comes to their donors.

The next step in non-profit strategy (as in military strategy) is the training of your own people. Everyone in the hospital must be patient-conscious. That's a training job—not just preaching. It isn't attitude, it's behaviour. In fact, we have learned that attitude training is not very effective. The way to train people is behaviourally: *This is what you do*. With that kind of specific training, even hospital workers who are very far away from the customer—the billing office, the janitorial workers—do things that satisfy the customers: the physicians, the patients.

In non-profit management, training doesn't apply only to the employees; training volunteers may be even more essential, especially in an organisation in which volunteers are the interface with the customers, with the public.

When it comes to introducing something new, when it comes to innovation, non-profit strategy requires careful thought and planning: where to start and with whom. Start with people who want the new to succeed. Don't try to have everybody in the organisation run with the new first. That route always gets into trouble.

Look for a target of opportunity, for somebody in the organisation who wants the new, who is convinced of it, who is committed to it. The strategy in innovation is to think through this process at the start, so that you can identify somebody willing to work hard at making the new successful, and somebody whose success then becomes a multiplier in the organisation.

The worst thing in strategy is to introduce something with great fanfare and great hope that it is going to change the world, and five years later say, "Well, it's doing all right. It's a little specialty." That's failure. That's misallocation of resources.

Knowing the customer also enables the non-profit organisation—whether it's the church, the synagogue, the Scouts, a hospital, a college—to know what results to expect. It is important to define goals and know what realistically should work. What are we trying to do? This college is trying to get in so many applicants, of what quality, so that it can maintain its size and quality. Then one can feed back from results. Then one can say, "Well, we are doing quite well here, but not really well over there. Let's put in a little more effort." Or, "We need a stronger person in charge." Or, "We need to offer something additional that will bring in the kind of students we need."

Strategy also demands that the non-profit institution organise itself to abandon what no longer works, what no longer contributes, what no longer serves. A church must get out of the singles ministry if it doesn't have the right person to run it and cannot guarantee a quality service. The American Heart Association must be willing to play down older people as potential donors because to people over seventy-five or eighty, death by heart attack is not the worst of all possible ways to go. That's abandonment. If you don't build it in, you'll soon overload your organisation and put good resources where the results don't follow.

The question always before the non-profit executive is: What should our service do for the customer that is of importance to that customer? Then think through how the service should be structured, be offered, be staffed. End up with nuts and bolts: What to do, when to do, where to do. And most importantly, who is to do it?

Strategy begins with the mission. It leads to a work plan. It ends with the right tools—a kit, say for volunteers, which tells them who to call on, what to say, and how much money to get. Without that kit, there is no strategy.

The last thing to say about strategy is that it exploits opportunity, the right moment. Greek theologians called it *Kairos*, the point when the new is received. Most of the needs non-profit institutions fill are likely to be there forever in one form or another; they are parts of the human condition. But the need presents itself in a specific form, and it is the function of research to find out, at this time, what that form is. Especially for the ones who should be customers but aren't because the service is not available in a form that serves them. Ask: "Is this something that fits our strengths? Can we develop the service that satisfies?" Then comes that third element, the right moment to seize the opportunity by the forelock, to run with success.

Strategy commits the non-profit executive and the organisation to action. Its essence is action—putting together mission, objectives, the market—and the right moment. The tests of strategy are results. It begins with needs and ends with satisfactions. For this you need to know what the satisfactions should be for *your* customers: the parishioners in your church, the sick in your hospital, the boys and girls in your Scout troops, and the volunteers who lead them. What is really meaningful to them? Non-profit people must respect their customers and their donors enough to listen to *their* values and understand *their* satisfactions. They do not impose the executive's or the organisation's own views and egos on those they serve.

Source: Peter F. Drucker, Managing the Non-profit Organisation, Harper Collins Publishers, New York.

CHAPTER 14

Understanding Client's Needs through Social Research Methodology

It is desirable to carry out social research to get facts about what are client's needs or what are real causes for certain problems.

James M. Henslin, in his book "Essentials of Sociology", writes that around the globe, people make assumptions about the way the world "is." Common sense, the things that "every-one knows are true," may or may not be true, however, it takes research to find out. To test your own "common sense," read the Down-to-Earth Sociology mentioned in Boxes 1 and 2 at the end. According to him, common sense is undependable. Objective research often shows that common sense ideas are highly limited or false.

In this chapter we shall discuss following aspects of social research survey methodology:

(a) A research model,
(b) Six methods of collecting data,
(c) Ethics in sociological research,
(d) Values in sociological research, and
(e) Summary.

Regardless of the topic that we want to investigate, we need to move beyond guesswork and common sense. We must need to know what really is going on.

(A) A RESEARCH MODEL

As shown in Figure 1 social survey follows 10 basic steps. This is however, and in the real world of research some of these steps may be even omitted.

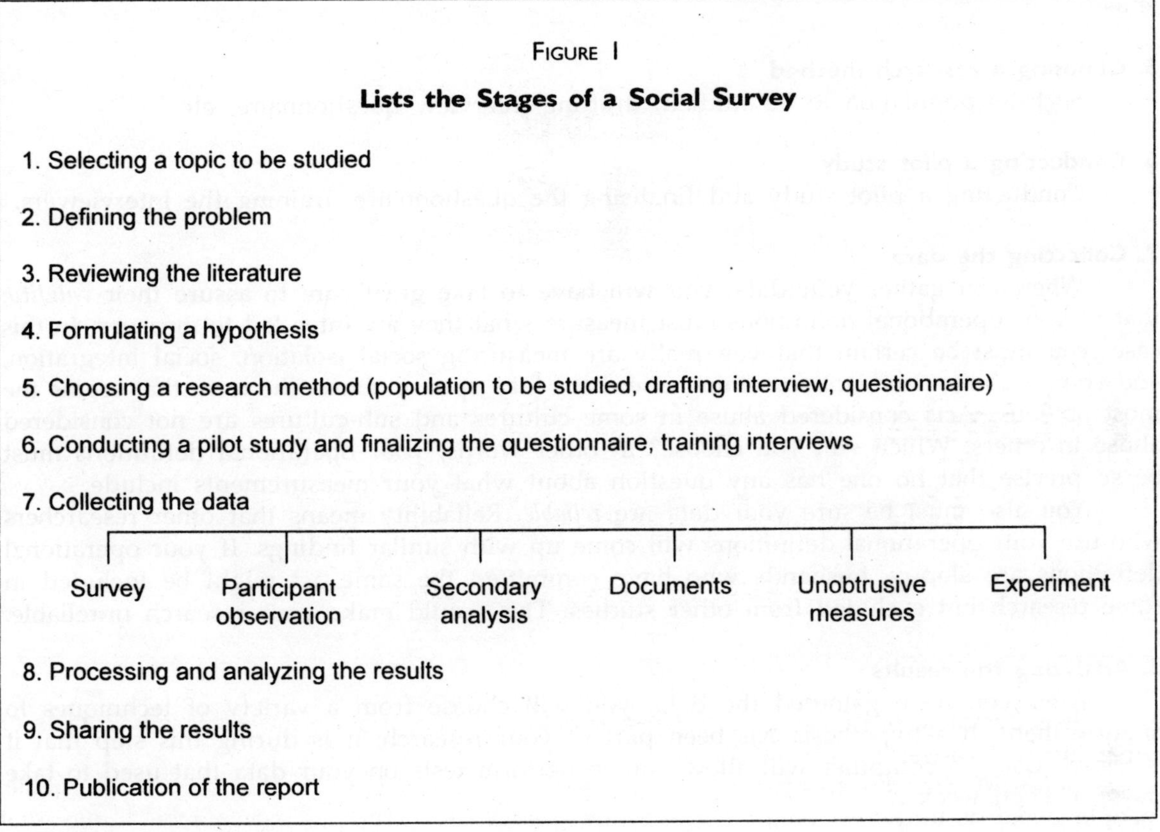

FIGURE I

Lists the Stages of a Social Survey

1. Selecting a topic to be studied
2. Defining the problem
3. Reviewing the literature
4. Formulating a hypothesis
5. Choosing a research method (population to be studied, drafting interview, questionnaire)
6. Conducting a pilot study and finalizing the questionnaire, training interviews
7. Collecting the data

8. Processing and analyzing the results
9. Sharing the results
10. Publication of the report

1. Selecting a topic

First, what do you want to know more about?

2. Defining the problem

The next step is to narrow the topic. We need to focus on a specific area. For example, you want to know what can be done to reduce domestic violence.

3. Reviewing the literature

You must review the literature to find out what is already known about the problem. You don't want to waste your time rediscovering what is already known.

4. Formulating a hypothesis

The fourth step is to formulate a hypothesis, a statement of what you expect to find according to predictions that are based on a theory. A hypothesis predicts a relationship between or among *variables,* factors that change, or vary from one person or situation to another. For example, the statements who are more socially isolated are more likely to abuse their wives than are men who are more socially integrated is a hypothesis.

We need precise ways to measure the variables. In this example, you would need operational definitions for three variables: social isolation, social integration, and spouse abuse.

5. Choosing a research method

Such as population to be studied, drafting interview questionnaire, etc.

6. Conducting a pilot study

Conducting a pilot study and finalising the questionnaire, training the interviewers.

7. Collecting the data

When you gather your data, you will have to take great care to assure their *validity;* that is, your operational definitions must measure what they are intended to measure. In this case, you must be certain that you really are measuring social isolation, social integration, and spouse abuse—and not something else. Let's take spouse abuse, the term that seems the most obvious. Acts considered abuse in some cultures and sub-cultures are not considered abuse in others. Which will you choose? In other words, your operational definitions must be so precise that no one has any question about what your measurements include.

You also must be sure your data are *reliable.* Reliability means that other researchers who use your operational definitions will come up with similar findings. If your operational definitions are sloppy, husbands who have committed the same act might be included in some research but excluded from other studies. This would make your research unreliable.

8. Analyzing the results

After you have gathered the data, you will choose from a variety of techniques to analyze them. If a hypothesis has been part of your research, it is during this step that it is tested. Using a computer will allow you to perform tests on your data that used to take days, or even weeks.

9. and 10. Sharing the results

Now it is time to wrap up your research. You will write a report that shares your findings with the scientific community. You will review how you did the research, including your operational definitions. You also will show how your findings relate to the published literature. In addition, you will show how your findings support or refute the theories that apply to your topic.

Let's look in greater detail at the fifth step and examine the research methods that sociologists use.

(B) SIX METHODS OF COLLECTING DATA

Choice of method will depend on the questions one wants to answer. Because many research methods require that you determine what "average" is in order to have a basis for comparison, the measures of average are to be specified.

Surveys

Let's suppose you want to know how many wives are abused each year. The survey, asking people a series of questions would be appropriate. Before you begin survey, we must deal with the practical matters.

(a) Selecting a Sample

Ideally, you might want to learn out all wives throughout the world. Obviously, your resources will not permit such a study, and you must narrow your population, the target group that you will study.

Let us assume that your resources allow you to investigate spouse abuse only on your campus.

Because.you want to generalize your findings to your campus, you need a sample that is representative of the entire people.

The best is a *random sample*. In a random sample, everyone in your population has the same chance of being included in the study.

We assign a number to each name on the list. Using a table of random numbers, then determine which person become part of our sample. (Random numbers are available in tables in statistics books, or they can be generated by a computer.) Because a random sample represents the overall population.

Asking Neutral Questions

After you have decided on your population and sample, your next task is to make certain that your questions are neutral. Your questions must allow *respondents,* the people who respond to a survey, to express their own opinions. Otherwise you will end up with biased findings, which are worth-less. For example, if you were to ask, "Don't you agree that men who beat their wives deserve to go to prison?" you would be tilting the answers toward agreement with a prison sentence.

Decide whether to use open- or closed-ended questions. *Closed-ended questions* are followed by a list of possible answers. This format would work for questions about someone's age (the possible answers would reflect a series of age ranges), but it wouldn't work for many other items. For example, how could you list all possible opinions that people hold regarding what causes spouse abuse? The alternative is open-ended questions, which allow people to answer in their own words. Although open-ended questions allow you to tap the full range of people opinions they make it difficult to compare answers.

Establishing Rapport

Will victims of abuse really give honest answers to strangers? The answer is yes, but first you must establish *rapport,* a feeling of trust, with your respondents. This is true in all research or surveys.

(b) Participant Observation

In participant observation, the researcher participates in a research setting while observing what is happening in that setting.

(c) Secondary Analysis

It is to analyse data that someone else has already collected, then one would be doing secondary analysis.

(d) Documents

Documents include books, newspapers, bank records, immigration files, and so on. To study spouse abuse, you might examine police reports to find out how many men in your community have been arrested for abuse. You might also want to find out what proportion of those men were charged, convicted, and sentenced.

(e) Unobtrusive Measures

Researchers sometimes use unobtrusive measures to observe people who do not know they are being studied.

(f) Experiments

To know if therapy for abusers actually works. One could conduct an experiment to find out. This is done through experimental group and control group technique.

(C) ETHICS IN SOCIOLOGICAL RESEARCH

In addition to choosing an appropriate research method, we must also follow the ethics of sociology, which center on assumptions of science and morality. Research ethics require openness (sharing findings with the scientific community), honesty, and truth. Ethics clearly forbid the falsification of results. They also condemn plagiarism, that is, stealing someone else's work. Another ethical guideline is that research subjects should not be harmed by the research. Ethics further require that researchers protect the anonymity of people who provide private, sometimes intimate, and often potentially embarrassing or otherwise harmful information. Finally, it generally is considered unethical for researchers to misrepresent themselves to keep confidentiality and avoid misrepresentation.

Sociologist to take these ethical criteria seriously. Confidential information provided by research participants must be treated as such by sociologists, even when this information enjoys no legal protection or privilege and legal force is applied. Sociologist agree on the necessity to protect respondents.

(D) VALUES IN SOCIOLOGICAL RESEARCH

Max Weber raised an issue that remains controversial among sociologists. *He declared* that sociology should be *value free*. By this he meant that a sociologist's values—personal beliefs about what is good or worthwhile in life—should not affect research. Instead, he said, we need objectivity, total *neutrality*, for if values influence research, sociological findings will be biased.

Objectivity as an ideal is not a matter of debate in sociology All sociologists agree that no one should distort data to make them fit preconceived notions or values, and that research must report actual, not desired, findings. It is equally clear, however, that, like everyone else, sociologists are members of a particular society at a given point in history and are, therefore, infused with values of all sorts. These values inevitably play a role in our research.

(E) SUMMARY

(a) We summarise the research methodology as under:

What are the basic steps in sociological research survey?

1. Selecting a topic.
2. Defining the problem.
3. Reviewing the literature.
4. Formulating a hypothesis.
5. Choosing a research method.
6. Conducting a pilot study.
7. Collecting the data.
8. Analyzing the results.
9. Sharing the results.
10. Publication of the report.

(b) How do sociologists gather data? Six research methods

Sociologists use six research methods (or research designs) for gathering data: **surveys,** participant observation, secondary analysis, documents, unobtrusive measures, and experiments.

(c) Issues and Ethics in Sociological Research

How do ethics affect?

Ethics are of fundamental concern to sociologists, who are committed to openness, honesty, truth, and protecting their subjects from harm.

(d) What value dilemma do sociologists face?

Max Weber stressed that social research should be *value free.*

The researcher's personal beliefs must be set aside in order to permit objective findings. Like everyone else, however, sociologists are members of a particular society at a given point in history and therefore are infused with values of all soils. To overcome the distortions that values can cause, sociologists stress replication, the repetition of a study by other researchers in order to compare results. Values present a second dilemma for researchers—whether to do research solely to analyze basic or (pure sociology) or in order to reform harmful social arrangements.

Box I

A Sociological Quiz—Sociological Findings Versus Common Sense

Some sociological findings support common sense understandings of social life, while others contradict them. Can you tell the difference? If you want to enjoy this quiz fully, complete all the questions before looking at the next page to check your answers.

1. *True/False*: The earnings of U.S. women have just about caught up with those of U.S. men.
2. *True/False*: When faced with natural disasters such as floods and earthquakes, people panic and social organisation disintegrates.
3. *True/False*: Revolutions are more likely to occur when conditions remain bad than when they begin to improve.
4. *True/False*: Most people on welfare are lazy and looking for a handout. They could work if they wanted to.
5. *True/False*: Compared with men, women touch each other more while they are talking to one another.
6. *True/False*: Compared with women, men maintain more eye contact while they are conversing.
7. *True/False*: The more available alcohol is (as measured by the number of places to buy alcohol per one hundred people), the more alcohol-related injuries and fatalities occur on U.S. highways.
8. *True/False*: Couples who live together before marriage are usually more satisfied with their marriages than couples who do not live together before marriage.
9. *True/False*: The reason people discriminate against minorities is prejudice; unprejudiced people don't discriminate.
10. *True/False*: Students in Japan are under such intense pressure to do well in school that their suicide rate is about double that of U.S. students.

Box 2

Sociological Findings Versus Common Sense—Answers to the Sociology Quiz

1. *False*: Over the years, the income gap has narrowed, but only slightly. On average, full-time working women earn only 65 to 70 percent of what full-time working men earn; this low figure is actually an improvement, for in the 1970s women's incomes averaged about 60 percent of men's.
2. *False*: Following such disasters, people develop greater cohesion, cooperation, and social organisation to deal with the catastrophe.
3. *False*: Just the opposite is true. When conditions are consistently bad, people are more likely to be resigned to their fate. Rapid improvement causes their aspirations to outpace their changing circumstances, which can increase frustration and foment revolution.
4. *False*: Most people on welfare are children, the old, the sick, the mentally and physically handicapped, or young mothers with few skills. Less than 2 percent meet the common stereotype of an able-bodied man.
5. *False*: Men touch each other more during conversations (Whyte, 1989).
6. *False*: Women maintain considerably more eye contact (Henley, *et al.*, 1985).
7. *False*: Researchers in California compared the number of alcohol outlets per population with the alcohol-related highway injuries and fatalities. They found that counties in which alcohol is more readily available do not have more alcohol-related injuries and fatalities (Kohfeld and Leip, 1991).

8. *False*: The opposite is true. The reason, researchers suggest, is that many couples who marry after cohabiting are less committed to marriage in the first place and a key to marital success is firm commitment to one another (Larson, 1988).
9. *False*: When racial was legal in the United States, sociologists found that due to business reasons and peer pressure some unprejudiced people did discriminate (LaPiere, 1934). For these same reasons, some prejudiced people do not discriminate, although they want to.
10. *False*: The suicide rate of U.S. students is about double that of Japanese students (Haynes and Chalker, 1997).

Source: James M. Henslin, "Essentials of Sociology: A Down to Earth Approach", Allyn and Bacon, Boston.

References

Patrick McNeill, Research Methods, Routledge, London.
James M. Henslin, Essentials of Sociology, Allyn and Bacon, Boston.

CHAPTER 15

Concepts in Staffing

In this chapter following sub-functions of staffing are covered:

1. Importance and advantages of staffing.
2. Human resource planning.
3. Job analysis, job descriptions and job specifications.
4. Recruitment or getting applicants for the jobs.
5. Selection of the best qualified from those who seek the jobs.
6. Placement and orientation.
7. Training and development of those who need further instruction to perform their work effectively or to qualify for promotions.
8. Performance appraisal.
9. Administration of compensation plans as these are important for getting and retaining competent employees.
10. To conclude.

I. IMPORTANCE AND ADVANTAGES OF STAFFING

It is important to fill jobs with the right people. All managers have a responsibility for staffing. The board of directors performs the staffing function by selecting the chief executive. The chief executive discharges this function when he selects a production, finance or a marketing manager and the manager does likewise when he selects his subordinates. Even the foreman or first level supervisors have a staffing responsibility when they select the rank and file workers.

Advantages of staffing are:

(a) It helps in locating competent employees and developing them for advancement in corporate ladder.

(b) It ensures greater performance by putting the right man in the right job.
(c) It helps to avoid a sudden disruption of an enterprise's operation run by indicating shortages of personnel, if any, in advance.
(d) It helps to prevent under-utilisation of personnel through overmanning and the resultant high labour cost and low profit margins.
(e) It provides information to management for the internal succession of managerial personnel in the event of an unanticipated turnover.

2. HUMAN RESOURCE PLANNING (HRP)

Human resource planning is an essential requirement of successful staffing. Human resource planning ensures right places at the right time. They also perform their work economically. Thus, human resource planning enable management to control employee cost by avoiding both shortages and surpluses of personnel in an organisation.

Human resource planning involves *forecasting* of requirements, developing employee and controling personnel according to requirements.

(i) The first step is to determine the requirements of manpower for a particular period. This is done by making forecasts. Forecasts of future manpower requirements can be made for a period of two to five years. If the periods selected are too long, it is difficult to have an accurate manpower forecast in view of the inability to predict effectively the likely changes in the economic, social and technological spheres.

For forecasting the number of rank and file workers it is better first to make a forecast of sales. On the basis of the sales forecast, we know the schedule of production for various products and the total quantity required to be produced during the particular period. When the output of various departments is ascertained, the requirements of manpower to enable the various departments to attain the required output can be very easily estimated.

To make a forecast of the number of executives needed at the end of a particular period, the number of managerial positions that currently exist should first of all be counted with the help of a complete and up-to-date organisation chart. In the next step, allowance should be made for (a) foreseeable expansion or contraction in the organisation structure on the basis of plans, if any; and (b) estimated deaths, retirements and turnover in managerial personnel on the basis of an annual average calculated, say, for the preceding five years.

(ii) The second step is to ascertain the existing number of rank and file workers in each section, department and unit and to compare it with the required number. In case the required number is more than the available number, the next step would be to consider, how such shortages are to be provided for—whether through recruitment or through promotion. In case, the available number is more than the number required, the next step would be to consider how to get rid of the excess hands, i.e. whether through premature retirement or discharge or lay-off, etc.

(iii) The third step is to determine the need and the kind of training to be given to the existing and new employees.

In fact, the HRP involves the undernoted steps:

- Marketing and production work load plans.
- Demand of manpower.
- Availability of manpower including forecast of wastages due to retirements, deaths, terminations, promotions.

- Gap between demand and availability forecasts, i.e. shortages or surpluses.
- Action plan for recruitment, training and productivity improvements, etc.

3. JOB ANALYSIS, JOB DESCRIPTIONS AND JOB SPECIFICATIONS

In order to be able to determine the qualifications needed to meet the requirements of jobs, the company has first of all to analyse the jobs, write job descriptions and prepare jobs specifications.

(a) Job Analysis

Job analysis is the process by means of which a description is developed of the present methods and procedures of doing a job, physical conditions in which the job is done, relation of the job to other jobs and other conditions of employment. Job analysis is intended to reveal what is *actually* done as opposed to what *should* be done.

The information concerning the job can be obtained from a number of sources such as observation of workers, interviews, questionnaire responses, published manuals, bulletins. It has been found that whereas the questionnaire is best suited to clerical workers, interviewing is best suited to shop workers. Observation is particularly desirable where manual operations are prominent and where the work cycle is short. Working conditions and hazards are better described when viewed personally by the analyst.

(b) Job Description

The results of a job analysis are set down in job description. Writing job description for production workers, clerical people and first-line supervisors is a fairy established practice. A more recent development is job role clarification for managers.

The job description is a written statement that describes in brief the tasks, duties and responsibilities which need to be discharged for effective job performance.

Role Description or Role Clarification for Managers

It involves undernoted steps as per role analysis technique:

(a) The manager lists his activities consisting of the prescribed and discretionary elements. Other role incumbents, and his immediate superior question him on the definition of his task and if there is confusion in their perceptions, the ambiguity is cleared.

(b) The manager lists his expectations from each of those other roles in the group which he feels most directly affect his own work. Others in the group also state their expectations and after a discussion, all of them arrive at an agreement among themselves on their mutual expectations.

(c) The manager then writes up his role which consists of all aspects of his work.

This technique allows the managerial group to work out interpersonal problems more effectively than is otherwise possible through a job description.

(c) Job Specification

A job specification (also called man specification) is a statement of the minimum acceptable human qualities necessary to perform a job satisfactorily. Making job description as its base, it lays down the abilities and qualities that employee should possess in order to hold the job in question. The exact list of these abilities and qualities varies according to the company and the uses to which the job specification is to be put. It contains the personal attributes in terms of education, training, experience, aptitudes and personal characteristics required to perform the job. Job specification serves as a guide for the selection, training and development of employees.

4. RECRUITMENT

Once the requirement of manpower is known, the process of recruitment starts. It can be defined as the process of identifying the sources for prospective candidates and to stimulate them to apply for the jobs. In other words, recruitment is the generating of applications or applicants for specific positions. It is the process of attracting potential employees to the company.

4.1 Sources of Recruitment

The sources of recruitment can be broadly classified into two categories: internal and external. Internal sources refer to the present working force of a company. Vacancies other than at the lowest level may be filled by selecting individuals from amongst the existing employees of the company. Among the more commonly used external sources are the following:

(a) *Re-employing former employees.* Former employees who have been laid-off or have left for personal reasons may be re-employed. These people may require less initial training than that needed by total strangers to the enterprise.

(b) *Friends and relatives of present employees.* Some industries with a record of good personnel relations encourage their employees to recommend their friends and relatives for appointment in the concern where they are employed.

(c) *Applicants at the gate.* Unemployed persons who call at the gates of the factories are interviewed by the factory representative and those who are found suitable for the existing vacancies are selected. This is an important source in countries where there is a lot of unemployment.

(d) *College and technical institutions.* Many big companies remain in touch with the colleges and technical institutions from where young and talented persons may be recruited. This type of source is more popular in advanced countries where there is a shortage of highly qualified technical people.

(e) *Employment exchanges.* Employment exchanges also serve as an important source of recruitment for a number of business concerns. They are considered a useful source for the recruitment of clerks, accountants, typists, etc.

(f) *Advertising the vacancy.* One more source that is tapped by the companies is advertising the vacancy in leading papers? This source may be used in case the company requires the services of persons possessing certain special skills or if there is an acute shortage of labour force.

(g) *Web-sites such as naukari.com, etc.* At present majority of recruitment is done on line.

4.2 Advantages and Disadvantages of Internal and External Sources of Recruitments

Advantages

Some of the advantages of internal recruitment are as under:

(a) A sense of security develops among the employees.
(b) Employee remain loyal to the organisation.
(c) People recruited from within the organisation do not need induction training.
(d) Employees in the lower ranks are encouraged to look forward to rising to higher positions in the concern.
(e) Labour turnover is reduced.
(f) People are motivated to become efficient.
(g) Valuable contacts with major suppliers and customers remain intact.
(h) A better employer-employee relationship is established.

Disadvantages

The method of internal recruitment suffers from certain disadvantages. These are:

(a) This method limits the choice of selection to the few candidates available within the enterprise.
(b) It may encourage favouritism and nepotism.
(c) It may lead to 'inbreeding', resulting in promotion of people who have developed a respect for the tradition and who have no new ideas of their own. It is generally the new blood which brings in new ideas.
(d) If a concern is extending its activities into new lines, internal candidates may prove unsuitable for new positions. This may involve extra expenditure in imparting necessary training to them.

Advantages and Disadvantages of External Recruitment

Advantages

Some of the advantages of making recruitment from outside sources are as follows:

(a) Under this method, new blood brings with it a fresh outlook, originality and new ideas. Old habits are replaced by new ones and the concern becomes more dynamic.
(b) The field of choice becomes very wide. Hence there is the possibility of selecting people with rich and varied experience.

Disadvantages

This method also suffers from certain disadvantages:

(a) If a concern makes recruitment from external sources, its employees generally feel frustrated and their morale is adversely affected.
(b) The present employees may lose their sense of security and become disloyal to the employer.

(c) There is a greater turnover of labour.
(d) There is deterioration in the employer-employee relationship, resulting in industrial unrest, strikes and lock-outs.

5. SELECTION OF THE BEST QUALIFIED FROM THOSE WHO SEEK JOBS

Importance of the Selection Process

Whereas under recruitment the manager identifies the sources for prospective candidates and stimulates them to apply for various openings in his organisation, under selection he compares their qualifications with the requirements of a job and eliminates all those who do not stand up to this comparison. There are several advantages of a proper selection procedure. As the employees are placed in the jobs for which they are best suited, they derive maximum job satisfaction and reap maximum wages. Employee turnover is reduced and the overall efficiency of the concern is increased. And finally, a good relationship develops between the employer and his employees.

There is no standard selection procedure followed by all organisations. However, the steps commonly followed are as under:

(a) Application blank and its security.
(b) Initial interview of the candidate.
(c) Employment tests.
(d) Checking references.
(e) Physical or medical examination.
(f) Final interview.

(a) Application blank and its security

Filling of the 'application blank' by the candidate is the first step in the process of selection. In this form, the applicant gives relevant personal data such as his qualification, specialisation, experience, firms in which he has worked, etc. The application blanks are carefully scrutinised by the company with reference to the specifications prescribed for the jobs to decide the applicants who are to be called for interview.

(b) Initial interview

Those who are selected for interview on the basis of particulars furnished in the application blank are called for initial interview by the company. This interview is the most important means of evaluating the poise or appearance of the candidate. It is also used for establishing a friendly relationship between the candidate and the company and for obtaining additional information or clarification on the information already on the application blank. The interview must be properly planned and the interviewers, consisting of specialists in different fields, must make the applicants feel at ease, discount personal prejudices and note their opinion about the applicants interviewed.

(c) Employment tests

For further assessment of a candidate's nature and abilities, some tests are used in the selection procedure. Psychologists and other experts have developed certain tests by which a candidate's particular traits or abilities, his likes and dislikes, his intelligence, manual dexteity, his capacity to learn and to benefit from training, his adaptability, etc. can be estimated. There are several types of tests at are used in selection procedure. The more commonly used are:

(i) Aptitude test

This test measures the applicant's capacity to learn the skill required for a job. It helps in finding out whether a candidate is suitable for a clerical or a mechanical job. This test helps in assessing before training as to how well the candidate will perform on a job after he is given the necessary training.

(ii) Interest test

This test is used to find out the type of work in which the candidate has an interest. For example, whether a candidate has a liking for a sales job requiring contact with other people can be assessed by means of this test. An interest test only indicates the interest of a candidate for a particular job. It does not reveal his ability to do it. Interest tests are generally used for vocational counselling. Usually, well-prepared questionnaires are used in interest tests.

(iii) Intelligence test

This test is used to find out the candidate's intelligence. By using this test, the candidate's mental alertness, reasoning ability, power of understanding, etc. are judged. Some examples of intelligence tests are: reading and summarising a paragraph in the allotted time, writing 10 to 15 words that begin with the same letter in one minute, adding up of some figures in the allotted time and so on.

(iv) Trade or performance or achievement test

This test is used to measure the candidate's level of knowledge and skill in the particular trade or occupation in which he will be appointed, in case he is finally selected. In this test, the candidate is asked to do a simple operation which is a part of, or similar to his proposed job. For example, a candidate for a driver's post may be asked to drive the vehicle to assess his proficiency, or a typist may be asked to type out some letters to find out his speed and accuracy, or a candidate for a post of salesman may be asked to attend to a prospective customer who enters the shop.

(v) Personality test

Personality test is used to measure those characteristics of a candidate which constitute his personality, e.g. self-confidence, temperament, initiative, judgement, dominance, integrity, originality, etc. Personality tests are very important in the selection process, particularly in the case of appointments to the posts of supervisors and higher executives. In a personality test, the candidate may be asked to answer a series of questions and from his response, his personality may be judged or in some special test situations, the candidate's reaction may be assessed, or the candidate may be asked to grade his own examination papers in order know his honesty.

(d) Checking References

If the candidate has been found satisfactory at the interview and if his performance is good in employment or proficiency tests, the employer would like to get some important personal details about the candidate, such as his character, past history, background, etc. verified from the people mentioned in the application. For this purpose, the employer may also contact his friends residing in the locality where the candidate is residing or he may contact the present or former employers of the candidate.

(e) Physical or Medical Examination

Physical or medical examination is another step in the selection procedure. The objectives of this examination are: (i) to check the physical fitness of the applicant for the job applied for; (ii) to protect the company against the unwarranted claims for compensation under certain legislative enactments, such as Workmen's Compensation Act; and (iii) to prevent communicable diseases entering the business concern.

(f) Final interview

This interview is conducted for those who are ultimately selected for employment. In this interview, the selected candidates are given an idea about their future prospects within the organisation.

6. PLACEMENT AND ORIENTATION

Placement

The process of placing the right man on the right job is called placement. Placement means "the determination of the job to which an accepted candidate is to be assigned and his assignment to that job." Placement is an important aspect of the selection process. An employee should be placed on a position where there is full use of his strengths and all his weaknesses become irrelevant. A misplaced person is always a frustrated individual.

His morale being low, he never gives his best to the organisation. Not only this, such an individual also hampers the work of his colleagues in the organisation. Proper placement reduces labour turnover, absenteeism and accidents.

Orientation

At the time of the placement of the employee, attention is also given to the special programmes such as orientation and training to the employee in order to enable him to adjust himself to the work in the organisation and to make him feel at home with his associates. Usually, large concerns provide formal training, consisting of lectures, plan tour and the presentation of pamphlets explaining the history and prospects of the organisation and its policies regarding employment, products, etc.

7. TRAINING AND DEVELOPMENT

Employee training is distinct from management development. Training is a short-term process utilising a systematic and organised procedure by which non-managerial personnel learn technical knowledge and skills for a definite purpose. It refers to instructions in technical and mechanical operations like operation of a machine. It is designed primarily for non-managers. It is for a short duration and for a specific job-related purpose.

On the other hand, development is a long-term educational process utilising a systematic and organised procedure by which managerial personnel learn conceptual and theoretical knowledge for general purpose. It involves philosophical and theoretical educational concepts and it is designed for managers. It involves broader education and its purpose is long-term development.

In the words of Campbell, "training courses are typically deigned for a short-term, stated set purpose, such as the operation of some piece(s) of machinery while development involves a broader education for long-term purposes."

Training involves helping an individual learn how to perform his present job satisfactorily. Development involves preparing the individual for a future job and growth of the individual in all respects. Development complements training because human resources can exert their full potential only when the learning processes far beyond simple routine.

7.1 Distinction between Training and Development

Sl. No.	*Point of Distinction*	*Training*	*Development*
(i)	Contents	Technical and mechanical operations.	Conceptual and philosophical concepts.
(ii)	Participants	Non-managerial personnel.	Managerial personnel.
(iii)	Time period	Short-term one shot affair.	Long-term continuous process.
(iv)	Purpose	Specific, job-related skills.	Total personality.
(v)	Initiative	From management external motivation.	From individual himself—internal motivation.
(vi)	Nature of the process	Relative process to meet current need.	Proactive process to meet future needs.

7.2 Importance of Training

(i) Higher Productivity

Training helps to improve the level of performance. Trained employees perform better by using better method of work. Improvements in manpower productivity in developed nations can be attributed in no small measure to their education and industrial training programmes.

(ii) Better Quality of Work

In formal training, the best methods are standardised and taught to employees. Uniformity of work methods and procedures helps to improve the quality of product or service. Trained employees are less likely to make operational mistakes.

(iii) Less Learning Period

A systematic training programme helps to reduce the time and cost involved in learning. Employees can more quickly reach the acceptable level of performance. They need not waste their time and efforts in learning through trial and error.

(iv) Cost Reduction

Trained employees make more economical use of materials and machinery. Reduction in wastage and spoilage together with increase in productivity help to minimise cost of operations per unit. Maintenance cost is also reduced due to fewer machine breakdowns and better handling of equipments. Plant capacity can be put to the optimum use.

(v) Reduced Supervision

Well-trained employees tend to be self-reliant and motivated. They need less guidance and control. Therefore, supervisory burden is reduced and the span of supervision can be enlarged.

(vi) Low Accident Rate

Trained personnel adopt the right work methods and make use of the prescribed safety devices. Therefore, the frequency of accidents is reduced. Health and safety of employees can be improved.

(vii) High Morale

Proper training can develop positive attitudes among employees. Job satisfaction and morale are improved due to a rise in the earnings and job security of employees. Training reduces employee grievances because opportunities for internal promotion are available to well trained personnel.

(viii) Personal Growth

Training enlarges the knowledge and skills of the participants. Therefore, well trained personnel can grow faster in their career. Training prevents obsolescence of knowledge and skills. Trained employees are a more valuable asset to any organisation. Training helps to develop people for promotion to higher posts and to develop future managers.

(ix) Organisational Climate

A sound training programme helps to improve the climate of an organisation. Industrial relations and discipline are improved. Therefore, decentralisation of authority and participative management can be introduced. Resistance to change is reduced. Organisations having regular training programmes can fulfil their future needs for personnel from internal sources. Organisational stability is enhanced because training helps to reduce employee turnover and absenteeism.

Training is an investment in people and, therefore, systematic training is a sound business investment. In fact, "no organisation can choose whether or not to train employees . . . the only choice left to management is whether training shall be haphazard, casual and possibly misdirected or whether it shall be made a carefully planned part of an integrated programme of personnel administration."

7.3 Training Methods and Evaluation of Training

(a) Training is the act of increasing the knowledge and skill of an employee for doing a particular job. Development implies an employee's growth and maturisation. A systematic training programme helps in improving the quality and quantity of a worker's output, make the worker committed and loyal to the organisation, facilitates promotion and replacement and reduces spoiled work and accident rate. A training programme can be of any of the following types: induction or orientation training; job training; promotional training; reframe; and corrective training.

(b) *All training methods can be grouped* into two categories: (a) training methods for operatives, and (b) training methods for managers. On-the-job training method is by far the commonly used method for training the rank and file workers in a factory. There are several methods, such as vestibule training, apprenticeship training and internship training . . . . make use of on-the-job training concept. Training methods used for manager's observation, assignment, position rotation, serving on committees, assignment of special projects, conferences and seminars, case study, incident method, role playing, sensitivity training and autonomy training.

(c) *Selection of an appropriate training method* depends upon the nature of the problem level of trainees. the method's ability to hold and arouse the interest of trainees during training period, availability of competent trainees, finance and time.

(d) *Evaluation of training methods* can be done in one of the following ways: (a) opinion of participants; (b) measurement of participants' performance when they are back on job; (c) evaluation of performance appraisals; and (d) overall look at the aggregate of people in the total organisation.

8. PERFORMANCE APPRAISAL

1. Performance appraisal refers to the assessment of an employee's actual performance, behaviour on jobs and his or potential for future performance. Appraisal has several objectives but the main purposes are to assess training needs, to effect promotions and to give pay increases.

2. Appraisal of performance proceeds in a set pattern. The steps involved are: defining appraisal objectives, establishing job expectations, designing the appraisal programme, conducting performance interview and using appraisal data for different human resource activities.

3. Performance appraisals are an integral part of every organization. Properly developed and implemented, the performance appraisal can help an organization achieve its goals by developing productive employees. While there are many types of performance appraisal systems, each having its own advantages and disadvantages.

To evaluate employees on behaviourally desired measures, use multiple raters, include peer assessments and self-assessments, reward accurate appraisers, and, above all, communicate the results of the evaluation to the employee.

4. The appraisal process consists of six steps:

(a) Establish performance standards
(b) Communicate performance expectations to employees
(c) Measure actual performance
(d) Compare actual performance with standards
(e) Discuss the appraisal with the employee
(f) If necessary, initiate corrective action

5. Appraisals can be distorted by:

(a) Leniency error
(b) Halo error

(c) Similarity error
(d) Central tendency
(e) Forcing information to match performance criteria
(f) Low appraiser motivation

6. Requirements of a Sound Performance Appraisal Programme

A sound system of performance appraisal must fulfil the following essentials:

(i) The appraisal plan should be simple to operate and easy to understand. When the appraisal system is complicated, employees may not understand it fully and may look at the plan with suspicion. The plan should not be very time-consuming.
(ii) The performance appraisal system should be performance-based, uniform and non-variable, fair, just and equitable. It should be ensured that the appraisers are honest, rational and objective in their approach, judgement and behavioural orientation.
(iii) The employees should be made aware of the performance in terms of goals, target, behaviour, etc. expected of them. A personal equation between the appraiser and the employee has to be developed to achieve mutual understanding of the criteria of evaluation.
(iv) The appraisal plan should be devised in consultation with the subordinates. This will increase their commitment to the plan and their understanding of expected performance.
(v) The top management must create a climate of reliable appraisal throughout the organisation. Goal-orientation, open communications, mutual trust informal relationships, etc. are the basic elements of such a climate.
(vi) The appraisal plan should be designed to achieve specific objectives. The objectives of the appraisal programme may be to evaluate current performance on the job and to determine the potential for higher jobs. In some cases, performance appraisal is linked with specific objectives like pay raise, training, promotion, transfer, etc. The number of factors to be considered and the data to be collected should be tailormade to achieve the objective of the appraisal.
(vii) The appraisers should be selected and trained properly so that they have no personal bias and possess the necessary capabilities for objective evaluation of employees. In order to ensure objectivity in appraisal, an individual may be rated by more persons independently.
(viii) There should be provision of appeals against appraisals to ensure confidence of the employees and their associations or unions. The results of appraisal must be discussed with the rates so that they may get an opportunity to express their feelings on their progress reports.

9. ADMINISTRATION OF COMPENSATION PLAN

Compensation plan is one of the most important areas of human resource management. Every human resource manager is entrusted with the responsibility of establishing equitable wage and salary structure on one hand and maintaining an equitable labour cost structure on the other.

Wages and salaries represent a substantial part of total costs in most of the organisations.

Objectives of Compensation Plan

(a) Reward employees according to merit.
(b) Attract and retain the services of desirable employees.
(c) Get improved employee moral and productivity.
(d) Keep labour cost within reasonable limits so as to safeguard the interests of shareholders, competitive worth of the organisation and its product and profitability.
(e) Pay employees according to the importance and difficulty of the job.
(f) Incorporate legal requirements.
(g) Facilitate payroll administration and exercising control.

A good compensation plan makes employee happier in their work, raises their output and quality and makes them loyal to the organisation.

The components of compensation can be: (a) primary compensation, (b) incentive compensation, and (c) non-monetary incentives.

(a) Primary compensation comprises of basic pay. This is determined through job evaluation. The compensation structure is a function of internal and external alignments. Internal alignment means that there has to be a proper relationship between the wages and salaries of various positions within the organisation. External alignment means that the company wages and salaries are comparable with the rates in other companies.
    - Factory-wide rates in other companies.
    - Payment by result to indirect employees.
(b) Payment of bonus is regulated under payment of Bonus Act.
(c) Non-monetary incentives are necessary to satisfy the social and egoistic needs of employees.

We have number of laws which regulate wages. These are: Minimum Wages Act, Payment of Wages Act.

10. TO CONCLUDE

Staffing is to be performed and conducted in a satisfactory manner. It must contribute towards accomplishment of overall objectives of organisation. Some basic guidelines could be as under:

(a) The staffing function must be set in such a way so as to contribute maximum to organisational objectives.
(b) Jobs should be well defined in terms of role, relationship, duties and responsibilities involved in the job, so that right type persons are selected to perform their jobs for achieving organisational objectives.
(c) Training should be organisation need-oriented and not a ritual or formality.
(d) Performance appraisal should be goals-oriented, objective and free from personal bias of managers.

CHAPTER

16

Managing Concerns in Human Resources in NPO

We shall discuss here some basic concerns in human resources, specifically in recruitment of employees under following headings:

1. Non-profit organisation's problems of staffing.
2. Sources of recruitment of manpower to be considered in NPO.
3. Critical points for recruitment process.
4. Women in the non-profit workforce in USA.

1. NON-PROFIT ORGANISATION'S PROBLEMS OF STAFFING

Some problems faced by non-profit organisations are as under:

(i) First, staff who should be committed to the 'cause' of NPO and have reasonable level of 'competence', and it is difficult to find this combination, due to growing materialism.

(ii) Second, staff should have strong sense of morality and ethics. It is difficult to find persons who are sincere and honest. We find instances where employees are stealing from blind and orphan schools for children, etc.

(iii) Third, non-profit organisations tend to offer salaries out of line with going market rates. It implies employee's willingness to sacrifice higher pay for the sake of noble cause. However, there is maximum gap between going rates of salaries in the country. Thus, NPOs can hardly ensure salary equal to government and semi-government institutions. However, NPOs have to provide salary and perks for acceptable standard of life and responsibilities of family.

(iv) Fourth, NPOs carry out review of the salary and compensation levels periodically say five years as is the practice with the corporate sectors.
(v) Fifth, consider any schemes like provident fund or pension scheme with employee's contribution and gratuity.
(vi) Sixth, reasonable provision for housing or subsidy in loans or payment of rent, etc.
(vii) Seventh, a provision for cumulated earned leave.
(viii) Eighth, medical assistance on pattern of Employee's Insurance Scheme (ESI), or group insurance scheme, or insurance through medical claim.
(ix) Ninth, arrangements for lunch facilities, etc.

These facilities make a difference in employees morale and job attraction inspite of lower salaries than going rates. NPOs can seek help of professional consultants for setting up employee's salaries and compensation pattern.

2. SOURCES OF RECRUITMENT OF MANPOWER TO BE CONSIDERED IN NPO

Since competing on salaries at going market rates is hardly feasible, but non-profit organisations have to attract manpower at higher levels of professional competence, particularly, for medical, teaching areas. Some specific segments can be targeted as under:

(a) Persons in higher age group say sixties, but have considerable service potential in them. Non-profit society can generate motivation of persons who are available at salaries that NPOs can afford.
(b) Ex-defence service officers who enjoy good health and have strong sense of discipline. They can be useful source for responsible positions.
(c) Those who have retired on voluntary retirement schemes may be attracted and may be satisfied with a lower than market rate of compensation. In view of the fact they have earnings through lum-sum amount received by them as VRS.
(d) Non-profit organisation can lay emphasis on commitment to the cause which may be motivating factor.
(e) It is useful to ask some responsible persons to recommend suitable candidates, as they may be able to say about their capabilities. Then these individuals can be considered for selection.

3. CRITICAL POINTS FOR RECRUITMENT PROCESS

Some aspects to be considered at the time of hiring employees can be:

(a) Recruitment should be on *objective basis*.
(b) A *job description* is essential to precisely know the job requirements of the position at the time of selection of suitable candidates.
(c) A good *upbringing makes* a difference. So family background, institutions attended for academic record, extra-curricular activities may be considered. These are helpful in selection process.
(d) Ability to judge people is important in candidates and service background helps.

(e) Employee to have a clear idea as to what services he has to render and supposed to do the job. If the position requires continuous interaction with clients or public, a proven extrovert is obviously at an advantage.

(f) An ideal selection committee to comprise of three or four members. Each member can rate candidates independently and then rating reviewed at the end of each interview for finalisation of the selection.

(g) It is desirable that appointment letters to contain a clause for *probation period.*

(h) Programme for *orientation of new employees* is very helpful:
- Towards mission and goals of organisation,
- Helping in removing their difficulties in adjusting, and
- Shaping the new comer's in NPOs cultural mould.

(i) Provision for *performance evaluation and feedback system*:
- Assessment of performance to be against pre-determined targets which mat be discussed and agreed between the employee and his supervisor. The appraisal session then becomes a joint review of plan agreed earlier. Role of the supervisor is more like that of a coach.
- Focus on developing the employee for better performance.
- Remove his weaknesses for better future performance.
- Potential of employees to be assessed for growth.

(j) Development process of employees, such as interaction skills, inter-personal development, leadership and team working are helpful in their job performance. Focus has to be given on all round development of employee for different jobs.

(k) Succession planning policy will facilitate development of employees for career in NPO. It will provide ability to shoulder responsibilities and challenges facing the organisation.

(l) Retaining of good people is a continuous process and has to be given utmost importance.

(m) The delected candidates should be able to keep regular interaction with other groups such as general public, donor groups to raise funds, professionals and public figures to be approached for attracting to NPOs cause.

These steps will help in motivating, developing commitment of employees to non-profit organisations.

4. WOMEN IN THE NON-PROFIT WORKFORCE IN USA

The sheer number of women working in the non-profit sector would seem to imply that women have met influence and equity there; however, research shows that although they make up more than sixty percent of the non-profit workforce, women still lack access to the top managerial positions and board participation.

Some statistics about the position of women and the non-profit sector is as under:

- Women constitute 45.5 percent of the total workforce.
- Women are paid seventy cents on the dollar as compared to men, according to Maggie Mohar in Working Woman (April 1993). Mohar explains that the gains that appear to be narrowing the gap between men and women's wages are due to men's

wages dropping, not women's wages rising. The divide between men's and women's wages is consistent regardless of profession. Wages of women just out of college are close to being equal to their male counterparts, but the gap widens over time.
- Sexual harassment is an active problem, and blatant discrimination is not a thing of the past.
- Female executives in top NPOs are still very rare.
- NPOs have been slow to adapt the workplace to women's needs in terms of flexible work conditions, self-actualization, benefits that fit the concerns of working mothers, etc. They need the support for a better balance between work and family.

Women make up approximately two-thirds of the non-profit labour force. They are concentrated in health, social services, legal and foundation organisations, while male employees constitute the majority in research, religious, arts and cultural organisations.

CHAPTER

17

Organisation Excellence through HRM

In this chapter following aspects of 'Organisation Excellence through HRM' are discussed:

1. High degree of achievement and motivation of human resources is important for organisation excellence.
2. Model for organisation excellence.
3. HR issues in achieving excellence.
4. Sustainable competitive development for excellent organisation.

1. HIGH DEGREE OF ACHIEVEMENT AND MOTIVATION OF HUMAN RESOURCES IS IMPORTANT FOR ORGANISATION EXCELLENCE

Organisations to a large extent depend on an entrepreneurial behaviour which calls for a high degree of achievement and motivation to engender organisation excellence. *Corporations need to shift from* physical technology to information *technology,* from capital centred economy to *human centred economy,* from material growth to *sustainable development,* from hierarchical pattern to *decentralized organisation* and from conflict to *cooperative working* relationship. Peter Drucker (2000) has rightly observed that to make the organisation excellent we need to change the organisation from flow of things to 'ranks', and 'powers' have to be replaced by mutual understanding and responsibility.

The nature of work, workforce, workplace and psychological environment in organisations have undergone and will continue to undergo enormous change, bringing both opportunities and challenges for those involved.

These organisations have to ensure that they maximize the use of technology to create an effective work environment and improve their products and services, human and technological resources. Similarly, the managers in the organisation should learn to deal with a very *diversified workforce* characterized by changing attitudes and values. They will be more effective if they can develop sensitivity towards people in the organisation. Today, organisations have to ensure both qualities of products and services offered by them and the quality of *work life for employees.*

2. MODEL FOR ORGANISATION EXCELLENCE

Organisation excellence is the combination of people, system, product and marketing excellence. Out of these, *people excellence is important* because it has a direct bearing on the system, product and marketing. In any organisation the 10P's are considered to be most important to bring excellence-purpose, perspective, positioning, politics, partnership, plans or policies, product, principles or (philosophy), people and performance (Figure 1).

(i) Purpose

Purpose basically is the goal, vision and service aim of the organisation.

(ii) Perspective

It is the direction—a mental view of the relative importance of things.

(iii) Positioning

The image of the company and its services to the client.

(iv) Politics

Judicious and expedient behaviour of people in the organisation.

FIGURE I

Model of Organisation Excellence

Purpose
Perspective
Positioning
Politics
Organisation
People
Performance
Organisation Excellence
Partnership
Planning
Service/Product
Principles

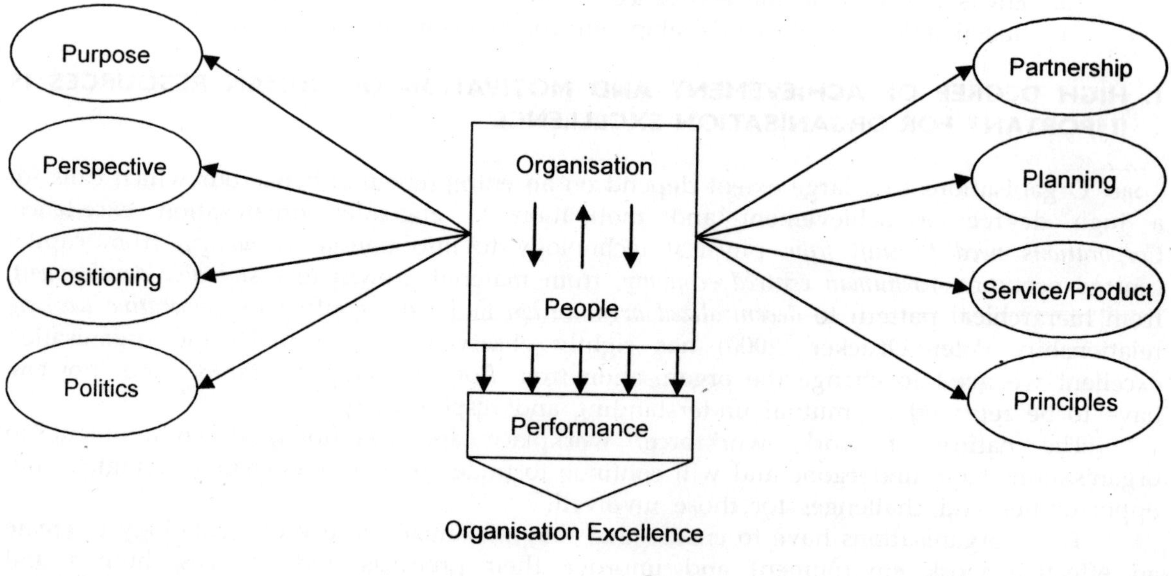

(v) Partnership

The state of being a partner or partners, a joint collaboration, within or outside the organisation.

(vi) Plans

Proper plans of action, translated to organisation policies.

(vii) Product

The product source should be innovative, qualitative and cost-effective.

(viii) Principles

Set of values, culture and philosophy.

(ix) People

Challenging, ethical, committed, high performance, self-driven.

(x) Performance

Output of the organisation, rests, in terms of both quality and quantity.

3. HR ISSUES IN ACHIEVING EXCELLENCE

Human resource management is now a strategically important area of corporate governance, which indicates that HRD policies need to be integrated into the overall policies of the organisation. To be precise, it is a cyclic process of developing mission, vision and service or business plan through people, and translating those to action through policies, ensuring results and redefining the objectives again.

HR is no more a support service but it is the partner in the organisational strategic function.

Organisations follow a combination of growth policies related to efficiency, productivity and human resource development. The following are the important HR issues in achieving corporate excellence:

(i) Aligning organisation strategy with HR strategy.
(ii) Knowledge management and creating learning organisation.
(iii) Competence mapping and skill development through assessment centres.
(iv) Developing moral excellence through ethics audit; and creating a value-based culture.
(v) Reorganisation of work through job enlargement and enrichment.
(vi) Development of mutual trust and synergy among work teams.
(vii) Managing change through people.
(viii) Restructuring and bringing about transformation in the organisation to add value to the service.
(ix) Bringing about rationalization of workforce through internal transfers.
(x) Holding opinion surveys to get a feel of the perception of employees and applying mid-course correction, if necessary.

4. SUSTAINABLE COMPETITIVE DEVELOPMENT OF EXCELLENT ORGANISATION

(i) In the dynamic world, competition is inevitable. Yesterday's best organisations are disappearing from today's list of the best. Every year the name of the Fortune 500 companies reflects how competition impacts the fate of the organisations. Gone are those days when excellent organisations used to have a life cycle of excellence for a very long period. Climbing to the top is relatively easy than staying at the top. Many organisations have grown at a very faster speed but simultaneously they have failed to sustain their growth. *Sustenance of growth requires proportionate development*. There is a qualitative difference between growth and development. A bright example could be the growth of a filariasis patient who adds some kilograms to his body weight because of the elephant leg, which is a growth but not development. Similarly, organisations may have assets worth of crores, but if their turnover and profitability are not remarkable they may loose in the race.

The world-class organisations are those who are *ahead of competitions* have managed to maintain sustainable competitive growth. The success stories of these organisations have proved that *people make the difference,* not the technology. It is the superior talent in the organisations, which will make the organisation different and will tomorrow's prime source of competitive advantage. The CEO of Allied Signal Larry Bossidy has rightly pointed it out: *At the end of the day we bet on people, not on strategies*. A high-speed positive culture enables an organisation to be more competitive and development-oriented.

(ii) Excellent organisations do not aim just to achieve one-time profitability; rather they *focus on excellence in every aspect of the organisation* including people, technology and performance and also to maintain it at an optimum level.

(iii) An employee satisfies the desire for achieving the goal and self-actualization. At the end of the day, the individual feels that he has *done something worthwhile* which gives him immense satisfaction. This has a lot of positive influence on the health of the organisation.

The key approach is that the employee must take a decision that cannot be taken at a lower level and nor does it need to be taken at a higher level. This precisely means that in the organisational hierarchy, each individual holding a position and discharging his role should *add value to the organisation* through his decisions. A layer of management can be created only when the boss really is accountable to take a decision that cannot be taken by the subordinates. The *decision-making accountability differentiates the healthy organisation* from the unhealthy one.

(iv) In order to be effective in the competitive environment, the successful organisations need to be *healthy to sustain their growth and development in the long-run*. Each successful organisation, instead of feeling complacent with the profitability they have achieved, needs to introspect and look within to identify the presence as well as absence of the *attributes of a healthy organisation*. Probably they need to ask many questions related to their structure and functional processes to understand the real value addition in the *decision-making process*. They should satisfy themselves regarding the flatness of the organisation in terms of layers to extend enough space to each individual to be accountable and add substantial value through his decision-making to achieve the ultimate goal of the organisation. Moreover, it is also essential to understand whether the decision-making accountability is being linked to the performance and reward system of the organisation or just the conventional way of linking the pay to performance, overlooking the value addition in terms of accountability. If all these things are not practised in the organisation, then definitely it is a matter of great concern because the future of organisation would then be a jeopardy. This throws a challenge to each organisation to transform themselves from unhealthy to a healthy one to have a longer life span.

(v) Further, *HRM is more crucial today for the success of any organisation* than ever before. The question that arises at this point is—what measures should the organisation take to influence the human resource outputs. The issues that need to be considered to move towards this goal are:

(a) *Employees* must no longer be seen as liability, but as a *key resource* which needs to be carefully nurtured and constantly developed.
(b) While organisations are becoming conscious of the potential of new technologies, they must also realize the crucial role that human being plays in *managing that technology.*
(c) Those organisations which are able to give relevant training to their personnel and maintain their willingness to *learn new ways to do things* can hope to survive in today's economic environment.
(d) There is serious need for all of us to *try and transform* at least that part of the organisation, where we have the power, into learning segments which could then be synthesized into a learning whole.

Box I

Business Practices and Strategies for Maximizing Stake and Shareholder's Wealth for Sustainable Indian Growth

In this competitive and dynamic world, any organisation, in order to take a lead over its competitors needs to focus on the contemporary and innovative HR practices. Some of the innovative practices can be as enumerated below which will help in maximizing Stake and Shareholder's wealth.

(i) Making Individuals a part of Vision and Objective

Making individuals a part of the vision begins with the top management and includes not only laying down the strategy, but also articulating the vision. After the shared vision is established, the vision should be clearly communicated to everyone in the organisation. Shared vision and value provide a direction; commitment and the driving force to all team members, and also build a culture for the organisation. The vision inspires the team members to achieve desired results.

Involving the team members in the vision and the objectives of the organisation leads to contribution in a better way, towards the development of the organisation.

A uniform culture has to be transplanted across the organisation. Once the vision is clearly understood by every team member, action plan needs to be put in place to take this shared vision forward in the organisation. Apart from a clear vision, Visible Management Commitment is very important in transforming the culture of an organisation. At least twenty-five percent of the time should be spent in order to further the vision and the values of the organisation. The top management should ensure that the team members are suitably rewarded for their efforts in implementing the shared values successfully.

Culture is a permanent character of the company. Employees come and go but the culture lives on.

(ii) Capturing and Sharing Knowledge will be Key Ingredients to Success

Tapping the potential of the employees and bringing the workforce and management to work together has to be an ongoing process. Set clear objectives, obtain commitment, provide proper support and work in line with the vision towards achieving desired objectives. Managing knowledge and determining techniques for capturing, distributing and sharing knowledge in the organisation will be the key ingredients to success. Many companies have kept a dedicated team, which continuously updates and maintains knowledge.

Knowledge is your assets.

This century belongs to those organisations, which have learned to utilize knowledge for competitive advantage. It is no longer true that a single person can deliver the goods at all times and that he is indispensable. Leader of the team should ensure that all information, data and knowledge is communicated to team members in order to enhance their contributions, even latest trends and good practices should be shared with the team. New methods of training like online discussion boards, or the conventional classrooms could be turned into a knowledge sharing room.

(iii) Shifting the Attitude from Control to Support

There needs to be a shift in the attitude of the management from the one that exercises control to the one that supports the team members. The strategies need to be redesigned, in order to make it more of a support function than a control function.

Anything which is forced, cannot be forceful.

The crux of the strategy will be to give highest value to humanity, treating people with dignity and respect and recognizing and rewarding their potential. Individuals want to work in a free environment. It has been proved that when autonomy and freedom is given to individuals, their efficiency and effectiveness increases. In the present context, the management should, through innovative techniques, enable support to the team members rather than controlling them, thereby, making them winner. The role of the leader is not just to create checks and balances but also to create an organisation that focuses on effective performance.

(iv) Developing Global Managers in a Cross Cultural Environment

In the present scenario, when the world has been transformed into a competitive global village, it becomes extremely important for the managers to transact globally besides transacting in their own regions. Therefore, to be successful globally, the managers need to learn the cultures of different parts of the world.

Leaders must be conscious of the expectations and the needs of the foreign counterparts.

The process of developing globally competent managers could be initiated by putting emphasis on the following sets of skills:

- Global managers have to constantly upgrade their awareness and knowledge, according to the latest trends and innovations taking place across the international market. Managers need to adjust and improvise accordingly, to match the required international standards.
- Developing a universally acceptable working culture: Efficiency, competency, punctuality and the application of the total quality management are some basic issues, which no manager of the present times could afford to overlook. To gain an international standing, it is essential to incorporate these standards in the day-to-day working.

  Success in the global market place depends on effective cross-cultural exchange. Knowledge of different management styles, such as, the Japanese, Korean and American styles and the ability to distinguish between them is absolutely essential for the managers to gain a competitive edge in the global market.
- Leaders must be conscious of the expectations and the needs of the foreign counterparts. It is imperative for the managers to understand the behavioural intricacies of different working cultures, especially taking into view the body language, postures, customs and certain ethics, specific to the working cultures.

(v) Getting Non-Hierarchical

More and more organisations are paving the way for a flat structured organisation. The idea is to facilitate faster decision-making, by providing more empowerment and autonomy to the employees. Flat structures and adaptive people shall be the slogan for the future.

CHAPTER

18

Working with New Generation Empoyees and Retaining them

Following aspects of new generation employees are covered as under:

(1) Characteristics of new generation employees.
(2) Retention strategies.

(I) CHARACTERISTICS OF NEW GENERATION EMPLOYEES

A breed of employees, that are between 18-24 years of age are smart, practical, *fiercely ambitious* and restless. They have inquiring minds and zealous spirit. They have *obsession to acquire* higher and more saleable skills. This is, their only guarantee to a better job and the *recipe to speedy success* in a fast changing world.

They are used to *offices interiors* which are inviting, comfortable, yet *formal work spaces.* Lounging areas, jukeboxes, food courts, gymnasium, etc. they have got all. They are more comfortable with informal, flexible roles rather than a fixed set of responsibilities. They thrive on *multi-tasking*. This also makes them more vulnerable to changing jobs, or switching careers.

A *less hierarchical* workplaces suit them best and they would prefer to converse on first name basis. Their workplace need to be fun, relaxed and unconventional. They do not need stuffy cabins for them, as they have to spend 12 hours a day there, five days a week. They work hard and harder.

(2) RETENTION STRATEGIES

(i) It is quite a task to keep Generation 'Y' hooked to one job and one employer for long. Because they do not identify with old-fashioned jargon like loyalty. Their *primary commitment is "we, me and my career success . . .* the faster I get there, the better." *So how to retain them. Best bet would be to appreciate their unique areas of strengths and build on those.*

(ii) *Ambition* is second nature to today's young workforce. They are used to aiming for the stars and believe they can go places, much faster than their predecessors. One youngman says, my father built a home when he retired, I can do it by the time I am 30 years. They have *over-confidence* and are optimistic. They want to be at the top from day one. What makes them think they can get to the top fast? Here is a tip. Be generous with some *direct and objective feedback,* while ensuring that it does not wash away that bubbly spirit. The trick is to help them start with smaller, attainable goals and be more practical about taking on higher levels of responsibility. Tap the potential of that limitless energy by assigning multiple projects.

(iii) Generation 'Y' employees are perfect *team players.* In fact, they would rather work in a team, rather than be singled out for an individual function. The opportunity to interface with intelligent and innovative colleagues can act a huge motivator for these people.

(iv) Another hint is *to build trust* with sincere, open and honest communication, share information and encourage two-way flow of ideas. Help them get a taste of loyalty, by offering *involvement in participative forums.* Office functions and events like annual days are great platforms for freshers to show their abilities.

(v) *Time-bound assignments* where they can prove their mettle to handle complexities are perfect. Facilitate them in assessing and identifying their hidden potential, and challenge them to make effective use of their special skills and talents. Generation 'Y' have a tendency to get *bored easily,* so make sure you keep them on their toes, with pressure and excitement.

(vi) *Coaching and mentoring* can be useful tools when it comes to moulding them. Their raw energy and unending enthusiasm, when tempered with appropriate guidance and encouragement from seasoned and respected professionals, can provide these youngsters, an ideal foundation that will ultimately transform them into smart managers of tomorrow.

(vii) They can flourish, if they are provided with state-of-the-art resources. The lack of high tech environment will not be welcome for them. Provide *state-of-art training to retain them.* Allow ample breathing space . . . *autonomy* and *independence* to experiment in their area, and learn from their mistakes. *Listen* to them as they recount their experience of last weekend.

(viii) Their *dreams* may be different from yours, and their work styles too, but they may score as high as yours, in much lesser time, because they mean business.

PART III

FINANCE FUNCTION

CHAPTER

19

Finance Functions in NPOs

Availability of finance is required to start up, to expand and carry on. If buildings have to be built, equipment to be installed, these have to be paid for. Finance is also required to pay for regular supplies of consumables, for energy (power), communications (telephone, postage, etc.)

Some fundamental functions in a non-profit organisation are covered as under:

(a) Sources of funds:
  (i) Donations
  (ii) Fees
  (iii) Endowments
  (iv) Loans
  (v) Cash generated through sale of paid services
  (vi) Interest income

(b) Outflow of funds:
  (i) Salaries and related expenses
  (ii) Expenses
  (iii) Capital expenditures
  (iv) Debit services
  (v) Two other aspects

(c) Functions of finance section in a NPO:
  (i) Raising funds
  (ii) Allocation of funds
  (iii) Balancing inflow and outflow

(d) Types of financial statements:
  (i) The balance sheet
  (ii) The operating statement of profit and loss statement
  (iii) The cash flow statements

Some fundamental finance functions in a non-profit organisation are:

(A) SOURCES OF FUNDS

The inflow of funds to the organisation is from the following sources:

(i) Donations

Donations may be for specific purpose or general purpose. They do not usually carry the restriction that the original corpus must be preserved, and only interest can be used.

(ii) Fees

Non-profit organisations normally tend to charge fees much below the cost of training, based on government restrictions or other reasons. The educational or training activity of the non-profit institutions rarely breaks even based on the income from the fees. This is in contrast to commercial institutions active in training or education, generating substantial surplus or profit. However, even for the non-profit institutions, fees are a source of funds. Several of them now-a-days offer a mix of 'traditional' and 'self-financing' courses. Fees are a significant portion of income for the latter.

(iii) Endowments

These are usually for a specific purpose. Scholarships, prizes for special achievements are the usual purposes. Sometimes an endowment is for a chair in a subject, or for research in a particular area. They are for specific purpose and they are often endowed with the proviso that the endowment be invested and the earnings utilized for the particular purpose. They are restricted as to usage.

(iv) Loans

Generally non-profit organisations do not borrow commercially. They may borrow under special equipment finance schemes or housing programmes. In such cases, these loans are a source of funds.

(v) Cash Generated through Sale of Paid Services

In the case of medical institutions, a part of the services that are generated are supplied free. Another part may be provided below cost to the deserving. However, a part of the services in most cases sold to the paying clients or patients. Even in the case of other types of institutions, to the extent to which some services are sold, it is a source of funds.

(vi) Interest Income

Endowment funds generally tend to be invested in fixed income securities. In addition, a non-profit organisation may have accumulated funds over a period of time awaiting investment in buildings or equipment. These would also be kept in fixed deposits with banks. All these produce income. In many cases both the investments and the income from them are quite substantial.

(vii) Income from Property

Income from property of NGO and contributions are exempt to the extent the same is applied to the purposes of NGO.

(B) OUTFLOW OF FUNDS

The major uses of funds are:

(i) Salaries and Related Expenses

These include all personnel-related costs, including salaries, other benefits including retirement programmes and perquisites. Many of the non-profit organisations are 'service' organisations and consequently personnel costs form a high proportion of their total requirements for funds on a regular month-to-month basis.

(ii) Expenses

These include all operating expenses. This would include materials, water, power, communications, repairs and maintenance. Most of these are regular recurring costs and have to be met and payments made promptly to keep the operation going.

(iii) Capital Expenditure

Capital expenditure fall into two broad categories. The first is replacement of worn out or obsolete equipment or buildings. The second category is the totally new acquisition. It may be to make an existing operation more efficient or to start a new product. Capital expenditure is under the control of the organisation.

(iv) Debt Servicing

These include interest payment and return of the principal. The quantum and timing are covered by the loan agreement and there is usually very little flexibility.

(v) Two Other Aspects

First, all these expenses go towards generating the services offered by the organisation. Of these services, a portion is free and represents a continuous drain on the funds. The second portion, 'paid services' is what results in an inflow of funds. The second aspect is a portion of the total funding marked off as 'working capital'. This consists of minimum cash required to keep going inventory and receivables.

The actual minimum balances to be maintained depends on several factors related to the nature of the operations. However, some payments such as salaries and wages cannot be postponed. Enough cash balances have to be maintained to meet such needs as they arise with predictable regularity.

(C) FUNCTIONS OF FINANCE SECTION IN A NON-PROFIT ORGANISATION

The responsibilities of the finance function in a non-profit organisation are relating to:

(i) Raising Funds

Initial funding of non-profit organisations is usually by the sponsoring donor. The sponsors do not expect a return on investment. This is a significant difference. The funds can be raised on a convincing 'cause' and not on the basis of expected returns. However, stating expected results in convincing quantitative terms could often be a significant requirement for funding commitments. Commitment is almost always for an indefinite period.

Loan funds can be availed of provided the ability to repay can be demonstrated to the lending agency. However, lending agencies are not too happy if the projected repayment is from donations. The loan would also have to be secured by fixed assets, preferably land and buildings. Sponsoring agencies have been known to provide loans at nominal rates of interest.

Institutions having a regular income accruing from the day-to-day operations, such as hospitals or educational establishments, may find loan funds available for expansion or new projects. Specialized agencies such as Housing Development Corporations are willing to extend loans on relatively soft terms, but for specific purposes.

(ii) Allocation of Funds

The non-profit organisations have much less flexibility in the allocation of funds. Funds are usually donated and earmarked for a building or a specific piece of equipment. Endowment income is usually earmarked for a specific activity or programme. Consequently, the finance function in a non-profit institution has very limited flexibility in the allocation of available funds.

(iii) Balancing Inflow and Outflow in a Non-profit Operation

A non-profit organisation does not have the same pressure to maximize profits. Hence, the managing of inflow and outflow could be less of a challenge from day-to-day. This may very well be true in the short-term. However, sooner or later, the question will arise if some of the idle finds could not be deployed to provide more or better service to whomever the organisation is supposed to serve. But, the challenge to the non-profit finance executive in short-term cash management arises more from the inflexibility of his finds being 'designated' or earmarked for specific purposes.

(D) UNDERSTANDING FINANCIAL STATEMENTS

All organisations, commercial as well as non-profit, report their financial status periodically as of a particular date and their performance as of a period, ending with that particular date. The principles governing such reporting are not very different for the commercial and non-profit organisations. However, there are differences in reporting practices as followed by different organisations. Non-profit organisations follow varying methods depending on the legal structure. Many of them find it convenient to follow one pattern for internal reporting and reporting to donors and a different one to meet statutory requirements.

Types of Financial Statements

There are three kinds of financial statements that the executive should be familiar with. These are:

(i) The balance sheet,
(ii) The operating statement of profit and loss statement, and
(iii) The cash flow statement.

(i) The Balance Sheet

Every entity keeping accounts produces a balance sheet as of the last day of an accounting period. Such a statement is produced at the end of the fiscal year.

The balance sheet presents a picture, as of that day, of the position of the entity in financial terms. Basically it consists of two sides. One side is called 'assets' and the other 'liabilities and equity'. The assets side is a listing of all the resources owned by the entity. This includes cash, bank balances, inventories (stock of goods), land and buildings, machinery and equipment. The other side titled liabilities and equity lists the amounts owed by the entity to outsiders (creditors) under liabilities. Equity is the net balance of assets-liabilities.

Assets and liabilities are reported in more or less the same way in the balance sheets of both commercial entities and non-profit entities. However, in reporting there is a basic difference. In commercial or profit-seeking entities, equity reports capital obtained from two sources the capital contributed by the investors and the capital obtained through profit from the operations. Investors (shareholders) would have contributed money in return for stocks or shares in the company. This part of the equity is referred to as the 'paid up capital'. The portion of equity that arises from the operations is referred to as 'retained earnings'. A portion of the earnings from operations may be paid out as 'dividends' to the shareholders and the balance is retained in the business. This is referred to as retained earnings.

A non-profit entity does not raise capital from investors. Therefore, there is no such item as 'paid up capital'. They do not payout dividends. All the net earnings (if any) are retained in the operation. However, this is not referred to as retained earnings, instead, the usual nomenclature is 'net assets' or 'find balance'. Many non-profit entities obtains capital contributions. These, if made as money, are referred to as 'endowments'. If contributed in the form of goods or other assets, they are identified as 'contributed plant' or 'contributed equipment'. In any case it is essential that contributed capital should be separately identified from operating capital. A separate statement of contributed capital is maintained. This type of capital contributions for acquisition of assets or for endowments is not a feature of commercial operations and finds no place in commercial accounting.

(ii) Operating Statement

A balance sheet presents the financial picture of the entity as of a point of time. As against this concept an operating statement summarizes the operations of the entity over a period, describes the events that have taken place between the balance sheets and the reason behind the changes in the balance sheet.

The operating statement starts with 'revenues'. They are increases in equity associated with the operations during the period. Revenues arise when an increase in assets is not accompanied by an equivalent decrease in another assets or an equivalent increase in liabilities. From the revenues expenses are deducted. Expenses are decreases in equity associated with operations during the period. They represent decreases in assets with no equivalent increase in another asset or an equivalent decrease in liabilities.

Some of the non-profit organisations show expenses as incurred by each department or activity and matches them against the income from that particular department or activity. In addition, where service has been rendered on a no charge basis, for example, in hospitals, the free work is shown in the same format along with income. Depreciation figures are shown in the 'other' column in the expenses. In most commercial operations and many of the non-profit operations, depreciation being a non-cash expense, is added on to expenses at the end as one single number or a group of numbers. (Buildings, machinery, equipment, etc. being separated). From a management point of view there is merit to this treatment since management can immediately identify the non-cash expenses.

(iii) Cash Flow Statements

The balancing of inflow and outflow of cash is a major finance function. An inability to meet payments as they become due cannot only be embarrassing but may lead to legal problems. For executives with responsibility for the longer term sustainability of a project or a non-profit operation, the cash flow statement is very significant source of information.

CHAPTER

20

Deferred Donations

DEFERRED GIVING OF DONATIONS

In most organisations, individuals provide a substantial number of the large gifts, and in many instances, innovative ways are found to extend the advantages of giving to this very important segment of donors. Deferred giving offers many contribution vehicles that provide substantial benefits to a number of different kinds of donors.

Deferred gifts involve arrangements by which a donor makes a commitment of funds but defers the actual transfer of cash, securities, or tangible assets for a period of time. On the surface, it would appear that deferred gifts would be discouraged by non-profit organisations, especially those that have a need for immediate cash. However, deferred gifts can be so advantageous for donors that these individuals may make much more substantial contributions under such arrangements. Ultimately, non-profit organisations can benefit handsomely and many build endowments almost entirely through gifts of this type.

What are some situations in which a deferred gift might be appropriate?

- An individual would like to make substantial contribution to a non-profit organisation but feels that he cannot give up the security of the income that these funds would provide him and his wife during their lifetimes.
- Another donor would like to establish a scholarship fund in honor of her husband but feels that she must hold on to her assets while her aged parents are still living in case they incur large medical bills.
- A businessperson who has just sold his company wishes to receive a large charitable income tax deduction in a particular year but does not have enough cash to make a gift that would be sizable enough to realize such a large deduction.
- A fifty-year-old woman has just been named president of a company and wants to defer income during her peak earning years; she wants to enjoy this income later when she is in a lower tax bracket.

- A forty-year-old man wants to set-up an endowment to honor his father but does not have enough cash for an outright gift; he wants to find some way to make annual payments toward the endowment but he wants the fund guaranteed should he die before all the money has been provided.
- A woman has inherited stock that has appreciated tremendously in value but that pays no dividend; she does not want to incur substantial capital gains taxes by selling the stock but she would like to figure out some way she could derive income from it.

For each of these individuals—and for many others—there are a variety of deferred giving instruments that allow them to accomplish their goals and help a non-profit organisation at the same time. A few of the most important deferred instrument are discussed below:

(i) Bequests

A bequest is a gift that is made through a donor's will. The advantages to the donor are as follows:

- By deferring the gift until after a donor's death, the individual has the use of the assets during his or her lifetime.
- A bequest usually provides a tax savings because the gift is deductible from the adjusted gross estate.
- A bequest can be changed during the donor's lifetime; it is not an irrevocable gift until the donor dies.

From the non-profit organisation's point of view, a bequest can be welcome but its revocable nature is problematic. Whereas a donor may feel positively toward an organisation today, he or she may feel less so at a later date and may change the will. A second disadvantage of a bequest is that there is no guarantee that there will be adequate money in an estate to provide the specified funds. Indeed in some cases, such as a residuary bequest (in which a non-profit is named to receive the remainder of an estate after specific legacies have been fulfilled), the assets of the estate may be inadequate to provide any funds. Nevertheless, bequests have provided the major portion of endowment funds held by non-profit organisations and their importance in fund raising from individuals should not be underestimate.

(ii) Gifts of Life Insurance

Gifts of whole life insurance policies, those that buy protection for a lifetime rather than for a limited time period (as is the case with term insurance), are another important type of deferred gift. Commonly an individual will purchase a policy with a certain face value (the amount the company will pay when the individual dies) and a schedule of premium payments. The individual who wishes to make a gift of life insurance must assign ownership of the policy to a non-profit organisation making it the beneficiary of the policy as well. In order to secure a tax deduction, the individual will make a contribution of the premium payments to the non-profit organisation, which in turn pays the insurance company.

A gift of life insurance offers the following advantages to donors:

- As soon as the policy is purchased, the gift is secured; thus even if the individual dies immediately after making the first premium payment, the organisation is assured of the gift in full.
- The donor enjoys the pleasure of planning the uses of the gift during his or her lifetime.
- In the case of younger donors (those under forty-five years of age), a sizable fund can be created with a rather modest investment.

Life insurance gifts also offer benefits to the non-profit organisation. The cash value of the life insurance policy can be listed as an asset on the organisation's balance sheet even during the donors lifetime and this can be used as equity against loans. A life insurance gift can be an excellent way to develop an ongoing relationship and other cultivation opportunities with a donor. The most substantial disadvantage is that the donor can choose to stop paying premium before the policy is paid up. Under these circumstances, the non-profit organisation itself can choose to pay the premiums or it can cash in the policy for whatever its cash value is at the time.

(iii) Charitable Trusts

(a) Charitable Remainder Trust

There are several types of charitable trusts that are used as deferred gifts. The most important is the *charitable remainder trust*, which allows a donor to make a substantial gift but to receive income based on the value of that gift for a period of time—either a fixed number of years or the balance of a lifetime (or lifetimes). The donor creates a formal trust and provides a certain sum which is often given in the form of securities although it can be cash or even real estate). The asset is transferred to the trustee who is responsible for managing the funds during the specified time period of the trust. When the specified period is over, the asset passes to the non-profit organisation. To be noted that a variety of other special pay-out arrangements can be arranged to meet the needs of specific donors.

There are several advantages to donors:

- The most obvious advantage is that the donors need not give up potential income by making a large gift; an income stream can be directed to designated beneficiaries for a specified amount of time thus reducing the risks involved in giving up capital.
- Donors get an immediate tax deduction.
- Unlike with charitable remainder trusts, individuals can participate for a relatively small investment—some non-profit organisations price a unit.
  Unlike a charitable remainder trust, a pooled-income fund allows donors to add to their initial contribution as often as they wish.

(b) For non-profit organisations, *pooled-income funds offer* the same advantages as charitable remainder trusts in that the gifts made to them are irrevocable and they often encourage larger and more frequent gifts from major contributors. However, there are some disadvantages. Perhaps the most serious one is the requirement that the organisation must either manage the pooled-income fund or find a trustee to do so. Unless a pooled-income fund is sizable and will end up paying a large return to the institution, it may not be worth the effort and responsibility associated with its management.

Deferred gifts represent one of the most important sources of long-term, substantial gifts to non-profit organisations over the next few decades. Although technical in nature, few non-profits can afford to ignore this source of funding, especially in the area of endowment building and finding funds for substantial facilities and projects.

CHAPTER

21

Financial Systems in NPOs

In this chapter we shall cover following aspects of financial systems in NPOs;

I. Budgets.
II. Costing concepts.
III. Pricing principles for investments.
IV. Managing of investments.
V. Tax exemptions.

I. BUDGETS

Budgets represent a plan for future action. Factors that are likely to influence the assumptions underlying the budget preparation are normally laid down. These days budget process has become participative so that departments can exercise better control. Budget process must be related with some measure of performance.

Budgets are of two types:

(i) Operating Budgets

It indicate the goods and services organisations expects to consume in a budget period. They list both physical quantities and cost figures. Common type of budgets are:

(a) *Expense budgets.* These contain planned expenses.
(b) *Revenue budgets.* These indicate expected sales with selling price.
(c) *Profit budgets.* These combines both (a) and (b). They assign responsibility of each manager. Provide also bench mark for regulating (a) and (b).

(ii) Financial Budgets

These spell out the money which organisation intends to spend in the same period and sources where from money will come. Different types of financial budgets are:

(a) Capital expenditure budgets

These relating to future investments in buildings, equipment and other physical assets/projects.

(b) Cash budgets

These indicate level of funds flowing through organisation and pattern of disbursements and receipts. It may reveal more cash than using in next year and organisation can plan capital expenditure investment.

(c) Financial budgets

These assure the availability of funds to meet the shortfall of revenues relative to expenses. These help to know funds organisation needs at a time.

(d) Balance sheet budgets

These may indicate company has planned to borrow more heavily than is prudent and then decide to reduction in planned borrowing.

(e) Zero-based budgeting

It enables organisation to look at its activities and priorities a fresh. Previous year's allocations are not automatically considered the basis of this year's allocations instead each department has to justify a new entire budget request. It is based on cost-benefit analysis of major activities.

Advantages of Budget Systems

Some benefits of budget systems are:

(i) Budgets can have positive impact on motivation and morale as they clarify common goals for everyone who is working towards them.
(ii) These help in coordination of work in organisation.
(iii) Budget is a device for taking corrective action if budget exceeds.
(iv) Budget helps people to learn from experience.
(v) Budget improves resource allocation.
(vi) Budget improves communication.
(vii) Budget helps people see where organisation is going. Further it enhances morale of managers.
(viii) Budget is a means of evaluation.

II. COSTING CONCEPTS

Non-profit organisation may be offering products or services to meet their resources. Manager must understand the correct cost of its goods or services. This serves various purposes.

Advantages of Costing

Simply put it, cost means expenditures (not price) to obtain more desirable resources. These resources may be money, material, time, or expertise. Frequently departments are treated as cost centres.

Type of Costs

(a) Cost may be fixed costs. The fixed costs are such as on labour, material, over-head expenses. Fixed costs are also referred as "overhead" costs. Cost workout statement/ estimate is given in Table 1.

TABLE I

Cost Workout Statement/Estimate

	Cost Per Unit (Rs.)	*Total for 1000 Units (Rs.)*
(i) Cost of raw materials	20	20,000
(ii) Labour cost	12	12,000
(iii) Prime cost	32	32,000
(iv) Factory overheads:		
50% Fixed Rs. 4,000		
50% Variables 4,000	8	8,000
(v) Works costs (i)+(ii)+(iii)	40	40,000
(vi) Office overheads:		
50% Fixed Rs. 2,000		
50% Variables 2,000	4	4,000
(vii) Cost of production (v)+(vi)	44	44,000
(viii) Selling expenses	1	1,000
(ix) Total costs (vii)+(viii)	45	45,000
(x) Profit (25% on selling price)	15	15,000
(xi) Sales (selling price)	60	60,000

(b) Cost may be *variable costs* depending on volume of work.

(c) *Standard costs.* In simple terms standard cost is a 'target' cost for product. Standard costing system calls for a pre-determined cost to be estimated for each unit of product. This will take into account the cost of estimated direct material, direct labour and an allocated overhead. The total output multiplied by the standard cost per unit is compared to actual total cost incurred in production. The usefulness of standard costing system depends on the 'analysis of variance' which is used to understand why actual cost has varied from estimate based on the standard cost.

(d) Methods of costing may be:

(i) *Job costing*. This is more often used in a hospital for patients or a school. For example, costs are accumulated on the patient card for direct and indirect costs, when patient is treated by different departments.

(ii) *Process costing*. This is used in manufacturing process where the output is uniform, or standardised. The total cost is divided during the period.

III. PRICING PRINCIPLES FOR INVESTMENTS

Some Usual Problems

Non-profit organisations do not as a general rule price their services or products in such a way as to maximize the net return. On the other hand, their pricing may be targeted towards what the poorest of users can afford. Sometimes they are based on an external subsidy, which has been promised conditional to the product being priced at a certain level. In any case it is not unusual for non-profit organisations to find themselves faced with a continuous loss on certain products. It is not unusual to find that those very products are making a contribution to the overheads and thereby making some of the other services lower priced.

Different Pricing Bases

A non-profit organisation may be planning to launch a new service and would like to set the price on a basis other than 'what the market will bear'. Or it may be already in the market and wondering if they are under pricing or over pricing their product. In either case it is important to have an appreciation for the various pricing bases that can be considered:

(a) Full cost,
(b) Full cost plus,
(c) Market base, and
(d) Inducement.

(a) Full Cost Pricing

Many non-profit organisations use full cost as a basis of setting the norm for prices. The rationale is fairly simple. Non-profit organisations are not set-up to make a profit or a surplus. Therefore, there is no reason to price the products/services at more than full cost. On the other hand, continuous pricing of products below the full cost will result in slow liquidation of the organisation unless there are specific schemes of subsidy. Many of the programmes managed by non-profit organisations, such as sponsoring research for employees, health care for employees, are customarily based on full cost reimbursement.

(b) Full Cost Plus as Basis

Many non-profit organisations find themselves compelled to set prices to include an element of profit or surplus over full cost. The surplus is what adds to the equity or funding. Such addition to the equity enables the organisation to replace assets and/or provide for additional working capital. Assets as they become work out or obsolete, will have to be placed. A combination of inflation and technological changes almost invariably results in the cost of replacement being higher than the replacement of the original equipment. A continuous build up of a 'replacement fund' is almost unavoidable. In fact, the formulation of the policy regarding replacements and financing of replacement of buildings and equipment should be a matter of careful thought within the management of all non-profit organisations.

Justification for cost plus pricing is that non-profit organisations, particularly in the area of health care or education, are often committed to support the user who cannot afford full cost pricing. Such users have to be subsidized. There may be specific donor arrangements to fund these requirements. However, one way to find such subsidy is to charge the paying customers on a full cost plus basis. While this is obvious in the case of health care and education, the same principle is applicable to many other areas of service.

Some non-profit hospitals have over a period evolved a system of varying prices based on the paying ability of the patient. One rational way to do this is to charge a higher rate for all services availed of by the patients using special ward facilities. Often these institutions end up with three rates, one for special ward, one for general ward and a third one involving partial write off. These are over and above the sub-sized free patient.

Two points of caution are in order. First, full cost plus pricing cannot be independent of the market prices for equivalent or similar products. These must be kept in view as possible ceiling to the prices. Second, organisations adopting a full cost plus formula for pricing a product, perhaps for a segment of the market, should do a reasonable study of costs. Then from time to time they tend to raise prices based on index of inflation or just 'gut feeling'.

(c) Market-based Pricing

Medical and educational services are examples of areas where market price may be a consideration, but not a determining factor. Many of them will have a semi-monopolistic position due to location, specialization in product offered, quality, etc., optimum pricing calls for very careful examination of all these factors.

The situation becomes problematic when competition (or legislation) forces the institution to set prices at market rates below full cost. Many colleges in India are in this situation where actual operating costs are well above the fees charged to the student, primarily as a consequence of government or university regulations. The question is how does the organisation cover its losses. Many professional colleges have taken the route of 'self-financing'.

'Self-financing' may be based on higher fees or on 'capitation' fees, a form of compulsory donation. Cross subsidy is also possible if one operation can subsidize the other. Medical college can be subsidized by an attached hospital. Annual donations from committed donor organisations particularly for a specific campaign, for example, eradication of leprosy or leprosy or immunization from polio, enables an institution to carry on a subsidized operation below full cost.

(d) Inducement Pricing

There could be situations in which a non-profit organisation purposely sets a price in order to induce the other suppliers to reduce their prices. In the case of the essential drug project, the promoters were clear from the beginning that their intention was not to force market prices down, but only to supply to select hospitals and medical centers for passing on the benefit to the poor patients. However, if it was a well organised scheme with a generous budget, it could influence market prices of essential drugs in the down-ward direction. We have not come across a successful operation of this kind yet. Availability of a service at a lower cost will, *per se*, influence prices set under monopoly or semi-monopoly conditions.

A subsidized price is offered mostly in situations where the organisation is anxious to ensure the use of the service irrespective of the ability to meet the full cost. It is always better to charge at least a nominal price instead of giving it away free. Many public authorities are on this basis of subsidized pricing. Where possible, it would be still advantageous to indicate and charge full cost and then deduct the subsidy to arrive at the selling price.

In conclusion, it may be mentioned that there is a good case for full cost plus pricing where it is possible, so long as the effective demand for product is not highly elastic to price.

Price Inflation

Prices do not remain constant over a period of time. They change due to various economic, social or political factors. *Changing in price level* cause two types of economic condition, inflation and deflation. *Inflation* is a period of general increase in prices of factors of production/consumption whereas *deflation* means a general fall in price level.

These changes lead to inaccurate presentation of *financial statements* and do not present true view of organisation's financial health. Financial statements are prepared on static or historical costs. So there is need for inflation accounting, also, which takes into consideration expenses incurred, incomes earned and liabilities incurred at different points of time. Thus, value of money does not remain the same over a period of time. It changes to price levels.

IV. MANAGEMENT OF INVESTMENTS

(i) Need for Managing Investments

Specific research or development grants are also available as funds to be invested for income or for temporary safe keeping while being drawn down to meet the related expenses as they arise. Some non-profit organisations fund their legal obligations to employees, such as gratuity or provident fund, by handing it over to external agencies such as Life Insurance Corporation or Provident Fund Commissioner's Office. Many organisations do not, because self-financing of these obligations (pay as you go) would be cheaper by managing the funds internally. LIC computes the annual premium for gratuity liability based on projected retirement age of employees and a notional return on the premiums cumulatively, in addition, there is an administrative charge. In fact by investing the equivalent premiums prudently, it is not difficult to reduce the total cost of gratuity benefit to the employer, assuming normal retirement patterns. Managing the provident fund liability internally gives the same advantage. Market returns on investments are generally higher than the LIC notional return. In addition, it is convenient for the employee to deal with the treasurer's office as against running around in government or LIC offices and greasing palms.

Non-profit organisations face a special challenge in managing their investments. Often they have property funded by the original promoters. Such property may consist of land, buildings and equipment. In addition, themes are usually endowments of various amounts the income from them being earmarked for designated purposes. Specific guiding principles are laid down by the board or management. Rather, the board tend to decide on investment on a situation-to-situation basis at board meetings. These meetings may take place only after a lapse of several weeks or months (three months is customary). Consequently, the organisation could find itself sitting with large amounts held in short-term bank deposits earning nominal interest or seeking advice from the banker.

(ii) General principles for investment

Some principles for investment are:

(a) Liquidity

There should be enough liquidity in the system to meet day-to-day obligations. The outgo of cash is usually easier to predict. Mostly theme is a pattern. Wages and salaries have to met on a monthly and weekly basis. Other bills-supplier's, telephone, wage and salary-related legal payments (PF, ESIC, etc.) are predictable. If construction work is going on, there is usually an agreed schedule of payment. If equipment has been ordered the delivery dates are known, at least approximately, and terms of payment (credit, discounts) are known early. A detailed projection of anticipated payments for three months on a weekly basis and for another three months on a monthly basis is not difficult. It is a good system for non-profit organisations to set-up at an early date, such forecasts.

The inflows are usually more difficult to predict. Educational institutions have a pattern of collecting fees and are predictable. Investment income is also predictable as to quantum and time.

Hospitals or medical services charging a fee for services rendered have a problem Hospital outpatient departments or clinical services will generate cash on a day-to-day basis. However, the amount of cash receipts will depend on the number of patients taking advantage of the facilities. Weather, political disturbances, local calamities will all affect the turnout and the collections. Inpatients are often billed only at the time of their discharge. Most commercial hospitals have a weekly billing system.

Depending on the matching if the inflow and outflow of cash, it is a general rule of thumb, to hold in current account or very short-term bank deposits, enough funds to meet a month's normal expenses. However, this is a very general rule and each organisation can decide, based on its particular circumstances and experience, how much liquidity is required for carrying on its operations without financial embarrassment.

Since banks now tend to offer term deposits with facility for withdrawal at short notice without penalty, considerably greater flexibility is available for managing short-term investments.

(b) Legal Constraints

Depending on the legal structure of the organisation, there could be constraints. Many trusts have to confine themselves to government securities or government guaranteed debt instruments. Some of the trusts having invested in land and buildings have done quite well on the rental income. If they have excess land, building commercial premises will prove to be good investments. 'Societies' registered under the Societies Act have more flexibility.

Some of the bonds issued by financial institutions such as ICICI or IDBL were also found to be rather attractive. They offered good returns and received high rating from the rating agencies. Similarly, bonds issued by government-sponsored corporations or public sector companies were considered good investments. In the United States and UK, it is not unusual for non-profit organisations to invest in the stock market and some of them have done quite well. In India it is not very common.

(c) Safety versus Returns

Non-profit organisations generally tend to consider safety of the principal to be more important than the actual return. This is very correct. Funds provided for a 'cause' is not suitable vehicle for anything that seems speculative.

(iii) Challenges for Management of Funds

Funds managers must now anticipate the following difficulties:

(a) Substantial decline in interest earnings.
(b) Erosion of principal on investments in mutual funds.
(c) Possible default on interest payments on fixed deposits placed with public sector or other corporations, or bonds issued by them. Ownership or guarantee by government may provide ultimate safety but will not prevent default in the short run.
(d) Funds manager to keep in close touch with *business environments* in India and abroad and take calculated decisions.
(e) If certain endowments have been made on *certain return,* it is desirable to ensure whether current yield will cover expenses.
(f) To consider *appointing a financial consultant* as retainer who can be a banker or broker can be considered.

V. SUMMARY OF INCOME TAX EXEMPTIONS

Exemptions under section 10 are available as under, subject to certain conditions:

(i) *Scientific research associations*: The association can claim exemption under section 10(21) if the income is applied or accumulated for research.
(ii) Professional associations, viz., law, medicines, architecture, engineering, accountancy, etc. except the income from property, for rendering any specific services, income as interest or divided. The exemptions are available only, when the association is approved by Central Government in terms of section 10(23A) and only for specified duration.
(iii) *Charitable or Public Religious Trusts*: The exemption is available under section 10(23C).
(iv) *Educational and Medical Institutions*, established solely for charity and not for profit.
(v) *Khadi or Village Institutions trust or society*: The income is exempt under section 10(23B), for strictly production and sale of Khadi and Village Industries product. Also the NGO applies to the relevant Khadi and Village Industries Commission for registration. Profit should not be the motive.

Exemptions under Sections 11 and 12: Registration with the Commissioner of Income Tax and Auditing

(i) NGO for wholly charitable or religious purpose for public benefit or religious within India or outside India. Where NGO is established partly for charitable purpose and a part of the income is used by the author of trust or his relatives, the exemption is not available.
(ii) NGO for the exclusive benefit of Scheduled Caste/Tribe, Backward Classes, Women, Children, etc.

(iii) The NGOs that are not eligible for exemption under sections 10, 11, 12 and whose part income is eligible, can be examined under section 164.

Rebate under Section 80G

Subject to this registration by the CIT, the donors to such an NGO can get tax rebate under section 80G(5C), to the extent of 50 to 100% on the amount of cash donations (donations in kind not exempt). The application for such an approval is made in Form 10G [under section 80G(5)] of I.T. Act, 1961. After the approval is made, the NGO can issue a certificate to the donor, to claim rebate. The amount so donated should not exceed 10% of the gross income of donor (minus allowable deductions) for tax rebate. Such exemptions are given for a specific period.

Rebate under Section 35(1)

Income tax rebate is available to scientific research associations, institutions of higher education and learning, research in social sciences, etc.

PART IV

MANAGEMENT AND FINANCIAL CONTROLS

CHAPTER

22

Management Control and Process

In this chapter, following aspects of control process are discussed:

1. Introduction.
2. Concept of control.
3. Management control process: meaning and features.
4. Importance of control.
5. Steps in control process.
6. Types of control methods.
7. Control areas.
8. Three basic components of control systems.
9. Levels of control.
10. Designing control systems.
11. Symptoms of inadequate control.
12. Preventive control.
13. Limitations of controlling.
14. To conclude.

1. INTRODUCTION

Control is an essential function of management in every organisation. The management process is incomplete and sometimes useless without the control function. The management process includes planning, organizing, staffing, leading, and controlling. Planning sets forth the objectives a manager intends to achieve. Organizing provides the structure of an organisation by determining how and where the employees will be placed in the organisation and the responsibilities that they will need to fulfil to attain predefined objectives. Staffing involves the managerial function of placing the right person in the right job in the organisation. Leading involves the managerial function of influencing, motivating and directing the human resources of the organisation to achieve organisational goals. The control function is concerned with ensuring that the planning, organizing, staffing and leading functions result in the attainment of organisational objectives. In other words, control is a tool that helps organisations measure and compare their actual progress with their established plan.

The term 'control' has different meanings in different contexts. In the management context, 'control' refers to the evaluation of performance and the implementation of corrective actions to accomplish organisational objectives. Some people confuse 'control' with 'supervision.' Supervision is a part of control; it helps identify deviations from the established standards of performance.

The modern concept of control envisages a system that not only provides a historical record of what has happened to the business as a whole but also pinpoints the reasons why it has happened and provides data that enables the management to take corrective steps, if there is any deviation from the plan. It also enables managers to identify trends in costs, markets, and other aspects of the business, and acts as a guide for future action.

Thus, control ensures that what is done is what is intended. Control must be exercised by everyone in the organisation, from the top level to the bottom level. There is a misconception that it is the duty of only the top level of an organisation to exercise control. This is because many managers see control, discipline and supervision as the same thing. Control is also perceived as tight supervision by others. Such misconceptions must be removed, if the control function is to contribute to the betterment of the organisation.

According to Robert J. Mockler, "Management control is a systematic effort to set performance standards with planning objectives, to design information feedback systems, to compare actual performance with these predetermined standards, to determine whether there are any deviations and to measure their significance, and to take any action required to assure that all corporate resources are being used in the most effective and efficient way possible in achieving corporate objectives."

Control is the process of taking the necessary preventive or corrective actions to ensure that the organisation's mission and objectives are accomplished as effectively and efficiently as possible. Objectives are yardsticks against which actual performance can be measured. If actual performance is consistent with the appropriate objective, things will proceed as planned. If not, changes must be made. Successful manage detect deviations from desirable standards and make appropriate adjustments. The purpose of the control function is always the same: *get the job done despite environmental, organisational, and behavioural obstacles and uncertainties.*

2. CONCEPT OF CONTROL

Managerial function of control implies measurement of actual performance, comparing it with the standards set by plans, and correction of deviations to ensure attainment of objectives according to plans. (Figure 1)

Action is the essence of controlling. It is this feature of control that makes it *forward looking.* Action to correct the error or to prevent such error to arise in future.

Planning without control is meaningless and control without planning is blind. There is relationship between control and planning.

Control action is guided by adequate information. This information is used as a guide as to what action can be taken. Control functions effectively on basis of information.

FIGURE I
Control is Always Based on Planning

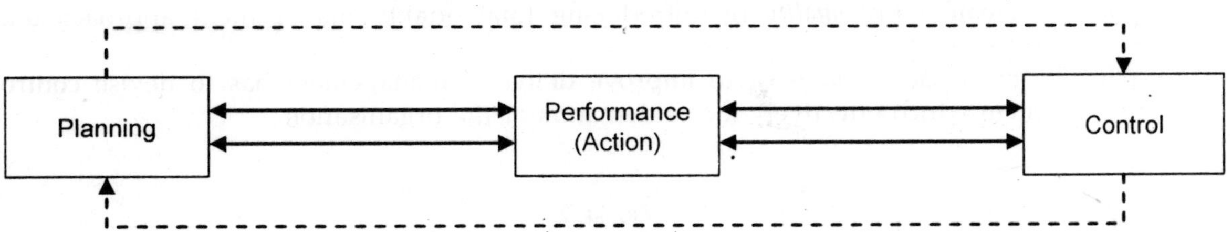

3. MANAGEMENT CONTROL PROCESS: MEANING AND FEATURES

Meaning

Management control is the process through which managers assure that actual activities conform to planned activities. Controlling is the process of ensuring that the organisation is moving in the desired direction and *progress is being made towards the achievement of goals.*

Features

(a) Controlling involves *monitoring/measuring performance* to minimise the gap between planned and actual performance. Control is based on comparing it with the standards set by plans.
(b) Control function *reveals bottlenecks* so that suitable corrective action may be taken in time to ensure attainment of objectives as per plan.
(c) Control is function of all managers and control is forward looking as well as preventive.
(d) Availability of information is guide to control.
(e) Control is continuous process and review of past activities.

4. IMPORTANCE OF CONTROL

Some factors that make control necessary are:

(i) *Changing environment of organisation and cope with uncertainty*, e.g. market shift, new products emerge, new materials, new regulations are passed by government. When manger detect changes to be made adjustment in operations are made to cope with change.
(ii) *Increasing complexity of organisations*, e.g. diversified product lines require sales, costs, quality to be analysed and monitored. Decentralises organisation set-up needs to be watched.
(iii) A control system helps detect mistakes and irregularities before they are critical and thus helps in coordination in action. (See Figure 2)
(iv) Delegation of powers require controls to be checked for accomplishing of tasks. Controls also help managers decentralise authority.

(v) Organisation can *verify its policies* are being followed.

(vi) Control process puts a *psychological pressure* on individuals for better performance and maximum contribution. It leads to organisation's efficiency and effectiveness.

(vii) To create *better quality* by introducing total quality management approach and reduce costs.

(viii) To create *faster cycles* or to improve delivery, management has to devise control system which effectively meets demands of the organisation.

FIGURE 2

Planning and Controlling Link

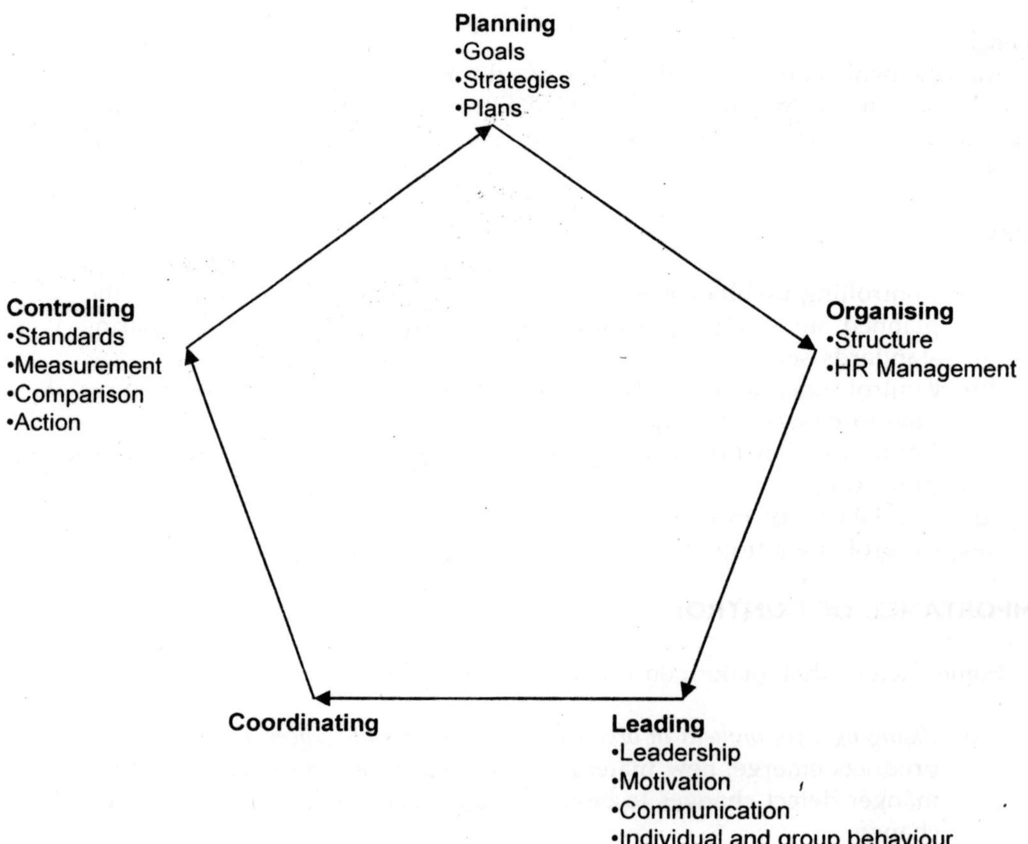

5. STEPS IN CONTROL PROCESS

Various activities to be carried out while introducing control process are: (See Figure 3)

FIGURE 3

Steps in Control Process

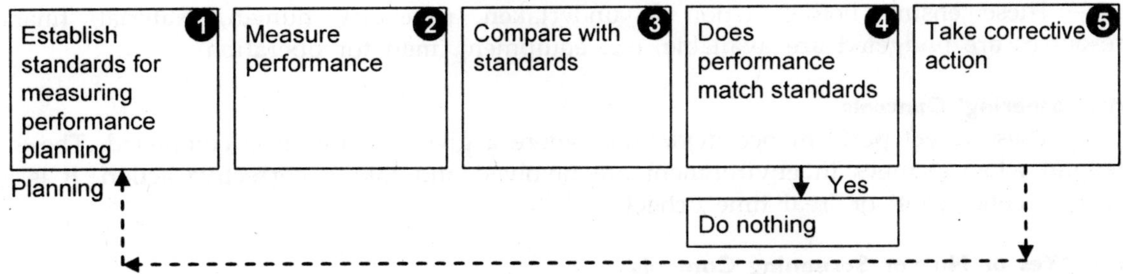

Step I: Establish the Standards for Measuring Work Performance

Standards should be clearly specified. These standards may be *quantitative* or *qualitative.*

(a) *Quantitative standards* may be such as:
 Physical standard for knowing output, sales, etc.
 Cost standards for assessing material cost, labour cost per unit.
 Capital standards to know rate of return.

(b) Qualitative standards deal with company image, attitudes, position of leader in the field. As such standards should identify the key areas and strategic points for control.

Step II: Measurement of Actual Performance

It is *ongoing repetitive process,* e.g. safe levels of gas particles in air may be continuously monitored in manufacturing plant or in some case after a year in a project.

Step III: Comparing with Standards

To check whether performance matches the standards.

Step IV: Finding Variance between the Two and Analysis of Reasons

The information must be communicated to the person who has to take corrective action. He will also exercise self-control. This is called *feed-back.*

Step V: Taking Corrective or Remedial Action

So as to attainment of objectives.

Note:
- Planning and controlling are closely related as explained in Figure 3. Elements of control. After a plan becomes operational, control is necessary to measure progress, to uncover deviation from targets and to take corrective steps. Control is always based on planning.
- Controlling and coordination are closely related as both are needed to achieve organisation goals. Both aspects will free it from chaos and conflict.

6. TYPES OF CONTROL METHODS

Some kinds of control methods are:

(a) Pre-action Controls

These ensure before action is undertaken, necessary human, material, financial resources are budgeted are available, e.g. equipment, men for operation.

(b) 'Steering' Controls

These direct performance deviations before a given operation is completed. These are helpful when changes in environment are involved and taking corrective action. It is also known 'concurrent' or 'real time', check.

(c) "Yes or No" or Screening Controls

These ensure specific conditions are met before an operation proceeds further where safety is key factor such as in aircraft design, "feed foreword control" is introduced.

(d) Post-action (Feed-back) Controls

These measures result on a completed action. Deviations are determined and corrective steps taken to avoid in future also.

(e) Strategic and Operational Control

(i) Strategic control

Strategic control is the process of taking into account the changing planning premises, both external and internal to the organisation, on which strategy is based, and continuously evaluating the strategy, as it is being implemented, and taking corrective actions to adjust strategy to the new requirements. Various factors indicating difference in strategic control and operational control are summarised in Figure 5.

(ii) Operational control

Operational control is concerned with *performance* and its evaluation. This control can be exercised at *different stages* of work performance. Stages of control in operation control are given in Figure 4.

FIGURE 4

Stages in Operational Control

(a) Feed forward control	(b) Concurrent control	(c) Feedback control
↓	↓	↓
On inputs	In processing	On outputs

Feed-Forward Control

In this control inputs are identified that are required in an action. It attempts to identify and prevent deviations, before they occur. It is preventive control.

FIGURE 5

Difference in Strategic Control and Operational Control

Sl. No.	*Factors*	*Strategic Control*	*Operational Control*
(i)	Basic question	Are we moving in right direction?	How we are performing?
(ii)	Aim	Proactive, continuous questioning of direction of strategy.	Allocation and use of resources.
(iii)	Concern	Steering future direction of organisation.	Action control.
(iv)	Focus	External environment.	Internal organisation.
(v)	Exercise of control	Top management.	Middle management.
(vi)	Main techniques	Environmental scanning, Information gathering, reviews.	Budgets, schedules, MBO.

Concurrent Control

In this control of inputs that are required in operation of work and making adjustments before any major damage is done.

Feedback Control

This post-action control is based on feedback from completed action based on measurement of results so that corrective action is taken.

7. CONTROL AREAS

Major areas of controlling are:

(i) Control over policies to ensure action taken by the people.
(ii) Control over organisation structure to solve organisation problems and conflicts.
(iii) Control over personnel to ensure required strength of manpower.
(iv) Control over cost. Cost control is supplemented with budgetary control system.
(v) Control over salaries.
(vi) Control over capital expenditure by evaluation of the project by capital budget monitoring.
(vii) Control over external relation by reviewing programmes.

8. THREE BASIC COMPONENTS OF CONTROL SYSTEMS

Complex organisational control systems such as these help keep things on the right track because they embrace three basic components, common to all control systems: *objectives, standards,* and an *evaluation-reward* system.

(i) Objectives

Objective as a target signifying what should be accomplished and when. Objectives are an indispensable part of any control system because they provide measurable reference points for corrective action. To help Chrysler get back on the road to profitability, former chairman Lee Iacocca set the objective of committing his company in 1990 to cutting $3 billion in costs by July 1991. That particular objective served as a focal point and measuring stick for wide-ranging cost reductions, including layoffs and smaller buyer rebates.

(ii) Standards

Whereas objectives serve as measurable targets, standards serve as guideposts on the way to reaching those targets. Standards provide feed forward control by warning people when they are off the track. Businesses rely on many kinds of standards, including those in purchasing, engineering, time, safety, accounting, and quality.

A proven téchnique for establishing challenging standards is benchmarking identifying and imitating the business practices of market leaders. The central idea in benchmarking is to be competitive by striving to be as good as or better than the best in the business. The search for benchmarks is not restricted to a single industry. Many companies in many industries are presently emulating the world-class service standards of Scandinavian Airlines (SAS).

(iii) An Evaluation-Reward System

Because employees do not get equal results, some sort of performance review is required to document individual contributions to organisational objectives. Extrinsic rewards need to be tied equitably to documented results and improvement. A carefully conceived and clearly communicated evaluation-reward scheme can shape favourable effort-reward expectancies, hence motivating better performance.

9. LEVELS OF CONTROL

The various managerial levels—strategic, tactical and operational—have different planning and control responsibilities. The presence of various degrees of control at each level of management increases the probability of the successful implementation of plans at these levels. (Figure 6)

FIGURE 6

Levels of Control

Levels of Management	*Type of Planning*	*Type of Control*
Top management • Organisation-wide perspective • Concerned with strategic issues • Long time frame	Strategic planning	Strategic control
Middle management • Department perspective • Concerned with department goals and objectives, programmes and budgets • Medium time frame	Tactical planning	Tactical control
First level management • Unit/individual perspective • Concerned with schedules, budgets, rules, and specific individual output requirements • Short time frame	Operational planning	Operational control

(a) Strategic Control

Strategic control involves monitoring critical environmental factors to ensure that strategic plans are implemented as intended, assessing the impact of strategic plans. and adjusting such plans when necessary. Top-level managers usually view things from an organisational perspective and are concerned with strategic issues. They usually have a long-term focus except in situations involving unstable environmental conditions and/or intense competition which necessitate shorter reporting cycles. Thus, strategic control is mainly the function of top-level managers. These managers may also exercise tactical or operational control to monitor the implementation of plans at the middle and lower levels of management to ensure that strategic plans are being implemented as intended or planned.

(b) Tactical Control

Tactical control focuses on assessing the implementation of tactical plans at department levels, monitoring associated periodic results, and taking corrective action when necessary. Middle-level managers are concerned with department-level goals and objectives, and programmes and budgets. They concentrate on medium time frames and therefore use weekly, fortnightly, and monthly reporting cycles in their plans. Middle-level managers exercise tactical control to test the impact of tactical initiatives of their departments on the organisational environment. Middle-level managers also exercise operational control by monitoring critical aspects of the implementation of operational plans. They are also involved in strategic control to a certain extent, because they provide information to top-level managers on strategic issues.

(c) Operational Control

Operational control involves overseeing the implementation of operational plans, monitoring day-to-day results, and taking corrective action when necessary. Lower-level managers concerned with schedules, budgets, rules, and specific individual output requirements make use of operational control. Using operational control, a lower-level manager provides feedback regarding the tasks being carried out on a day-to-day basis (in the very near term) in order to achieve the short-term and long-term goals of the organisation.

10. DESIGNING CONTROL SYSTEMS

Managers face number of challenges in designing control systems that provide accurate feedback to organisation. These problems can be avoided by an analysis that identifies: (a) Key performance areas, and (b) Strategic control points.

(a) Identifying key performance areas—KPAs are areas to gauge performance such as sales volume, quality standard, sales expense for each department so that organisation to succeed.

(b) Identifying strategic control points—These are *critical points* in a system at which monitoring or collecting information should occur, for example, 10% of products may yield 60% on sales.

11. SYMPTOMS OF INADEQUATE CONTROL

When a comprehensive internal audit is not available, a general check list of symptoms of inadequate control can be a useful diagnostic tool. While every situation has some unusual problems, certain symptoms are common:

- An unexplained decline in revenues or profits.
- A degradation of service (customer complaints).
- Employee dissatisfaction (complaints grievances turnover).
- Cash shortages caused by bloated inventories or delinquent accounts receivable.
- Idle facilities or personnel.
- Disorganised operations (work flow bottlenecks excessive paperwork).
- Excessive costs.
- Evidence of waste and inefficiency (scrap, rework).

Problems in one or more of these areas may be a signal that things are getting out of control.

12. PREVENTIVE CONTROL

The preventive control means that higher the quality of managers and their subordinates, the less will be the need for direct controls.

The extensive adoption of preventive control must await a wider understanding of managerial principles, functions, and techniques as well as management philosophy. While such an understanding is not achieved easily it can be gained through training, on-the-job experience, coaching by a knowledgeable superior, and constant self-education. Moreover, as progress is made in appraising managers as managers, preventive control can be expected to have more practical meaning and effectiveness.

Assumptions of the Principle of Preventive Control

The desirability of preventive control rests upon three assumptions: These hold that (1) qualified managers make a minimum of errors, (2) managerial performance can be measured and management concepts, principles, and techniques are useful diagnostic standards in measuring managerial performance, and (3) the application of management fundamentals can be evaluated.

Advantages of Preventive Control

Controlling the quality of managers and thus minimizing errors has several advantages. First, greater accuracy is achieved in assigning personal responsibility: The ongoing evaluation of managers is practically certain to uncover deficiencies and should provide a basis for specific training to eliminate them.

Second, preventive control should hasten corrective action and make it more effective. It encourages control by self-control. Knowing that errors will be uncovered in an evaluation, managers will themselves try to determine their responsibility and make voluntary corrections.

Third, preventive control may lighten the managerial burden now caused by direct controls.

Fourth, the psychological advantage of preventive control is impressive. Many subordinates feel that superiors do not rate fairly that they rely on hunch and personality and that they use improper measuring standards, but performance appraisal can go far in removing this feeling. Subordinate managers know what is expected of them, understand the nature of managing, and feel a close relationship between performance and measurement.

13. LIMITATIONS OF CONTROLLING

These can be:

(i) It is difficult to establish standards for intangible activities.

(ii) Control cannot be effectively exercised over external factors which are uncontrollable.

(iii) Intensive control measure may be listed by employees as it interferers with their freedom of individual thinking and action.

14. TO CONCLUDE

Control is an essential function for managing an organisation. It is used to ensure that what is done is what was intended. The control function plays an important role from the top to the bottom level of an organisation.

Controlling involves the comparison of actual results with planned results. Thus, there is considerable overlap between the planning, organizing and leading functions of a manager. Coinciding with the three levels of management, there are three levels of control—strategic, tactical and operational.

Although control systems must be tailored to specific situations, they generally follow the same basic process. The control process consists of seven steps: determining the areas to control, establishing standards, measuring performance and comparing it against the standards, recognizing good or positive performance, taking corrective action when necessary, and adjusting standards and measures when necessary.

Organisations implement control in a number of different ways and at different levels. Along with determining the areas in which they wish to use controls, managers need to also consider the types of control they wish to use. There are various types of control based on the stage in the production process when they are used, and on the degree of human discretion they require to be effective, control systems should reflect organisational plans, positions and structure; should be understandable; should be cost-effective; should identify only important exceptions; should be flexible; and should provide accurate information.

CHAPTER

23

Effective and Reliable Controls

In this chapter we have covered following aspects of effective and reliable controls:

1. Characteristics of effective and reliable control system.
2. Benefits of effective control system.
3. Reasons for human resistance to controls.
4. Overcoming resistance to controls.

I. CHARACTERISTICS OF EFFECTIVE AND RELIABLE CONTROL SYSTEM

Some essential features of effective control system are:

(a) Ensuring *accuracy* of information.
(b) *Timely* information is collected.
(c) Control system is *understandable* and seen as *objective* by individuals.
(d) Control system is focused on *strategic control points* where deviations lead to harm.
(e) *Cost of implementing* controls is economical.
(f) Control system must *have flexibility* built into them to meet changing conditions.
(g) Control system should *indicate deviation* from standards, and what corrective action to be taken.
(h) Control by exception, i.e. significant deviations are to be only reported.
(i) Controls accepted by *various levels*. For example:
- Top management is concerned with financial performance—budget.
- Supervisors—exercise control on such as percentage of rejects, down-time, material wastage, number of items produced.

(j) The control system must *also be consistent* with organisation culture, or it is likely be ineffective. Normally, *easily measured* factors receive much weight, while *difficult to measure items do not get much attention.*
(k) Self-control means units may plan to control themselves.

2. BENEFITS OF EFFECTIVE CONTROL SYSTEM

An effective control system will help in achieving:

(i) Better coordination
(ii) Corrective action and decision-making.
(iii) Better planning.
(iv) Decentralisation of authority without adequate controls cannot succeed.
(v) Timely action is the action of control.
(vi) Control standards should encourage compliance.
(vii) Control is viewed as fair, which is measurable, specific, participatively set, fit the amount of control to the task.

3. REASONS FOR HUMAN RESISTANCE TO CONTROLS

Some individuals adjust to controls while others resist one way or the other. People dislike controls for following reasons:

(i) Controls are perceived as *curbs to freedom* of individuals.
(ii) Controls may *suppress* the creative and innovative abilities of employees.
(iii) In controls, standards of performance may be *imposed from the top* and subordinates are not involved in determination of standards. Standards may be rigid and unrealistic.
(iv) Performance appraised may be *fault finding* rather than guiding for better action.
(v) Controls may be based on *assumptions* 'X' and involves close and strict compliance. In such case there is no place for individual for exercising self-control.
(vi) Controls may be *administered in discriminatory* or arbitrary manner.

4. OVERCOMING RESISTANCE TO CONTROLS

Controls are aimed at getting results through people. Behaviour towards controls may range from acceptance or to total rejection. Following measures are suggested to avoid resistance to controls by workers:

(i) Controls should be realistic.
(ii) Control should allow for creativity and self-expression.
(iii) People to have say in determination of standards and its administration.
(iv) Control by exception to be the rule.
(v) Reward system to be integrated with controls. Offer reward for acceptable behaviour so that they get positive reinforcement.
(vi) Should be consistently operated and no discrimination to be made.
(vii) Manager to explain and communicate that controls are intended to achieve goals and not to curb freedom of individuals.

Box

Funds to Charitable Bodies to be Tracked

Finance Minister P. Chidambaram on Tuesday said the government proposes to amend tax laws to increase the accountabilIty of charitable organisations.

Responding to a question in the Rajya Sabha on Tuesday Chidambaram said a Bill to amend tax laws would be introduced in the Lok Sabha by Friday to bring the funds received by charitable organisations under the government scanner.

Seeking the support of the House, the Finance Minister said, "it is a sensitive subject and I want to approach it with caution and sensitivity". "Our aim will be only to ensure there is a trail of the financial transactions in such organisations and not any form of harassment".

—HT Correspondent, New Delhi, May 10, 2005

CHAPTER

24

Techniques of Managerial Control

In this chapter techniques of managerial control are covered as under:

1. Financial control methods:
   - (a) Financial statements.
   - (b) Ratio analysis.
   - (c) Break-even analysis.
   - (d) Budgetary control methods.
   - (e) Auditing accounts:
     - (i) External auditing, and
     - (ii) Internal auditing.
2. Managerial controls
   - (i) Management information systems (MIS).
   - (ii) Decision support systems (DSS).
   - (iii) Net working.
   - (iv) Expert systems.
   - (v) Benchmarking.
   - (vi) Role of top managers.
   - (vii) Quality control.
   - (viii) Inventory control.
   - (ix) Management by exception.
3. Management audit and enterprise self-audit.
4. To conclude.
5. Principles of Control. (Box 1)
   - (a) Purpose and nature of control.
   - (b) Structure of control.
   - (c) Process of control.
6. Points of control. (Box 2)

Management has to make optimal decisions in utilising the assets of the organisation. Managers use a variety of control methods and systems to deal with various problems in their organisations.

It is the top-level management that monitors the overall financial health of an organisation. Hence, the financial control system is used by and large by the top-level management. However, middle level managers also monitor financial matters that affect their areas of specialization. The budgetary control system is used by middle-level and lower-level managers to ensure that the activities of the organisation are carried out according to the budgets allocated. The top management occasionally uses the system to monitor the overall budget performance and check any major deviation from the original budget plan. Quality control systems, since they are strategically important, are used by all levels of managers, especially by the top management. Inventory control systems are used largely by lower-level and middle-level managers. However, some indexes may be used by the top management to evaluate the cost of inventory. (Figure 1)

FIGURE 1

Managerial Levels and Control Systems

Level of Management	*Type of Control*
Top level management Middle level management Lower level management	Financial control Budgetary control Quality control Inventory control

1. FINANCIAL CONTROL METHODS

Include:

(a) Financial statements/written reports.
(b) Ratio analysis (Key ratios).
(c) Break-even analysis.
(d) Budgetary control methods.
(e) Audits.

(a) Financial Statements

These analyse in monetary terms of the flow of goods and services to and from the organisation. They are key summaries of the *firm's accounting records.* These are prepared after events have occurred, for example, financial statement for previous year or quarter period. Its usefulness as control measure is limited.

Some commonly used financial statements are *balance sheets, income statements, cash flow* and *sources,* uses of funds statements. These are used by managers to control their organisations activities and by individuals outside the organisation to evaluate its effectiveness.

(b) Ratio Analysis

It can provide quick assessment of financial performance. Ratio analysis comparisons can be made in two ways:

(i) Comparison over a time period—present ratio with ratio in the past in same organisation.
(ii) Comparison with similar organisations.

These indicate change as well as how it compares with competitors. Some examples of ratios are:

Ratios	*Measures*	*Calculation*
Return on investment	Profitability	$\frac{\text{Profits after taxes}}{\text{Total assets}}$
Inventory turnover	Efficiency of inventory management	$\frac{\text{Sales}}{\text{Inventory}}$
Current ratio	Liquidity (Solvency)	$\frac{\text{Current assets}}{\text{Current liabilities}}$
Debt to assets	Utilisation of borrowed fund	$\frac{\text{Total debt}}{\text{Total assets}}$

(c) Break-even Analysis

With this managers can study relationship between costs, sales volume and profits. It can give rough *profit and loss estimate for* different sales volumes.

It can be used to identify the minimum sales volume necessary to meet profit margin and also to provides data in deciding to drop or add product lines. It is a control device to evaluate company performance. It provides basis for corrective action to improve performance. It is a good operational tool and procedure is simple.

(d) Budgetary Control Methods

- Budgets are formal *quantitative statements or resources allocated* for carrying out planned activities over a given period of time.
- They are most widely used means of planning and controlling activities at every level of the organisation.
- A budget indicates the expenditures, revenues, profits planned for some futures data. The planned figures become the standard by which future performance is measured. Deviations can be detected.
- Budgets are favoured by all companies as control device. Budgets are also major means of coordinating the activities of organisations as lot of interaction during budget development process defines and integrates activities.

(e) Auditing Accounts

Auditing serves many important functions in organisation, from validating the accuracy of financial statements, uncovering fraud to providing a critical basis for management decisions. Auditing is of two types:

(i) *External auditing* is an independent appraisal of a firm's financial accounts and statements. Auditor's purpose is not to prepare the company's financial reports. Their job is to verify that company in preparing its own financial statements and valuing its assets and liabilities, has followed accepted accounting principles as well as applied them correctly. Idea is to ensure financial statements are accurate for public purpose.

(ii) *Internal auditing* is carried out within the organisation to assure proper safeguards for company's assets exist. It confirms that records are being accurately kept, and to seek ways of improving organisation efficiency.

(iii) *Cost audit.*

(iv) *Management audit* for resource utilisation.

2. MANAGERIAL CONTROLS

Some managerial controls are as under:

(i) Management Information Systems (MIS)

MIS is formal method of making available to the management the accurate and timely information, necessary to facilitate the decision-making process. MIS enables the organisation planning, control and operational functions to be carried out effectively.

Information needs of managers differ with hierarchial level:

- *Top managers* require information on strategic planning. Thus, there information sources will be largely external.
- *Middle level managers* require both from external and internal sources information. They require more rapid information flow.
- *Lower level managers* are concerned with operational control and will require frequent, detailed as well as accurate information mostly from internal sources.

(ii) Decision Support Systems (DSS)

DSS is direct user-access information system that permits managers to manipulate data and create models in order to assist them in making decisions. A DSS differs from MIS because it involves the interaction of users with data.

(iii) Net Working

It refers to group of computers that can communicate with each other and share common resources, data bases, hardware, etc. Lan is used within the organisation. PERT, CPM, PRIM VERA (Microsoft) is for project control.

(iv) Expert Systems

These are used as tools for improving organisation decision-making and control. They are called artificial intelligence that can exhibit many features of human experts. These systems are distinctly user-oriented and through prompting as well as questioning the user. Expert systems can diagnose problems, recommend solutions. Expert systems are concurrently being applied to resource allocations, problem diagnosis, personnel assignments, etc. Similarly, SAP integrates all functional activities.

Thus, MIS, DSS, Expert Systems offer managers ability to receive filtered, condensed and analysed information that can enhance their job performance.

(v) Benchmarking

This is best practice to monitoring and measuring organisational performance gaps and areas of improvement.

(vi) Role of Top Managers

Role of top managers to help managers to make right choices during periods of change and creating an atmosphere in which employees turn ideas into action.

(vii) Quality Control

Traditionally, financial control and budgetary control have been given considerable importance in most organisations. Of late, quality control too has been receiving considerable attention. This happened after many Japanese companies entered the global markets, offering products and services of superior quality, and posed a challenge to the existing players. US-based companies, in particular, suffered major setbacks on account of comparatively poor quality. A gallop poll conducted in the 1980s indicated that top executives of major US companies rated improvements in service quality and product quality as the most critical challenges facing their companies.

Quality means different things to different people and can be defined in numerous ways. According to the American Society for quality control, "Quality is the totality of features and characteristics of a product or service that bear on its ability to satisfy stated or implied needs."

(viii) Inventory Control

Inventory control is another important control system adopted by organisations. It involves decisions regarding the amount of assets that should be held in inventory. Inventory is a stock of materials that are used to facilitate production or to satisfy customer demand. Inventory helps managers deal with uncertainties in supply and demand. Organisations generally maintain three kinds of inventory: raw materials, work-in-progress and finished goods, and each is affected by different factors.

Raw material inventory is the stock of parts, ingredients and other basic inputs to a production or service process. Work-in-progress inventory is the stock of items currently being transformed into a final product or service. Finished goods inventory is the stock of items that have been produced and are awaiting sale or transit to a customer.

The level of raw materials in inventory is determined by such factors as reliability of supply sources, seasonal nature of production and anticipated sales. Work-in-progress is affected by the length of production cycles.

(ix) Management by Exception

Management by exception is an important principle of organisational control put forward by classical management writers. This principle holds that only significant deviations (i.e., exceptions) from standards of performance should be brought to the management's attention. Factual performance is according to the planned performance (i.e., standards already laid down), it need not be brought to the attention of the concerned manager as no follow up action is necessary. But if there is a major deviation from the standard, it should be reported to the manager. For example, a manager establishes a quality control standards which lays down that five defects per 100 units produced are permissible. Under the management by exception principle, only significant deviations from the standard—six or more defects per 100 units in this case—should be brought to the notice of the manager concerned.

Minor deviations from the standards are usually given less attention. But in some cases, small deviation may mean a great deal and have greater significance than large deviations in other cases. For instance, management will be more concerned if the cost of labour is five per cent more than the budgeted labour-cost as compared to cost of postage stamps which is fifteen per cent more than the budgeted one. So the principle of management by exception must be practised in conjunction with the principle of critical or strategic point control In other words, management should be selective in exercising control. It should select key areas of activity on which the performance of the entire organisation depends and concentrate more on these areas. The exception principle logically refers to the size of deviations from the standards in the critical control points or areas.

Management by exception is an attempt to conserve managerial time, effort and talent and apply these in more important areas. It is a technique of separating important information from the unimportant information. Only such information which is critical for managerial control action is sent to the management. This facilitates the installation of an effective control system.

3. MANAGEMENT AUDIT AND ENTERPRISE SELF-AUDIT

An organisation can have two types of audit: management audit and enterprise self-audit. A management audit aims at evaluating the quality of management and the quality of managing a system. An enterprise self-audit is a much broader type of audit. It evaluates where an organisation is and where it is going, keeping in view present and future economic, social and political developments. It is, in fact, an indirect means of auditing the managerial system.

The Certified Management Audit

A certified management audit may be defined as an independent appraisal of an organisation's management by an outside firm. For years, investors and others have relied on an independent certified accounting audit designed to ensure that an organisation's reports and records reflect sound accounting principles. From the point of view of investors and managers, an audit of the quality of management is extremely important. As the future of an organisation depends on the quality of managers, we can say that a certified management audit would provide more value than a certified accounting audit.

The responsibility of conducting a certified management audit should be given to an outside firm which is staffed by individuals who have sufficient knowledge and are qualified to appraise a company's managerial system. Employing an outside firm ensures the objectivity of the audit. The employees of the auditing firm should be accountable to the auditee firm's board of directors or other senior executives. As a management audit requires a thorough understanding of the internal and external environment of an organisation, it takes a longer time to carry out than an accounting audit. But once auditors become familiar within an organisation, the management audit can be carried out easily and efficiently.

The Enterprise Self-audit

According to J.O. McKinsey, a business organisation should carry out an audit on a periodic basis in order to appraise the organisation and all its aspects in light of its present and probable future environment. He termed this appraisal 'management audit'. An enterprise self-audit appraises an organisation's position and helps it determine where it (the organisation) is, where it is heading with its current plans and programmes, whether it is meeting its objectives, and whether any revision of plans is required to enable the organisation to achieve its predefined goals and objectives. For an organisation to survive and be competitive, it must adapt to the changing social and technological environment. If the organisation does not adapt to these changes in the environment, its objectives may not be achieved and its plans may become obsolete. The enterprise self-audit is designed to force managers to overcome such problems and adapt to the changing external environment.

4. TO CONCLUDE

Managers use a series of control methods and systems to deal with the various problems of their organisations. The major control systems that assist a manager in exercising control are financial control, budgetary control, quality control, inventory control, operations management and computer-based information systems.

Control systems are classified into feedforward, concurrent and feedback control systems based on the management level at which they are used, as well as on the nature of their timing. Financial control systems are feedback control systems.

While financial controls are a major tool of top management, budgetary controls are used by middle managers. Budgets are a widely used means for planning and control at every level of the organisation. Budgeting is the formulation and quantification of future plans for the organisation. Organisations divide their units into responsibility centers to facilitate budgeting. The responsibility centers are classified as standard cost centers, discretionary expense centers, revenue centers, profit centers and investment centers, depending on the degree to which they have control on inputs and outputs and their contribution to the organisation. Quality control and inventory control help organisations reduce costs considerably by preventing products and services of inferior quality from leaving the organisation, and excess raw material from entering the organisation (or accumulation of excess products in the warehouse).

Two methods of control can be—direct control and preventive control. In direct control the cause of an unsatisfactory outcome is traced back to the individuals responsible for it and they are made to correct their practices. Preventive control, however, focuses on developing better managers who will skillfully apply concepts, principles and techniques and view managing and managerial problems from a systems point of view, so that the undesirable outcomes caused by poor management are eliminated.

5. PRINCIPLES OF CONTROL (BOX I)

Box I

Principles of Control

Principles of control can be grouped into three categories, reflecting their:

(a) purpose and nature of control,
(b) structure, and
(c) process.

(a) The Purpose and Nature of Control

The purpose and nature of control may be summarized by the principles listed below.

1. Principle of the Purpose of Control

The task of control is to ensure that plans succeed by detecting deviations from plans and furnishing a basis for taking action to correct potential or actual undesired deviations.

2. Principle of Future-directed Controls

Because of time lags in the total system of control, the more a control system is based on feed-forward rather than simple feedback of information, the more managers have the opportunity to perceive undesirable deviations from plans before they occur and to take action in time to prevent them.

These two principles emphasize that the purpose of control in any system of managerial action is ensuring that objectives are achieved through detecting deviations and taking action designed to correct or prevent them. Control, like planning, should ideally be forward-looking. This principle is often disregarded in practice, largely because the present state of the art in managing has not regularly provided for systems of feed-forward control. Managers have generally been dependent on historical data, which may be adequate for collecting taxes and determining stockholders' earnings but are not good enough for the most effective control. If means of looking forward are lacking, reference to history, on the questionable assumption that "what is past is prologue," is better than not looking at all. But time lags in the system of management control make it imperative that greater efforts be undertaken to make future-directed control a reality.

3. Principle of Control Responsibility

The primary responsibility for the exercise of control rests in the manager charged with the performance of the particular plans involved.

Since delegation of authority, assignment of tasks, and responsibility for certain objectives rest individual managers, it follows that control over this work should be exercised by each of these managers. An individual manager's responsibility cannot be waived or rescinded without changes in the organisation structure.

4. Principle of Efficiency of Controls

Control techniques and approaches are efficient if they detect and illuminate the nature and causes of deviations from plans with a minimum of costs or other unsought consequences.

Control techniques have a way of becoming costly, complex, and burdensome. Managers may become so engrossed in control that they spend more than it is worth to detect a deviation.

Detailed budget controls that hamstring a subordinate, complex mathematical controls that thwart innovation, and purchasing controls that delay deliveries and cost more than the item purchased are examples of inefficient controls.

5. Principle of Preventive Control

The higher the quality of managers in a managerial system, the less will be the need for direct controls.

Most controls are based in large part on the fact that human beings make mistakes and often do not react to problems by undertaking their correction adequately and promptly. The more qualified managers are, the more they will perceive deviations from plans and take timely action to prevent them.

(b) The Structure of Control

The principles that follow are aimed at pointing out how control systems and techniques can be designed to improve the quality of managerial control.

6. Principle of Reflection of Plans

The more that plans are clear, complete, and integrated, and the more that controls are designed to reflect such plans, the more effectively controls will serve the needs of managers.

It is not possible for a system of controls to be devised without plans, since the task of control is to ensure that plans work out as intended. There can be no doubt that the more clear, complete, and integrated these plans are, and the more that control techniques are designed to follow the progress of these plans, the more effective the controls will be.

7. Principle of Organisational Suitability

The more that an organisational structure is clear, complete, and integrated, and the more that controls are designed to reflect the place in the organisation structure where responsibility for action lies, the more controls will facilitate correction of deviations from plans.

Plans are implemented by people. Deviations from plans must be the responsibility primarily of managers who are entrusted with the task of executing planning programmes. Since it is the function of an organisation structure to define a system of roles, it follows that controls must be designed to affect the role in which responsibility for performance of a plan lies.

8. Principle of Individuality of Controls

The more that control techniques and information are understandable to individual managers who must utilize them, the more they will actually be used and the more they will result in effective control.

Although some control techniques and information can be utilized in the same form by various kinds of enterprises and managers, as a general rule controls should be tailored to meet the individual needs of managers. Some of this individuality is related to position in the organisation structure, as noted, in the previous principle. Another aspect of individuality is the tailoring of controls to the kind and level of managers' understanding. Company presidents as well as supervisors have thrown up their hands in dismay (often for quite different reasons) at the unintelligible nature and inappropriate form of control information. Control information that a manager cannot or will not use has little practical value.

(c) The Process of Control

Control, often being so much a matter of technique, rests heavily on the art of managing, on know-how in given instances. However, there are certain principles that experience has shown have wide applicability.

9. Principle of Standards

Effective control requires objective, accurate, and suitable standards.

There should be a simple, specific, and verifiable way to measure whether a planning programme is being accomplished. Control is accomplished through people. Even the best manager cannot help being influenced by personal factors, and actual performance is sometimes camouflaged by a dull or a sparkling personality or by a subordinate's ability to "sell" a deficient performance. Good standards of performance, objectively applied, will more likely be accepted by subordinates as fair and reasonable.

10. Principle of Critical-point Control

Effective control requires special attention to those factors critical to evaluating performance against plans.

It would ordinarily be wasteful and unnecessary for managers to follow every detail of plan execution. What they must know is that plans are being implemented. Therefore, they concentrate attention on salient factors of performance that will indicate any important deviations from plans. Perhaps all managers can ask themselves what things in their operations will best show them whether the plans for which they are responsible are being accomplished.

11. The Exception Principle

The more that managers concentrate control efforts on significant exceptions, the more efficient will be the results of their control.

This principle holds that managers should concern themselves with significant deviations—the especially good or the especially bad situations. It is often confused with the principle of critical-point control, and the two do have some kinship. However, critical-point control has to do with recognizing the points to be watched, while the exception principle has to do with watching the size of deviations at these points.

12. Principle of Flexibility of Controls

If controls are to remain effective despite failure or unforeseen changes of plans, flexibility is required in their design.

According to this principle, controls must not be so inflexibly tied in with a plan as to be useless if the entire plan fails or is suddenly changed. Note that this principle applies to failures of plans, not failures of people operating under plans.

13. Principle of Action

Control is justified only if indicated or experienced deviations from plans are corrected through appropriate planning, organizing, staffing, and leading.

There are instances in practice in which this simple truth is forgotten. Control is a wasteful use of managerial and staff time unless it is followed by action. If deviations are found in experienced or projected performance, action is indicated, in the form of either redrawing plans or making additional plans to get back on course. The situation may call for reorganisation. It may require replacing subordinates or training them to do the task desired. Or it may indicate that the fault is a lack of direction and leadership in getting a subordinate to understand the plans or in motivating him or her to accomplish them. In any case, action is implied.

Source: Harold Koontz and Heinz Wehrich, 'Essentials of Management', International Perspective, Tata McGraw Hill, New Delhi.

6. POINTS OF CONTROL (BOX 2)

Box 2

Points of Control

1. Why managers believe they need control?

Control is the process through which managers ensure that actual activities conform to plans. As such, control is useful in evaluating the effectiveness of planning, organizing, and leading.

2. The steps in the control process

The control process consists of: (1) establishing standards and methods for measuring performance; (2) measuring the performance; (3) determining if performance matches the standards; and, if needed, (4) taking corrective action.

3. The importance of key performance areas and strategic control points to the design of effective control systems

Designing effective control systems can be difficult. If managers try to control too many elements in a rigid way, morale will probably suffer and valuable time, money, and energy will be wasted. These problems can be minimized if managers focus on controlling key performance areas and strategic control points.

4. Why financial controls are important to managers

Financial controls are important to managers because money is one of the most prominent and measured inputs and outputs for most organisations. Financial statements, which include balance sheets, income statements, and cash flow statements, provide snapshots of an organisation's liquidity, its general financial condition, and its profitability. This information is useful for managers and for outsiders who need to evaluate the organisation's performance.

5. Some of the reasons budgets are used so widely

Budgets, formal quantitative statements of resources set aside for a given activity and time period, are the most widely used means for planning and controlling. Because they are stated in monetary terms, budgets make it easy to compare dissimilar activities and their profit-loss potential; they establish clear standards of performance; and the interaction their creation requires helps coordinate activities within the organisation.

6. The main types of responsibility centers and the budget considerations associated with each

Although budgets can be established for specific projects, most budgets are devised for responsibility centers. The four types of responsibility centers are revenue centers, expense centers, profit centers, and investment centers.

7. The budgeting process

The budgeting process begins when top managers give lower-level managers their economic forecasts and objectives for the coming year. A few organisations use top-down budgeting, in which top management also completes the budgets; but most use bottom-up budgeting, in which lower-level managers, often with the help of their employees, create budgets and submit them to higher-level managers for approval on a specific timetable.

8. The uses of external and internal auditing

Auditing compares actual performance to budgets. External auditing, conducted by outside chartered accountant's firms, examines an organisation's financial reports to verify that the organisation has used generally accepted accounting principles in a proper way. As such, it can be used to detect fraud and encourage honesty and accuracy. Internal auditing, carried out by specially appointed members of the financial department or by an internal auditing staff, helps managers evaluate the organisation's operational efficiency, as well as the effectiveness of its policies, procedures, use of authority, and other managerial methods.

Source: James A.F. Stoner/Charles Wankel, Management, PHI, New Delhi.

CHAPTER

25

Accountability and Financial Transparency for NGOs

The role of Non-governmental Organisations (NGOs) in societal problem-solving, securing human rights, poverty alleviation, environmental issues, rural transformation, etc. is increasing. Most of the NGOs are controlled by people of genuine personal concern and commitment, functioning with a high standard of honesty and integrity. It is therefore necessary to maintain the integrity of the services and to provide proper and transparent accountability procedures to the people involved in the services. There is a need to enhance accountability and transparency in all NGOs in order to foster and consolidate greater democracy. This paper highlights the need for ethical issues in the governing principles of NGOs and certain best practices adopted by on NGO in achieving accountability and transparency. In this paper, a real life implementation, using an ERP-based system and web-enabled design is also discussed, for sharing with other NGOs in India/Overseas.

INTRODUCTION

In recent years, there is a witness of dramatic increase in the importance, number, and diversity of Non-governmental Organisations (NGOs). NGOs now influence policies and initiatives that were earlier the domain of governments and for profit corporations, and their humanitarian service has become vital to the well-being of individuals and societies throughout the globe. In many cases, NGOs have proven more adept than governments in responding to particular needs. As a powerful "third sector" existing between the realms of government and business, NGOs are bringing an unprecedented vitality and ability to bear on critical issues related to service and world peace. Their flexibility and connections to grass-roots communities aid them in mobilizing resources quickly to affected areas. Their single-minded commitment and strong motivation affords them a civic power that other institutions may lack.

However, with their increased importance comes increased responsibility. NGOs have the responsibility to be transparent, honest, accountable, and ethical to provide accurate information, and not to manipulate situations for the personal benefit of their boards and staff. NGOs have a calling to go beyond the boundaries of race, religion, ethnicity, culture and politics. They have the obligation to respect each person's fundamental human rights.

Globally, NGOs collect hundreds of billions of dollars annually from donors and distribute/utilize these funds to beneficiaries after paying for their own administrative costs. Transparency is in the interest of the public, donors, organisations, and authorities. However, the sheer volume of transactions conducted by NGOs combined with the desire not to unduly burden legitimate organisations, generally underscore the importance of risk and size-based proportionality in setting the appropriate level of rules and overseeing in this area.

NEED FOR ACCOUNTABILITY FOR NGOs

NGOs fulfil a number of functions in areas, which tend to be neglected by the private and public sectors. Due to declining public sector/governmental provision of services in many countries, NGOs have played an increasingly influential role in a variety of activities which impact upon the lives of many people. There are at least four features that portray the function of NGOs: (1) they exist to fulfil a charitable purpose; (2) they function without the use of coercion; (3) they operate without distributing profits to shareholders; and (4) they exist without simple and clear lines of ownership and accountability. One of the primary goals of assessing financial performance is to assess how well an organisation is fulfiling its mission and what are its prospects in future.

Reasons to Look at NGO Accountability?

There are a number of reasons: There has been a rising visibility and stakes of NGOs' work. A crisis of legitimacy in many sectors, especially business and government, has amplified the need for NGOs as a 'counterbalance'. More vocal advocacy by NGOs has also challenged the work of corporations, governments and international organisations, which in turn has elicited counterattacks. Their potential to address institutional failures (formal and/ or informal) for global problems is also being increasingly recognized. NGOs have also ignored the fact that they are answerable to key stakeholders and the constituency that they work with, for promises of performance.

Several major financial scandals have rocked the non-profit world, including embezzlement by the president of the United Way of America for (Murawski, 1995) investment fraud by the Head of the Foundation for New Era Philanthropy for perpetrating (Stecklow, 1997), theft by leaders of the Episcopal and Baptist churches (Greene, 1995; Fletcher, 1999), improper use of funds by the Head of the National Association for the Advancement of Colored People (NAACP) (Greene, 1995), and excessively generous compensation of the president of Adelphi University (Thornburg, 1997). In the past decade, the issue of the non-profit financial reporting and accountability of the non-profit sector has surfaced, including the adequacy of the current reporting and oversight mechanisms.

An important feature of non-profit and voluntary organisations is that they have unclear lines of ownership and accountability (Chisholm, 1995). This trait separates these entities from both business and government. Businesses must meet the expectations of shareholders or they risk financial ruin. The ownership question in the business sector is clear, shareholder's own larger or smaller amounts of equity in companies depending on the number of shares held. Similarly, government is tethered to a well-identified group of individuals namely voters. Government is traditionally conceived of as "belonging" to citizens, though the ways in which this ownership claim can be exercised are severely limited. The non-coercive feature of non-profits brings them closer to business and separates them from government; the non-distribution constraint pushes non-profits closer to the public sector and away from the private sector.

In the non-profit sector, there are no owners, and the accountability is absent. While these claims have rarely mounted to the level of ownership claims, the lines of accountability have been drawn more sharply, particularly as questions about the transfer of assets have come up when non-profit organisations have attempted to convert to for-profit status.

ETHICS FOR NGOs

NGOs need to have a system of proper governance. They must be careful to treat all public monies with utmost seriousness as a public trust. NGOs have an obligation to not align themselves with, or stand in opposition to, any particular government for purely selfish or shortsighted means, nor to become controlled by a governmental body. In short, NGOs have the responsibility to dedicate themselves for the sake of others and do so according to the highest code of ethical conduct. Some of the ethics are:

Financial Transparency and Accountability

(i) NGOs should strive for openness and honesty internally and towards donors and members of the public. Periodic accountings should be made.

(ii) An NGO should be accountable for its actions and decisions not only to its funding agencies and the government, but also to the people it serves, its staff and members, partner organisations, and the public at large.

What are the key principles of NGO accountability?

(a) One of the first principles is that responsibility and authority has to be clearly specified. The responsible person must be informed of the expected programme results and resources (financial and human) allocated for the purpose. Monitoring and evaluation systems should be clarified, along with organisational values, policies, rules and regulations, and the behavioural standards.

(b) The second principle calls for providing guidance and support to the responsible person in the form of regular and timely management information, training and development, access to senior managers, and advice from financial and human resource management experts.

(c) The third principle calls for the monitoring and assessment of the needs of responsibility and authority. This is done by an objective comparison of results against targets and standards, covering such issues as delivery of programme, cost and quality; management of human and financial resources; decision-making-authority fully exercised but not exceeded; and compliance with policies, values, rules and regulations, and behavioural standards.

(d) The final principle is on taking appropriate action. This deals with issues such as excellence, satisfactory performance, unsatisfactory execution of responsibility and authority as a result of carelessness or ignorance, unacceptable execution of responsibility and authority due to deliberate flouting of policies, rules and regulations, or exceeding the limits of decision-making authority.

APPLICATION OF KEY PRINCIPLES

(i) An NGO should be transparent in all of its dealings with the government, the public, donors, partners, and other interested parties, except for personnel matters and proprietary information. An NGOs basic financial information, governance structure, activities, and listing of officers and partnerships should be open and accessible to public scrutiny and the NGO should make effort to inform the public about its work and the origin and use of its resources.

(ii) NGOs should have proper financial and legal procedures and safeguards in place, not only to stay within the law, but also as a measure of the organisation's health and to assure donors, members, and the general public that investments in the organisation are safe and being correctly used. NGOs should employ sound internal financial procedures, maintain financial records carefully, and make available to the public financial statements. They should also have their financial records reviewed periodically by a qualified, independent, outside examiner who can certify that the organisation is operating legally and according to generally accepted accounting practices. NGOs must also be diligent that they are complying with applicable laws of the land. Various issues that relate to NGOs are given in Figure 1.

(iii) Legal Compliance

Laws and regulations

An NGOs activities, governance, and other matters should confirm to the laws and regulations of its nation and locality. (An NGO may seek to change those laws and regulations, if such activity is consistent with its mission.)

Liability insurance

An NGO should consider having liability insurance, if available and applicable.

Internal review

An NGO should conduct an internal review regarding compliance of the organisation with current laws and regulations and summaries of this review should be presented to members of the governing body.

Legal review

An NGO should get a legal review of its organizing documents to make sure that they are in compliance with existing laws and regulations.

(iv) Independence and Autonomy

NGOs should not be controlled by any government or inter-governmental body, or by

FIGURE I

Issues Related to NGOs

Fiscal Responsibility	Members of the governing body hold ultimate fiscal responsibility for their organisations and should understand the organisation's financial statements and reporting requirements.
Annual Budget	An NGOs annual budget is to be approved by the governing body, and should outline projected expenses for programme activities, fund raising, and administration. The NGO should operate in accordance with that budget.
Internal Financial Statements	Internal financial statements should be prepared regularly and provided to the governing body. Any and all significant variations between budgeted expenses and actual expenditures, and between budgeted revenues and actual revenues, should be identified and explained to the governing body.
Financial Policies	An NGO should have established financial policies, suitable for the size of the organisation, regarding the receiving and disbursement of financial resources, investment of assets, purchasing practices, internal control procedures (such as policies for signing checks), and so forth.
Internal Control Procedures	An NGOs internal control procedures should have a safeguard against a person having the power to issue a cheque to himself or herself, such as requiring a counter-signature on the cheque. An NGOs internal control procedures should have a safeguard against one person being able to issue a check over a certain amount (such as two signatures are needed over Rs. 1 lakh) and should have restrictions on cheques made out to cash.
Audit	For NGOs with substantial annual revenue, the accuracy of the financial reports should be subject to audit by an independent, qualified accountant. NGOs with small gross incomes should have a review by a qualified accountant. NGOs with very small revenues may suffice with an internally produced, complete financial statement.
Professional Standards	An NGO should adhere to professional standards of accountancy and audit procedures as stipulated by the law in its nation, and fulfil all financial and reporting requirements.

Source: http://www.wango.orglactivities/codeofethics/financialandlegal.htm

corporate interests. NGOs have a responsibility to not rigidly align themselves with, or stand in opposition to any particular government or political party, but should focus instead on principles and policies.

Truthfulness and Legality

An NGO should be honest and truthful in its dealings with its donors, project beneficiaries, staff, members, partner organisations, government, and the public in general, and should respect the laws of any jurisdiction in which it is active.

- An NGO should give out accurate information, whether regarding itself and its projects, or regarding any individual, organisation, project, or legislation it opposes or is discussing.

- An NGO should not engage in any activities that are unlawful under the laws of the nation in which it is organised or works, and should be strongly opposed to, and not be a willing partner to corruption, bribery, and other financial improprieties or illegalities.
- An NGO should have a policy for staff and volunteers to confidentially bring evidence to the governing body of misconduct of anyone associated with the organisation.
- An NGO should meet all of the legal obligations in their country. Such obligations may include laws of incorporation, fund-raising legislation, equal employment opportunity principles, health and safety standards, privacy rules, trademark and copyright legislation, and so forth. An NGO should take prompt corrective action whenever wrongdoing is discovered among its staff, governing body, volunteers, contractors, and partners.

(v) Financial Transparency for Beneficiaries

There is no external pressure for NGOs to provide financial reports to their beneficiaries (as opposed to donors, for instance). But financial transparency at the local level puts poor people at the centre of NGOs' accountability systems. It strengthens respect and

FIGURE 2

Desired Financial Reporting System

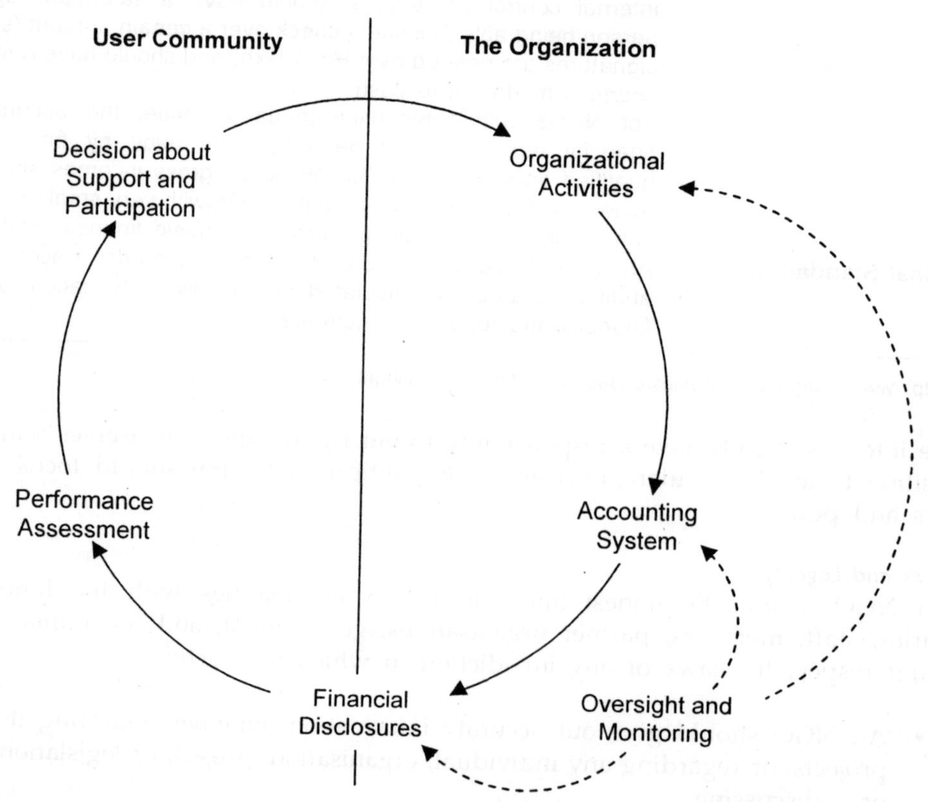

collaboration between NGOs, partner organisations and the people they aim to help. As a result, financial transparency can transform the effectiveness and efficiency of NGO interventions. (Figure 2)

Why should NGOs Provide Financial Reports to their Beneficiaries?

By providing simple financial reports to their beneficiaries, NGOs can:

- Increase their accountability and transparency to their beneficiaries, who are their primary stakeholders;
- Empower beneficiaries (particularly in discussions with NGO staff) and demonstrate that NGOs respect them;
- Strengthen NGOs' relationship with beneficiaries, providing the foundations for longer-term interventions;
- Improve the quality of programme decisions, as beneficiaries provide feedback on how funds are being spent; and
- Reduce the possibility of inefficiencies or fraud.

Examples of Good Practice

Some practical examples of best practices in this area are given below:

- *Using white-boards outside offices*: Outside its offices in the Western Region of Kenya, Action-Aid has put up public information boards that display the budgets, the amounts of funds available for each area and a monthly update of expenditure. The boards are simple white-boards mounted on a frame and covered by a small roof.
- *Presenting information in a simple graphical way*: Working with aboriginal communities in Australia, an organisation called Littlefish has developed a way of presenting financial information in a simple graphical way. They turn expenditure and budget reports into colourful bar charts which show how much have been spent on what. The reports are printed out on to A3 poster-size paper and displayed publicly.
- *Using activity-based reports*: In the district of Mai Son in Vietnam, Action-Aid reviewed how much it spent on each different activity it carried out, and compared it to a ranking given to the activity by local communities:

The total costs column shows the total amount spent on each activity over the period 1992-2003 (Figure 3). The ranking column shows the ranked priority that the communities affected by the projects assigned democratically to each activity in 2003. The combined table provides important information for discussing Action-Aid's activities in the past and the future.

(vi) Financial Transparency for Donor

NGOs raise large sums of money and, donors want to know how the NGO spends the money it collects and whether the programme it runs makes a difference to the target group. Thus, NGOs should strive to provide all details about the utilization of the funds to the maximum possible extent.

FIGURE 3

Action-Aid Activities—Rankings

Activities	*Total costs*	*Ranking*
Agriculture extension	2,483,566	1
Para-vet	1,397,934	4
Irrigation	2,932,218	5
Health	2,220,703	3
Savings & credit	5,371,105	2
Education	771,411	6

Source: www. mango.org.uk/pool/ Financial reports for beneficiaries Jan05.doc

REFERENCE

Sushiv S., Harsh Bhargava, G. Radha Krishna and J.K. Manivannan, The ICFAI Journal of Corporate Governance, Vol. V, No. 3, 2006.

PART V

EVALUATION OF PERFORMANCE

CHAPTER

26

Evaluation of NPOs Performance Process

Organisation performance process is the accumulated end results of all the organisation's work processes and activities. We shall discuss following aspects of evaluation of organisation performance:

(a) Benefits of measuring organisation performance.
(b) Organisation performance measures.
(c) Maintaining quality standards.
(d) Social audit.
(e) Concepts of EVA and economic contribution (EC) for NPO.
(f) The evaluation process.
(g) How to increase public trust or confidence in non-profit organisations.

(A) BENEFITS OF MEASURING ORGANISATION PERFORMANCE

It is important to measure organisation performance as it leads to:

- Better *assets management*.
- To an increased ability to provide *customer value*. (To solve customer's problems).
- To improved measures of *organisational knowledge* through information sharing and social interaction.
- Measuring process has an impact on organisation's reputation. (i.e. consumer trust and financial measures) (Figure 1).

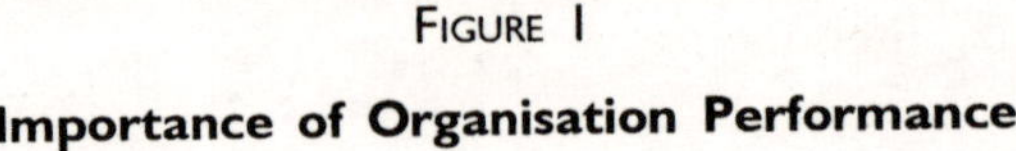

FIGURE I

Importance of Organisation Performance

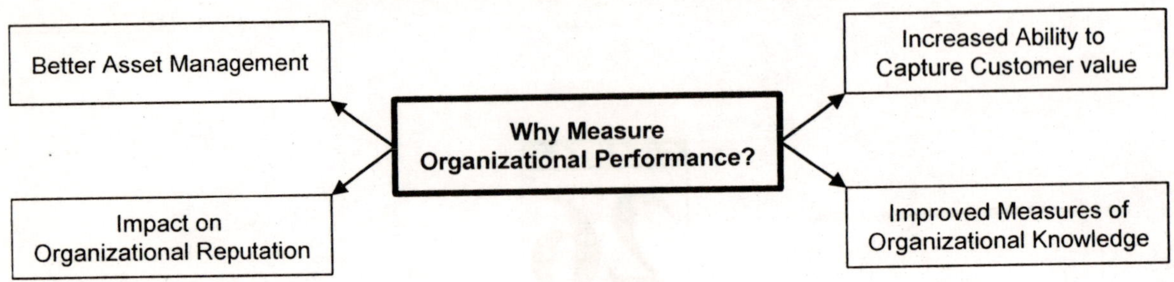

(B) ORGANISATIONAL PERFORMANCE MEASURES

Some measures for organisation performance can be:

(i) *Organisational productivity*, i.e.

$$= \frac{\text{Output (Goods \& Services)}}{\text{Inputs needed to generate}}$$

(ii) *Organisational effectiveness.* How effective are goal's and how well company is achieving them.

(iii) *Rankings* of NPO on different performance measures.

(iv) *Overall performance in summary* budget. It is summary of all operating revenue and expense budget.

(v) *ROI Financial ratios*, e.g. profit and loss control, services provided to community, etc.

(vi) Performance control through calculating and comparing return on investment (ROI).

(vii) Another control financial measure is *economic value added* (EVA) and *marketing value added* (MVA).

EVA is taking after-tax profit minus total annual cost of capital. EVA focuses on earning a rate of return over and above the cost of capital. The object of EVA is supposed to take in capital from investors and make it worth more.

(viii) *Balanced scorecard* is a performance measure that looks at four areas—financial, customer, internal processes and people innovation that contribute to NPOs performance. Goals are to be set in each of four areas and to measure these goals whether these are met.

(ix) *Identifying key performance areas* or key result areas (KRA). Key result areas are those aspects of the organisation that must function effectively for the entire organisation to succeed. These KRA's usually involve all major activities. Some KRA's for production and marketing can be:

Production	*Marketing of Services*
• Quality	• Expense of services/programming
• Cost	• Advertising expenditure
• Quantity	• Individual achievement of goals of performance

Another point worth mentioning is that performance reporting may create some problems. (Figure 2)

FIGURE 2

Performance Reporting

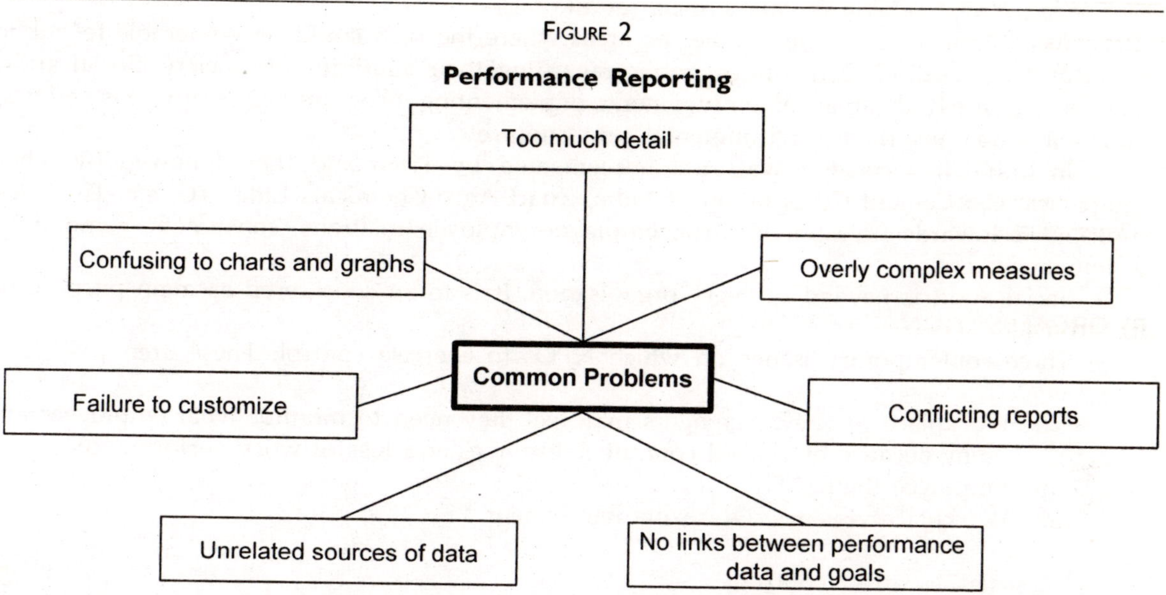

Source: Based on T. Leahy, "10 Cures for Performance Reporting Anxiety", *Business Finance*, December 1999, pp. 63-65.

(C) MAINTAINING QUALITY STANDARDS

All NPOs have to set-up quality-assurance programme to ensure measurements in the output. Some examples could be that *quality* could be more important than that of quantity. The number of students graduating from an institute is quantitative measures, while number of graduating in a *first class* is a qualitative measure. The quality of education in municipal schools may be of poor quality, while private schools have to maintain high quality standards by procuring required equipment or to keep qualified teachers, etc.

So quality is a matter of defining the *expectations* of quality standards of the institution. Such programmes have to be reviewed so that these are useful. The important point is for every one to know that there is an *established standard* which is documented and known to all:

- *Feedback* on quality standards is of value.
- A review committee should be set-up to look at matters of quality standards.
- Particular attention should be paid to complaints received.
- A random review of quality standards is desirable so that corrective steps can then be taken.
- To ensure quality standards any lapse in quality to be discussed. It should not be to blame individual but to ensure correction.

(D) SOCIAL AUDIT

The measurement, evaluation and reporting of performance of an organisation in the *area of social responsibility* is called social audit.

Social audit helps to determine the areas where the firm could be vulnerable to public criticism. Organisations can inform public regarding their activities for society. Social audit may be measured in areas of employment, implementing programmes, employees' efforts, donation funds absorbed, environmental protection, etc.

In India, this concept was first implemented by Tisco and then followed by other companies, e.g. Cement Corporation of India, Zuari Agro-Chemicals Ltd., ITC, etc. Tisco has contributed towards pollution control, employer-employee relations, consumers, community development, etc.

Social audit is needed in every organisation. It is to be considered as main purpose of its survival.

Three contemporary issues on which NPOs to exercise control. These are:

(i) Workplace privacy. Managers may feel they need to monitor what employees are doing because of wasted computer resources and loss of work performance.
(ii) Employee theft.
(iii) Workplace violence, i.e. sexual harassment.

These issues affect control.

(E) ECONOMIC VALUE ADDED (EVA) AND ECONOMIC CONTRIBUTION (EC) FOR NPO

(i) Economic Value Added (EVA)

Definition

Economic Value Added (EVA) — Subtracts the capital charge (the capital investment times the cost of capital) from the net financial benefits of the investment. Or the monetary value of an entity at the end of a time period minus the monetary value of that same entity at the beginning of that time period.

What it means

Economic profit is wealth treated above the capital cost of the investment. EVA prevents managers from thinking that the cost of capital is free. EVA is a measure of performance of the organisation based on what it is auditing over and above the cost of funds being used by it.

Strengths

EVA focuses managers on the question."For any given investment, will the company generate returns above the cost of capital?" Companies that embrace EVA have bonus compensation schemes that reward or punish managers for adding value to or subtracting value from the company.

Weaknesses

As with any metric, it's hard to link precise EVA returns to a specific technology investment. EVA is ideally suited to publicly traded companies, not private companies, because it deals with the cost of equity for shareholders, as opposed to debt capital.

If a company invests in manufacturing equipment or a warehouse, how much additional profit will be required to pay for it? Managers are intuitively aware of the importance of value creation to their businesses. EVA is a management philosophy and performance metric that elevates those goals from intuition to rigorous analysis and ensures that no investment escapes scrutiny.

Calculation

Net operating profit after taxes – capital charge (capital investment × cost of capital).

But, purely speaking, there is no net operating profit after taxes (NOPAT) arising out of an IT investment, so the net financial benefits of the IT investment are used as a replacement for NOPAT.

Consider, for instance, a case where the cost-benefit analysis reveals that a $50,000 IT investment will return $8,000 in net quantifiable benefits. The ROI is 16% ($8,000 divided by $50,000). The cost of capital in the company is 12%. Using the formula above, the EVA in this case is $2,000:

$8,000 net benefits – ($50,000 capital investment × 12% cost of capital) = $2,000 EVA

Another way to calculate EVA in this example is to simply deduct the 12% cost of capital from the 16% ROI, then multiply by the investment:

4% × $50,000 = $2,000 EVA
EVA is always expressed as a dollar amount.

"EVA doesn't make it easy to quantify IT benefits but creates clarity so that all the pluses and minuses of these IT decisions can be considered in ways that companies [that don't use EVA] find difficult to do," says Bennett Stewart, co-founder of Stern Stewart & Co., a New York-based consultancy that coined the term Economic Value Added, but not the concern.

(ii) Economic Contribution (EC) for Non-profit Organisation

Non-profit organisations normally justify their existence in emotional or moralistic terms. But non-profit organisations are also economic entities. Non-profit organisations have no shareholder interested in the enhancement of his economic value through his investment.

On the other hand, the promoters have invested in the project, expecting that the resources so mobilized will add to the well-being of a specific segment of society. The 'economic value of the contribution' from the project should exceed the 'total cost' of the resources. Otherwise the original contribution could have been simply distributed among potential beneficiaries. The contribution of the project (and the organisation managing it) must therefore be considered measurable as the difference between the cost of the funds utilized and the economic value of the product received by the beneficiaries.

Since the non-profit organisation provides a product (goods or services) we can estimate the contribution, provided we can attribute an economic or market value to the product. If there is an equivalent product available in the market at a price, the process of attributing a value is simple. It is assumed to be equal to the market price. For example, a charitable hospital provides a service, (a kidney transplant or a heart bypass) free of cost or at a subsidized cost. An equivalent service provided by the commercial hospital gives the market value of the service. If there is no market equivalent available, it may be necessary to use the full cost of the product as its economic value. We then take into consideration the 'value' (market price or full cost) as the gross contribution. However, if the product is not supplied free but at a subsidy, the 'value less the subsidy' is to be considered the actual contribution. This contribution can be calculated per unit of output.

When multiplied by the total units, the result gives us 'the contribution' of the organisation. We may designate this as the 'economic contribution of the organisation'.

In order to arrive at net economic contribution (NEC) we need to deduct the cost of capital employed from the EC.

EC can be compared to the average cost of capital to arrive at the Net Economic Contribution or NEC.

(F) THE EVALUATION PROCESS

Only those organisations succeed who are committed to evaluation process and identify problems and make things better. Some important steps are:

1. Accurately *diagnosing* the organisation's current situation and identifying areas, where there are opportunities for positive change. A 'SWOT' analysis helps, such as reassessment of mission, image and case for support.
   (a) Whether '*mission*' is relevant to current needs of concerned society or is it up-to-date or it has to be rewarded.
   (b) Whether *image* of organisation is well known and well respected in its community. To ensure people are well familiar with its activities and NPO enjoys good reputation.
   (c) When organisation must represent a *case for support* to contributors and clients.
2. Separating the problems into those that *need immediate attention* and those that are to be dealt later.
3. Build consensus of board of governors and the staff to *deal with problems* honestly in time.
4. Developing a *realistic schedule* for implementing change.
5. Continuing the diagnostic, evaluation, and self-improvement process year after year.

(G) HOW TO INCREASE PUBLIC TRUST OR CONFIDENCE IN NON-PROFIT ORGANISATION?

- One solution is to implement DADS, where

  D Disclosure of performance information, e.g. client satisfaction.

  A Analysis of adequate quantity of financial data for analysis.

  D Dissemination is normally meagure and slow to elected representatives.

S Sanctions against those who fail to disclose, analyse, and disseminate required information and some agency should be in a position to inflict capital punishment by revoking its tax-exempt status and criminal penalties for managers.

- Without information, the public cannot know if organisation is fulfiling its mission.
- Perhaps wide public disclosure of wrong doing is to some extent what strong sanction.
- Provide for steps for early warning signals, such as, are NPOs goals consistent with financial resources.
- Audits by government regulator on certain areas such as hospitals have been charged with providing too few services for the poor, or schools not allocating seats for reserved community, but are charging inflated tuition fees from poor students, etc.
- Pro-active role of directors, such as non-profits should not sacrifice present generations of users for the benefit of future generations. Inter-generational parity (equity) has to be ensured.

If boards of governors demonstrate that they can change effectively, the professional staff may follow suit. They need to divide what needs to be measured.

Box I

Points of Organisation Performance

1. Organisational performance is the accumulated end results of all the organisation's work processes and activities.
2. Measuring organisational performance is important because it leads to better asset management, to an increased ability to provide customer value, and to improved measures of organisational knowledge. In addition, measures of organisational performance have an impact on an organisation's reputation. Organisation knowledge is that it is created by collaborative information sharing and social interaction that leads to organisational members taking appropriate actions.
3. The most frequent used organisational performance measures include organisational productivity, organisational effectiveness, and industry rankings. Organisational productivity is the overall output of goods or services produced by an organisation divided by the inputs needed to generate that organisational effectiveness is a measure of how appropriate organisational goals are and how well an organisation is achieving those goals. Industry rankings are lists created by various business publications and organisations that rate organisations on different performance measures.
4. Traditional financial control measures include ratio analysis and budget analysis. Managers can use ratio analysis as internal control devices for monitoring how efficiently and profitably an organisation uses its assets, debt, inventories, and the like. Budgets managers with quantitative standards against which to measure and compare resource consumption. Other financial control, measures include economic value added (EVA) and market value added (MVA). EVA is calculated by taking after-tax operating profit minus the total annual cost of capital. As a control tool, EVA

focuses managers' attention on earning a rate of return over and above the cost of capital. MVA measures the stock market estimate of the value of a firm's past and expected capital investment projects. The fundamental concept behind both EVA and MVA is that companies are supposed to take in capital from investors and make it worth more.

5. A management information system can provide managers with the information they need to monitor organisational performance and to control organisational activities. Without information, they would find it difficult to measure actual performance, compare actual performance against the performance standards, or develop appropriate courses of action if there are significant deviations between actual and standard.
6. The balanced scorecard is a performance measurement tool that looks at four areas—financial, customer, internal processes, and people/innovation/growth assets—that contribute to a company's performance. According to this approach, managers should develop goals in each of the four areas and measures to determine if these goals are being met.
7. Benchmarking of best practices can be used for monitoring and measuring organisational performance because it can identify specific performance gaps and potential areas of improvement.
8. In their role of helping organisations achieve high levels of performance, managers have certain responsibilities including helping organisational members make the right choices during periods of organisational change, designing a performance management system that identifies appropriate performance measures and addresses common performance measurement problems, and creating an atmosphere in which employees turn ideas into action.

Box 2

Measuring Accountability

It is very important for NGOs to be accountable and during our restructuring programme we took a long hard look at ourselves. We arrived at a system of metrics, prepared our *own accountability chart and scored ourselves* (Exhibit 1). While we have scored well on getting citizens interested, putting processes and tools in place and for getting the system to accept citizen participation, we have still a long way to go on creating a visible change and in scaling our model. We do not have the wherewithal to scale.

We are in the process of *tackling the critical issues* that emerged during the restructuring programme. We decided not to be defined as a movement but rather as the Janaagraha Centre for Citizenship and Democracy (JCCD). Within the purview of citizenship and democracy, our activities fall into four kinds of programmes—core programmes, leadership programmes, partner programmes and resource.

EXHIBIT I

Restructuring—Measuring Ourselves

No explicit measurement at institutional level

Area	Assessment	Score
Getting citizens interested	Reasonable record. Good responses to various campaigns	6/10
Getting the poor interested	Difficult process; no consistent effort	2/10
Giving them the tools	The material is there; needs to be organized into a pedagogy	5/10
Getting the system to respond	Partial success; better than most civil society records	4/10
Creating visible change	Minimal; more attitudinal change than outcomes	3/10
Making this process irreversible	Asking for laws on citizen participation	5/10
Scaling this across other locations	Anecdotal experiences; no capacity to do this	1/10

Box 3

Views of Management Guru on Performance

Performance is the ultimate test of any institution. Every non-profit institution exists for the sake of performance in changing people and society. Yet, performance is also one of the truly difficult areas for the executive in the non-profit institution.

I'm always being asked what the differences are between business and non-profit institutions. There are few, but they are important. Perhaps the most important *is in the performance area*. Businesses usually define performance too narrowly-as the financial bottom line. If that's all you have as a performance measurement and performance goal in the business, you are not likely to do well or survive very long. It's too narrow. But it's very specific and concrete. You don't have to argue about whether we are doing better because results within terms of profitability or market standing or innovation or cash flow are easily quantifiable and very hard to ignore.

In a non-profit organisation, there is no such bottom line. But there is also a temptation to downplay results. There is the temptation to say: We are serving in a good cause. We are doing the Lord's work. Or we are doing something to make life a little better for people and that's a result in itself. *That is not enough*. If a business wastes its resources on non-results, by and large it loses its own money. In a non-profit institution, though, somebody else's money—the donors' money. Service organisations are accountable to donors, accountable for putting the money where the results are, and for performance. So, this is an area that needs special emphasis for non-profit executives. Good intentions only pave the way to Hell.

Nonetheless, non-profit institutions find it very hard to answer the question: What, then, are in our institution? It can be done, however. Indeed, results can even be quantified.

There are different kinds of results. First, you have immediate results. Then, you have the long-term job of building on those first results. Maybe it's not easy to define precisely what results you have, but it's got to be done in such a way that one can ask: "Are we getting better? Are we improving?" And: "Do we put our resources where the results are?"

We need to remind ourselves again and again that the results of a non-profit institution are always outside the organisation, not inside. Results for the Salvation Army are among the alcoholics and the prostitutes and the hungry. Results for the school teacher are kids who learn.

There is also, I am sure, joy over the right allocation of resources to the mission, to the goals, to results. And the Jesuits long ago stopped wasting brilliant members of their order on hopes.

One starts with the mission, and that is exceedingly important. What do you want to be remembered for as an organisation—but also as an individual? The mission is something that transcends today, but guides today, informs today. The moment we lose sight of the mission, we begin to stray, we waste resources. From the mission, one goes to very concrete goals.

Only when a non-profit's key performance areas are defined can it really set goals. Only then can the non-profit ask: "Are we doing what we are supposed to be doing? Is it still the right activity? Does it still serve a need?" And, above all, "Do we still produce results that are sufficiently outstanding, sufficiently different for us to justify putting our talents to use in that area?" Then, you can do the next important thing, which is every so often to ask: "Are we still in the right areas? Should we change? Should we abandon?"

Results are achieved, too, by concentration, not by splintering. That enormous organisation the Salvation Army concentrates on only four or five programmes. Its executives have the courage to say, "This is not for us. Other people do it better." Or, "This is not really what we are good at." Or, "This is not where we can make the greatest contribution. It does not really fit the strength we have. One of the most important things for a non-profit executive to be able to acknowledge is that we are not competent; we can only do harm. Need alone does not justify our moving in. We must match our strength, our mission, our concentration, our value."

Good intentions, good policies, good decisions must turn into effective actions. Work is only done when it's done. Done by people. By people with a deadline. By people who are trained. By people who are monitored and evaluated. By people who hold themselves responsible for results.

The ultimate question, which I think people in the non-profit organisation should ask again and again and again, both of themselves and of the institution, is: "What should I hold myself accountable for by way of contribution and results? What should this institution hold itself accountable for by way of contribution and results? What should both this institution and I be remembered for?"

Source: Peter F. Drucker, Managing the Non-profit Organisation, Harper-Collins Publishers, New York.

CHAPTER

27

A Model for Performance Assessment of NGOs

In this chapter following aspects of a 'model' for performance assessment of NGOs are covered:

1. Introduction.
2. Need for performance assessment of NGOs.
3. NGO map model for performance Assessment.
4. Applicability of the model.
5. To sum up.

1. INTRODUCTION

Non-government sector or not-for-profit sector plays a pivotal role in the society along with government and corporate sector. The need for evaluating the performance of NGOs has been felt both by the donors and the organisations themselves. NGOs have mushroomed in India during the past few years. An NGO which is small in size but working effectively and efficiently is better than a bigger NGO which is not so effective and efficient.

NGOs are doing a great service for the society. The irony is that both the sides of the gap i.e., the government and the corporate sector are liable, answerable to the people, stakeholders and society at large. But the most important link between the two i.e., the NGO sector surprisingly is not very answerable, transparent and there are hardly any measures to evaluate their performance (both efficiency and effectiveness). Just because they (NGOs) work for the society, makes them rather more responsible and credible towards the society.

2. NEED FOR PERFORMANCE ASSESSMENT OF NGOs

The need for performance assessments is increased due to following reasons:

- Lack of time to think about some strategy. Further they do not see any incentive to grow.
- Donors have difficulty in identifying and rewarding the most successful NGO.
- Absence of clear performance measures to know how effective they are.
- *Mushrooming of similar NGOs*: In recent years as many as 30,000 new non-profit organisations have been created annually worldwide. Small organisations can no doubt provide services to local needs and allow individual social entrepreneurs to try innovative approaches, but the non-profit sector as a whole would benefit from consolidation.
- Increasingly funding agencies and donors are requesting non-profits to better measure the impact of their work.

There is a need for a tool, which can assess the performance of an NGO. Although there are few models already existing to measure the performance for example, foreign aid model, CAMEL, PEARLS, UTI credibility forum, etc. but none of them is standardized like there is the CRISIL Ratings in the corporate sector. Also models like Camel and Pearl are meant only for micro-finance institutions and credit unions respectively.

3. NGO-MAP MODEL FOR PERFORMANCE ASSESSMENT

Model "NGO-MAP" attempts to capture both efficiency and effectiveness of NGOs through some broad indicators. The basic structure of the NGO-MAP is shown in Figure 1. Each of the four main indicators is further divided into sub-parameters and these sub-parameters again have some details within them (not shown in the diagram).

FIGURE I

Details of the Main Indicators and their Sub-parameters

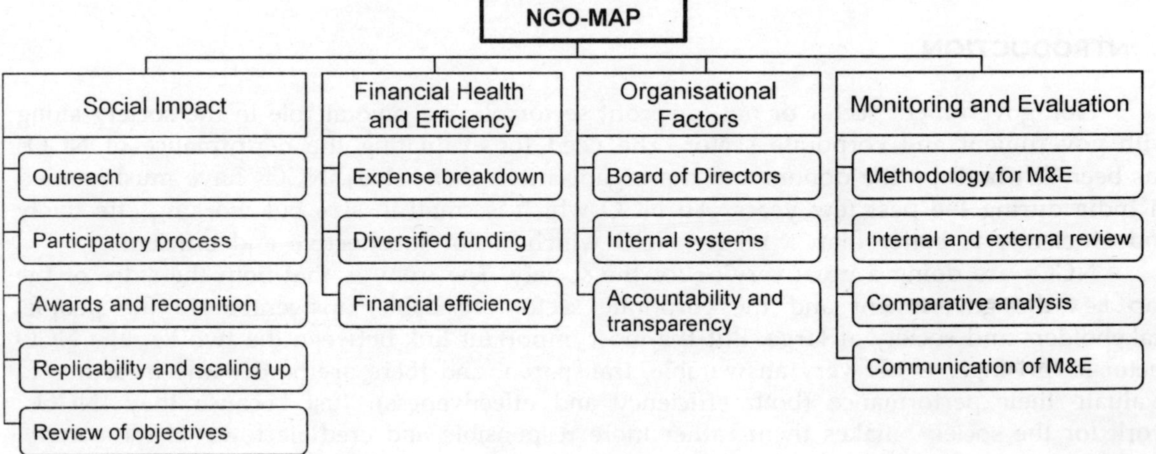

3.1. Main Indicators

NGO-MAP has four broad indicators, which attempt to capture the overall performance of an NGO. These indicators and their weights are as follows:

(a) Social Impact (25%)

This parameter measures the impact, which the programmes run by the organisation, have on its beneficiaries. The goals or objectives which were set for a particular community or an area have been achieved or not, how participatory are the programmes, how many lives directly or indirectly are touched by the NGO, etc., are all measured under this indicator.

(b) Financial Health and Efficiency (25%)

Be it a corporate or government or even an NGO measuring how well the organisation is doing financially is very important. This indicator measures the financial health of NGO by measuring expense breakdown, how diversified are the funding sources, how much is the financial efficiency and transparency of financial results, etc.

(c) Organisational Factors (30%)

The factors which are crucial from the organisational point of view like the structure and membership of board of directors, how efficient is the internal working of the organisation, how much transparency is there in overall working of the organisation and so on, form the metrics under this indicator.

(d) Monitoring and Evaluation (20%)

After a programme or project is implemented how is the monitoring of that programme done, data collection is properly done and documented or not, how many times internal and external review of the programme is carried out, before implementing same programme a study of similar programmes by other NGO should be done and better points should be implemented, etc. This indicator has been given a lesser weightage than other indicators because monitoring and evaluation is dependent on other three indicators. This may not be an independent indicator.

3.2 Working of the Model

Once the information regarding the different parameters of the model is collected from the NGOs through e-mail, personal interviews, etc. it is entered in an excel sheet with the help of a Manual created to make the data-entry convenient. The excel sheet has same calculations and equations which automatically generates a score for a particular parameter in a scale of 0-3. This score is then multiplied by the weights that have been assigned to each parameter depending on its importance and relevance to the model. This is repeated for all the parameters and then they are added to compute an Overall Composite Score out of the total score of 500.

4. APPLICABILITY OF THE MODEL

The NGO-MAP model can be applied to assess the performance and effectiveness of an NGO. However, while applying the model to real life NGOs, following characteristics may please be kept in mind:

- The model is meant for assessment of own performance of an NGO. Such assessment can then be utilized for comparing the performance in subsequent periods/years.
- The model may also be applied to such NGOs who have more than one activity domain e.g., primary education, healthcare, sanitation, etc.
- The Model is not meant for rank ordering of different NGOs.
- It is simple and can be adaptable to various sectors of NGOs. It is computer-based.

5. TO SUM UP

The NGO-MAP is meant to evaluate the performance of an NGO, i.e., the efficiency and effectiveness for better governance. The four broad indicators form the pillars of the model covering most of the crucial aspects essential to evaluate an NGOs performance. It can also be used as a self-assessing tool by the NGOs to evaluate their own performance.

Reference

This NGO-MAP, Performance Assessment Model for NGOs is by Harash Bhargava and Maneet Chandok. This an abstract of an article in *ICFAI Journal of Corporate Governance*, July 2005. Gratefully acknowledged.

CHAPTER

28

Mutual Expectations: Society and Organisations

In this chapter we have discussed following aspects:

1. Concept of corporate social responsibility and current concerns.
2. Linkage of organisation and society.
3. Managing stakeholders' interest.
4. Mutual expectations—society and the organisation.
5. Emerging indications.

I. CONCEPT OF CORPORATE SOCIAL RESPONSIBILITY AND CURRENT CONCERNS

The concept of corporate social responsibility is not new; its origin can be traced back to the evolution of the concept of 'welfare state'. Corporate social responsibility is concerned with the impact of the company's actions on society. Social responsiveness is the ability of a corporation to relate its operations and policies to the social environment in ways that are mutually beneficial to the company and society. According to Keith Davis, the term 'social responsibility' refers to two types of business obligations viz.:

(i) The socio-economic obligation, to see that the economic consequences of its actions do not adversely affect public welfare.

(ii) The socio-human obligation of every business is to nurture and develop human values such as morale, cooperation, motivation and self-realization in work.

Peter F. Drucker (1998) is of the view that 'an enterprise is an organ of society and that its actions have a decisive impact on the social scene. Business must consider the impact of every business policy and business actions upon society'.

The importance of the external environment and the influence of stakeholders have been increased by the social issues and problems, giving rise to the demands for high levels of appropriate social responsibility. The debate as the role of business in society has created an agenda of social problems that includes environmental pollution, equal employment opportunity for women and minority workers, consumer safety and many other concerns reflecting the moral and social aims of stakeholders (Stoner, J.A.F. & Wankel Clares, 1987).

"A business is only a sub-organisation of the society. The society is the largest possible kind of organisation with goals of production, distribution and harmonizing individual relationships. If the organisational aims part runs contrary to those of society, the organisation part will die out sooner or later. Therefore, we need managers who don't think only in terms of business and organisations but also of social welfare. Towards this end, we require managers with social concern, social awareness/responsibility.

Current concerns

In recent years, corporate social responsibility (CSR) has become one of the top boardroom agenda and gained more visibility as the regulatory pressure, strong advocacy from NGOs and the pressure from collective movement have put companies firmly on the defensive front just to think holistically that the business of business is not just business. And at some forum, policy-makers are even going further to discuss that profit at what cost-end of living and beginning of business. This stimulates intellectual debates so as to understand different approaches and modes of business operations in a society at large. In this context, the two most talked about approaches of business social responsibility, are:

(a) Corporate philanthropy (CP).
(b) Social responsibility.

As the corporate philanthropy (CP) is concerned with the improvement of the competitive context—benefiting both the company and society whereas social responsibility, the integration of "social and environmental concerns in the daily operations and interactions with the stakeholders on a voluntary basis".

Recent surveys confirm that the correlation between the social and financial performance is either positive or neutral (Margolis and Walsh, 2003). This negates the very statement of Fredman, i.e. any kind of social initiative will affect profits negatively. Nevertheless, one central question is raised on how the relationship between business society can be made more symbiotic, each contributing and harvesting benefits from the development of the other. The business environment of the present scenario is becoming more volatile, and the challenges of change are becoming more turbulent. Thus, directly or indirectly business organisations started realizing the need to become more caring and contributing to society.

2. LINKAGE OF ORGANISATION AND SOCIETY

(a) Organisation

Organisation as an association of the employees excluding the owner of the organisation. An organisation is made up of people. It is said that the organisation makes the people, and people make the organisation. Existence of the individuals comes to a standstill without organisation.

(b) Characteristics of a Good Organisation

Following are the characteristics of a good organisation:

- It should be well structured.
- It should have common objectives.
- It has its own mission.
- It has its own long-term plan.
- Maximum welfare of everyone.
- It has responsibility towards society.
- Innovative approach.

Apart from the organisation's objectives, responsibility towards society should be taken as one of the prominent characteristics. No organisation can function in isolation, since it is part and parcel of society.

The need for developing a social concept and a social framework for guiding economic activity has been reinforced as a result of the adoption of economic planning for the nation as a whole.

(c) Organisation and Society

Organisation and society has a gap in its goal and structure, but organisation and society are linked to some extent forming a network of structure. The person from any organisation can be a part of a society. But the same person working in organisation has to perform different role which he usually performs in society. If at all the persons who works in the organisation can contribute to the welfare of society by implementing new method and techniques, the society can be totally revolutionized. It is every organisation, which contributes for the society, and it is the society, which produce the efficient person for the organisation.

Responsibility towards society is one of the important attributes of professionalism. There should be co-ordination between the organisation and the society. The relationship between organisation and society is interwoven. Multiple relationships exist between the members of the organisation and the society of course the organisation is the inseparable part of the society. Organisation should behave as the guardian for the society.

Customers are the best judges for the assessment of the organisation. They can give the best feedback to the organisation. So, SWOT analysis is the trusted way to know about the current status about the image of the organisation and certainly it will help in building its image for further development.

3. MANAGING STAKEHOLDER'S INTEREST

An organisation must carefully balance the claims of its stakeholders when choosing criteria for evaluating its performance. However, the interest of managers and shareholders are most commonly used to give direction to the organisation activities because satisfying those stakeholders has the greatest effect on the survival and prosperity of the organisation. If the satisfaction of managerial and shareholder interests is the organisation's ultimate goal, then satisfying the interest of customers, employees, the govenment and other stakeholders can be seen as the means of reaching that goal. Although high quality products and services at treasonable prices may be the criteria that customers use to evaluate the organisation and thus are goals from the customer's perspective. From the manager's perspective customer satisfaction and customer revenues become the means of maximising long-term organisational profitability and sustainability.

4. MUTUAL EXPECTATIONS—SOCIETY AND THE ORGANISATION

4.1 Society's expectations from the organisation

Society expects following benefits from the organisation:

(i) Quality products at reasonable prices.
(ii) Health Services.
(iii) Educational Services.
(iv) Sports Facilities.
(v) Recreational Facilities.
(vi) Better customer Services
(vii) Fast Emergency Services like Fire, Police, and Ambulance.
(viii) Efficient Postal Services.
(ix) High Speed Communication Facilities.
(x) Various Mass-media Facilities.
(vi) Entertainment & Fun Facilities like Cinemas, Exhibition, Playing Parks for Childrens.
(xii) Tourism facilities.
(xiii) Good Judicial departments.

Apart from the above services, the organisation should adopt the villages for their alround development.

4.2 Organisation's expectations from society

(a) Organisation expects better academic potential from the individuals in the society.
(b) Organisation expects the people to avail the facilities provided to them by the organisation.
(c) Organisation should expect that the society should suggest the ways and measures for the improvement of the organisation, e.g.,
  - Brand Suggestion competition.
  - Slogan competitions.
  - Trade Marks suggestion competition.
  - Advertisement copy competition, etc.

(d) It expects healthy feedback from the society related to their product or services.
(e) To help the organisation to keep the environment conducive.

5. EMERGING INDICATIONS

There is emerging pattern of paradigm shift and its concomitant influence in CSR. This paradigm shift in CSR is explained in Figure 1.

FIGURE I

Emerging Pattern of Paradigm Shift and its Concomitant Influence in CSR

CSR Now	*A Paradigm Shift*
1. **Commitment**: Superficial and marginal towards the society. Short-term commitment.	Moderate and symbiotic. Long-term commitment.
2. **Concern**: Shows concerns and responsiveness to complaints to build the corporate image and property. Lukewarm concern on social or environmental progress. (voluntary obligations to maintain their license to operate)	Pro-responsiveness, prevention is better than cause and address. The chief concern will be to collaborate and create niches in certain areas of CSR- corporate citizenship through knowledge and relationship.
3. **CSR Strategy**: Not much.	Deep concern to improve social and environmental conditions.
4. **Structure of the organisation**: Structure supporting profit through production.	Sustainable development, sustainable consumption, and intergenerational equity.
5. **Corporate move**: The primary emphasis of this move is on economic performance—profit is on end in itself. Companies' involvement in philanthropic activities with a motive of doing good to get good in terms of business development and reputation.	Structure supporting profit through societal involvement and development in consortium with NGOs.
6. **NGO's Partnership**: Remains primarily with business houses.	Corporate indulgence will look forward to achieve full integration—jointly of social and environmental concern. Economic profit will be a means to an end. NGO's Partnership with business houses will be secondary. Corporates will be stretching their hands for meaningful partnership with NGOs or network of NGOs to bridge the gap between community and corporates.
7. **Investment**: Capital investment.	Socially responsible investment. In the future more investors and analysts would integrate social and environmental criterion into their financial assessment. Thus, a sustainable investment will be encouraged between company and stockholders to stimulate large scale societal change.
8. **Recruitment conditions**: Skill and knowledge-based.	CSR-based, skill and knowledge will not be adequate. Emphasis will be on value creation, not just a value preservation.

9. **Business education**: Focused on fast creation of wealth and resource consumption to address social responsibility.	Focused on understanding, CSR issues related to business management. CSR issues gradually will be finding place in the heart of business theory and practice. Enterprise success will be walking hand in hand with ethics and social responsibility.
10. **Ethical adherence**: (Shallow) Social and cultural and environment are primordial to humans, biophysical environment is not.	Deep ecological consideration will find important place in overall functioning of CSR.

(1) In India we find many public and private sector organisations. In both the types some organisations are growing fast and many have come to closure. If we critically analyze these organisations then we come to know that the sinking organisation and their sound policies and programmemes but they lack in the responsibility for the society.

(2) Organisation should always think that it is a part and parcel of the society it should try to meet society's expectations. Similarly, it is the responsibility of society to co-operate with the organisation. Consumers, which are a very important part of society, should also be aware about the rights and duties of the consumers.

The companies TISCO, HLL and WIPRO integrate CSR into their own strategic planning. They engage in a host of improvement initiatives, from school education to income generation to public health (Sinha and Mohanty, 2004), thus slowly shifting the business strength from short-term 'Fancy-Philanthropy' to deep involvement and capacity building at the bottom of the pyramid (Prahalad, 2004).

Let us take the example from the western world and its changing demographic trends. Most of the mega cities in the western part of the world have a multicultural society, aging population, a decline trend in birth-rates and increase in youngster population of ethnic minorities. Thus, the people of ethnic minority communities are going to make a significant percentage of future employees in most of the organisations there. Managing a diverse work culture will be having its own complex questions *vis-a-vis* corporate social responsibility.

Thus companies will require deep knowledge of both market and society where they will be operating, because the race will be that of the "yolk and shell" kind of reward-companies that innovate fast and reap the benefit as early birds.

Thus, corporate have to rethink about western emulation and way of doing business. The wisdom lies not in "more" and "faster" (Senge, 1998) way of innovation and technological breakthrough rather in minimizing the gap between quality of life and speed of technology. Thus, business organisations will have to acquire fundamentally new capabilities for understanding and dealing with this complexity.

To conclude, the purpose of CSR is to have a better society to give business a new filip and a new way to innovate. Society's recommendation is the most important asset of any organisation.

PART VI

ENVIRONMENT CONTEXT

CHAPTER

29

Corporate Social Responsibility and Leadership

Corporate Social Responsibility (CSR) has become topic of worldwide importance in present times. This has become top concern at International Business community level. Social responsibility is not new to our country. In olden days, whenever famine, floods, etc., occurred leading business of area would provide food and other assistance to needy.

As Mc Williams & Siegel have said, "Corporate Social Responsibility are actions above and beyond that required by law." The voluntary actions of the companies for the benefit of the community is what CSR is about. CSR is designed to deliver sustainable value not only to the shareholders but also to the society at large.

We shall discuss this vital topic under broad headings to promote understanding of CSR issues:

1. External Environment affects business.
2. Corporate Social Responsibility (CSR): Meaning and Importance.
3. Arguments for and against CSR.
4. Corporate Social Responsibility towards various interest groups.
5. Role of Leadership.
6. Trend towards measuring social responsibilities, focusing on what to measure? and how to measure?
7. To sum up.

1. EXTERNAL ENVIRONMENT AFFECTS BUSINESS

Since organisations are affected by changes in the external environment, managers must understand the nature of this environment. (Figure 1)

FIGURE I

External Environment of an Organisation

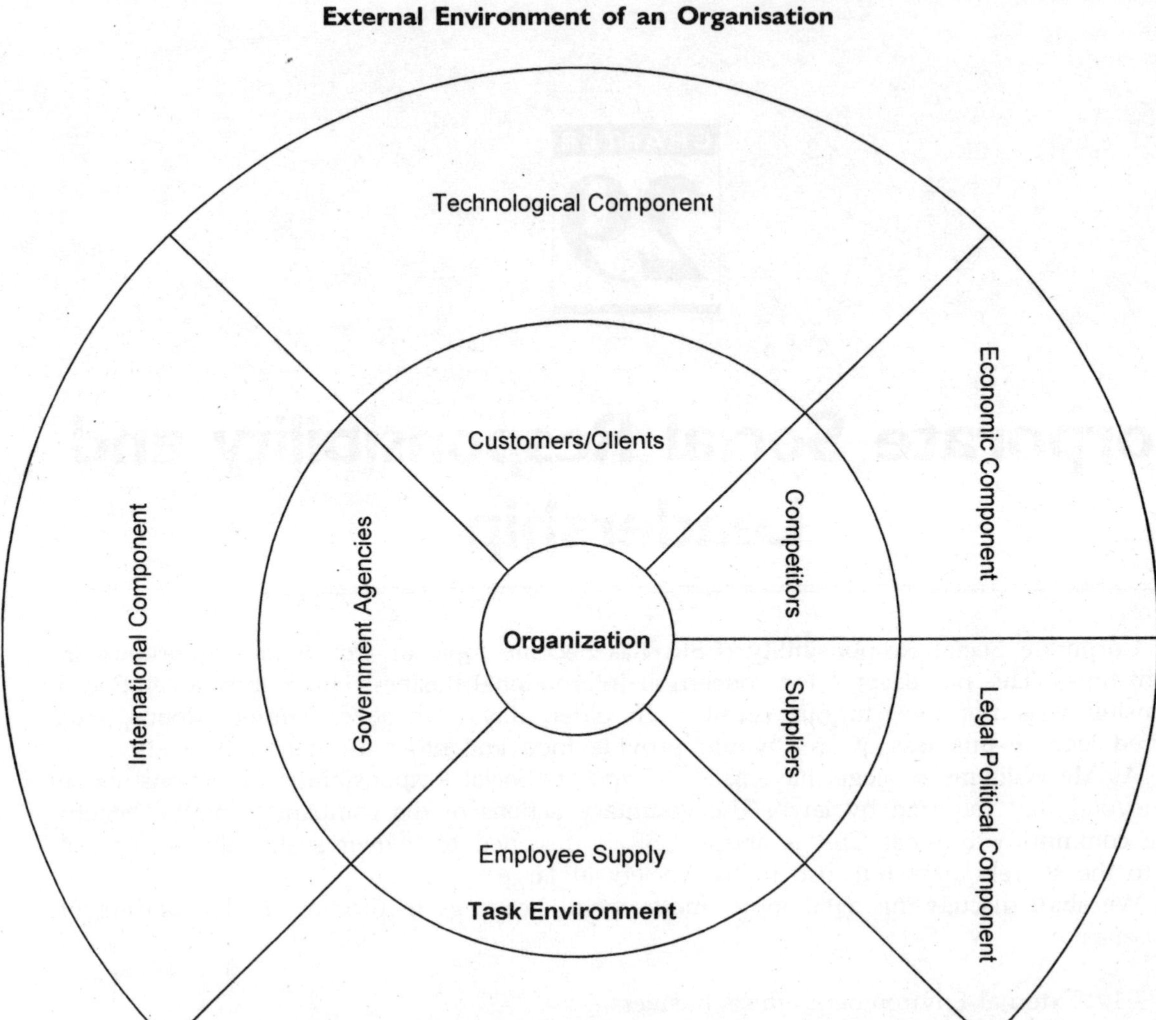

The external environment of an organisation consists of the mega environment and the task environment as shown in Figure 1. The mega environment reflects the major trends in the societies within which the organisation operates. These societies have the following components: technological, economic, socio-cultural, and international. The task environment consists of specific external elements with which an organisation interacts while conducting its business. These include customers and clients, competitors, suppliers, labour supply and government agencies. The task environment, which depends largely on the products and services offered by the firm and its business location, may vary from firm to firm. While a firm may not be able to directly influence its mega environment, it can certainly influence its task environment.

Working within a large and complex external environment affects a business in terms of its social responsibility, its social responsiveness and role of leadership. The Operational Definition of Corporate Social Responsibility is:

> Corporate Social Responsibility contends that management is responsible to the organisation itself and to all the interest groups with which it interacts. Other interest groups such as workers, customers, creditors, suppliers, government and society in general are placed essentially equal with shareholders.

2. CORPORATE SOCIAL RESPONSIBILITY—MEANING AND IMPORTANCE

In the early 20th century, business firms were predominantly concerned with maximizing their profits. In the 1950s, social activists began to question business enterprises' singular objective, of profit maximization. They argued that since business derive their existence from society, they have some obligations towards it. The concept of social responsibility became popular after the publication of Howard R. Bowen's Social Responsibilities of Business. Bowen argued that business enterprises should consider the impact of their decisions on society.

Corporate Social Responsibility has its origin in USA about seven decades ago. It is an obligation of decision-makers to take actions which protect and improve the welfare of society as a whole along with their own interests. Such decisions may affect environment, consumers and community. It was Peter Drucker who later emphatically argued that management should assume social responsibility. Management should consider the impact of every business policy and action upon society. It has to consider the actions that are likely to promote the public good and to advance the basic beliefs of society, and to contribute to its stability, strength and harmony. He laid emphasis on "Quality of product and customer service."

Later on Sandra Holmes in her study of 540 top executives emphasized that in addition to making profit, business should help solve special problems whether or not business creates these problems.

Companies operating in globalised markets are increasingly required to balance the financial and economic considerations of their business with social, community and environmental aspects as well, while building shareholder value.

The socially responsible business is attracting some of the best business minds, as numerous initiatives seek to identify the issues and create the tools to implement programmes at the company level. For different industries, responsible business practice involves different-issues.

According to the CSR Survey 2002 (India), Report, Indian companies see corporate social responsibility as central to corporate action, with "excessive philanthropy" no longer a sufficient response to rising expectations of the society. The above mentioned report surveyed 102 Indian companies and was conducted jointly by the United Nations

Development Programme, the British Council, Confederation of Indian Industry and Pricewaterhouse Coopers. The report found that the most important driver for involvement in CSR within Indian industry was the desire to be a good corporate citizen, linked to company as well as Product/brand reputation. Improved ties with local communities was also seen as a strong factor. (Box 1)

Box I

Corporate Social Responsibility in the Indian IT Sector

Corporate social responsibility (CSR) has become the buzz word among companies in the Information technology sector. Corporate Social Responsibility denotes the commitment of organisations to uphold the interests of direct stakeholders and also behave in an environmentally and economically responsible manner. Many Indian IT firms have realized the important role of corporate social responsibility in improving a company's image. They have donated a sizable chunk of their profits for the betterment of the society. Notable among them are Polaris Software Labs, NIIT, and Satyam Infoway (Sify).

IT firms are recognizing the importance of being good corporate citizens as it not only enhances their public image but also helps them, to create a cordial relationship with society.

3. ARGUMENTS FOR AND AGAINST CORPORATE SOCIAL RESPONSIBILITY

Today, many organisations are involved in social activities. Since the expectations of the society have changed, organisations have become more aware of their social responsibilities. A careful analysis of arguments for and against time involvement of organisations in social welfare is necessary to determine whether an organisation should implement social initiatives.

Arguments for Social Responsibilities of Business

(i) Change in Public Expectations

The needs of today's consumers have changed, resulting in a change in their expectations of businesses. Since businesses owe their profits to society, they have to therefore respond to the needs of society.

(ii) Business is a Part of Society

Society and business are benefited when there is a symbiotic relationship between the two. Society gains through economic development and the provision of employment opportunities and business benefits through the workforce and consumers provided by society.

(iii) Avoiding Intervention by Government

By being socially responsible, organisations attract less attention from regulatory agencies. This gives them greater freedom and flexibility in their operations.

(iv) Balance of Responsibility and Power

Businesses have considerable power and authority. The exercise of this power should be accompanied by a corresponding amount of responsibility.

(v) Impact of internal activities of the organisation on the external environment

Most firms are open systems, i.e., they interact with the external environment. The internal activities of such firms have an impact on the external environment. To avoid a negative impact on the external environment, firms should be socially responsible.

(vi) Protecting shareholder interests

By being socially involved, a company can improve its image and thus protect its shareholders' interests.

(vii) New avenues to create profits

Social responsibility involves the conservation of natural resources. Conservation can be beneficial for firms. Items that had been considered waste earlier (for example, empty soft drink cans) can be recycled and profitably used again.

(viii) Favourable public image

Through social involvement, a firm can create a favourable public image for itself and endear itself to society. By so doing, a firm can attract customers, employees, and investors.

(ix) Endeavor to find new solutions

Businesses have a history of coming up with innovative ideas. Therefore, they are likely to come up with solutions for social problems, which other institutions were unable to tackle.

(x) Best use of resources of a business

Businesses should make optimum use of the skills amid talent of its managerial personnel as well as its capital resources to produce good quality products and services. By so doing, the business will be able to fulfil their obligations toward society.

(xi) Prevention is better than cure

It is in the interests of business organisations to prevent social problems. Instead of allowing large-scale unemployment to lead to social interest (which will harm business interests), businesses can be sources of employment for eligible youth.

Arguments against Social Responsibility of Business

(a) Opposes the principle of profit maximization

The main motive of a business is profit maximization. Social involvement may not be economically viable for a business.

(b) Excessive costs

When a business incurs excessive costs for social involvement, it passes the cost on to its customers in the form of higher prices. Society, therefore, has to bear the burden of the social involvement of business by paying higher prices for its products and services.

(c) Weakened international balance of payments

A weakened international balance of payments situation may be created by the social involvement of organisations. Since the cost of social initiatives would be added to the price of the products, the multinational companies selling in international markets would be at a disadvantage when competing with domestic companies which may not be involved in social activities.

(d) Increase in the firm's power and influence

Businesses are inherently equipped within a certain amount of power. Their involvement in social activities can lead to an increase in their power and influence. Such influence and power may corrupt them.

(e) Lack of necessary skills among business people

Business people do not possess the necessary skill to handle the problems of society. Their expertise and knowledge may not be relevant to deal with social problems.

(f) Lack of accountability to society

Until a proper mechanism to establish the accountability of business is developed, they should not get involved in social activities.

(g) Lack of consensus on social involvement

There is no agreement regarding the type of socially responsible actions that a business should undertake.

Considering the above arguments for and against social responsibilities of business, it can be stated:

> Business depends on society for the needed inputs like money, men and skills, business also depends on society for market where products may be sold, thus, business depends on society for existence, substance and encouragement, and being so much dependent, business has definite responsibility towards society.
> IBM's corporate citizenship report rightly sums up its perspective on philanthropic activities, "it is not just good deeds, it's good business."

4. CORPORATE SOCIAL RESPONSIBILITY TOWARDS VARIOUS INTEREST GROUPS

Managers who are concerned about social responsibility need to identify various interest groups which may influence the functioning of a firm and which, in turn, may be affected by the firm's decisions. Business enterprises are primarily accountable to six major interest groups: (a) shareholders, (b) employees, (c) customers, (d) creditors and suppliers, (e) society, and (f) government. These groups are also known social stakeholders.

(a) Shareholders

The primary responsibility of a business is to protect the interests of its shareholders. The shareholders provide the core resource—the capital—that enables an organisation to operate and grow. They expect the management to use the capital judiciously and operate the business in a way that ensures a good return on their investment, both through dividends and through increase in stock value. Shareholders should be provided with adequate and timely information about the functioning of the organisation.

(b) Employees

Employees are an organisation's biggest asset. Traditionally, managers regarded employees only as factors of production and denied them their rightful share in the distribution of income. However, in the present times, it is mandatory for business firms to protect the interests of their employees. Laws and government regulations now define the responsibilities of the employer: ensuring equal employment for men and women, offering pensions and other retirement benefits, and providing a safe and healthy work environment. To protect the interests of employees, management must:

(i) Develop administrative processes that promote cooperation between employers and employees.
(ii) Foster a harmonious work atmosphere by adopting a progressive labour policy. This includes allowing the participation of workers in management, creating a sense of involvement, and improving the working conditions and living standards of workers.
(iii) Provide fair wages and other financial benefits to workers to keep them motivated.

(c) Customers

In recent years, customers have received great attention. Firms have begun to realize the importance of keeping customers happy. Moreover, the growth of consumerism has made firms more aware of their duties towards consumers. Business firms can fulfil their obligations to their customers by:

(i) Charging reasonable prices for their products.
(ii) Ensuring the provision of standardized and quality goods and services.
(iii) Ensuring the easy availability of goods and services, so that customers do not have to spend too much time and energy in procuring them.
(iv) Abstaining from unethical practices like hoarding, profiteering or creating artificial scarcity.
(v) Refraining from deceiving customers by making false or misleading claims.

(d) Creditors and Suppliers

Creditors and suppliers are responsible for providing inputs for production process in the form of raw materials and capital. Management is responsible for fulfiling its obligations to its creditors and suppliers. This can be done by:

(i) Creating a long-term and healthy business relationship with them.
(ii) Making prompt payments to creditors and suppliers
(iii) Providing them with accurate, relevant and needed information.

(e) Society

Organisations function within a social system and draw their resources from this system. Therefore, they have certain obligations towards society. The management of business organisations can fulfil their obligations toward society by preserving and enhancing the well-being of the members of society. Management can do so in the following ways:

(i) Using its technical expertise to solve local problems.

(ii) Setting socially desirable standards of living and avoiding unnecessary and wasteful expenditure.

(iii) Playing an important role in civic affairs. Volunteers from some companies help the traffic police regulate traffic at busy intersections. Pizza Corner in Hyderabad is one such company. Many companies also put up road signs along highways to encourage safe driving habits. For example, liquor companies such as Shaw Wallace and United Breweries have put up road signs on mountain roads in India. These road signs caution drivers against driving under the influence of alcohol.

(iv) Providing basic amenities, healthcare and education facilities, thus creating better living conditions. (For example, the Tata group has set-up the Tata Memorial Hospital and Cancer Research Institute and the 'Tata Institute for Social Sciences,' to meet its obligation toward society.)

(v) Establishing development programmes for the benefit of economically weaker sections of society.

(f) Government

The government of a country provides the basic facilities required for the survival and growth of businesses. The government monitors and, to a certain extent, controls the business systems of the country. Most of the controls imposed by the government are in the best interests of businesses. To fulfil its obligations to the government, the management of business organisations should:

(i) Be law-abiding.

(ii) Pay taxes and other duties fully, timely and honestly.

(iii) Not bribe government servants to obtain favours for the company.

(iv) Not try to use political influence in its favour.

5. ROLE OF LEADERSHIP

A company is limited closely to the communities in which it operates locally, nationally or globally. It cannot exist in isolation.

—*Sir Richard Skyes*, Chairman, Glaxo Wellcome
At Glaxo Smith Kline Pharmaceuticals Limited, India

Throughout history the difference between success and failure, whether in a war, a business or non-profit organisation or games has been attributed to leadership. In fact towering personalities make real difference such as J.R.D. Tata, Bill Gates, Mahatma Gandhi, Mother Teresa, Obroi, Naryanamurthy and many more. Leaders with transformational style are people-oriented, visionary, passionate, creative, inspirational, imaginative, independent, courageous and experimental. They are super leaders who show others how to lead themselves. Such leaders have knowledge of constituents needs and have an instinct for how to service them in a way that they will consider effective. These leaders practice personal values, voice passion in their social work and are creative agents of change. Thus, right leadership with integrity, honesty, commitment to social values are vital for social responsibility of business.

For example, J.R.D. Tata, an outstanding entrepreneur had contributed towards various social causes such as funding in population control, establishing cancer institute in 1941, employee welfare schemes which were later adopted as statutory requirement, corporate governance, etc. He was epitome of achievement of CSR and business ethics in Indian industry. Likewise, Microsoft Founder, Bill Gates has donated more money to charity than anyone in history and is regarded as good corporate citizen on various counts. Recently on 01.11.05 lie donated $ 258 million to fight malaria disease and earlier gave huge sum for AIDS cure. Similarly Hindustan Lever Chairman, M.S. Bhanga in his address at CII leadership summit on September 18, 2002 highlighted his organisation's role in fulfiling its Corporate Social Responsibilities which make impact on social development of community.

6. TREND TOWARDS MEASURING SOCIAL RESPONSIBILITIES

According to Keith Davis and William C. Frederick, social responsiveness (SR) is "the ability of a corporation to relate its operations and policies to the social environment in ways that are mutually beneficial to the company and to society." In other words, it refers to the development of organisational decision processes that enable managers to anticipate, respond to and manage the areas of social responsibility. Though the term 'social responsiveness' is generally applied to business organisations, it is also applicable to not-for-profit organisations.

What should be Measured?

Many attempts have been made to measure social responsiveness. Some companies establish special committees to evaluate their social responsiveness. What should be measured when measuring social responsiveness? The various categories for measuring the social responsiveness of organisations are discussed below (these can vary depending on the industry or company):

(i) Contributions

Companies make direct financial contributions to charitable and civic projects. The Hyundai Motor Company donated $ 5,00,000 for public education in Montgomery, Alabama where it plans to build its new $1 billion plant. Many companies made financial contributions towards relief and rehabilitation work after Gujarat earthquake (January 2001). Infosys foundation, set-up by Infosys, provides financial assistance to war widows.

(ii) Fund-raising

This involves fund-raising for a social cause, either by the organisation itself or by assisting voluntary social organisations in fund-raising. McDonald's raised an approximate $15-20 million in a day during its first ever World's Children Day fund raising effort on 20 November, 2002. The proceeds of the fund would be used by Ronald McDonald House Charities for children's causes worldwide. In India, newspaper companies such as *The Times of India* and the *Indian Express* participate fund raising campaigns to help people affected by natural disasters. Companies such as Reliance India Ltd. (RIL) and Satyam Infoway (Sify) collected money from all their employees to contribute to the Gujarat Relief Fund.

(iii) Volunteerism

Volunteerism refers to the involvement of employees in civic activities. Boots Company has a volunteering programme called 'Skills for Life,' which gives employees a host of opportunities to get involved in community activities in company time. These include giving career talks; conducting mock interviews; supervising students during their work experience period; sharing business skills with local small businesses; and planting gardens and decorating community centers. Many Indian companies such as Voltas are involved in voluntary activities. The Voltas company, belonging to the Tata group, has adopted ANZA, a school for mentally handicapped children in Mumbai. Volunteers from Voltas provide their support to workshops organised in the school and also help sell the handicrafts produced by the children of this school.

(iv) Recycling

To conserve the environment, materials like plastic, paper, etc. can and should be recycled into useful products. Nike and The National Recycling Coalition have decided to expand their 'Reuse-a-shoe' programme to 25 community centers across the United States. This will allow athletic footwear to be recycled into new products like sports surfaces. In India, companies such as Garware and Indian Organic Chemicals, etc. have worked out an arrangement under which they recycle used Pepsi bottles and generate polyester fibre. This fibre is then used by Garware company in pillows. The recycling efforts of these companies reduce the accumulation of plastic waste in lands.

(v) Valuing Diversity

Companies that value diversity voluntarily take measures to promote equal employment opportunities irrespective of gender, race, religion. In the US, it also involves taking affirmative action. Affirmative action refers to the set of policies and initiatives designed to eliminate past and present discriminations based on race, colour, religion, sex or national origin. Such measures are an attempt on the part of companies to ensure equality in all aspects of employment. In India, some of the companies that have well-developed diversity policies are Hewlett-Packard, Philips Software Mind Tree Consulting, IBM, Motorola, Oracle and Microsoft.

(vi) Direct Corporate Investment

Often, companies make direct investments to provide facilities for a locality or a community. Hewlett-Packard has launched three digital villages across the United States, which will provide local schools, businesses and community technology centers with equipment and training in the latest digital technology. The purpose of these schools, businesses and community technology centers is to offer technological literacy to residents of under-served communities, regardless of their income or educational background.

In India, many companies make direct investments in programmes and projects to meet their social obligations. For example, Oil India Limited (OIL) sets aside a significant sum of money towards community development, development of educational institutions, sports and cultural organisations, building mobile dispensaries and setting up medical camps that offer child and family healthcare services. OIL has also invested in gobar gas plants for rural areas, and tubewells and sanitation services for the economically weaker sections of society. In addition, the company helps universities, colleges and schools develop their facilities. It also supplies them with equipment and books, and awards scholarships to needy and meritorious students.

Box 2

IBM's Commitment to Giving

IBM, not only reacted quickly to the terrorist attacks on September 11, 2001, it continued to help victims even a year after the attack. The company created a database of the bereaved families and invited them for a memorial service making the first anniversary of the attacks.

IBM has shown its commitment to the community by its noble actions. It not only donated money, but also its best resources—IBM-technology and the skill and generosity of its employees—to aid the victims of the attack.

Adapted from "One Year Later. A Commitment To Giving", IBM, <http://www. ibm. com/ibm/ibmgives/news/pedge.shtml>

(vii) Quality of Worklife

Apart from ensuring *fair pay*, the fair *treatment of employees* and *safe working* conditions, many companies respond to *specific employee needs*.

Some Companies in India emphasize the quality of work life are Hewlett-Packard, Smithkline Beecham, American Express, Colgate Palmolive, Gillette, Dr. Reddy's Laboratories, Reliance and Maruti Udyog Limited. HP allows flexible working arrangements for its employees and follows certain innovative practices such as allowing employees to avail leave for special occasions (marriage, exam preparation, adoption of a child, bereavement in the family; and paternity), Smithkline Beecham encourages its employees to balance their work life with their personal life through arrangements such as compressed work week, flexitime amid work from home. Dr. Reddy's Laboratories tries to bring about the overall development of its employees by encouraging their participation in cultural and outdoor activities. The company organises outdoor expeditions for its employees on a regular basis. It has also set-up interest clubs such as a music forum, a performing arts club, etc.

(viii) Attention to Consumers

Consumers prefer to buy products that are of good quality and are safe to use. Bajaj Auto aims at designing vehicles which give excellent performance and cause the least harm to the environment. It has a well-equipped laboratory to assess vehicle performance and emission standards. Apart from testing the vehicles in the laboratory, Bajaj Auto also employs test riders who test the vehicles on all types of terrain and weather conditions to ensure the suitability of the design before its commercialization.

(ix) Pollution Control

Pollution is a major problem caused by rapid industrialization. Increasing public awareness and government pressure have made corporations more environment conscious.

GVK Industries' first power plant near the Krishna-Godavari gas fields observes stringent pollution control standards. The plant uses natural gas or naptha (instead of coal) to produce electricity, thereby, causing significantly less pollution. Moreover, of the 72 hectares of land acquired for the project, only one-third of it used by the power plant. The remainder has been used to construct a greenbelt to curb pollution.

How to Measure Social Responsiveness?

Social audits arose from the need to measure the social responsiveness of organisations. Let us examine the meaning and significance of social audits.

Social Audits

The concept of social audit was first proposed in the 1950s by Howard R. Bowen. He defined it as "a commitment to systematic assessment of and reporting on some meaningful, definable domain of the company's activities that have a social impact." Louis E. Boone and David L. Kurtz defined, "social audit as the efforts made within the firm to evaluate its own social responsiveness." Social audits enable management to identify the direct financial benefits as well as the intangible benefits to the organisation from socially responsible behaviour. Firms such as General Motors and American Express have published social audits in the past. A survey of Fortune 500 firms showed that 456 companies (91.2 percent) have made social responsibility disclosures in their annual reports.

Social audits can be broadly distinguished into two types: (i) those required by the government, and (ii) voluntary social programmes. The audits imposed by the government involves the audit of pollution control measures, audit of product performance, and audit of equal employment standards. The second type includes voluntary audits made by companies to identify the extent of their social responsiveness.

Social audits are difficult to carry out. The categories for measuring social responsiveness discussed earlier in the article determine the areas which should be included in the social audit. As disagreements can arise over areas of social responsiveness to be measured, results can be somewhat intangible and or difficult to measure. Also, assessments of the quality of social programmes are likely to vary. Despite the problems of carrying out a social audit, the concept is gaining popularity. Many companies are now assessing their social performance through social audits.

Many large enterprises in India have emphasized their social responsibility in their annual reports, e.g. TISCO, ITC, SAIL, BHEL ONGC, etc. have developed neighbourhood projects.

The corporations are now doing 'social audit', i.e. presenting additional objectives and comprehensive information about organisation's social performance which reflect social responsibilities. Some areas covered in social audit are, i.e.

(a) Social benefits to the staff—various facilities, etc.
(b) Social benefits to the community—local taxes paid to panchayat, municipality, environmental improvements, generation of job potential.
(c) Social benefits to the public—taxes paid and follow the duties toward government.

7. TO SUM UP

To be truly effective, organisations should interact with their external environment. The external environment can be divided into the general or mega environment and the specific task environment. Social responsibility refers to the obligation of a business firm to enhance the condition of society along with its own interests. Business firms are accountable to six major stakeholder groups: shareholders, employees, customers, creditors and suppliers, society and the government.

Social responsiveness refer to the ability of a firm to implement policies and take part in activities that would benefit both society and the firm. The following categories are generally considered when measuring social responsiveness: contributions, fund-raising, volunteerism, recycling, diversity policies, direct corporate investment, quality of work life, attention to consumers and pollution control. The need to measure social responsiveness led to the development of social audits. Social audits are of two types—audits required by the government and voluntary audits. Although Social Audits are not legally mandatory, many organisations make social involvement disclosures in the annual reports. This shows the growing concern among major firms about their social responsibility.

To conclude, it has been realised that the future of business depends on its ability and willingness to respond to the changing expectations of society. Corporations must present themselves as being committed to social causes. A global company has to develop global sensitivity.

CHAPTER

30

Managing Cultural Diversity in NPO's Operations

There have been considerable changes, in almost all societies, brought about by technological advances, social alterations, economic influences and political and environmental pressures. The existing and future trends will throw new challenges in managing cultural diversity in organisations.

(a) Some major forces for change currently happening are:

(i) Technological:
- Artificial organs and transplants
- The space shuttle
- IT and internet revolutions
- Biotechnological revolution

(ii) Social:
- Women's movement
- Human rights movement
- Growth in higher education
- Stress and tensions

(iii) Economic:
- Rise in living standards
- Rapid expansion of the checkless society (i.e., credit cards)
- Fluctuating interest rates and inflation rate
- Global competition
- Tax rates

(iv) Political:
- Religious "terrorism"

- Medicare for the aged
- "Star Wars" space defence system

(v) Environment:
- Pollution, wild-life protection
- Customers and employee protection

(b) Further *societal trends* will vitally influence peoples' cultural norms and values. Some trends and practices are seen in organisations are:

- *Creation of bio-modal workforce of the future*: With distribution in two large groups with very different earnings and professional backgrounds. The tensions between two groups, i.e. workforce and professionals will grow. There is need for more employee participation and non-financial rewards by the organisations.
- *Management's move to make their organisations 'lean and mean'*: Employees are getting less secure in their jobs. There will be "corporate divorce" in the decades to come, when they early retire their employees to improve productivity and at the same time outsourcing young employees.
- *Dual career couples* as the one-bread-winner household is rapidly disappearing. This will decrease employees mobility and focus will be on the local job markets. To attract and retain female employees, the organisations will provide more day care services. Work-related health problems, especially back strain, eye strain may have to be reduced by having ergonomically designed furniture in offices.
- *Working at home* by IT savvy workforce: More people will be employed in this manner and through part-time service.
- Though there will be fewer people unionised, the rift between unions and management will continue.

The *environment* in which managers work today is *more dynamic than in the past*. The individuals with whom they work in future will be *diverse in intents, abilities, values and motivations*. Thus, there will be challenges in managing its people and culture diversity in organisations.

In the remaining part of this chapter we shall attempt to summarise our thinking on managing cultural diversity under following headings:

(i) Meaning of cultural diversity.
(ii) Importance of cultural diversity.
(iii) Two aspects of cultural diversity:
   (a) global business operations, and
   (b) work place diversity in organisation.
(iv) Managing cultural diversity.
(v) Advantages of managing cultural diversity.
(vi) To conclude.

(I) MEANING OF CULTURAL DIVERSITY

Culture is "software of the mind", the way people think, act and perceive others and it is shared by societies. Three primary components of culture, relevant to international business are language, religion and attitudes.

Cultural diversity (CD) indicates the characteristics that may make an individual culturally different from another. These differences may be:

(a) Cultural differences involving patterns of life styles, values, beliefs, ideals, practices.
(b) Differences may include race, national origin, language, religion, age, etc.
(c) Differences in views held about the world, codes of social behaviour, communication styles.

(II) IMPORTANCE OF CULTURAL DIVERSITY

1. Cultural diversity is one of the major challenges facing global business organisations, as it is important for success and vitality of the organisation.
2. Management process is increasingly becoming cross-cultural with opening of Indian economy and globalisation. It becomes necessary to have an understanding of various cultures, and the ways to manage the cultural diversity for achieving competitive advantage. This brings one of the major challenges for the MNCs, exporters, tourists, sportsmen, entrepreneurs, artists, diplomats of foreign service, financial experts, researchers, etc. who operate in diverse cultures.
3. It has importance in all activities of life and more so in international business operations, such as:

   cross-cultural differences in communication can be source of problem due to different meaning and tone of words to different people. So awareness of certain characteristics of other culture reduces misinterpretation and thus in improving communication in business introductions, telephonic conversations and meetings is important.
4. It has implications in all fields of management, such as:
   - in international marketing practices
   - in international advertising
   - in international business negotiations
   - in international human resource management
   - in international practices in industrial relations
   - in international management functions (PODCC)
   - in international developing strategies in global
   - in international organisation structure
   - in international manager's role (MNCs) in global market.

(III) TWO ASPECTS OF CULTURAL DIVERSITY

(a) First Aspect Relates to Global Cultural Diversity

People of one country have common characteristics that differentiate them from people of other countries. This is called international diversity.

Understanding of common characteristics within a particular country is important if we are going to successfully manage in an international business environment.

For example:

- Manager with awareness of national differences knows that British protect their privacy, so Indians would avoid asking British personal questions. In contrast, asking personal questions in India is acceptable. It is sign of showing interest.
- Communication is often difficult with Japanese, Americans value directness. Japanese are more subtle and view directness as not proper.
- Further, Japanese believe in group consensus in decision-making which does not fit well with Americans who are used to making fast decisions.
- In greetings Americans are smiling, firm handshake and eye contact, while Japanese bowing, exchange business cards.
- In U.S.A. women in business have equal rights, opportunities and treated seriously, while in Japan women are not considered for higher management positions. In middle-east women stand to disadvantage.

So MNCs have to develop global strategies to take advantage world-wide by properly managing cultural diversity. This calls for the need to design country specific management practices for each country in which the organisation wants to operate.

(b) Second Aspect Refers to Workforce Diversity in an Organisation

- This aspect looks at differences between people inside the work organisation. The composition of employees is changing to show heterogeneity of whole population. Thus, employee mix is undergoing change and no exclusive population in organisation.
- Workforce is now multi-lingual, multi-racial which have different life-styles, values, beliefs, ideals and practices.
- Even, language, religion, codes of social behaviour, custom, festivals are diverse.
- Workforce includes more women now, older persons. Women require protection against gender discrimination, flexible work schedules, and child care programmes.
- In addition, there are minority workers and disabled individuals.
- Diverse workforce is more educated.
- So the aim is not to remove the differences in cultures, but managers to respond to individual expectations and valuing differences to learn the details of different cultural norms which will help employees to bring out best in them.

(IV) MANAGING CULTURAL DIVERSITY

1. Thus, there is need for *preparing managers for foreign assignments through cross-cultural training* such as in history, culture, religions, values, political, legal, economy of that country to overcome cultural shock.
2. *To develop international business negotiations strategies* such as positive overtures, dealing problems and not personalities, emphasis on win-win solutions, create an open and trusting climate, build lasting relationships.

3. *To develop second generation organisation structures* which (in addition to strategy and structure) take two other aspects:
   (i) Strategic flexibility, and
   (ii) Management process.
4. *Train transnational managers with competencies in understanding* of:
   (a) Global perspective of world market business environment.
   (b) Knowledge for cultural responsiveness.
   (c) Cross-cultural interaction skills with foreign clients.
   (d) Global strategist to identify unique business opportunities, technologies, etc.
5. *Avoiding discrimination in policies, to make a harmonious work place* so that all employees benefit from wider range of experiences and ideas. Discrimination can be identified in practices of the organisation, such as racial discrimination in recruitment, employee training and career development opportunities. For example, wearing of turban by Sikhs in U.K. was discriminated. Differences in job prospects among England's ethnic minorities are now almost as big as differences between them and the majority. White community, according to a Cabinet Office strategy unit study published in March 2003. The Report emphasises that employers still discriminate on basis of ethnicity.
6. *To develop policies on sexual harassment, grievance systems* and for equal opportunities.
7. *Barrier in this change is mind-set.* It has to be recognised that such as prejudice against other cultural and racial groups, unknown fear of their dominance, avoidance of contact, lack of integration, etc. to be eliminated.
8. In managing diversity, *ethics programmes* are useful in acknowledging different values and perspectives.
9. To develop *organisation culture* for valuing differences.
10. *HR management systems to be bias free.*
11. Some other steps such as: *Involvement of women,* cultural differences knowledge to be imparted and accepting for higher career assignments.
12. *Education of employees for mind-set* about diversity.

(V) ADVANTAGES OF MANAGING CULTURAL DIVERSITY ARE THAT IT CAN IMPROVE ORGANISATIONAL PERFORMANCE

- Groups of people from diverse backgrounds can be *more creative and better at problem-solving.*
- Companies which manage cultural diversity can develop *favourable reputation* of good prospective employers of minorities such as Tata, HLL and many more.
- Cultural diversity can *get better customers* which has a variety of people.
- Organisations which *handle multiculturalism well,* create cost advantages over those who do not.
- Ability to manage cultural diversity *increases the adaptability and flexibility* of management to react to environment changes.
- Belief that people of many different backgrounds *can work together and lead to coexistence* is now university accepted. In nut shell managers must take positive steps to manage issues of cultural diversity.

Infact, successfully managing cultural diversity can lead to global business advantages. Indian IT sector, which have successful in their global operations, have to be careful in developing cultural sensitivity and preemptive in understanding political and economic environment of the host country.

(VI) TO CONCLUDE

1. Organisations are increasingly becoming multicultural and it is one of its major challenge to have competitive global advantage.
2. Managements have to understand different cultures where they do business and respect each other.
3. Organisations not only to adapt to local culture but also to design practices to suit the culture of each country.
4. Take positive steps:
    - Prepare transnational managers for foreign assignments.
    - Develop HR policies and practices (bias free).
    - Avoid discrimination and provide equal opportunities.
    - Educate employees to change mind-set and prejudice.
    - Develop organisation culture for valuing differences. Open culture develops tolerance for cultures of their employees.
    - To foster mutual adaptation is the only approach works in managing diversity. To make harmonious work place people and employees try to keep "their identity" while on the other hand they are being "homogenised."
    - Top management to support the company's multi-cultural events and encourage employees to attend.
    - Managements must recognise that a heterogenous group will produce better ideas and strategies than homogenous group.
    - A "world culture is a dream." We have to be more realist in taking above steps.

REFERENCE

S.K. Bhatia and Poonam Chaudhary, Managing Cultural Diversity in Globalisation, Deep & Deep Publications Pvt. Ltd., New Delhi.

CHAPTER

31

Counselling for Re-assurance to Face Problem

Following aspects of counselling are covered in this chapter:

1. Meaning of counselling.
2. Functions of counselling.
3. Why need for counselling?
4. Counselling system in organisations.
5. Guidelines for counselling process.
6. Is advice giving counselling?
7. An experience in counselling.

I. MEANING OF COUNSELLING

Keith Davis has defined counselling as *'discussion of an emotional problem with an employee with the general objective of decreasing it.'* The implications of this definition are as under:

(a) Counselling Involves Discussion or Communication

Successful counselling depends upon communication skills of the counsellor to share the emotions of the depressed person.

(b) Counselling is Concerned with Emotional Problem or Disorder

It has no concern with other problems like technical, methodological, job inconvenience or occupational. But any emotional problem will require *'counselling'*. The main purpose of counselling is to understand and check an employee's emotional disorder.

(c) Objective is to Reduce the Emotional Problem

The origin of counselling can be traced back to the work of Freud. Freud's method of psycho-analysis dominated the field of psychotherapy for half a century which emphasised the relationship between the therapist and the client (or doctor and patient). Carl Rogers appeared a little later on the scene and worked extensively towards understanding counselling process. He was a pioneer in advocating the counselling method and showed that a constructive approach to the patient brings about a change in personality. He advocated a strong relationship between the client and the counsellor by developing and expressing attitudes of congruence, acceptance and empathy.

2. FUNCTIONS OF COUNSELLING

The general objective of counselling is to help the employee in dealing with their emotional problems so that they can work well for the accomplishment of common goals and gain self-confidence, self-control, understanding and ability to work effectively. This objective can be achieved through performance of the following counselling functions:

(i) Re-assurance

Re-assurance is a way of giving courage to a worker to face a problem or to pose a confidence in himself that he is following the right path. Sometimes, supervisors are heard saying, *'Well, you are making good progress'* or *'don't worry, go ahead'* or *'You are right'*. These are all re-assurances.

(ii) Release of Tension

One of the important functions of counselling is to release the employee's emotional tension. It is also called *'emotional catharsis'*. People tend to get an emotional release from their frustration and all other problems as soon as they tell these to some sympathetic listener. They feel relaxed. The release of tension does not necessarily solve the problems, but it removes mental blockade and gives courage to the individual to face the problem boldly and think constructively.

(iii) Re-orientation

Re-orientation involves a change in the employee's psychic self through change in basic goals and values.

(iv) Clarified Thinking

Facilitation of realistic thinking is also an important function of counselling. Counselling encourages clarified thinking because mental blocks are cleared and the counsel is made to think rationally.

Thus, counselling through the above noted functions improves the organisational climate by solving the emotional problems of the workers in the organisation.

3. WHY NEED FOR COUNSELLING?

Counselling may be required in any situation, both on-the-job and off-the-job. The need for counselling is required because of the following factors:

(i) Conflict

Emotional disorder may be caused by interpersonal and inter-group conflicts. The conflicts are due to different backgrounds, points of view, values, needs and personality of the fellow men or due to organisational change. Thus, conflicts are inevitable in an organisation, sometimes substantial. Counselling assists conflict resolution by reducing emotional blockages.

(ii) Frustration

Frustration is the result of motivation drive being blocked to prevent one from reaching a desired goal. For example, a worker while on work is interrupted time and again and his goal for the day remains unfulfilled, he will feel irritated and frustrated. The situation becomes more serious when it is long-run frustration such as blocked opportunity for promotion. Reaction to frustration such as irritation, uneasy feeling or some other reactions are known as defence mechanism. Reactions of frustrated behaviour are aggression, apathy, withdrawal, resignation, fixation, physical disorders, substitute goals and compromise. These reactions are in no way favourable to the individual or the organisation; so it is desirable to reduce the frustrating conditions in the organisation.

(iii) Stress

Stress is a condition of strain on one's emotions, thought processes and/or physical conditions that seem to threaten one's ability to cope with environment. Excessive stress or stress over a long period of time may result in physical and emotional disorders and lowered effectiveness. Stress is also affected by the tolerance power of the person concerned.

Stress may be on-the-job and off-the-job. The main causes of stress on-the-job are job itself (work overload, pressure of work, tension and insecurity), role conflicts and role ambiguity, conflicts with people (mainly when it is with the supervisor or any other authority), etc. Off-the-job stress may be caused by family and financial problems.

Stress is a major contributor to emotional disorder of employees. It leads to physical disorder such as stomach disorder, bodyache or headache and much permanent disorder. Counselling is necessary to disperse the emotional disorders caused by stress.

4. COUNSELLING SYSTEM IN ORGANISATIONS

(i) Manager's Role in Performance Review Counselling

It requires manager to allow participation of subordinate in performance review discussions and goal-setting process. This has almost become a part of performance appraisal system in the organisations.

(ii) Supervisor to Help Employees

In guidance and coaching on-the-job, assisting them in their efforts to grow and develop, improve their interpersonal relations at work. He can also help in dealing personal problems of employees such as alcoholism, indebtedness, family relations, children vocational guidance, etc.

(iii) Counselling through Experts

Human resource department can also organise *counselling through experts* to help employees on various aspects.

5. GUIDELINES FOR COUNSELLING PROCESS

(a) Create the right environment.
(b) Listen actively.
(c) Identify the real problem.
(d) Clarify expectations and roles.
(e) Get the person to:
- talk,
- recognise the existence of a problem,
- identify solutions,
- identify the preferred solution,
- accept responsibility, and
- decide what to do.

(f) Follow up on actions agreed.

6. IS ADVICE GIVING COUNSELLING?

Many persons look upon counselling primarily an advice-giving activity but in reality this is one of several functions that counselling can perform. The giving of advice requires a counsellor to make judgements about a counsellee's emotional problems and to lay out a course of action. Herein lies the difficulty because it is almost impossible to understand another person's complicated emotions, much less to tell that person what to do with them. Advice giving may lead to a relationship in which the counsellee feels inferior and emotionally dependent on the counsellor. In spite of all its ills, advice giving occurs in routine counselling particularly performance counselling between managers and employees, because employees expect it and managers tend to provide it. Advice may have to be used with a lot of discretion and discrimination.

7. AN EXPERIENCE IN COUNSELLING

It may be pertinent to narrate here an experience of a large organisation which had taken up a project for control of absenteeism. Over 600 habitual absentees were identified and they were counselled. Follow-up of these employees was carried out, this constructive approach revealed encouraging results in reduction of overall absenteeism rate from 20 per cent to 16 per cent in the plant in two years, and considerable improvement in the attendance of habitual absentees. Counselling also helped in rehabilitating employees suffering from social evils such as drinking, gambling family disharmony, etc.

To summarise, employ counselling is discussion of an emotional problem with person with the objective of decreasing it. This is essentially a process of adjustment of seeking a new emotional equilibrium for person. Frustration, conflict, and stress are important causes of emotional problems, and bio-feedback and meditation are being experimented with as additional ways to deal with these conditions. The functions that counselling accomplishes are emotional release, clarified thinking, re-assurance and communication.

REFERENCE

S.K. Bhatia and Poonam Chaudhary, Managing Cultural Diversity in Globalisation, Deep & Deep Publications Pvt. Ltd., New Delhi.

CHAPTER

32

Ethical Concerns

In this vital chapter we have covered some aspects relating to ethical conerns as under:

(a) Meaning of business ethics.
(b) Objectives of business ethics.
(c) Scope of business ethics.
(d) Why ethical behaviour is important?
(e) Essential principles of a highly ethical organisation.
(f) To build commitment to ethics in organisation, i.e. institutionalising ethics.
(g) Benefits of teaching business ethics to students.
(h) Three similar concepts.

(A) MEANING OF BUSINESS ETHICS

Carter McNamara has defined: "Business ethics is generally *coming to know what is right or wrong in the work place and doing what is right*—this is in regard to effects of products/services and in relationships with stakeholders." "Attention to ethics in the work place sensitizes managers and staff to how they should act so that they retain a strong moral compass. Consequently, business ethics can be strong preventive medicine."

- Business ethics is *application of moral or ethical principles to business problems.* Morals are basically accepted customs in a society.
- Business ethics also relates to the behaviour of manager. It can be defined as an attempt to ascertain the responsibilities and ethical obligations of business professionals. Here the focus is on people, how individuals should conduct themselves in fulfilling the ethical requirements of business?

One writer (Deepak Parekh, CMO HDFC in his J.R.D. Tata Corporate Leadership Award lecture in 27.2.1997) has given one line definition of ethics: "Do not do something that you would be ashamed of, if it becomes public." It is not too difficult to achieve this reality. There is no pillow as soft as a clear conscience.

(B) OBJECTIVES OF BUSINESS ETHICS

It has following objectives:

- It *evaluate human practices*, i.e. actions and events by calling upon moral standards. The analysis consists of clarifying standards and lines of arguments.
- Another objective is *curative advice*. How to act morally in a special kind of situation, i.e. answering the present and future issues. It suggests solutions and policies when facing the present dilemmas and future dangers, based on balanced judgements.
- Further, business ethics is now considered a management discipline. The subject is receiving serious attention in management circles these days all over the world. Business executives have to observe *high ethical and honesty standards*.
- Business ethics involves *personal and professional conduct* and as such *requires high standards* of ethics. As business leaders are involved in social good, their responsibilities go far beyond of running the business.
- The *government, laws and lawyers cannot resolve certain key problems of business and protect the society: ethics can*. Ethics can only resolve futuristic issues. Regulations almost always lag behind. That companies social responsibility extends beyond what the law strictly requires.
- *Ethical activity is valuable in itself*, for its own sake, because it *enhances the quality of lives* and the work we do—business has an ethical responsibility for fairness for humanity, e.g. employees.
- Thomas Donaldson (Ethics in Business: A New Look) sums up that "There is a growing realisation all over the world that ethics is vitally important for any business and *for the progress of any society*. Ethics makes for an efficient economy; ethics alone, not government or laws, can protect society; ethics is good in itself; ethics and profits go together in the long-run. An ethically responsible company is one which has developed a culture of caring for people and for the environment; a culture which flows downwards from the top managers and leaders."

(C) SCOPE OF BUSINESS ETHICS

Ethical issues are there everywhere, at all levels of business activity. Business ethics concern the ground rules of individual company and societal behaviour.

(a) Societal Level

- Concern for poor and down-trodden.
- No discrimination against any particular section or group.
- Concern for clean environment.

- Preservation of scarce resources for posterity.
- Contributing to better quality of life.

(b) Stakeholder's Level

(i) Employees

- Security of job.
- Better working conditions.
- Better recommendation.
- Participative management.
- Welfare facilities.

(ii) Customers

- Better quality of goods.
- Goods and services at reasonably price.
- Not to corner stocks and create securities.
- Not to practice discriminatory pricing.
- Not to make false claims about products in advertisements.

(iii) Shareholders

- Ensure capital appreciation.
- Ensure steady and regular dividends.
- Disclose all relevant information.
- Protect minority shareholders' interests.
- Not to window dress balance sheets.
- Protect interests in times of mergers, amalgamations and takeovers.

(iv) Banks and other Lending Institutions

- Guarantee safety of borrowed funds.
- Prompt repayment of loans.

(v) Government

- Complying with rules and regulations.
- Honesty in paying taxes and other dues.
- Acting as partner in the progress of the country.

(c) Internal Policy Level

- Fair practices relating to recruitment, compensation, lay-offs, perks, promotion, etc.
- Transformational leadership to motivate employees to aim at better and higher things in life.
- Better communication at all levels.

(d) Personnel Policy Level

- Not to misuse others for personal ends.
- Not to indulge in politics to gain power.
- Not to spoil promotional chances of others.
- Not to use office car, stationery and other facilities for personal use.
- Not to fall prey to shortcuts and easy money.
- Promise keeping.
- No violence, i.e. preventing or not causing physical harm to others.
- Mutual help.
- Respect for persons and property.

(D) WHY ETHICAL BEHAVIOUR IS IMPORTANT?

There are several compelling reasons:

- First, *ethical behaviour is usually associated with important positive consequences.* Honesty in one's professional dealings promotes trust and establishes the foundation for relationship development and positive future interactions. Business in particular depends on the acceptance of rules and expectations, mutual trust and fairness. Thus, ethical business is good business. In contrast, unethical behaviour can cause serious damage affecting both the person committing the behaviour and the people touched by it.
- Second, from a personal perspective, *ethical errors end careers more quickly* than any other mistakes in judgment and accounting. Lying, stealing, cheating, on contracts, and so on undermine the very foundation upon which the business and professional world is built. Ethical behaviour is especially important for organisational leaders because they influence the ethical climate for everyone.
- Third, *ethical behaviour is empowering for all parties.* The manager who behaves ethically establishes an organisational climate of supportiveness, honesty, and trust. This climate in turn empowers employees to try out new ideas, take risks, express dissent, and generally assume enhanced responsibility.
- Fourthly, *ethical behaviour is intrinsically valuable.* Those who know that they are honest, who behave humanely in their dealings with others, who are fair in their evaluations of others, and who are concerned for the welfare of the organisation as a whole and the society it serves are rewarded with a peace of mind that carries no price tag.
- Fifthly, managers who treat other people with unimpeachable integrity thereby *earn those people's trust and make them more willing to support the organisation.* Conversely, managers who lack integrity promote mistrust among those with whom they deal and make their employees ashamed of their organisation and the products and services they provide. Since workers feel their work is unworthy, they stop caring.
- Sixthly, attention to business ethics has *improved society.*
- Seventhly, business ethics cultivates strong team work, productivity and maintans a moral course in turbulent times. Ethical principles in business ensure that policies are legal in future.
- Adherence to business ethics *promotes a strong public image.*

Azim Prem Ji, recently said that in his journey from tiny business of Rs. 5 crores to Wipro's net worth today touching some Rs. 3500 crores, everything in Wipro but *for values and integrity*, has undergone a drastic change. He cautioned the emerging breed of entrepreneurs and business managers to *desist from temptation of shortcuts and windfall gains.*

(E) ESSENTIAL PRINCIPLES OF A HIGHLY ETHICAL ORGANISATION

Some principles follwed by managers in ethical organisation are:

1. *Protect stakeholders' interest.* They are at *ease interacting with diverse inter2nal and external stakeholder groups.* The ground rules of these firms make the good of these stakeholder groups part of the organisations' own good.
2. *Fitness in decisions.* They are *obsessed with fairness.* Their ground rules emphasize that the other persons' interests count as much as their own. Treat them with fairness and justice.
3. *Responsibility is individual* rather than collective, with individuals assuming personal responsibility for actions of the organisation.
4. *They see their activities in terms of purpose.* This purpose is a way of operating that members of the organisation highly value. And purpose ties the organisation to its environment.
5. There exists a *clear vision* and picture of *integrity* throughout the organisation.
6. *Follow the laws* of land both in letter and spirit.
7. *Protect rights of others.* Do unto others as you would have them do to you.

(F) INSTITUTIONALISING ETHICS, i.e. BUILD COMMITMENT TO ETHICS IN ORGANISATION

Managers, and especially top managers, do have a responsibility to create an organisational environment that fosters ethical decision-making by institutionalizing ethics. This means applying and integrating ethical concepts into daily action. This can be accomplished in seven ways:

(1) By establishing appropriate company policy or a code of ethics,

(2) By using a formally appointed ethics committee,

(3) By teaching ethics in management development programmes. The most common way to institutionalize ethics is to establish a code of ethics; much less common is the use of ethics board committee,

(4) Appointing an *ombuds person.* He is an executive outside the normal chain of command who handles serious ethical problems in an impartial way (a type of vigilence officer).

(5) *Protecting whistle blower,* who reports perceived unethical organisational practice to outside authorities (Press, Government).

(6) Assigning responsibility for implementation of ethics programme in the organisation, such as top level manager or director.

(7) Building systems and policies that support ethical behaviour.

To raise ethical standards some measures are (Gellerman):

(i) Provide clear guidelines for ethical behaviour clarifying company's ethical standards.
(ii) Teach ethical standards and values in business in schools and organisations.
(iii) In gray areas where there *are* questions about the ethics of an action, refrain from it.
(iv) Set up controls (e.g., establish an auditing agency reporting to outside directors) that check on illegal or unethical deeds.
(v) Conduct frequent and unpredictable audits.
(vi) Punish trespassers in a meaningful way and make it public so that it may deter others.
(vii) Emphasize regularly that loyalty to the company does not excuse improper behaviour or actions.
(viii) Ethical codes to be enforced and unethical persons should be held responsible for their actions. (Box 1)

Box 1

Code of Ethics and Its Implementation through a Formal Committee

A code is a statement of policies, principles, or rules that guide behaviour. Certainly, codes of ethics do not apply only to business enterprises; they should guide the behaviour of persons in all organisations and in *everyday life*.

CODE OF ETHICS FOR GOVERNMENT SERVICE

The federal government in USA has established the following code. Any person in government service should:

1. Put loyalty to the highest moral principles and to country above loyalty to persons, party, or Government department.
2. Uphold the Constitution, laws, and regulations of the United States and of all governments therein and never be a party to their evasion.
3. Give a full day's labour for a full day's pay; giving earnest effort and best thought to the performance of duties.
4. Seek to find and employ more efficient and economical ways of getting tasks accomplished.
5. Never discriminate unfairly by the dispensing of special favours or privileges to anyone, whether for remuneration or not; and never accept, for himself or herself or for family members, favours or benefits under circumstances which might be construed by reasonable persons as influencing the performance of governmental duties.
6. Make no private promises of any kind binding upon the duties of office, since a Government employee has no private word which can be binding on public duty.
7. Engage in no business with the Government either directly or indirectly, which is inconsistent with the conscientious performance of governmental duties.
8. Never use any information gained confidentially in the performance of governmental duties as a means of making private profit.
9. Expose corruption wherever discovered.
10. Uphold these principles, ever conscious that public office is a public trust.

Simply stating a code of ethics is not enough, and the appointment of an ethics committee, consisting of internal and external directors, is considered essential for institutionalizing ethical behaviour. The functions of such a committee may include:

(1) holding regular meetings to discuss ethical issues, (2) dealing with "gray areas," (3) communicating the code to all members of the organisation, (4) checking for possible violations of the code, (5) enforcing the code, (6) rewarding compliance and punishing violations, (7) reviewing and updating the code, and (8) reporting activities of the committee to the board of directors.

FACTORS THAT RAISE ETHICAL STANDARDS

The two factors that raise ethical standards the most, according to the respondents in one study, are: (1) public disclosure and publicity, and (2) the increased concern of a well-informed public. These factors are followed by government regulations and by education to increase the professionalism of business

For ethical codes to be effective, provisions must be made for their enforcement. Unethical managers should be held responsible for their actions. This means that privileges and benefits should be withdrawn and sanctions should be applied. Although Factors that Raise Ethical Standards.

Source: Harold Koontz/H. Weihrich, Essentials of Management, 6th Edition, Tata McGraw Hill, New Delhi.

(G) BENEFITS OF TEACHING BUSINESS ETHICS TO STUDENTS

Some benefits for the student young managers are:

(i) Young managers should understand and be aware of the reasons that underlie moral principles. These are helpful in fostering *ability to reason* when applying these principles. It is vital part of ensuring compliance by managers with company standards for conduct.

(ii) Knowledge of business ethics will help managers in *resolving ethical issues/dilemmas* as they arise.

(iii) Knowledge will help managers in setting highly *responsible tone for the organisation*-- in individual judgements and decisions whether ethical or not.

(iv) The study of business ethics will *provide conscientious managers* with morally responsible approach to business. The need for responsible managers is acute as questions of business ethics cannot wholly be determined by law or government regulations, but must remain the concern of individual manager.

(v) It helps *managers to realise their social responsibility*. Many organisations find it wise to go beyond their primary mission and take into account needs of the community. Business ethics makes managers more accountable for social responsibility.

(vi) The study of business ethics *inculcates high level of integrity in managers*. Goal of ethics education is to share knowledge, build skills and develop minds. It helps to gain clarity and insight into business ethics and avoid business misconduct in organisations. The study of business ethics helps manager arrive at a decision that he feels to be "right and proper" 'just'. It facilitates individual's to understand their moral standards and ethical norms, beliefs and values so that they can decide when faced with business dilemma.

(vii) Business ethics *creates awareness of social and moral values* through education (value education) because erosion of essential values and increasing cynicism in society is leading to violence, superstition and fatalism.

In view of aforesaid benefits, majority of business management institutes in India have now introduced a separate course on business ethics for management students. Knowledge and awareness of the concepts and practices of business ethics is equally helpful to practicing managers in managerial conduct and decision-making. Business ethics improve the skills of reflective managers both in analyzing concrete moral issues and in deliberating and deciding upon strategies for solving moral dilemmas.

In nutshell, business ethics provides a basic outlook to the training of a business manager. He would enter the bad word with fortified set of values and less of doubts.

(H) THREE SIMILAR CONCEPTS

Three major concepts which are almost similar in approach in protecting various interests. These are:

- *Corporate Social Responsibility,* which has its origin in USA and Government had passed Anti-Trust Act against monopolistic practices, so as to protect and improve the welfare of society.
- *Business Ethics,* which highlighted social values and society's concerns in the 1970s and forced corporates in the USA to abstain in their policies which violated consumer protection and environmental protection, etc.
- *Corporate Governance* commenced in the UK (1990s) for improved accountability of directors to shareholders, emphasised for more trnansparent auditing and increased responsibilities of independent directors, division of rules of chairman and managing directors for safeguarding interests of shareholders.

REFERENCE

S.K. Bhatia, Business Ethics and Corporate Governance, 2004, Deep & Deep Publications Pvt. Ltd., New Delhi.

CHAPTER

33

Trends in NGO's

The typical image associated with NGO (non-government organisation) workers of yesteryears, khadi-clad individuals with a 'jhola' slung over their shoulders, has been replaced with a more urbane look. We find many donning the regular pant-shirt today and portraying the office look (although many continue to carry the 'jhola' citing the promotion of their NGOs wares as a reason).

(i) Working for an NGO is *no longer merely a philanthropic activity undertaken* by retired individuals who feel it's their duty to give back to the community or spirited individuals driven to create a more equitable society. Today, several MBA graduates from institutions even like the IIM are opting for the non-profit sector as a career option as are several other corporate drop outs.

(ii) The *non-profit sector has assumed a more corporate outlook*. The work they do has remained the same. "The role of the NGO is critical in carrying out the entire financial and non-financial transaction between "the underprivileged and the privileged" or "the donors and the community". It is not possible for any organised or individual donor to reach out to the last "man/woman," says Sanjay Bapat, founder and managing director, IndianNGOs.com. But it's the manner in which NGOs are executing the work that is different. It's more professionalised, with transparent systems of accounting and accountability. Several are functioning like companies with timeliness, budgets, fund raising and market research.

(iii) A *possible reason for this change* is that *several companies have begun to get more involved NGOs*. Some merely to provide funds for its activities while many have partnered with them to run programmes together and lend their expertise to them. "Companies can play a significant role by ramping up the capabilities of an NGO since the very nature of corporate interactions expect high standards of reporting and accounting practices. They can also bring in the culture of corporate ethics and corporate mindset", says Rohini Nilekani, chairperson Akshara Foundation and Arghyam. Adds Bapat,"Companies can share their core competencies in marketing, finance, HR systems and administration with NGOs. This way they are building the capacities of the NGOs and helping them towards sustainability."

(iv) On the other hand, *NGOs can make an equal contribution by counselling corporate professionals on issues* like child adoption, sexual harassment, addressing the needs of old people at home or the children at risk, how to be positive if you are HIV positive human rights.

(v) Clearly, a *collaboration between NGOs and companies has several benefits*. However, it is important first to select the appropriate NGO to collaborate with. "Getting the right NGO who shares the same vision, ideas and commitment is critical and very difficult too," says Sudha Murthy, chairperson, Infosys Foundation. Sometimes companies choose NGOs that have a different vision from theirs and try to impose their agenda on to the organisation. NGOs, in turn also sometimes allow themselves to be swayed. "NGOs in need of funds sometimes shift focus from their core competencies to run projects different from their area of functioning to appease companies to obtain funds", says Deval Sanghavi, founder, Dasra. This doesn't always lead to positive results. (Boxes 1, 2 and 3)

(vi) Often the *credibility of NGOs is also a question*. Advises Murthy, "It is important to start on a small scale with an NGO, *monitor their work closely* for a couple of years. and only then go on to bigger projects with them." Monitoring is necessary because there are cases of several NGOs indulging in unethical practices. "Often companies are concerned that their donations may not be used for the purpose for which they are given. The concerns revolve around many issues like credibility of the NGO, financial management, possibility of siphoning funds, governance issues or inefficiency of the NGO," says Bapat. Lending business knowledge and skills in these areas to *inculcate accountability in the non-profit organisations* can become a key contribution of the corporate sector.

(vii) *Assisting in the recruitment of talent* is another area where companies can help out. As NGOs become *more professionalised*, the management team and its leader become a core element of the organisation. Several organisations fall through because the individuals who began them are no longer invoked in them. In such a scenario, if organisations had a strong team in place to take over the reins from the leader, the issue of succession wouldn't arise. Since companies are well versed in the field of HR, they can be of tremendous help. "Just the way HR is critical in business, it is also important in the social sector because if the management of an organisation is good, the quality of programmes and their execution will also be good," says Sanghavi. "*Companies can help NGOs build management* expertise. This however cannot be done in isolation. The corporate executives must have knowledge of the various issues peculiar to this work before handling out advice to the NGOs," says Anurag Behar, corporate vice-president (community initiatives), Wipro.

(viii) *Wipro is working on a Fellowship plan* to encourage professionals from the corporate world to work in the NGO sector. Expected to be rolled out over the next three-four months, the Wipro Fellowship will invite executives with a minimum of three to four years work experience who have an inclination towards social development work. Those selected for the Fellowship will be placed in different NGOs identified with Wipro for a period of two years. During this period the remuneration will be paid by Wipro. Structured on a similar concept is Dasra, a non-profit organisation begun by an NRI couple with business degrees from the University of Texas Austin and Harvard Business School. Disillusioned by the lack of professionalism in the non-profit sector, the mission of Dasra is to provide managerial support and technical assistance to other NGOs.

(ix) Some *innovative ideas to nurture the NGO-corporate relationship* are: There is no doubt that the partnership can bring about immense change in our society. Nevertheless, both parties have issues they need to consider in order to ensure the equation remains positive. Some information about NGO's is as under: (Boxes 1 to 5)

Box 1

Sector-wise Concentration of NGOs

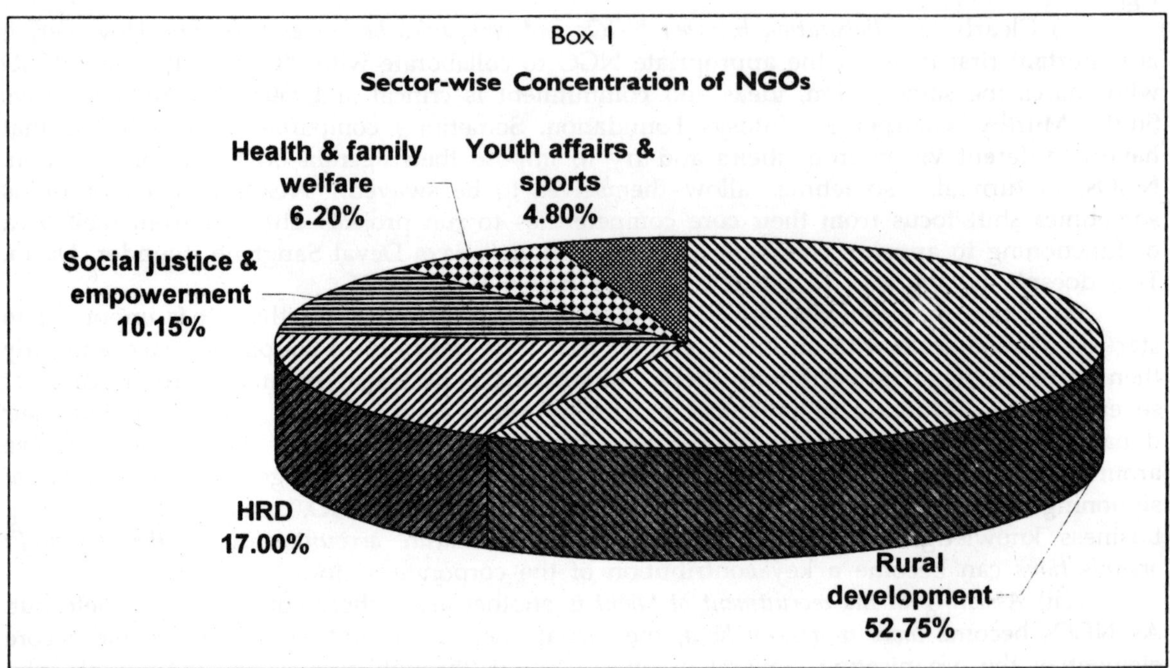

Box 2

NGO Facts

- 25 percent NGOs work in the southern states—10.4 in Andhra Pradesh; 4.15 in Karnataka, 2.84 in Kerala and 7.85 in Tamil Nadu.
- 36 percent NGOs are active in the demographically weak states including newly formed states—15.84 per cent in UP, 4.5 in MP, 9.33 in Bihar, 2.9 in Rajasthan, 1.7 in Jharkhand, 1.3 in Uttaranchal and 0.35 in Chhattisgarh.
- 30 percent NGOs work in other major states—West Bengal (9.73), Orissa (6.78), Maharashtra (4.95), Delhi (4.08), Gujarat (2.59), Haryana (1.5) and Punjab (0.36).
- 7.35 percent NGOs are active in North East—Assam (2.1%), Manipur (2.9%), Meghalaya (0.18), Mizoram (0.28), Nagaland (0.47), Arunachal Pradesh (0.2) and Tripura (0.37).

Source: Population Commission.

Box 3

Definition of a Social Entrepreneur

- Identifies and applies practical solutions to social problems.
- Innovates new products and services, or a new approach to a social problem.
- Focuses on social value creation and is ready to share innovations and initiatives.
- Doesn't wait to secure resources before undertaking innovations.
- Is fully accountable to the constituencies she/he serves.
- Resists being trapped by constraints of ideologies.
- Continuously refines approach in response to feedback.
- Has a vision, and a well-thought out roadmap to attain goals.

Source: Schwab Foundation

Box 4

NGOs most Trusted Organisations

According to the new Edelman Trust Barometer Survey carried out for the World Economic Forum, NGOs are the most trusted institutions worldwide. Edelman, which describes itself as "the largest independent PR firm" in the world, has been polling over 2,000 opinion leaders annually over the last seven years about their take on the state of trust in four sectors—business, government, media and NGOs.

By way of illustration, trust in NGOs in the US has gone up by 13 percentage points in the post-five years, while trust in business has increased only by five points in the same period. In Europe, trust in business has actually declined by three percentage points since 2002, according to the Edelman survey, while trust in NGOs across Europe has gone up by one point from 2004 to 2005.

Source: Business Line, March 13, 2006.

Box 5

Research has Determined that among U.S. Companies—Types of Corporate Giving

Research has determined over 82 percent of U.S. companies have a volunteer programme; 62 percent offer awards and benefits to employees who volunteer; 46 percent loan executives to non-profit organisations; and 26 percent compensate employees for time off for volunteer work.

Another way to classify socially responsible actions is according to the *beneficiaries* of each action. In some instances, the organisation's *customers* benefit; in other instances, the *employees* benefit. Beyond employees and customers are definable interest groups, such as racial and ethnic groups, women's groups, etc.

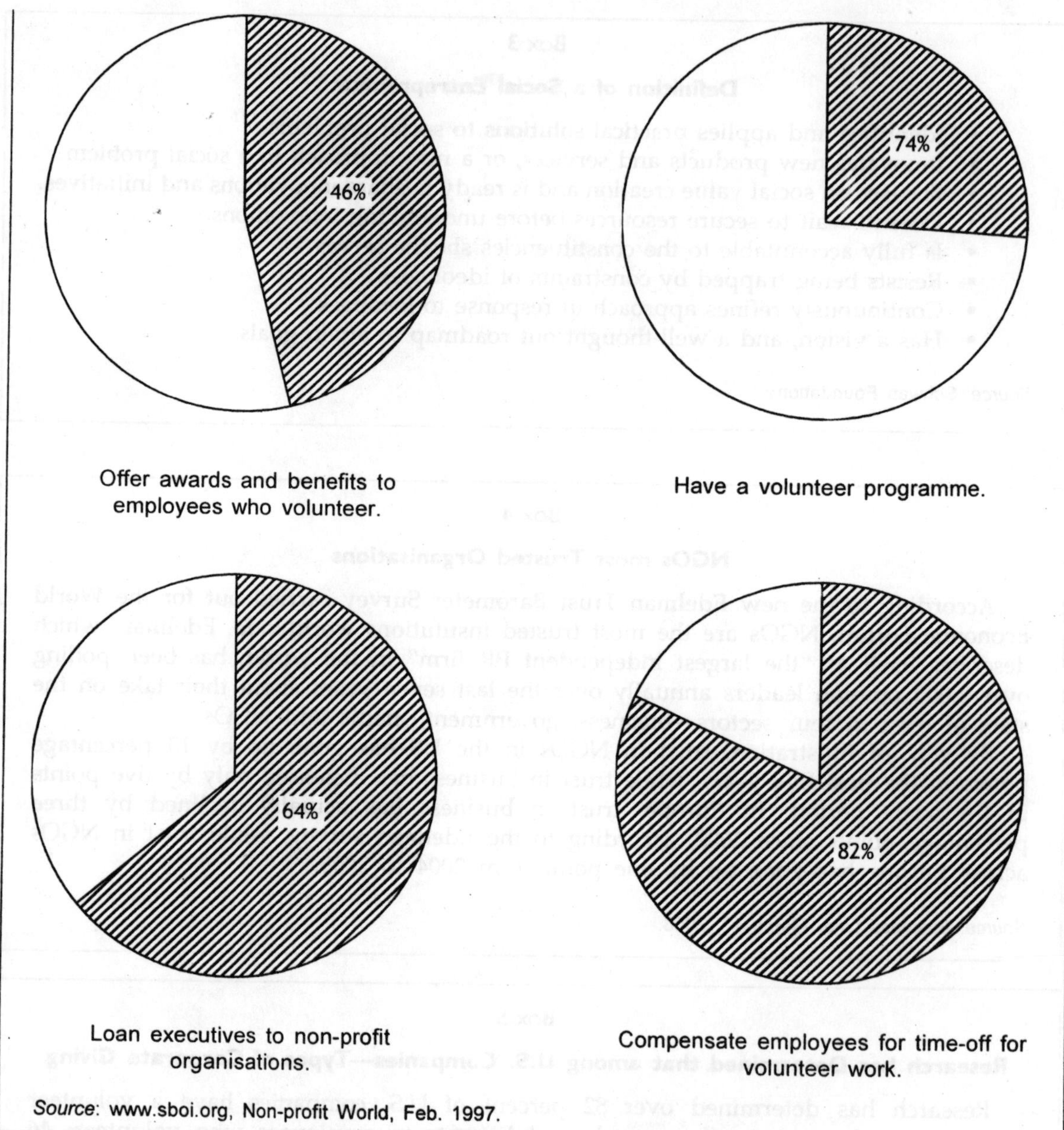

Source: www.sboi.org, Non-profit World, Feb. 1997.

Reference

Hiral Saeth, Business India, April 9, 2006.

PART VII

ANNEXURES

ANNEXURE I

SOCIETIES REGISTRATION ACT, 1860

(An Act for the Registration of Literary, Scientific and Charitable Societies)

Preamble

Whereas it is expedient that provision should be made for improving the legal condition of societies established for the promotion of literature, science, or the fine arts, or for the diffusion of useful knowledge, the diffusion of political education, or for charitable purposes. It is enacted as follows:

1. Societies formed by memorandum of association and registration

Any seven or more persons associated for any literary, scientific or charitable purpose, or for any such purpose as is described in Section 20 of this Act, may, by subscribing their names to a memorandum of association, and filing the same with the Registrar of Joint Stock Companies form themselves into a society under this Act.

2. Memorandum of association

The memorandum of association shall contain the following things, that is to say—

(i) the name of the society;
(ii) the objects of the society;

the names, addresses and occupations of the governors, council, directors, committee, or other governing body to whom, by the rules of the society, the management of its affairs is entrusted.

A copy of the rules and regulations of the society, certified to be a correct copy by not less than three of the members of the governing body, shall be filed with the memorandum of association.

3. Registration and fees

Upon such memorandum and certified copy being filed, the Registrar shall certify under his hand that the society is registered under this Act. There shall be paid to the Registrar for every such registration—a fee of fifty rupees, or such smaller fee as the State Government may, from time to time, direct; and all fees so paid shall be accounted for to the. State Government.

4. Annual list of managing body to be flied

Once in every year, on or before the fourteenth day succeeding the day on which, according to the rules of society, the annual general meeting of the society is held, or, if the rules do not provide for an annual general meeting, in the month of January, a list shall be filed with the Registrar of Joint Stock Companies, of the names, addresses and occupations of the governors, council, directors, committee or other governing body then entrusted with the management of the affairs of the society.

5. Property of society how vested

The property, movable and immovable, belonging to a society registered under this Act, if not vested in trustees, shall be deemed to be vested, for the time being, in the governing body of such society, and in all proceedings, civil and criminal; may be described as the property of the governing body of such society by their proper title.

6. Suits by and against societies

Every society registered under this Act may sue or be sued in the name of the president, chairman, or principal secretary, or trustees, as shall be determined by the rules and regulations of the society, and, in default of such determination, in the name of such person as shall be appointed by the governing body for the occasion:

Provided that it shall be competent for any person having a claim or demand against the society, to sue the president or chairman, or principal secretary or the trustees thereof, if on application to the governing body some other officer or person be not nominated to be the defendant.

7. Suits not to abate

No suit or proceeding in any Civil Court shall abate or discontinue by reason of the person, by or against whom such suit or proceedings shall have been brought or continued, dying or ceasing to fill the character in the name whereof he shall have sued or been sued, but the same suit or proceeding shall be continued in the name of or against the successor of such person.

8. Enforcement of judgment against society

If a judgment shall be recovered against the person or officer named on behalf of the society, such judgment shall not be put in force against the property, movable or immovable, or against the body of such person or officer, but against the property of the society.

The application for execution shall set forth the judgment, the fact of the party against whom it shall have been recovered having sued or having been sued, as the case may be, on behalf of the society only, and shall require to have the judgment enforced against the property of the society.

9. Recovery of penalty accruing under bye-law

Whenever by any bye-law duly made in accordance with the rules and regulations of the society, or, if the rules do not provide for the making of bye-laws, by any bye-law made at a general meeting of the members of the society convened for the purpose (for the making of which the concurrent votes of three-fifths of the members present at such meeting shall be necessary), any pecuniary penalty is imposed for the breach of any rule or bye-law of the society, such penalty, when accrued may be recovered in any Court having jurisdiction the defendants shall reside, or the society shall be situate, as the governing body thereof shall deem expedient.

10. Members liable to be sued as strangers

Any member who may be in arrear of a subscription which according to the rules of the society he is bound to pay, or who shall possess himself or detain any property of the society in a manner or for a time contrary to such rules, or shall injure or destroy any property of the society, may be sued for such arrear or for the damage accruing from such detention, injury, or destruction of property in the manner hereinbefore provided.

Recovery by successful defendant of costs adjudged

But if the defendant shall be successful in any suit or other proceeding brought against him at the instance of the society, and shall be adjudged to recover his costs, he may elect to proceed to recover the same from the officer in whose name the suit shall be brought, or from the society, and in the later case shall have process against the property of the society in the manner above described.

11. Members guilty of offences punishable as strangers

Any member of the society who shall steal, purloin, or embezzle any money or other property, or wilfully and maliciously destroy or injure any property of such society, or shall forge any deed, bond, security for money, receipt, or other instrument, whereby the funds of the society may be exposed to loss, shall be subject to the same prosecution, and, if convicted, shall be liable to be punished in like manner, as any person not a member would be subject and liable to in respect of the like offence.

12. Societies enabled to alter, extend or abridge their purposes

Whenever it shall appear to the governing body of any society registered under this Act, which has been established for any particular purpose or purposes, that it is advisable to alter, extend, or abridge such purpose to or for other purposes within the meaning of this Act, or to amalgamate such society either wholly or partially with any other society such governing body may submit the proposition to the members of the society in a written or printed report, and may convene a special meeting for the consideration thereof according to the regulations of the society.

But no such proposition shall be carried into effect unless such report shall have been delivered or sent by post to every member of the society ten days previous to the special meeting convened by the governing body for the consideration thereof, nor unless such proposition shall have been agreed to by the votes of three-fifths of the members delivered in person or by proxy, and confirmed by the votes of three-fifths of the members present at a second special meeting convened by the governing body at an interval of one month after the former meeting.

13. Provision for dissolution of societies and adjustment of their affairs

Any number not less than three-fifths of the members of any society may determine that it shall be dissolved and thereupon it shall be dissolved forthwith, or at the time then agreed upon, and all necessary steps shall be taken for the disposal and settlement of the property of the society, its claims and liabilities, according to the rules of the said society applicable thereto, if any, and, if not, then as the governing body shall find expedient, provided that, in the event of any dispute arising among the said governing body or the members of the society, the adjustment of its affairs shall be referred to the principal Court of original civil jurisdiction of the district in which the chief building of the society is situate; and the Court shall make such order in the matter as it shall deem requisite:

Assent required

Provided that no society shall be dissolved unless three-fifths of the members shall have expressed a wish for such dissolution by their votes delivered in person, or by proxy, at a general meeting convened for the purpose.

Government consent

Provided that whenever any Government is a member of or a contributor to, or otherwise interested in, any society registered under this Act, such society shall not be dissolved without the consent of the Government of the State of registration.

14. Upon a dissolution no member to receive profit

If upon the dissolution of any society registered under this Act there shall remain, after the satisfaction of all its debts and liabilities, any property whatsoever, the same shall not be paid to or distributed among the members of the said society or any of them, but shall be given to some other society, to be determined by the votes of not less than three-fifths of the members present personally or by proxy at the time of the dissolution, or, in default thereof, by such Court as aforesaid.

Clause not to apply to Joint Stock Companies

Provided, however, that this clause shall not apply to any society which shall have been founded or established by the contributions of shareholders in the nature of a Joint Stock Company.

15. Member defined

For the purposes of this Act a member of a society shall be a person, who, having been admitted therein according to the rules and regulations thereof, shall have paid a subscription, or shall have signed the roll or list of members thereof, and shall not have resigned in accordance with such rules and regulations; but in all proceedings under this Act no person shall be entitled to vote or be counted as a member whose subscription at the time shall have been in arrear for a period exceeding three months.

16. Governing body defined

The governing body of the society shall be the governors, council, directors, committee, trustees or other body to whom by the rules and regulations of the society the management of its affairs is entrusted.

17. Registration of societies formed before Act

Any company or society established for a literary, scientific or charitable purpose, and registered under Act 43 of 1850, or any such society established and constituted previously to the passing of this Act but not registered under the said Act 43 of 1850, may at any time hereafter be registered as a society under this Act; subject to the proviso that no such company or society shall be registered under this Act unless an assent to its being so registered has been given by three-fifths of the members present personally, or by proxy, at some general meeting convened for that purpose by the governing body.

In the case of a company or society registered under Act 43 of 1850 the directors shall be deemed to be such governing body.

In the case of a society not so registered, if no such body shall have been constituted on the establishment of the society, it shall be competent for the members thereof, upon due notice, to create for itself a governing body to act for the society thenceforth.

18. Such societies to file memorandum, etc., with Registrar of Joint Stock Companies

In order to any such society as is mentioned in the last preceding section obtaining registry under this Act, it shall be sufficient that the governing body file with the Registrar of Joint Stock Companies a memorandum showing the name of the society, the objects of the society and the names, addresses and occupations of the governing body, together with a copy of the rules and regulations of the society certified as provided in Section 2, and a copy of the report of the proceedings of the general meeting at which the registration was resolved on.

19. Inspection of documents, certified copies

Any person may inspect all documents filed with the Registrar under this Act on payment of a fee of one rupee for each inspection; and any person may require a copy or extract of any document or any part of any document, to be certified by the Registrar on payment of fifteen paise for every hundred words of such copy or extract; and such certified copy shall be *prima facie* evidence of the matters therein contained in all legal proceedings whatever.

20. To what Societies Act applies

The following societies may be registered under this Act:

Charitable societies, the military orphan funds or societies established at the several presidencies of India, societies established for the promotion of science, literature, or the fine arts, for instruction, the diffusion of useful knowledge, the diffusion of political education, the foundation or maintenance of libraries or reading rooms for general use among the members or open to the public or public museums and galleries of paintings and other works of art, collections of natural history, mechanical and philosophical inventions, instruments, or designs.

Annexure II

SAMPLE QUESTIONS

10 Questions

1. Explain problems commonly faced by non-profit organisations?
2. Discuss the importance of key performance areas and strategic control points to the design of effective control systems?
3. Explain different financial control methods.
4. What is the purpose of auditing and how is it achieved?
5. Explain characteristics of effective and reliable control systems?
6. Explain why managers believe they need control?
7. Why are budgets so widely used by NPOs?
8. What are ways to increase public confidence in NPOs?
9. Explain financial reporting system in NPOs?
10. Explain methods of evaluation of performance of NPOs?

10 Questions

1. What is a non-profit organisation? Explain characteristics of NPO?
2. Explain emerging trends in NPO?
3. Define principle activities of management process?
4. Describe the steps in the control process?
5. What is the importance for managers of vision, mission, ethics, cultural diversity, and changing workplace.
6. Describe the budgeting process.
7. Explain techniques of managerial controls.
8. Explain the use of external and internal auditing?
9. What are reasons for human resistance to controls.
10. Discuss the different skills that managers must have and roles they can fill.

10 Questions

1. Explain major areas of control in NPO?
2. Discuss various stages in operation control such as:
   (a) Feed-forward control,
   (b) Concurrent control, and
   (c) Feedback control.
3. Explain the control process and its features in NPO.
4. Explain challenges of managers in NPO?
5. Discuss values of studying management?
6. Explain importance of NPO.
7. List some of the reasons budgets are used so widely?
8. Explain MIS?
9. Explain link between planning and controlling.
10. Explain procedure for formation of non-profit organisation.

Annexure III

QUESTION PAPER

Master of Business Administration (MBA)

SEMESTER-II
END SEMESTER EXAMINATION, APRIL-2005
NON-PROFIT ORGANISATION (NPO)

Time: 3 Hours Total Marks: 100

Note:

1. Attempt all questions.
2. Marks carried by the questions are shown against it.

I. Attempt any FOUR of the following: **4×5=20**

What is the difference between:

(a) Internal and External Audit
(b) Ethics and Social Responsibility
(c) Concurrent Control and Feedback Control
(d) Procedure for formation of Non-profit Organisation and Commercial Company.
(e) Vision and Mission in NPO
(f) Skills and knowledge managers

II. Attempt any FOUR of the following: **4×5=20**

Write a note on:

(a) Emerging trends in Not-Profit Organisations.
(b) Human resistance to controls
(c) Explain details of action plan to collect donations/contributions for NPO.
(d) Purpose of Auditing and how it is achieved?
(e) Characteristics of NPO.
(f) To have good public relations in NPO, is it advisable to associate a politician or political party in its activities.

III. Attempt any TWO of the following: **2×10=20**

(a) Today there is stronger emphasis on "Doing Well" while "Doing Good". Do Non-profit Organisations need management practices. Discuss some management approaches which are for NPO.

(b) Why are budgets so widely used by NPO?
(c) Explain methods of evaluation of performance of NPO.

IV. Attempt any TWO of the following: **2×10=20**

(a) Handling of personnel in Non-profit Organisation is often more difficult than in a commercial operation. Explain some significant Human Resource practices followed in NPO.
(b) Are external relations required for all welfare organisations? Explain reasons.
(c) Explain different financial control methods.

V. Attempt any TWO of the following: **2×10=20**

(a) Case Study

Let us assume that a school has been identified as having a large proportion of the students who go without lunch on account of poverty. Enough research has been conducted to know that such children would welcome the idea of lunch being provided in school. If a philanthropist is willing to underwrite the lunch and one has to fix a lunch menu for the children, one must wonder, will the menu be acceptable to the children's palate? Would they like milk or would they prefer yogurt and buttermilk? Are there vegetarians who do not eat eggs? What would a good combination of food items be such that their nutritional requirements and taste buds (developed on the basis of a very poor diet) are taken care of?

The experiences of the Tamil Nadu mid-day meal scheme at the micro-level at different school locations indicated how annoyingly fussy the poorest children could be on a free meal. It does not in any way, diminish the value of the scheme itself. It is, however, also important to make sure that the children get optimum nutrition and enjoy the meal.

Questions

1. Explain how NPO should proceed to ensure that menu school provides will have wider assurance of children acceptability?
2. Explain details of your suggested approach.

(b) Case Study

There is a section of persons who feel that they have worked hard and long; and earned enough, and would now like to do some 'good'. In the US this category of persons form a substantial proportion workers' at various non-profit organisations. In India, the concept of the voluntary worker is still to catch up. However, the 'let me now try to pay my debt to society' motivation does generate a number of persons who are available at salaries that the non-profit organisation can afford.

Question

1. Can we identify certain categories of persons who can be willing to serve for the 'cause' of NPO.
2. Why NPOs should utilize their services?

(c) Case Study

A medical professional of above average competence today has several markets to choose from. There is the US market where he can aspire to be a millionaire. Next comes the Middle East where the earnings are a bit lower, but has also the disadvantage that his knowledge and skills will become obsolete rather quickly.

There is the Commonwealth market where the money is quite good, even if it is not a good as the US. Finally, there are the Indian commercial hospitals where they can get high salaries and substantial 'tax avoided' cash compensations. The charity hospitals have to rely on the commitment to the cause.

In medical colleges some seats are given to students who contribute as donations in return for a commitment to serve such institutions for an agreed number of years. The system works, but not satisfactorily. Many of the graduates look for loop-holes to escape from the commitment, but the moral pressures from the peer groups are usually adequate to hold the majority to their commitment.

The salary and compensation pattern of a very reputed charitable medical colleges and hospitals are not attractive. These institutions are doing emeplary service both in training and patient care.

Questions

1. How is that some charity hospitals can retain doctors and para-medical staff to stay, even when the salaries are not so attractive?
2. What remuneration policies charitable hospital should follow to retain doctors, etc.?

ANNEXURE IV

Assignment I: INDUSTRY BASED PROJECT

Subject:	**Non-profit Organisation (NPO)**		
Programme:		*Semester:*	**II**
Faculty Name:		*Date of Submission:*	**15.03.2005**
Assignment Issue Date:	**19.02.2005**	*Marks:*	**10**

After studying the various concepts in Non-profit Organisation, it is necessary to understand practices followed in Indian NPOs. This practical based project will help you to appreciate different practices, policies and innovations followed by the Indian NPO have to attain survival. You will carry out in-depth study of at least any two areas of Indian NPO in the industry-based project. These areas of study include such as:

1. Formation procedure followed by NPO. It's mission and objectives (Long-term and Short-term)
2. Sources of funds and marketing strategies to get contributions.
3. Techniques of Management and Financial Control System in NPO.
4. Organisation Structure and Management working system.
5. System of monitoring and evaluation of performance.

Description of the Project

This assignment requires you to—

- Select NPO in India.
- Examine its history, growth, organisation, collaboration, etc.
- Conduct in-depth study of *any two* areas as in project brief above.

Evaluation Criteria

- Creativity/innovativeness of report—20%
- Substance/task submitted—40%
- Presentation of the report—20%
- Oral Presentation of assignment—20%

PS: The project submitted should be presented in the following order:
Cover sheet/certificate from the company/contents/acknowledgement/company profile/findings/conclusion/recommendations/bibliography/annexure/visiting care of one manager contracted.

Assignment 2: IT WAS A VERY GOOD YEAR

Remember that song by Frank Sinatra? In that very popular number, Old Blue Eyes celebrated different stages of his life—his teens, 20s, 30s and middle age.

Throughout SHRM's existence, we've enjoyed significant success in many years. But 2004 was exceptional—a very good year, indeed.

As 2004 began, we faced the challenge of implementing a new volunteer leadership structure—putting it in place to serve our mission of serving the HR professional and advancing the profession. That we pulled it off is testimony to the dedication of literally hundreds of people.

We created five new domestic and two new international regions, new regional councils, and a Membership Advisory Council to serve as liaison between members and the SHRM Board of Directors and staff.

Early in the year, we launched eight new virtual forums that provide, free to all members, information and tools previously available only to those who paid additional fees.

We formed 12 special-expertise panels, covering the full spectrum of HR interest and activity, whose members serve as subject-matter experts and help SHRM identify emerging trends.

Working with our chapters and volunteer leaders, we established special-interest chapters, which allow like-minded HR professionals to affiliate around specific topic areas, and special-interest groups within chapters.

To increase awareness of global HR issues and to be a valuable resource to HR professionals worldwide, we refocused our internationalization efforts to examine additional member services, explore opportunities in other countries and expand the global orientation of SHRM's staff. As a key step in this process, we redefined the SHRM Global Forum, previously a separate membership category, to allow all members to access international HR content.

We also enjoyed a phenomenal conference season in 2004. Our Annual Conference and Exposition was an overwhelming success, while ours discipline-specific conferences hit the mark. We also staged a brand-new event, a Strategic HR Conference that drew HR leaders interested in acquiring more knowledge about HR's strategic contribution to business success.

While there were many other successes this year, I've focused on these because they are prime examples of what can be achieved by dedicated people—SHRM members, the Board of Directors, volunteers and staff—all working together. Without their collective talent, energy and commitment, none of this could have been accomplished. My thanks to everyone.

Frank Sinatra had many good years during his illustrious career. We've also enjoyed many very good years and, with the continued commitment of our members, volunteer leaders and the board, many more lie ahead.

1. Explain the mission of SHRMs.
2. How SHRM expanded the global orientation of SHRM's staff?
3. Explain various initiatives taken by SHRM's staff for its success in 2004.

Source: *HR Magazine*, December 2004 by Susan Meisinger, President, SHRM.

Assignment 3: A CASE STUDY OF SOUTH CENTRAL RAILWAY: A SERVICE ORGANISATION

Subject: **Non-profit Organisation**
Programme: MBA *Semester*: II
Faculty Name: *Marks*: 5
Assignment Issue Date: **23.12.2004** *Date of Submission*: **13.01.2005**

Assignment Brief

Problems of South Central Railway are brought out. As a service organisation it has to evolve an action plan to improve its image.

Evaluation Criteria

- 2 marks for each correct answer to questions.
- 1 mark for right grasp of concepts and problems.
- 5 marks for all correct answers, plus right grasp of concepts and systematic presentation.

A case study of South Central Railway—a Service Organisation

(I) The Indian Railways are Asia's largest and world's second largest railway system under one management, next to the rail network of Soviet Russia. The Railways in India provide the principal mode of transport for freight and passengers and remain as the backbone of the county's transport infrastructure. The Indian Railways has grown substantially since the commencement of the planning era. The Indian Railways have attempted modernization and technological upgradation of the system to generate maximum capacity with minimum investment to provide Railway transport at the least cost to rail users.

The South Central Railway was formed on 2nd October 1966. SCR has emerged as the third largest zone of Indian Railways in terms of originating freight tariff, achieved a three-fold increase in passenger traffic and stupendous improvement in earnings. It is playing a vital role as a catalyst for agricultural and industrial development in the southern peninsula by providing a customer-friendly transport network. In its 37 years, SCR has achieved more than 95% of consumers'/rail user's requirements. SCR has always been stead fast in bettering its performance every year.

(II) Today many developments have taken place in transport industry. Developments in South Central Railway have also been very rapid. Modernization and technological upgradation of its services have made the SCR to occupy the prime place in the India Railways.

(III) The demand and expectations of customers are increasing tremendously day-by-day, the railways are expected to and are trying to make all out efforts to reach the country side.

(IV) *Statement of problem*: There has been a phenomenal growth in the movement of men, machine and materials. The primary, secondary and tertiary sectors are witnessing radical changes. The product development strategy would make possible equilibrium between the transportation, demand and supply. Transport facilities help greatly in widening the size of the market. The widening of the size of the market rests on the creation of a network of transport and communication. In a developing country like India, it is very much significant that policy decisions are made keeping in view the needs and requirements of both general customers and the industrial users.

(V) *Some findings*: The South Central Railway has been acknowledged as one of the best zones of Indian Railways and has been awarded, the Railway minister's safety shield several times. Yet it suffers from the following deficiencies in some sectors/areas.

1. South Central Railway is more product-oriented than customer-oriented. Marketing is peripheral activity and the commercial department is engaged only in selling business.
2. The advertisement released by SCR is not creative enough in messages, appeals and slogans to become effective in informing serving to persuading the users.
3. In South Central Railway there is inadequate management of service promises. There is discrepancy between service delivery and service promises made through promotional programmes.
4. Inadequacy of proper motivational and encouragement set-up to reward employees who excel in their endeavors.
5. There is deficiency in customer service skills among the personnel at the enquiry counters. Inadequate customer-orientation among the personnel exists and persists.
6. Customer-focus is missing and customer-satisfaction is not an organisational mission and vision.

Assignment Questions

1. Suggest steps to improve the image of South Central Railway as Service Organisation.
2. Evolve an action-plan of action, which links the human resources strategy to the business strategy of SCR?

Assignment 4: BEN JERRY'S SUPER AUDIT CRUNCH

Subject:	**Non-profit Organisation**		
Programme:	**MBA**	*Semester*:	**II**
Faculty Name:		*Marks*:	**5**
Assignment Issue Date:	**31.01.2005**	*Date of Submission*:	**15.02.2005**

Assignment Brief

Ben and Jerry's Homemade Company wants to measure success both by financial performance and audit of social mission. Can non-profit organisations follow such type of control system?

Evaluation Criteria:

- 1 mark for each correct answer to questions.
- 1 mark for right grasp of concepts and problems.
- 5 marks for all correct answers, plus right grasp of concepts and systematic presentation.

BEN JERRY'S SUPER AUDIT CRUNCH

Organisations' annual reports typically consist of a combination of SEC filings and glossy photographs. Numbers, audits, footnotes, and portraits of smiling executives all come together to produce an organisation's "best side," then presented to stockholders as the actual status of the company. Failures, financial or otherwise, are often sugar-coated or ignored altogether. Promises of growth and improvements abound with little attention to troubles the company may be experiencing. Moreover, annual reports tend to focus on only one aspect of an organisation's well-being: the financials. "One of the problems is that annual reports only tell part of the story and they only talk to one audience—the financial community," noted Robert Rosen, president of Health Companies, a not-for-profit, Washington D.C.-based group that strives to redefine how businesses are organised and run. "Companies do not report how well they are doing in terms of managing the human capital side of the business or whether they are building a health company."

Then there is Ben & Jerry's Homemade, Inc., the Waterbury, Vermont-based, super-premium ice cream maker renowned for its innovative and exceptionally tasty flavors, such as "Chocolate Chip Cookie Dough" and "Cherry Garcia" (named after Jerry Garcia of the Grateful Dead). Ben & Jerry's annual reports fall somewhere outside the norm. Since 1988, Ben & Jerry's has published two types of bottom lines in its annual report: one, financial, the other, social.

At Ben & Jerry's, management believes that a company should be evaluated not only on its financial performance but on its social performance as well. "To be profitable for its shareholders and to be socially responsible, inside and outside the organisation" is an assertion boldly made in the company's mission statement. "We decided that we wanted to measure our success by changing the definition of our bottom line," explained co-founder Jerry Greenfield. "For most businesses, their bottom line is just their profits, how much money is left over at the end of the year. We said we're going to have a two-part bottom line. We'll measure our success both by how we do financially and how we do with our social mission."

The Ben & Jerry's social audit rates the company in areas such as employee benefits, plant safety, ecology, community involvement, and customer service. In order to make sure that no stone is left unturned, the auditor, an outside export not employed with Ben & Jerry's, is given access to all employee and corporate documents during the conducting of the review.

"It's all in keeping with our two-part bottom line," noted Mitch Curren, P.R. Info Queen: at Ben & Jerry's types, that is her real title. The findings of the audit, positive or negative, are then published, unedited, so as to guarantee complete candor.

As a result, Ben & Jerry's annual reports tend toward brutal honesty. The 1992 social audit, for example, openly criticized the company for poor plant safety. At two plants, the number of injuries suffered had increased from 52 in 1991 to 75 in 1992. According to Paul Hawken, noted author and speaker on social responsibility and conductor of the 1992 audit, the number of days lost as a result of injuries or accidents during this period showed an 87% increase, far in excess of increased sales and production. Hawken also examined Ben & Jerry's unique "7:1 (RATIO)" salary ratio, which prevented the highest-paid employee from making more than 7 times the salary of the lowest-paid employee. While Hawken admired the willingness of Ben & Jerry's board of directors to set such a cap on executive salaries ($100,000 as of 1992), he pointed out that the policy left a number of key positions vacant since many qualified applicants were able to find much higher salaries elsewhere. All of these criticisms found their way into Ben & Jerry's annual report, intact and unedited.

Even Ben & Jerry's charitable efforts have been attacked in the social audits. "One of the year's (1991) unmitigated flops was the 'Save the Family Farm' campaign," said Milton Moskowitz, author of the social audit in Ben & Jerry's 1991 annual report. Originally designed to rally support for independent farmers, Moskowitz criticized the campaign's vague directives such as "write your Senators and Representatives to tell them to support a dairy programme that provides farmers with a decent living." Moskowitz likened the "Save the Family Farm" effort to "a drive for motherhood: everyone's for it but what do you do about it?" While this review was somewhat chafing, it did alert all of Ben & Jerry's stakeholders to the presence of a problem in need of correction—a problem, like plant safety and the salary cap, that might have remained unnoticed and. neglected had it not been for the published social audit, "One reason business is so good at making money is because that is what they measure," commented Greenfield. "We said, if we're ever going to get our social mission to be an important thing to the company, we have to be able to measure it."

While many people might criticize the practice of publishing corporate failures for the world to see. Corren argues that accountability is important, particularly in a business context. "We try to be up-front, to show whether we've walked the talk," Curren asserted. According to Dixie Watterson, executive vice-president of the Investors Relations Company in Northbrook, Illinois, publicly acknowledging its own shortcomings also serves to enhance Ben & Jerry's credibility. Investors may perceive such openness as something that sets the company apart from the pack, and a company that does not cover up its problems is apt to be admired by stockholders and consumers alike.

Still, inclusion of an uncensored social audit in an annual report is still a rare practice. "It's difficult for a company to allow that kind of criticism," commented Moskowitz.

Assignment Questions

1. Discuss what types of control process seems to be a past of the Ben & Jerry's way of doing business.
2. What are the benefits of Ben & Jerry's method of control?
3. What are its drawbacks?
4. In what other types of companies would Ben & Jerry's system work well?

ANNEXURE V

CASE STUDIES

(a) Gandhi Vikas Mandali.
(b) Tsunami disaster effect.
(c) Business fulfils its corporate social responsibilities—Hindustan Lever Limited.
(d) Glaxo Smith Kline Pharmaceuticals Ltd.—Role in corporate social responsibility.
(e) Microsoft larger donator to charity.
(f) Nelson Food Product Ltd.
(g) Tsunami and lessons for internal crisis communities.

(A) GANDHI VIKAS MANDALI*

Gandhi Vikas Mandali (GVM) is a voluntary organisation located in the picturesque surroundings of Periyar, a small village near the capital of a southern state in India. It is engaged in grass-root level development, training, and education. According to Rajen, the founder Director of GVM, "the mission of GVM is to aim at total development of man, and through him a fully developed community". GVM attempts to achieve its mission through its involvement in educational and rural development activities *endeavouring to practice the ideal of community-centred education in an education-centred community*. This strategy has guided GVM in all its efforts through three decades of its existence. Elaborating on this issue, Rajen says:

> "The journey so far had not been smooth and it is not going to be so in the future, GVM had faced many problems, but it always had the resilience to successfully overcome those problems. Availability of sufficient funds for all the programmes the GVM wants to take up was always a problem. Because the voluntary organisations that are affiliated to political parties, religious bodies, and the government are assured of financial help. They will get money easily. But voluntary organisations, like GVM, which declare themselves as secular and apolitical, face the financial crunch. It is therefore imperative that such voluntary organisations become financially strong if they want to implement programmes that are consistent with the objectives of their organisations. Five years from now I would like to see GVM to become financially fully self-sufficient or at least to a great extent."

---

* Prepared by Prof. K. Parthap Reddy, Institute of Rural Management, Anand. All the names in the case are disguised.

Case material of the Institute of Rural Management, Anand, is prepared as a basis for class discussion. Cases are not designed to present illustrations of correct or incorrect handling of administrative situations.

Background

Rajen founded GVM in 1956 as a small community centre at a corner of his parent's property graciously donated to him. It was housed in a thatched shed constructed with the help of his friends and family members. Now it has 65 acres of its own land planted with rubber, coconut, banana and other crops, and fully equipped buildings to meet the requirements of most of its programmes. It hosts several conferences and workshops conducted by various organisations every year. GVM is well-known all over India for its innovative programmes in different areas of rural development. Recalling the conditions in and around Periyar in 1950s, Rajen says,

> "The area in and around Periyar as well as in other villages in this part of the state was completely barren. The greenery now one sees all around was completely absent at that time. It took us almost three decades to educate the village and develop this area. In the beginning, I faced stiff resistance from the vested interests. It somehow persisted with my efforts and ultimately, I succeeded."

Rajen, as a student, was actively involved in socio-cultural and political activities of his locality. He left the state for his studies in social studies during 1949-56. During this time, he also visited Shantiniketan (West Bengal), Sevagram (Maharashtra), and other institutions in India, and some institutions in the UK, USA, Denmark, Holland and other European countries, studying education system, cooperation schemes, experiments in community development, and extension work. Gandhi's ideas also influenced the young Rajen to a great extent. One of the Gandhi's quotes prominently printed in GVM's brochure is reproduced below.

> "By education I mean an all-round drawing out of the best in child and man— body, mind, and spirit. Literacy is not the end of education, not even the beginning. It is only one of the means whereby man and woman can be educated. Literacy in itself is no education. I would therefore begin the child's education by teaching it a useful handicraft and enabling it to produce from the moment it begins its training . . ."

Rajen's studies and the ideas of great people like Gandhi convinced him that only a community-centred education in an education-centred community based in a natural environment can meet all the challenges of total education.

GVM celebrated its Silver Jubilee in 1982. The Indian Merchants Chamber conferred it the Platinum Jubilee Endowment Award in 1986 for its work in socio-economic and human resource development in rural areas.

Administrative Arrangements

GVM was registered under Literacy and Charitable Societies Act-XII of 1955 of the state. It had a General Council consisting of 21 members, a Chairman and a Member-Secretary. The General Council was a policy-making body. The day-to-day management of GVM was looked after by the Director (Rajen) assisted by an Executive Council of five members. Each major activity was managed as a separate centre headed by a senior manager.

All the centres, except the Rural Technology Centre (RTC) were headed by a retired personnel of the state, who were well known for the expertise in their respective fields. For example, the head of the Centre for Educational Research, Innovation, and Development (CERID) was an eminent educationist in the state. The RTC was the most important and the largest unit. Mrs Rajen headed the RTC as the Joint Director. Two of her three daughters attended to the work in the Director's office-*cum*-residence. Many guests visiting GVM often took food at the Director's office-*cum*-residence, which was also arranged by his daughters. The third daughter was a properly trained rural development professional helping her father in the administration and accounts section (which was also headed by a retired bureaucrat).

Low salaries was one of the major reasons for hiring the services of retired persons as head of the units. Most of the other staff was also recruited at very low salary levels—ranging from Rs. 500 to 1,000 per month. The qualified engineers and doctors received slightly better salaries—in the range of Rs. 3,000 to 4,000 per month. The non-supervisory staff was mostly the ex-trainees of the GVM. All the employees were provided accommodation in the campus. GVM ran a mess in which all the employees were allowed to eat on payment of nominal charges. Even Rajen and his wife were working on a small monthly salary. Rajen was willing to pay more than what he gets if he could find a good management graduate.

The organisational chart of GVM is given in Figure 1. In addition to the departments shown in Figure 1, GVM ran a Marketing Servicing Centre and a working-women's hostel, both in the state capital.

Activities of GVM

The major activities of GVM in 1992 are:

(a) Accounts and Administration

The administration and accounts were looked after by a retired bureaucrat, strangely designated as 'Advisor'. He worked full-time and took care of all the financial and administrative matters of the GVM. He was supported by a small staff, including one of the daughters of Rajen.

(b) Rural Technology Centre (RTC)

Joint Director, Mrs Rajen, headed the RTC. A qualified engineer assisted her. The RTC had five units:

(i) Carpentry unit

Four people were employed in this section. Its main activities include sawing and resawing of wood, making wooden furniture, and training people in these works. It had sawing, drilling, and polishing machines and instruments.

(ii) Metal fabrication unit

There were six people working in this section. It had facilities for fabricating various metals. It was equipped with welding, grinding, and lathe machines. Its main activity was training people in welding and fabrication works. Its products included chairs, almirahs, cots, and so forth.

(iii) Pottery unit

The unit had one potter. It had facilities for preparing various types of earthenware.

FIGURE 1

Organisational Chart of Gandhi Vikas Mandali

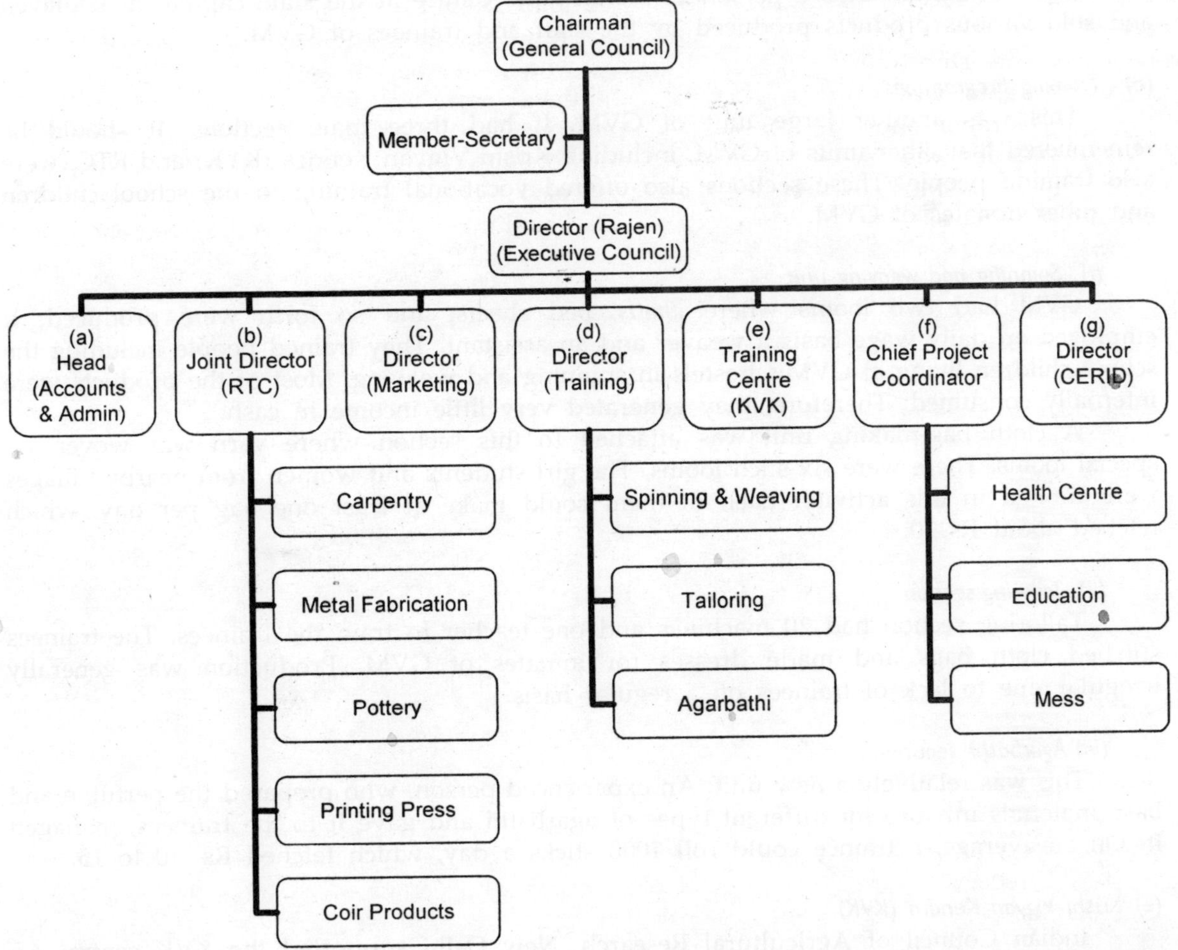

Its main activities included training people in improving their skills in pottery-making.

(iv) Printing press

Seven people were employed in this section. They undertook printing and binding works on custom basis and also trained people in these activities. It had four automatic and semi-automatic printing presses and two cutting machines.

(v) Coir products unit

There were two employees in this section including a diploma-holder in coir technology. They trained as well as produced various types of coir products. The coir products produced in this unit were regularly exported to France. GVM had also formed a separate trust to promote coir industry and coir products.

(c) Marketing

The marketing unit was headed by a retired bureaucrat. It had a Marketing Service Centre at the state capital and a Rural Marketing Service Centre at Periyar. A sales assistant and couple of administrative personnel manned the Centre at the state capital. It displayed and sold various products produced by the staff and trainees of GVM.

(d) Training Programmes

This was another large unit of GVM. It had three main sections. It should be remembered that other units of GVM, including Krishi Vigyan Kendra (KYK) and RTC, were also training people. These sections also offered vocational training to the school children and other inmates of GVM.

(i) Spinning and weaving unit

GVM had two looms where *dhotis,* bed sheets, and so forth were produced. It employed on daily wage basis a weaver and an assistant. They trained people including the school children living at GVM's hostels in spinning and weaving. Most of the products were internally consumed. Therefore, they generated very little income in cash.

A cloth bag-making unit was attached to this section where yarn was woven on special looms. There were six such looms. The girl students and women from nearby villages were trained in this activity. Each of them could make at least one bag per day, which fetched about Rs 20.

(ii) Tailoring section

Tailoring section had 20 machines and one teacher to train the trainees. The trainees stitched cloth bags and made dresses for inmates of GVM. Production was generally irregular due to lack of trainees on a regular basis.

(iii) Agarbathi section

This was relatively a new unit. An experienced person, who prepared the perfume and base materials mixture for different types of agarbathi and gave it to the trainees, managed it. On an average, a trainee could roll 1000 sticks a day, which fetched Rs. 10 to 15.

(e) Krishi Vigyan Kendra (KVK)

Indian Council of Agricultural Research, New Delhi supported the KVK centre. An agricultural expert, retired from the state government service, headed the KVK. In addition, it had a few agricultural officers and a couple of helpers. This unit was responsible for managing the GVM's farm. Besides, this unit also managed programmes on sericulture, biogas, poultry, dairy and bee-keeping.

(f) On-going Projects

GVM regularly added new programmes to the existing ones. A retired bureaucrat headed this unit. The main projects in 1992 were in the areas of health, education, and women welfare.

(i) Health centre

The health centre located in the GVM campus had its own regular doctor. In addition, there was at least one volunteer doctor from abroad at any given point of time. They took up two types of activities: conducting regular health camps in the neighbouring villages and nearby tribal areas for treating patients, and training health volunteers. Besides; they also maintained a Home for the Aged where 30 people were. living in 1992. The health centre also took care of the health needs of the students residing in the hostels. A nurse and a helper assisted the doctors.

(ii) Education programme

Education was the major programme of GVM. Rajen's plan was to set-up a replica of Shantiniketan. Accordingly, GVM started its activities with a school. The school was, however, closed down in 1980 when the teachers went on a strike demanding salaries and other service conditions at par with state government teachers. This clearly contradicted the philosophy of GVM. Even other programmes were stopped for a brief period. GVM re-started its activities using developmental projects and vocational training as main tools for achieving its objectives.

In 1992, GVM was providing only free boarding and lodging facilities to 90 boys and 60 girls housed in two separate hostels. They were mostly tribal children. They attended schools in the nearby villages. They were also trained in various activities like dramatics, sports, gardening, weaving, making cloth bags, agarbathi-making, and other trades for which facilities were available at GVM.

(iii) Working women's hostel

GVM was running a working women's hostel at the state capital housed in a four-storied building constructed with the financial assistance from Ministry of Welfare, government of India. The hostel was full in 1992.

(g) Centre for Educational Research, Innovation and Development (CERID)

An eminent retired educationist of the state headed the Centre for Education, Research, Innovation and Development (CERID). It was started in 1988. It had many Innovative programmes on hand. One such programme was using music and poetry to teach mathematics to school children. It was also a recognised centre for doctoral level studies in education. One student of CERID was awarded doctorate by 1992.

Organisation and Management

The activities of GVM were started on a small scale. It had only 10 employees working in 3 projects in 1956. The number of employees and the projects increased to 20 and 8 in 1960, 40 and 15 in 1965, and 123 and 21 in 1989 respectively. GVM received funding support for these programmes/projects from a variety of sources including from the state government, central government and international donor agencies. GVM was an approved turnkey agent for constructing biogas plants. Its Krishi Vigyan Kendra (KVK) got support from the central government. Council for Advancement of People's Action and Rural Technology (CAPART) extended support to a large number of projects. In fact, as part of its animal husbandry programme, GVM trained local youth and popularised artificial insemination (AI) much before AMUL introduced it on a large scale. Even now GVM trains local youth and supplies to them semen with 50 per cent subsidy. There was an offer to make the CERID an open university, which was rejected fearing government control over

GVM/CERID. All these suggest that GVM was doing very well. But many issues regarding the feature of GVM worried Rajen. Financial self-sufficiency was the most important issue.

With increase in number of employees and number of projects, the dependance of GVM on external sources for financial assistance also increased. While the external financial assistance was only 10 per cent of the annual budget in 1956, it increased to 50 per cent in 1960, and 84 per cent in 1989 (see Exhibit I). In absolute terms, the growth in internal revenue generation was also impressive. While it was Rs 18,000 in 1956, it increased to Rs. 25,000 in 1960, Rs. 50,000 in 1965, and Rs. 9,24,500 in 1989. Elaborating on this issue Rajen explained:

> "A considerable part of this revenue is generated from GVM's 65-acre farm (which also includes land occupied by office buildings, workshops, play-grounds, hostels and residential quarters). While income generation from this source can be increased, it is not going to be substantial. We have to tap our training and educational programmes to make GVM to ultimately become financially self-sufficient."

EXHIBIT I

Internal Revenue Generation by Gandhi Vikas Mandali

Year	*No. of programmes in operation generated (Rs.)*	*No. of employees*	*Annual budget (Rs.)*	*Income internally*
1956	3	10	20,000	18,000
1960	8	20	50,000	25,000
1965	15	40	1,50,000	50,000
1989-90	21	125	59,53,900	9,24,550

The details of the GVM's programmes in 1989-90, their annual budgets, and the income generated by them are given in Exhibit 2. For making GVM financially strong, Rajen had identified three areas for immediate attention. Firstly, GVM as a charitable and separate organisation cannot take up commercial/profit-oriented activities. Hence, there was a need for creating a separate organisation which could take up commercial activities on GVM's behalf and plough back the profits to GVM. Secondly, persons attending various training programmes carry out most of GVM's production activities. As a result, production was irregular and the product quality was not uniform. Therefore, there was a need for streamlining and standardising the products and their quality. Third, GVM had to strengthen its marketing activities. To this end they had recently converted the Rural Marketing Service Centre at Periyar into a marketing department, in addition to its already existing Marketing Service Centre at the state capital. Rajen had observed:

"As mentioned earlier, competent professionals who had either retired from government service or were on deputation head most of the departments/centres of GVM. They are well-known in their field of specialisation for their competence and expertise. But they are not able to give the type of thrust I would like to give for GVM. I need some people with management background to help me streamline the activities of GVM, especially the activities of Rural, Technology Centre (RTC) and its units under the administrative control of the Joint Director.

Besides, Rajen was a heart patient. Of late he was not keeping good health. He was an emotional person but could not afford to speak loudly or, shout at anyone. He was wondering if it was time to look for his successor who could also give the type of thrust he wanted to give to the activities of GVM. His wife too, was concerned about his failing health, three daughters of marriageable age and no savings of their own. The entire family gave their best to the organisation without receiving any remuneration, which could have helped them save some money.

The change efforts

It was in this context that in August 1989, Rajen was able to recruit one young, 25-year-old management graduate, Vinod, from a famous management institute. Vinod had about 1½ years' experience in finance and project management in a large organisation before joining GVM. Vinod had left that organisation because be had strong differences with his boss over a project. He joined GVM because his parents lived at the state capital, which was only about 40 km from Periyar. After joining GVM, Vinod preferred to stay with his parents and commuted from the state capital to Periyar daily.

EXHIBIT 2

Details of Expenditure Incurred and Income Generated from Each Programme

Sl. No.	*Name of the programme*	*Year of starting*	*No. of Project employees*	*Annual budget ('000 Rs.)*	*Income generated in 1989-90 ('000 Rs.)*
1.	Low Cost Houses for weaker Sections	1989	5	300	Nil
2.	Vanita Cooperative Society	1989	5	100	5
3.	Sericulture Project	1988	5	700	5
4.	CERID	1988	4	825	Nil
5.	Tree Lovers' Club	1987	33	544	Nil
6.	Coir Mat Weaving	1987	2	300	100
7.	Income Generation Programme for Women	1987	5	600	150
8.	Gandhi Bhavan (Old Age Home)	1985	1	92	Nil
9.	Krishi Vigyan Kendra	1985	21	700	130
10.	Kora Grass-Mat Weaving	1985	1	13	Nil
11.	Working Women's Hostel	1984	5	230	44
12.	Carpentry	1984	3	480	100
13.	Pottery	1984	1	60	10
14.	Biogas Technology	1983	4	240	40
15.	Low Cost Latrines in Rural Areas	1983	4	120	Nil
16.	Metal Fabrication Centre	1983	6	180	36
17.	Handloom Project	1972	2	2	Nil
18.	Rubber Plantation	1960	3	14	100
19.	Health Centre	1960	3	175	55
20.	Printing Press	1957	7	89	Nil

Before Vinod joined GVM, most of the products produced by GVM were sold through its Rural Marketing Service Centre in Periyar and Marketing Service Centre at the state capital. Wooden and steel furniture, coir products, shoulder bags, and agarbathis were the main items.

Rajen wanted Vinod to first streamline the training-*cum*-production activities of Rural Technology Centre and units, and ultimately, cover all other centres. Besides Rajen told him to get involved in the formation of a trust that was to take up marketing and commercial activities on behalf of GVM.

As soon as he joined GVM, Vinod started working on the tasks assigned to him. A meeting was held in November 1989 to review the progress of his work. Besides Rajen, Pillai, head of administrative and accounts section, Dr Kartikeyan, head of Krishi Vigyan Kendra, Sudasan, a member of the Executive Council, and Raman, who was visiting GVM to understand the working of voluntary agencies, were present in the meeting. Vinod explained the progress of his work in the formation of the trust. He said, "I have already prepared a letter to be mailed to the potential clients and well-wishers of GVM. I have also collected their addresses. However, I need the assistance of Pillai and Sudasan in the formation of the trust, especially to deal with the legal aspects". Rajen said that he had no objection. Both Pillai and Sudasan then readily agreed to extend their cooperation to Vinod in the formation of the trust.

Regarding the streamlining of the activities of RTC, Vinod told the members that he was concentrating on increasing the sale of chairs, tables, almirahs, and so on, being produced now in RTC. He said, "The state capital is a good potential market for these products. To convert this market potential into a reality requires lot of marketing effort." Explaining the results of his marketing efforts, Vinod said, "Sales during April-September 1989 were around Rs 1,500 per month while the expenditure of Marketing Service Centre at the state capital-alone was more than Rs. 1,500 per month: However, there was an increase in sales during October-November 1989 to Rs. 4,009 per month. But that is not enough. If we have to breakeven, the sales have to increase to Rs. 15,000 per month without covering the rent of the building and to Rs. 25,000 per month if the rent also is to be covered."

"Sales can be increased only if the production activities are streamline", explained Vinod. "Further, I have already started this work in the agarbathi section." I will take up this work in the Rural Technology Centre. Meanwhile, I am facing some problems in streamlining the production activities in agarbathi section." Then he listed the following problems:

(i) There are no norms and standards for production per worker. In fact, such norms and standards cannot be easily developed in this section because most of the people who roll agarbathis are trainees, and their skills in making agarbathis vary considerably.

(ii) The raw material cost of agarbathis cannot be ascertained accurately as the composition of the agarbathis, specially the perfume part, is known only to the person in-charge of this section. He does not want to disclose it to others.

(iii) Standardisation of agarbathis, branding them, and maintaining their quality is very difficult in view of the above two reasons.

(iv) Costing of agarbathis is also difficult for the same two reasons.

(v) The quantity of production of agarbathis is mainly dependent on the number of trainees working at a given point of lime in this section. Their number varies considerably from batch to batch. As a result, it is extremely difficult for people to commit a certain quantity and maintain its supply to the dealers on a continuous basis.

"These reasons are not unique to the agarbarthi section," Vinod continued. "They appear to apply to all the other sections of GVM where people are trained in producing various goods. In addition, in welding, fabrication, and carpentry sections of RTC, the quality of the product (furniture) produced by the trainees varies considerably not only across individuals but also at different time periods of their training. A list of the training programmes, their duration, and the number of participants per programme are given in Exhibit 3. Under these conditions how do I commit to any customer that we will supply a particular product of a particular quality on a particular date?" observed Vinod. Moreover, Vinod continued, "The person in charge of the agarbathi section (and probably other section-heads too), does not recognise the importance of modern techniques of planning, control, and monitoring systems. He is not conscious of cost control. Still I made m1, m2, and m3 forms for daily, fortnightly, and monthly reports. I hope he will use them."

Rajen did not agree with the observations of Vinod. He said, "I expected you to stay at GVM Periyar. It was necessary for you to stay at Periyar to understand the work culture

EXHIBIT 3

The Number and Duration of Various Training Programmes

Sl. No.	*Name of the Programme*	*Duration*	*# of People/Batch*	*# of Batches during 1988-90*
1.	Carpentry	1 Year	8	1
2.	Metal Fabrication	1 Year	12	1
3.	Health Worker Training	1 Year	4	1
4.	Garment Making	1 Year	19	1
5.	Training in Weaving	1 Year	6	1
6.	Printing	4 Month	10	3
7.	Binding	4 Month	10	3
8.	Composing	4 Month	10	3
9.	Shoulder Bag Weaving	3 Month	12	4
10.	Sericulture Field Staff Training	2 Month	10	1
11.	Kora Grass Mat Weaving	1 Month	25	10
12.	Sericulture Farmers' Training	1 Month	25	5
13.	Agarbathi Making	1 Month	25	10
14.	Horticulture	1 Month	25	9
15.	Livestock Production	1 Month	5	10
16.	Agricultural Engineering	15 Days	50	13
17.	Home Science	5 Days	35	11
18.	Mushroom Cultivation	3 Days	10	15
19.	Crop Production	3 Days	325	12

and work values of people at GVM and continuously monitor the progress of your effort. But you preferred to stay at the state capital with your parents. And you are concentrating on marketing efforts in the state capital instead of streamlining the training and production activities of RTC. You have taken up the study of smaller agarbathi section because you could manage it with occasional visits to Periyar. Even in the agarbathi section, you suggested some changes without considering the needs and values of the people working there and their competence to implement your suggestions."

"Also," continued Rajen, "Vinod, you are wrong when you observed that the Heads of Departments do not recognise the importance of planning, control, and monitoring systems and are not conscious of cost control. Though the theories of planning and other control systems and other accompanied jargons may not be familiar to them, they had applied them in practice." Vinod mumbled something and finally said that he will shift to GVM campus in the next few days. "Meanwhile", assured Rajen, "I will find you a suitable accommodation in the campus."

Vinod then raised the issue of payment of all the bills at Central Administrative and Accounts Section at Periyar. He said that he was finding it difficult to pay even small amounts of contingency expenses and cited the problems he had recently faced while dealing with the sale to some items of furniture. He suggested that he should be given some imprest money (advance), and he will settle the accounts once in a week. Rajen replied, "This is an important issue. While I have no objection to give you the imprest money, there may be many such issues, which come in the way of smooth functioning of the organisation. Why don't you take up the study of the activities needing money to be spent immediately from the imprest amount and suggest limit for each activity?" Vinod agreed to study it in a week's time. Then the meeting was closed.

Though Rajen did not agree with the method of Vinod's working, he did not doubt his competence. He told Raman, "Vinod is a capable, competent and hard working young man but he is a bit impatient. He wants to do things in a hurry. He does not pause to understand people. Here we have people with different levels of competence and understanding. We took them as they came along. If Vinod wants them to implement his ideas, he has to take them with him. Sometimes he may have to go back to their level, work with them at their pace, develop them and then carry them and get his ideas implemented. The modern planning and control techniques cannot be simply thrusted upon them."

After spending three days at GVM, Raman observed, "GVM is being managed like an extended joint family. I saw senior and junior employees freely walking in and having food in the Director's house. It is the same case with most guests. The main concern of the GVM's management seems to be the welfare and overall development of people. Commercial orientation is totally lacking. Then how can GVM become financially self-sufficient?" When Raman communicated his observations to Rajen, he replied, "GVM cannot be assessed or studied merely from business management angle as, it is a combination of social, economic cultural complex having creatively productive action programmes along with community living to provide stimulant environment, both human and nature. Community living gives the ideas of an extended family. The Director's residence provides not only for managers but also to junior officials, students, and guests to come together for informal, get together in smaller numbers either over a cup of tea, lunch, or supper. GVM has to become financially self-sufficient without unnecessarily disturbing this present work culture". He also informed Raman that Vinod left GVM in December 1989 leaving most of the tasks assigned to him unfinished.

(B) TSUNAMI EFFECT AND NPOs

Dreams of celebrating New Year 2005 were swept away when the dreaded Tsunami struck on 26 December, 2004 leaving millions of people stranded and hopeless. It wiped out scores of villages, altered the geography of entire islands, and created mountains of debris that could choke mangrove forests and destroy coral reefs. India's southernmost spot, Indira Point on Campbell Bay Island, has disappeared. The sand beaches which have always been the main attraction for tourists for different reasons, are the worst affected.

What is a Tsunami

Tsunami a Japanese term, which has been universally adopted to describe a large seismically generated sea wave is capable of considerable destruction in certain coastal areas, especially where underwater earthquakes occur. Although in the open ocean the wave height may be less than 1 m, it steepens to heights of 15 m or more on entering shallow water. They have been incorrectly referred to as tidal waves.

The recent earthquake originated in the Indian Ocean just north of Simeulue island, off the western coast of northern Sumatra, Indonesia. The resulting tsunami devastated the shores of Indonesia, Srilanka, South India, Thailand and other countries with waves of up to 15 m (50 feet) high. It caused serious damage and deaths as far as the east coast of Africa, with the furthest recorded death due to the tsunami occurring at East London in South Africa, 7800 km (4800 miles) away from the epicentre. Approximately, 270,000 people are thought to have died as a result of the tsunami. The true final toll may never be known due to bodies having been swept out to sea, but current estimates use conservative methodologies.

Tsunami of December 26

Death toll:	2,70,000
Indonesia:	1,27,420
Sri Lanka:	31,003
India:	10,273
Thailand:	5,395

Disaster have often played a spoilsport in the growth of tourism industry. After a lull of three years owing to September 11 attacks followed by SARS fear, the tourism industry had just begun to take off. More than 5.5 million Indians were expected to travel abroad—mostly to south east Asian destinations like Thailand, Malaysia and Singapore and even more were expected to reach India by the last week of December. But all hopes were shattered to this unprecedented turn of events.

The tourism insiders reveal the industry has been hit badly. Non-profit organisations have liberally come to rescue and long-term rehabilitation measures. Over 26 NPOs were operating to assist in terms of manpower and in kind, i.e. food, financial aspects. WHO gives priority to rapid health assessment by supporting the efforts of national and local counterparts. WHO is also working on strengthening health coordination and evidence-based decision-making in all affected countries in the region. It is also coordinating with UNDAC and other UN bodies.

Another Earthquake

A massive earthquake of at least 8.5-magnitude struck off Indonesia's Sumatra Island on Monday (28.3.2005) night spreading panic and triggering tsunami warnings in India, Indonesia, Thailand and Sri Lanka.

In India, the Home Ministry's emergency control room, set-up after the Boxing Day disaster, kicked into action and sounded a tsunami alert in the Andaman and Nicobar islands and the southern states

There was hectic activity also at the control room of the Integrated Defence Staff (IDS) in South Block as the brass led by IDS chief Vice-Admiral Raman Puri descended to monitor the situation. The IDS is mandated with coordinating relief operations by the armed forces in the event of calamity "The armed forces are on standby to meet any contingency," an official said.

The LAF also implemented the disaster drill at the Car Nicobar air base that was devastated in the December 26 tsunami. All personnel were moved to the airstrip, the highest point on the island and authorities are in constant touch with the base.

The earthquake was felt as far north as Bangkok, Thailand, peninsular Malaysia and Singapore, causing thousands of residents to flee high-rise apartment buildings and hotels.

Most governments were prompt in issuing tsunami alerts, with warnings going out shortly after the earthquake struck. Residents of coastal areas in Malaysia, Sri Lanka, Thailand and Indonesia were asked to move to higher ground as a precautionary measure.

Wiser, quicker this time

Earthquake struck off the coast of Sumatra, close to where a quake triggered a tsunami last December. The Pacific tsunami warning center said the quake had the potential to cause a "widely destructive tsunami" and authorities should take "immediate action", including evacuating coastlines within 960 km of the epicenter. Tsunami warnings were issued in Thailand, Japan and Sri Lanka.

(C) BUSINESS FULFILS ITS CORPORATE RESPONSIBILITIES: A CASE STUDY OF HLL

We discuss the role currently played by business and its leaders, and to assess how it should evolve, given the current global context.

Is shareholder value the singular measure of a business capability, success and contribution? Surely not. Recent events like the dotcom bust and events in corporate America have certainly shown that we need to move beyond the mere metric of the stock market. Business has several stakeholders—Employees, Customers, Suppliers, Government, and of course the Community at large, apart from our Shareholders. Each of these groups has different anticipations from us, each expects us to make a different kind of contribution. The sum total of these contributions, across all of business, can potentially have a very broad impact on society—and I dare say, even on the nation. This is not only true for India—it is true globally.

I were to share with you our perspective on how we in Hindustan Lever are trying to achieve this across our various constituencies. A key stakeholder for us is the Government. HLL has always believed and practised that "What is good for India, is good for HLL." We were the first company to voluntarily disinvest 10% of the Unilever holding in 1956 to local shareholders. Since then, there has been progressive disinvestment of the

Unilever shareholding, essentially to attract local ownership to a point where today only 52% of the company is held by Unilever and the rest by 350,000 local shareholders and financial institutions. Our local shareholding brings us several benefits—it helps us identify very clearly with national interest. It also provides a greater degree of accountability for performance.

Another example is our commitment to growing exports and foreign exchange earnings. We are already one of India's largest exporters with a total export of over Rs. 1500 crores last year, and have been rated a Super Star Trading House for several years by the Government of India. Indeed, we believe that we can grow our exports strongly and sustainably by leveraging on our strengths to source products for other Unilever countries, and also by focussing on areas where India has a natural country advantage like Marine Products.

A couple of years ago, we were the first company to avail of the Government's disinvestment policy with the acquisition of the loss-making Modern Foods. Within a couple of years, we have been able to double its sales, reduce its cost base and bring it to breakeven this year. We believe this is a good illustration of our professional management and of course, the very principles of disinvestment.

We are also collaborating with the Government and other agencies to uplift the general level of social development. Let me give you one example. Not many people know that diarrhoea is the largest cause of children's deaths, accounting for over 2 million fatalities globally each year, 30% of which are in India. The cause is poor hand hygiene—a large number of people do not wash their hands before eating or after personal hygiene practices. The result—germs are transferred from the hand to the mouth and the result is a disaster for human life. In October, we are launching a massive programme in the State of Kerala to educate the population on the need to wash their hands with soap.

Last, but not the least, we take very seriously our responsibility of associating with the Government in various forums, providing information, insight and advice on policy formation and implementation.

Another major stakeholder is the *Community at large*. We have, over the years, established 15 manufacturing units in various backward areas. Many of these were barren lands with no infrastructure when we arrived. It is today a source of great pride to see vibrant factories with skilled manpower, as well as local ancillary industries to support us, contributing to the local economy and prosperity. Importantly, these units are not merely cutting edge in India—they are world class both in quality and cost! Many of these units are also involved in several community initiatives—adult education, running of schools, etc.—and often become a catalyst for social improvement.

Another example of our commitment to the Community is the work we are doing with Self Help Groups in Andhra Pradesh, in partnership with several NGOs. The women in these Self Help Groups can access micro-credit from NABARD and are in search of a viable enterprise model. That is where we come in. We provide them with the opportunity to educate others in the villages on the nutritional and hygiene benefits of our brands and also to retail these.

We are totally committed to protecting our environment PTO. Several initiatives are under way. Our load on the environment has reduced dramatically—specifically, our energy and water requirements have halved in five years. Our plants do not discharge effluents and we are leading efforts towards harnessing water and greening the environment. In our tea plantations, we are working to ensure their sustainability. A good example is the conversion of waste from our workers' homes to natural fertiliser, using vermin composting, thereby reducing our use of chemical fertilisers.

Let me now turn to our *Shareholders.* They are obviously interested in a fair return on their capital. However, I believe our shareholders are not looking for a fast buck with the concomitant risks attached with it. They are interested in steady, long-term appreciation, and we are determined to deliver this—and we have. Over the last five years, we have delivered a growth of 300% to them. Our EVA has trebled over the last five years, growing consistently at over 30% p.a. But they also require transparency. They want information. They want to know how we are managing their company. What is the strategy that is being followed? How well is it being implemented? Who are the key people running it? And it is their right to know—after all, they are the owners. Many see this as an unnecessary intrusion—a burden. At HLL, we welcome this and indeed try and provide as much information as possible. We provide detailed financial updates every quarter. We were amongst the first to lead with segmental reporting. Our Balance Sheet runs into 50 pages and provides all the information we sensibly can. In January 2001, we developed a new strategy to take into account changes in the competitive environment in a more open India. We shared this with all our investors and now regularly review our progress against this. We hold analyst meets very six months, attend investor conferences and of course, meet individual investors as required. We also get them to meet our other senior people, and all that we say is immediately put on our web site making it available to every investor—current or potential. We never brief investors selectively. Our smaller individual shareholders also have several opportunities to access information, including at our AGMs, which are very well attended—the last one had 10,000 people. It is our practice to answer every single question that is raised, even if it means that our meeting often lasts for 6-8 hours.

Let me now turn to another important group—*our Employees.* Of course, we reward them well, and place a great emphasis on linking reward with performance. But what is only a small part of our contract with them. We do believe that people are not motivated by money alone. Their main motivation in working with us is to pursue their own development and growth. In this context, we provide a culture of complete meritocracy. Every individual manager, salesman, factory worker, joins after a very thorough selection process and justifiably feels an enormous sense of pride at being selected. Each manager's contribution in the year is thoroughly assessed against agreed targets and openly communicated to him, including areas of further development. All promotions are on merit. Each opportunity is advertised within the company and any manager who fulfils the required experience criteria can apply. A due selection process is followed—very similar to the one for entry to the company—and the best candidate selected. Each person who is not selected is told why he has not made it. Do people value this? Yes, definitely. Our attrition rate is relatively low at 6-7% p.a. Also, last year, we were rated as the No. 1 employer in a survey of all leading business schools.

I could go on like this about our other stakeholders . . . the Consumers, Customers, Suppliers, etc. . . . but shall not do so for want of time. Thus far, I have been telling you what we have done to meet the expectations of our various stakeholders. Let me now move to talking about how we have been able to create an *organisation culture of responsibility.*

HLL follows a very *strong Code of Business Principles*—a framework that is available to each of our employees. Every manager is given a copy as he joins and there are several forums at which these are discussed and reiterated. Violation of this code is simply not tolerated. You can make any number of mistakes in a business sense, as long as you learn from them. However, you cannot go against the code. Let me give you some examples that will show you how we enforce this.

A few years ago, the terrorists in North East India threatened the safety of our management unless we provided 'safety money'. It took us virtually no time to decide that we simply could never accede to such a request. Overnight, we decided to close down our plantations and fly our managers and their families to safety. We chartered an Indian Airlines plane and flew it into that area at night, and evacuated all our people under cover of the Indian Army. This, of course, had considerable implications, both in terms of cost and the publicity that we received, but we were simply not prepared to succumb to unlawful demands and operate under threat. We went back into Assam only several months later, when we were assured of the Government's intent and ability to protect our people.

In another case, we were opening a new factory. A Factory Inspector wanted us to employ a person known to him. The individual concerned was tested, but regrettably was not selected as he failed the skills test. We provided feedback, both to the candidate and the Inspector, and offered to re-test him after he had improved his skills base. The Inspector took great umbrage at this and refused to allow us to open the factory on some spurious technical grounds. Every week's delay cost us a lot as our investment was idle, but we stood our ground. We fought the matter all the way up the bureaucratic hierarchy till our stand was upheld.

Recently, we built a new office building of about 30,000 sq. ft. When it was ready, we discovered that we had inadvertently built about 300 sq. ft. extra which was not in the plan. This was, of course, challenged by the authorities who saw in this a way for them to seek favour. It would have been quite easy for us to resolve the matter in some way, but we chose not to do so. We appealed to the higher authorities that this was a genuine mistake. When this was not accepted, we decided to demolish the 300 sq. ft. that was extra so that there would then be no reason for them not to give us an occupancy certificate. The whole process delayed us by a few months, but we were determined to secure occupancy in the right way.

In each of these cases, we have had to bear a short-term cost. This has never impacted our determination to uphold our way of doing business. In general, today, there is a lot of cynicism about whether you can do business in the right way. Our experience is that you can. But only if you are prepared to fight for it. The good news is that once you establish a reputation for being principled, you are not persecuted—your reputation is your armour!

We have also identified and articulated a very clear set of values for the company. Why? Because these values provide a moral framework by which our people can view their own actions. Values also provide a very aspirational environment—they attract like-minded people into the company and help to bind them together. So what are the HLL values?

HLL Values

We expect our managers to live by the values of TRUTH, COURAGE, ACTION and CARING. At one level, these appear very naive words. However, when you think deeply about them, and then apply them to all situations, they have a very profound meaning.

Truth

What is truth? Some call it candour, honesty. What does it give us? Truth helps us acknowledge the problems as they arise, so that we spend the rest of our time dealing with them—not denying them.

Truth helps us to be honest with each other—to tell each other what we really feel, of course, to get truth, you have to be a good listener. We have to be open to feedback and pick up signals.

A very important precursor to truth is trust—and trust comes from knowing each other better. So we encourage our teams to really get to know each other—to spend time together, to eat together, to spend time outside the office together with their families. We are also using 360 degrees feedback throughout the entire organisation to bring about greater openness, greater trust, and greater truth.

Courage

Another value is Courage. Courage is about inner confidence. Courage is about conviction. Courage is about betting. Courage is about saying, "I will do this because it will work." But courage is not recklessness. Courage comes from knowledge. Courage comes from rigour. If you have done your homework, you will have plenty of courage. Courage is also about doing what is not obvious. We have recently decided to focus our attention and resource of key brands in our FMCG businesses. We had two very successful businesses—Seeds and Flavours and Fragrances—both growing and very profitable. A convenient decision would have been to keep them for now, at a time when growth is hard to come by. But we took the courageous decision to let them go—we parted with two highly successful businesses so we could concentrate our efforts on our key brands.

Action

Our third value is Action. This is quite simple. Wars are not won because of the battle plan. They are won in the trenches, on the hills of Kargil, by what people do. So we must move. We must move with great speed. We must move with great precision. We must move with great excellence. Last year, we faced the challenge of putting up additional capacity in a short time. Our teams took an impossible target, and put up 6 factories in different corners of India in just 9 months.

Caring

Last, but definitely not the least, is the value of Caring—caring for each other, for each other's families, sharing the joy of good times, sharing the sorrow of difficult times. Tragedies do happen everywhere. One thing is for sure—the HLL families are secure in the knowledge that they will be taken care of in every eventuality—the very best medical care in the world, a determination to protect the lifestyle of the family and children's education in the event of a premature death. But caring is not being soft. Caring is about really feeling for the other person. Caring is about being honest to a person about his potential, even if the truth is difficult. Caring is knowing that every person has only one life to live and you owe it to him or her to be totally honest.

So these then are the values of HLL. We expect all our managers to live by these. How do we ensure that? We have involved a large number of them in identifying the specific behaviours that best exemplify these values and also those that contradict them in each function. These desirable and undesirable behaviours have been widely publicised throughout the company. Those who live by these values are celebrated-eulogised, written about.

Cultures are built by leaders and driven by the people. I am here reminded of a wonderful story told to me by Prakash Tandon, the first Indian Chairman of HLL. He was once asked as to what qualities he would look for in his successor. He replied unhesitatingly, in one word—"character." Today when we recruit people, we of course look for professional competence, but much more that, we look for people who have integrity. Integrity, because they will have the ability to objectively assess reality and give both good and bad news. We also look for self-confidence. We need people who have faith in themselves, even in the face of immense adversity—people who can and will make a difference, to their organisations and to India.

In conclusion, I would say this. Business leaders can, of course, play a major role in driving shareholder value, but they can do much more. They can build a very positive relationship with all the other stakeholders—and through these wide ranging relationships, they can make a very broad impact on society, and indeed on India. I would also like to say that employees increasingly wish to work in organisations, which, of course, are commercially successful, but in addition, make a positive contribution to society. I have also no doubt that consumers too will increasingly choose brands, not just on the basis of the brand benefit, but on the value systems of the company behind the brand. The interest and appreciation that employees, consumers and shareholders show, in how a business fulfils its corporate responsibilities, helps build a virtuous cycle of greater commitment from the business and greater trust from the stakeholders.

Source: This is an Extract from the Text of the address delivered by Mr. M.S. Banga, Chairman, HLL at the CII Leadership Summit, New Delhi on September 18, 2002. Gratefully acknowledged.

(D) GLAXO SMITH KLINE PHARMACEUTICALS LIMITED, INDIA: ROLE IN CORPORATE SOCIAL RESPONSIBILITY

> A company is linked closely to the communities in which it operates locally, nationally or globally. It cannot exist in isolation.
>
> —*Sir Richard Skyes*, Chairman, GlaxoWellcome plc

I. Introduction to CSR

Companies operating in globalised markets are increasingly required to balance the financial and economic considerations of their business with social, community and environmental aspects as well, while building shareholder value.

The socially responsible business is attracting some of the best business minds, as numerous initiatives seek to identify the issues and create the tools to implement programmes at the company level. For different industries, responsible business practice involves different issues.

As Mc Williams & Siegel have said, "Corporate Social Responsibility are actions above and beyond that required by law." The voluntary actions of the companies for the benefit of the community is what CSR is about.

Corporate Reasons for Response

CSR is designed to deliver sustainable value not only to the shareholders but also to the society at large.

According to the CSR Survey 2002 (India) Report, Indian companies see corporate social responsibility as central to corporate action, with "excessive philanthropy" no longer a sufficient response to rising expectations of the society. The above mentioned report surveyed 102 Indian companies and was conducted jointly by the United Nations Development Programme, the British Council, Confederation of Indian Industry and Pricewaterhouse Coopers. The report found that the most important driver for involvement in CSR within Indian industry was the desire to be a good corporate citizen, linked to company as well as product/brand reputation. Improved ties with local communities was also seen as a strong factor.

The authors have surveyed most of the large corporates, both national and multinational, and have observed that corporates undertake CSR activities due to the feeling of community belongingness.

In this article presented a case of an Indian Pharmaceutical Company's responsibility towards the community through its CSR-related activities.

2. Glaxo Smith Kline Pharmaceuticals Limited, India

Gluxo Smith Kline Pharmaceuticals Ltd. is India's leading Pharmaceutical company with a market share of over 6.6 per cent. The company markets a wide range of ethical formulations and is the leader in therapeutic areas of respiratory, dermatology and vaccines, besides having a significant presence in areas of gastroenterology, dietary supplements, and intensive care. Glaxo Smith Kline (GSK) is also the undisputed leader in animal health and fine chemicals businesses. CSR's strategic intent is to become the undisputable leader in its industry—not simply in terms of size, but in how it uses that size to achieve its mission. Through its Global Community Partnerships function and Corporate Donations Committee, GSK partners wish and *supports organisations whose goals and objectives reflect its mission* of improving the quality of human life.

The company has manufacturing units in India, located at Thane, Nasik, Mysore and Bangalore. Operational Excellence is the buzzword at GMS, a new global improvement programme that will drive change, increase efficiency and raise quality standards in every process.

GSK employs over 4000 skilled persons across the country. The company has the largest field force in the industry and a nation-wide network of about 4000 dealers. This gives the company a wide reach across the nation in its efforts to strengthen the hands of the doctor in his fight against diseases. GSK is the largest prescription generator in the indusry.

Glaxo Smith Kline plc is the world's leading research-based pharmaceutical and healthcare company.

A truly global organisation with a wide geographical spread, Glaxo Smith Kline has its corporate headquarters in West London, UK. The company has over 1,00,000 employees and supplies its products to 140 markets around the world. It has one of the largest sales and marketing operations in the global pharmaceutical industry.

GSK's global quest is to improve the quality of human life by enabling people to do more, feel better and live longer.

GSK's *community investment programmes* represent a commitment that, as the company builds upon its successes and grows, it will continue to recognise the responsibility of leadership and the strength of partnership.

This commitment is maintained through a blend of innovative and more established philanthropy and sponsorships, and initiatives in global public health.

The company's flagship community programme is its key role in the Global Alliance to Eliminate Lymphatic Filariasis—a 20 year programme to eliminate one of the world's most disfiguring and disabling diseases.

3. GSK's Core Value—We Care

Being a premier pharmaceutical company in the country GSK's core value is to be a good corporate citizen. It is committed to the communities in which it works. Support to the community through charitable initiatives is the ways through which it invests in society.

To GSK being a good corporate citizen means:

- being proactive in improving the environment,
- participating in and contributing to the well-being of the local community, and
- actively contributing to national priorities in health and safety.

At Glaxo Smith Kline, India, the activities towards community development are attached to the Corporate Communications Department. There is also a Community Welfare and Social Activities Department.

Mr. N.Y. Sanglikar, Sr. G.M. states that the organisation performs Socially Responsible activities as a sincere attempt to give back to the society what it earns from it. GSK believes that it owes its services to the community.

Mr. Sanglikar stated that the initiatives are mainly towards Women and Children and the focus areas are Education, Hygiene and Health, because, the company believes that the three areas are related and of direct concern to GSK. If there is proper education will one eventually learn to be hygienic, and if one is hygienic will one remain healthy. He adds that the organisation facilitates towards educating masses on good practices of healthy living.

The assistance given is always need-based; there is no budget driven expenditure. This implies that there is no planned expenditure towards community development, but an impulsive attempt to uplift the needy whenever it is possible.

4. Programmes undertaken by the Social Work Unit of GSK

Since 1970's the company has been implementing various social responsibility programmes apart from the statutory ones. The following Communities Development activities are carried out:

(a) Child Welfare at Koliwada, Mumbai

In 1979, 'the International Year of the Child', the employees of the heritage company Glaxo India promoted this charitable trust for the development of the financially disadvantaged children deprived of opportunities such as basic education, healthcare and recreation. It aims at promoting the physical, intellectual, emotional and psychological development of needy children. The SSSS runs a Modern Care Centre which provides comprehensive health check-up and treatment.

An initiation of the social workers has enabled rehabilitation of a few mentally and physically challenged children, which was a task beyond the reach of the parents.

(b) Rural Development: Gramin Arogya Vikas Sanstha (GAVS) at Dhondbar Village

The Sanstha (Organisation) works in Dhondbar village in Sinnar taluka, Nasik district. Inaccessibility, low literacy level, absence of any NGO and paucity of basic healthcare facilities characterized the village. Ms. Pooja highlighted the fact that before their adoption of the villages, the literacy level was zero, today, many of the adolescents know to read and write. The trust, sanctioned of an amount of 11 crores and the organisation ensured that the funds were utilized in the most effective way.

(c) Quality Streets Circle at Worli, Mumbai

In 1990, Glaxo initiated a unique project—Quality Streets Circle (QSC), which is an association of over 25 business establishments located around the Glaxo & Wellcome headquarters in Worli. The objective of QSC is to maintain clean and healthy civic environment in the neighbourhood. It tackles various civic issues through collective action and so far has been successful in removal of some unauthorized construction, widening and beautification of the roads and pavements in the vicinity and installation of post boxes. QSC has developed a positive working relationship with the Mumbai Municipal Corporation, the local ward office.

(d) Glaxo HIV/AIDS Help Line

The company launched a 24 hours phone in help line in October 2000, as a unique and innovative initiative for counseling and dissemination of information on HIV/AIDS to the lay public in Mumbai. A highly trained and experienced team of counselor answers thousands of callers at the help line. GSK's help line was rated as the best help line on the subject in India. The organisation provides HIV/AIDS drugs at discounted price.

(e) Positive Action on HIV/AIDS

Positive Action is GSK's long-term, international programme of HIV education, care and community support.

(f) The Fight Against Malaria

GSK has been active in the fight against malaria for many years.

(g) Audio Visuals for Promoting Health Awareness

A series of public health audio visuals on balanced diet, prevention of TB and AIDS, environment protection, primary healthcare for infants and consumer rights and responsibilities have been produced by Glaxo. These are screened for various audiences including voluntary and Government bodies.

(h) Medical Education for Health Professionals

A subsidized teaching aids programme for doctors and health professionals was implemented by GSK.

(i) Science Education Programmes for the Youth.

(j) Product Donations for Humanitarian Relief Efforts

Such donations are made at the request of government and major charitable organisations.

(k) Eco Consciousness

Treating effluent, planting trees and energy conservation form the thrust of this programmes. The nature of the company's business points to the generation of effluents. Effluent Treatment Plants (ETP) are in operation at all sites and the treated water is used for gardening. Solid and chemical waste is also disposed-off in a way as to protect the environment from damage. Tree plantation is an ongoing process at GSK sites.

(l) Employee Development through Cultural, Social and Educational Programmes.

(m) Employee Involvement

GSK has more than 5000 employees in India, all of whom have been drawn together to assist in the fight against human disease and suffering. Employees are encouraged to take advantage of the company's employee volunteering support scheme.

(n) Helping the Physically Challenged

GSK has been the employer of a large number of disabled persons in all its four factories and has won awards from voluntary bodies and the Government in recognition for the same.

(o) Financial and Infrastructure Support to Voluntary Bodies

GSK supports the needy organisations and causes by way of cash donations, souvenir advertisements and medicines.

GSK's contribution to those affected by natural calamities, like the earthquake at Latur and the cyclone in Gujarat has always been swift.

5. Final Observations and Summary

- Most of the CSR activities revolve around their core business activity, mainly healthcare. GSK's products and business operations therefore focuses on improving the health and quality of life of people throughout the country.
- GSK stresses on the importance of education to lead a healthy life.
- The programme of charitable and community contribution is an aspect of the activity which the company regards as a proper part of its set role in society to be a good corporate citizen worldwide.
- In selecting projects towards social responsibility, equal priority is given to those activities which promote scientific and medical education.
- The presence of a team within GSK to work towards community development explains the organisations' long-term interest in the concept of CSR.

Source: This is an abstract of an article by N.M. Kandop, "Corporate Social Responsibilty" in *NMIMS Journal*, July-December 2003.

S.K. Bhatia, Business Ethics and Corporate Governance, 2004, Deep & Deep Publications Pvt. Ltd., New Delhi.

(E) A TAKE ON MICROSOFT AS A GOOD CITIZEN

In honour of my (John Caroll) one-time favourite late-night talk show, I present the top 10 reasons why Microsoft is a good corporate citizen.

10. Microsoft drives computing cost down

With all the rhetoric surrounding Linux and its "free" status, it is often forgotten why consumers (Linux users included) pay so little for computer hardware these days. Not only have Microsoft's desktop efforts led to greater hardware economics of scale, the company has actively worked to drive down hardware prices through standard PC specifications, including simple things like the WinModem.

Though WinModems drive Linux usefulness to distraction, the reason WinModems exist is that they cost less, saving consumers on new PCs.

Furthermore, let's not forget that Microsoft has historically charged far less than its proprietary cousins. Compared to Sun Microsystems' high-priced Unix servers. Oracle's incredibly expensive database and the price combo of Apple hardware with ANY Apple OS, Microsoft products have been an incredible bargain.

9. Microsoft has been instrumental in bringing computing to ordinary people

Although that might be a "negative" for those who don't want to be bothered by hordes of "newbies", non-technical computer users wouldn't be on the Internet if it weren't for hand-holding from companies such as AOL and, of course, Microsoft. Though its marketing and products, Microsoft has done more than any other company to help users find ways to integrate computing into their daily lives.

8. Microsoft employees absolutely love their company

Microsoft regularly is ranked one of the best places to work. Programmes are respected, and creativity is encouraged. Plus, the company pays well to boot. That leads to one of the lowest employee turnover rates in the industry, even at a time when the company is in the midst of a government suit which has dragged its name through the mud.

7. Microsoft pays loads in taxes

According to information found on Yahoo Financials, Microsoft paid $ 1.288 billion in income taxes for the fiscal quarter ended March 31.

6. Its founder has donated more money to charity than anyone in history

At the last count, Bill Gates, as an individual, has given about $ 22 billion—or just under 26 aircraft carriers—to charity. To put that in perspective, George Soros' donations as an individual total a "merely" $ 2 billion. Andrew Cornegie, the famed philanthropist, gave only $ 3 billion in current dollars over the course of his life.

5. Microsoft creates a computing economy worth far greater than its own net worth

If one counts up all the companies that develop Windows-compatible software (including such industry luminaries such as Oracle and IBM), all the hardware companies that make money selling to Windows users, and all the technicians engaged in writing software for Windows or providing technical support for it, you'll find that there is far more money made from Microsoft products outside of Redmond than is made of it.

4. One of the largest R&D budgets in the industry

In fiscal year 2001, Microsoft spent $ 4.4 billion, a spending total that rose to more than $ 5 billion in fiscal year 2002. R&D benefits us all through technological advancements. Though developing software that is more productive might not seem as earth-shattering as, say, finding a cure for cancer, such advances improve the efficiency of the digital infrastructure upon which we build our lives.

3. Microsoft takes risks

This might seem a strange reason to consider Microsoft a good corporate citizen, but consider the results. How many companies would have the courage—much less the stamina—to take on Sony in game consoles, Palm computing in handhelds, Sun in server operating systems, Oracle and IBM in databases, AOL in Internet access, and practically every wireless phone-maker in existence (Nokia and Ericsson among them) in the provision of operating systems for advanced cell phones? Not many.

Microsoft is the primary competitor to these leading companies in most of these markets, which helps boost quality and innovation. I might be going off on a tangent, but if Microsoft can enter already dominated markets and manage to keep its head above water, why can't other large companies compete in markets Microsoft dominates?

2. A beacon of profitability in a sea of red ink

Microsoft is one of the few companies to have managed to maintain robust sales throughout the current recession. That should matter to those who care about the health of the US economy. And last but not least . . .

1. No accounting scandals at Microsoft

In contrast to all the revenue-padding at Enron, WorldCom and even AOL, Microsoft was prompted by the Securities and Exchange Commission to adjust its past income upwards. So there you have it. My apologies to David Letterman for dragging him into the mother of all greek wars.

Box I

Some information about the Bill and Melinda Gates Foundation

The Bill and Melinda Gates Foundation is the world's largest charitable foundation. Endowed by Bill and Melinda Gates, it was created in January 2000 through the merger of Gates Learning Foundation and the William H. Gates Foundation. The foundation is based in Seattle, Washington and is led by William H. Gates, Sr. (Bill Gate's father) and Patty Stonesifer.

The foundation has an endowment of approximately $ 27 billion. To maintain its status as a charitable foundation, it must donate at least 5 percent of its assets each year. This amounts to over $ 1 billion.

The foundation focuses on the following areas:

- Global health
- Education
- Libraries
- Pacific Northwest

Source: John Carroll, www.zdetindia.com and *Economic Times*, New Delhi.

(F) CASE STUDY: NELSON FOOD PRODUCTS LIMITED

Nelson Food Products Limited is a super-premium chocolate-maker renowned for its innovative and exceptionally tasty flavours which are preferred by young and old in India. Besides, chocolates, they manufacture many other milk products including for babies.

Organisations annual reports normally highlight promises of growth and improvements in financial well-being of the corporation. However, companies do not report how well they are doing in terms of managing the human resources side of the business or whether they are building a health company. Nelson Food Products Ltd. annual reports fall somewhere outside the business norms. Nelson Foods have published two areas in its annual report, one financial, and the other social.

At Nelson Foods, management believes that a company should be evaluated not only on its financial performance but on its social performance as well. "To be profitable for its shareholders and to be socially responsible, inside and outside the organisation" is an assertion boldly made in the company's mission statement. "We decided that we wanted to measure our success by changing the definition of our bottom line," explained its Chairman. "For most businesses, their bottom line is just their profits, how much money is left over at the end of the year. We said we're going to have a two-part bottom line. We'll measure our success both by how we do financially and how we do with our social mission."

The Nelson Food's social audit rates the company in areas such as employee benefits, plant safety, ecology, community involvement, and customer service. In order to make sure that no stone is left unturned, the auditor, an outside export not employed with Nelson Foods, is given access to all employee and corporate documents during the conducting of the review.

"It's all in keeping with our two-part bottom line," states Chairman, Nelson Foods. The findings of the audit, positive or negative, are then published, unedited, so as to guarantee complete candor.

As a result, Nelson Foods annual reports tend toward honestly. For example, in their two plants safety standard showed increase in days lost as a result of injuries due to accidents. They also imposed a cap on executive salaries in order not to have salary system which does not exceed seven times the salary of the lowest-paid employee. This resulted in some key positions remaining vacant.

While many people criticize the practice of publishing corporate failures for the world to see. However, Nelson Food's Vice-President investor's relations asserts that publicly acknowledging its own shortcomings also serves to enhance our credibility. As we are going to get our 'social mission' to be important thing to the company and we have to measure it. Meeting corporation social responsibility (CSR) is of mutual benefits. Still, inclusion of social audit in an annual report is still a rare practice.

Questions

1. Discuss what types of control process seems to be a part of Nelson Food's of doing business.
2. Explain concept of social audit and its benefits.
3. Can NPOs adopt social audit as their control process.

(G) TSUNAMI AND LESSONS FOR INTERNAL CRISIS COMMUNICATIONS

The number of people dead in India:	12,450
Total population affected (in lakh):	27.92
Monetary damage in Tamil Nadu, the worst hit state (in Rs. Crore):	4,528.66
Total monetary damage to the country (in Rs. Crore):	11,544.91

In the wake of the destruction left behind by the quakes and tsunamis that struck recently, a few key learnings and lessons for internal communications can be derived and put to practice.

Most corporate houses have risen to the occasion and provided relief and support. but there are still many ways by which these entities can gain public respect and employee trust.

Numerous unique but touching examples are heard each day of individuals and companies using their core strengths to bring assistance to the needy. A car rental company using their vehicles to 'pick & drop' food, medicine and clothing. IT professionals and celebrities spending time to assess the damage and route essential material, airlines chartering flights for relief work, media firms setting up call centers and toll free numbers for relatives and well-wishers.

Companies who want to 'walk the talk' can do much more than extend 'cheque book' support to prove their integrity. Here are some ideas for building that feeling of oneness among employees during a crisis.

Trawl the database to match skills of employees to specific requirements

A quick scan of an employee database can reveal unique hobbies and interests which may be useful during a crisis. For example, an employee with an amateur HAM operator license would be of use in keeping devastated islands linked to the rest of the world. I can relate to this example, since a good friend of mine took leave to travel with the Indian Armed Forces rescue team and utilize his experience as a radio operator. His action was purely based on concern and individual drive but I am sure there may be many more such people who can contribute their talent. There may be employees trained as counselors who can help victims get over the trauma or those who can play the role of interpreters for international agencies and local administrators because they know a local language or dialect.

Opportunity for building employee morale

Its crises like these when employees judge the true commitment of their employer. It's the tact, the balance and the ability to empathize with the suffering that employees look forward to. Managers who show individual activism and take decisions to visit and support relief camps are respected. Senior leadership who make personal contributions is looked up to. Even by matching or exceeding employee contributions.

Assisting employee volunteerism

Routing energies of employees for the right causes can go along way in making them feel good about working for a socially responsible company. Firms should empower, reward and publicize the actions of these 'unsung heroes' internally.

Action-oriented support is expected

No action is too small in times of crises. Some methods are to set-up of online helpdesks or free access calls helping family, relatives and friends re-unite, helping employees adopt children and villages, investing in infrastructure and identifying reputed charities for employees to contribute. Some companies tracked each employee's whereabouts and reported them on the internal systems, which raised confidence among its employees.

Contribute your core strength

One enterprising networking firm provided free bandwidth and space on their servers for NGOs involved in relief work. If your core strength or value is innovation, invest time and people in developing a programme or software for early warning mechanisms working closely with the national or local administration.

Building a framework for internal communications during crises

Most companies scrambled to put together messages for internal circulation during crises. Putting together a framework involving crisis teams, leadership and department specific messages and action baskets were cases of employees duped by fake fund raisers. By anticipating, covering all angles of crisis communication and using the internal news channels like the intranet/portal/newsletters, companies can keep employees tip-to-speed on the do's and don'ts. During crises, keep in mind that usual channels of communication, e.g., telephone lines may be disrupted. Think of unique methods of reaching employees, may be via chat or sins or through families and friends.

While the world comes to grip with the disaster, organisations need to put comprehensive internal communications crisis support systems in place and keep a close watch over our shoulders for the next big challenge.

Reference: anish.busby@mailcity.com

Annexure VIA

LIST OF NPOs IN INDIA

Abhijit Nirmal
HAQ: Centre for Child Rights
208, Shahpur Jat,
New Delhi
Tel: 9899894234/26490136
Email: haqcrc@vsnl.net

Ardhendu Dakshi
CITU
13A, Rouse Avenue,
New Delhi-110002
Email: citu@bol.org.in

Asif Iqbal
SRUTI
Q-1, Hauz Khas Enclave,
New Delhi-110016
Tel: 26569023, 26926964926
Email: sruti@vsnl.com

Azad S.A.
PRASAR
G-12, 462-A, Sangam Vihar,
New Delhi-110062
Tel: 9811914329/26046374
Email: prasar@rediffmail.com

Bapi Carr
MM&P
C-308, Block, Pardesipara Sonari,
Jamshedpur-831 011
Tel: 29531814/09431372228
Email: bapikar@sify.com/
bapisdoc@yahoo.com

Davinder Kaur
KRITI
S-35, Tara Apartments,
Alaknanda, New Delhi
Tel: 26477845/26213088
Email: kritidpc@vsnl.com

Dr. Fatimi Shahnaz
India Peace Organisation
Tel: 22758577, 9818693855
Email: fashahnaz@yahoo.com

Joseph Xavier
SAPI-JESA
ISI, 10, Lodhi Institutional Area,
New Delhi-110003
Email: jesa@jesvits.net

Diana Khambatta
Guild of Service
C-25, Qutab Institutional Area
Email: gos@bol.net.org.in

Dolly Mishra
AVARD
5, CFF, Dean Dayal Upadhyay Marg,
New Delhi-110002
Email: agricodolly@yahoo.co.in

Harekrishna Dobnath
NFF
F-10-12, Malviya Nagar,
New Delhi-110017
Tel: 9434039599
Email: nffcal@vsnl.com

Jalees K.
Research Foundation for Science and Technology
A-6, Haus Khas,
New Delhi
Tel: 28535422

Jimmy Dabhi
ISI
10, Institutional Area
Lodhi Road,
New Delhi-110003
Email: jimmy@unv.ernet.in

Jitendra Singh
All India Trade Union Congress
24, Canning Lane,
New Delhi
Tel: 23387320
Email: aitucong@bol.net.in

John J.
Centre for Education and Communication
173-A, Khirki Village,
Malviya Nagar,
New Delhi - 110022
Tel: 29541841/58129545442
Email: jjojhn@labourfile.org

Murugan K.
AIYE
4/7, Asabali Road,
New Delhi-110002
Email: aiyf@hotmail.com

Kalyani Sen
JAGORI
C-54, South Extension-II,
New Delhi-110049
Email: kalyani@jaori.org

Kamal Mitra Chenoy
JNUTA
158, Uttrakhand, JNU,
New Delhi-67
Tel: 26177492/9810060481/ 26177492
Email: kamalchenoy@yahoo.com

Malvika Vartak
HIC-HRLN
B-28, Nizamuddin East,
New Delhi- 110013
Tel: 24358492
Email: mvartal@hic-sarp.org

Mansi
ANHAD
4, Windsor Place, New Delhi
Email: anhadinfo@yahoo.co.in

Mital R.A.
HMS
120, Babar Road
New Delhi - 110001
Tel: 23413519/23411037
Email: hms@nda.vsnl.net.in

Muqbil Ahmad
JNUSU
#36, Sabarmati Hostel,
JNU, New Delhi-110067
Tel: 9810458416
Email: ahmar_bluez@yahoo.com

Sadhana Arya
SAHELI
Above Shop Nos. 105-108,
Under Defence Colony Flyover,
Defence Colony,
New Delhi
Email: saheliwomen@hotmail.com

Nandini
JAGORI
C-54, South Extension-II,
New Delhi-110050
Email: jagori_jagori@yahoo.com

Pallavi Mansingh
Centre for Education and Communication
173-A Khirki Village,
Malviya Nagar,
New Delhi-110017
Tel: 29541841/58
Email: pallavi@labourfile.org

Rama Krishna Panda
AISF
4/7, Asabali Reed,
New Delhi-110003
Email: rkpodisha@yahoo.co.in

Ravi Hemadri
The Other Media
A1/125, FF
Safdurjung Enclave
New Delhi - 110029
Tel: 9811415186
Email: ravi@theothermedia.org

Rita Roy
Gandhi Peace Foundation
221/223 Deen Dayal Upadhyay Marg,
New Delhi
Tel: 23237491/23236734
Email: gpf@vsnl.net/gpf@rediffmail.com

Sreedhar R.
Environics Trust/MM&P
33-B, IIIrd Floor, Saidullajab,
New Delhi-110030
Tel: 9810708244/29531814
Email: environics@vsnl.com

Shabnam Hashmi
ANHAD
4, Windsor Place,
New Delhi
Email: anhadinfo@yahoo.co.in

Sharmila Bhagat
ANKUR
7/10, Sarvapriya Vihar,
New Delhi-110016
Email: ankureducation@vsnl.net

Sindhu Menon
Labour File
B-89, IInd Floor, Sarvodaya Enclave,
New Delhi- 110017
Tel: 30927311
Email: edit@labourfile.org

Souparna Lahiri
Delhi Forum
F-10/12, Malviya Nagar.
New Delhi
Email: defforum@vsnl.net

Vijayan M.J.
Pakistan-India Peoples' Forum for Peace and Democracy
Tel: 8182451/452

Vimila Pant
Guild of Service
C-25, Qutab Institutional Area
Tel: 51013416/17/18
Email: gos@bol.net.in

Dr. Swayam Prabha Das
Co-ordinator
Oceans & Costs Programme
WWF India Secretariat
172-B, Lodhi Estate
New Delhi-110003
Tel: 011 51504806/51504821
Email: sdas@wwfindia.net

Smitu Kothari
Lokayan
52, DD8
Nehru Enclave
Kalkaji Extn.
New Delhi
Tel: 9810619983
Email: smitukothari@vsnl.net

Rajeev Chourasia
KDK Infotech
3/31, Shivajik Road
Malviya Nagar
New Delhi
Tel: 26672652, 9810686305
Email: rajeev@kdkinfotech.com

Dr. S.K. Tiwari
Krishna Foundation
24, Kallol Appartment
35, I.P. Extension
Delhi-110092
Tel: 9810160677
Email: Krishnafoundation@yahoo.co.in

Payel Randhawa
PRAVAH
15/10, IInd Floor
Kalkaji, Opp. P Block Gurudwara
New Delhi-110019
Tel: 26440619/26213918

Sakarama
CSD
Council for Social Development
53, Lodhi Estate
New Delhi-110 003
Tel: 24615383

Non-profit Organisations

1. Bachpan
2. Associations for India's Development
3. Child Relief and You (CRY)
4. Force
5. Indian Children Fund
6. India Charity Net
7. India Development and Relief Fund
8. Jagriti
9. Pratham
10. Rajiv Gandhi Foundation
11. Tripura Foundation

NPO's in Delhi

1. Bapu Nature Cure Hospital and Yogashram
2. Kasturba Institute of Rural Studies
3. Harit Dhara Sanghatan
4. Society for Child Development
5. Indian National Trust for Welfare of Tribals

ANNEXURE VIB

PROFILES ON NPO's

I. PROFILE—CHILD RELIEF AND YOU (CRY)

Following aspects are covered in this profile of CRY:

(i) Mission of CRY.
(ii) Overview.
(iii) Tax exemption.
(iv) Organisation set-up.
(v) Sources of funds.
(vi) Development support and financial control support resources.
(vii) Human resources.
(viii) CRY America Inc.
(ix) CRY achievements.
(x) Summary of Balance Sheet.
(xi) Summary—Income and Expenditure Account

Introduction

CRY stands for Child Relief and You. CRY is an Indian non-government organisation (NGO) that works towards restoring basic rights to underprivileged Indian children.

CRY was started by seven young people in December 1978. One of them, an airline purser called Rippan Kapur, was the moving spirit behind the whole thing. Their objective to do what they could to improve the situation of underprivileged Indian children. Their first office—Rippan's mother's dining table.

Unusually, the founders of CRY chose not to found a grass-roots-level implementing organisation working directly with and for underprivileged children. Instead, they opted to make CRY a link between the millions of Indians who could provide resources and the thousands of dedicated fieldworkers struggling to function for lack of them. They saw their role as enablers and in so doing created an institution that is a unique model of a community movement that takes responsibility for its weakest and most vulnerable members and motivates and catalyses change on their behalf.

CRY focuses on the *4 basic rights of children* (or we say objective of CRY). These were defined in 1989, by the United Nations Convention on the Rights of the Child, an international human rights treaty to which 191 countries, including India, are signatories.

the right to survival—to life, health, nutrition, name and nationality
the right to development—to education, care, leisure, recreation

the right to protection—from exploitation, abuse, neglect
the right to participation—to expression, information, thought and religion.

CRY works to ensure that these rights are available to all categories of *underprivileged children*, including street children, girl children, children bonded in labour, children of commercial sex workers, physically and mentally challenged children and children in juvenile institutions. 25 years after it began work, CRY has made a profound difference to the lives of more than 1.25 million Indian children, by channelising the resources of over 100,000 individuals and organisations. In doing so, it has shown that lasting change happens when individuals believe it can happen and do what they can to make it happen.

(i) Mission of CRY

To enable people to take responsibility for the situation of the deprived Indian child and so motivate them to confront the situation through collective action thereby giving the child and themselves an opportunity to realise their full potential

For every underprivileged child, there are at least a handful of people who want to help. CRY acts as a "slink" between two groups:

(a) Development organisations and individuals working at grass-roots level with underprivileged children and communities,

AND

(b) People like you who wish to help but don't know how.

In this way, harness the money, time and skills of thousands of individuals and organisations to partner 171 child development initiatives across India. As such, they are an 'enabling' organisation, as opposed to an 'implementing' one.

Their emphasis is on supporting small, nascent initiatives. Over time, as each grows and achieves stability the nature and quantum of the support provided evolves. At the other end of the spectrum, the *Rippan Kapur CRY Fellowship Programme* seeks to enable motivated individuals starting a career in grass-roots development work to make a beginning.

(ii) Overview

They work by creating awareness (through Development Support Team) and raising resources (through Resource Mobilisation Team) and disbursing them to deserving grass-roots initiatives. Apart from these, they have teams working in the areas of organising material donations, developing fund raising products, sensitising specific target audiences and providing information on specific issues.

Internal support functions, like communications, Human Resources, Finance, Planning and Information Technology, also play a key role in organisation building efforts.

Support funds is accompanied by the non-financial inputs like in training, materials, infrastructure, organisation development and moral support.

Direct Action

Working with children, their parents and the community in which they live to ensure long-term viability by encouraging community ownership of the initiative.

Building capacities

Providing inputs in the areas of organisation building, programme development (especially with locally relevant tools), training, and perspective building in child rights and accountability.

Networking

Bringing together organisations and individuals working in the same area, so as to enhance their collective impact.

Influencing Policies

Playing an effective role in influencing government policies towards child rights.

This enabling position has determined our strategic choices at every juncture from the fund raising methods we' employ, to the nature of our relationship with the NGOs we partner.

(iii) Tax-related at CRY

Every donation made to CRY is granted a 100% tax exemption by the government.

The exemption works by reducing the donated amount from the taxable salary. Hence if the taxable income in a year is Rs. 2,00,000 then people make a donation of Rs.5,000. Then net taxable income will become Rs. 1,95,000. The tax will now be calculated on this new amount basis the prevailing tax rates. *All employers allow the 100% tax exemption to be considered in Form 16?*

While there is no maximum or minimum limit for 100% tax exemption, CRY recommends that people can donate over Rs. 250 to claim exemption as this would cover the cost of data processing, printing and mailing of the 58A exemption form and receipt and still leave a surplus that they can deploy towards our projects.

(iv) Organisation set-up

(a) CRY—Board of trustees

CRY has 6 trustees, each of whom brings a unique set of professional and personal skills to the team. Trustees hold CRY's interest before everything else, and share a firm belief in values of public trust, collective responsibility and transparency.

(b) CRY Management Committee

CRY's MANCOM team of 6 members is a close knit one that steers the organisation towards its objectives. At present the team has an excellent mix of the 'sold' and the 'new' people who have seen CRY from its inception and therefore shared and lived Rippan's passion for many years, and a set of committed individuals who are concerned about the situation of underprivileged children and bring a new perspective on how to change it. Both groups have a deep and abiding faith in CRY's mission—enabling more and more people to take responsibility for improving the situation of the underprivileged Indian child—and the combined strength of their perspectives adds tremendous value to the organisation.

(c) Organisation chart

One of CRY's greatest strengths has been the people associated with it over the years.

FIGURE I
Organisational Structure

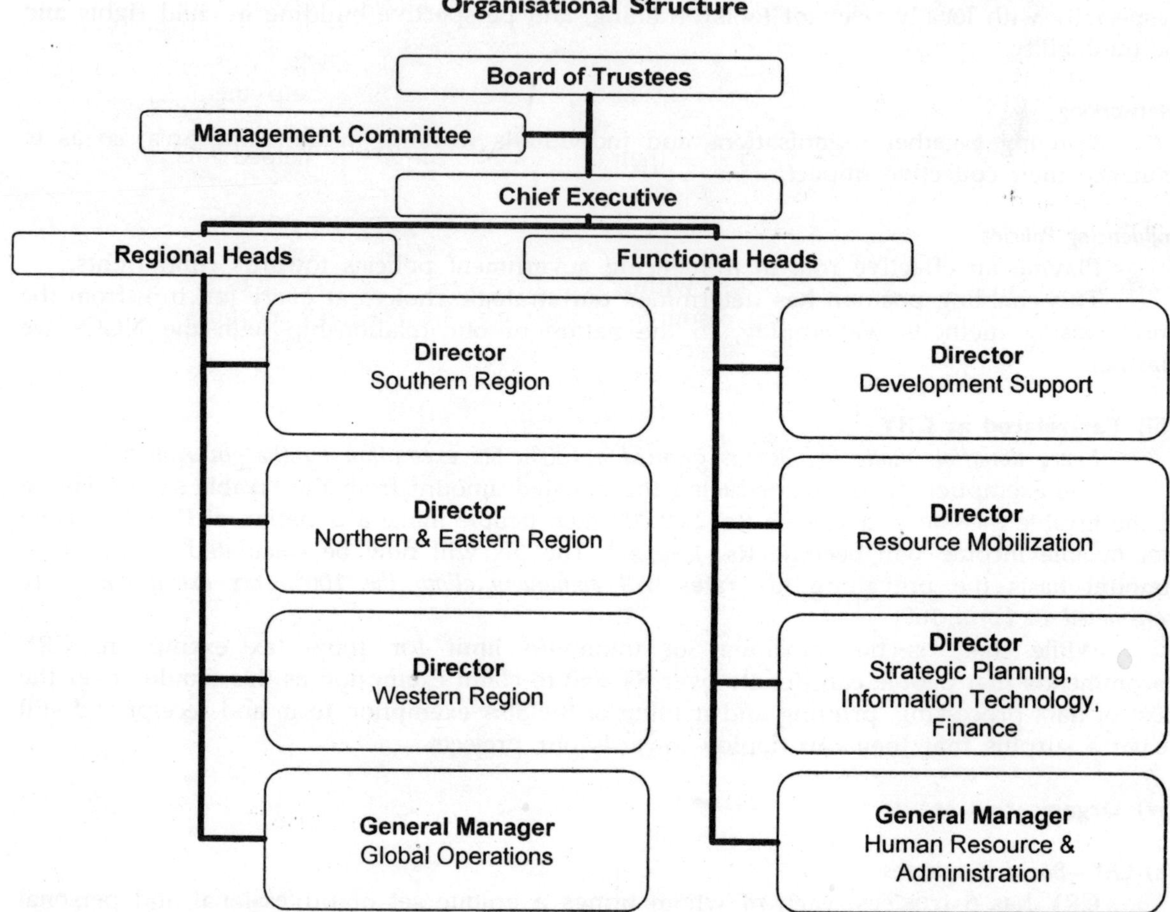

It has benefited from a wide range of dedicated individuals who have lent their expertise and skills to build the organisation. Be it the trustees who are the guardians of CRY's ethos, or the members of its Managing Committee (MANCOM) who steer the organisation to its designated goals, or the many employees and volunteers who use their time and skills to enable CRY's work or CRY's development partners, people who make extraordinary change possible through their work. All of these people make CRY what it is today—a true people's movement for India's children.

(v) Sources of funds

CRY's resources come mainly from individuals and organisations. In fact, in 2001-02, as much as 81% of the resources raised were from individual and corporate partnerships.

Greeting cards and other paper products that sell for Rs. 6 to Rs. 180 each, and donations from individuals averaging about Rs. 1500 per donor per year, are the mainstay of fund raising efforts.

This allows millions of middle-income Indians from every walk of life to become part of movement for children and builds an element of consciousness-raising into every fund raising activity.

Marketing tie-ins with corporations, events, school and college workshops, media campaigns, signature drives, the internet and street theatre also help them to mobilise resources.

Over the years, innovative, first-of-their-kind events have also helped raise resources. In 2001-02, events contributed to 6% of our resources.

In all resource mobilisation activities, the focus has always been to provide ways and means to involve as many people as they can, by providing opportunities for them to contribute in whatever way they can, within the context of their own lives.

People help them to mobilise resources through individual and corporate sponsorship, by purchasing their products, and supporting their events.

CRY underwent some remarkable changes in 2001-02 that they covered in their last annual report. They restructured the organisation, reduced their employees numbers, outsourced operations and streamlined processes. The year, 2002-03 was the year they started to reap the benefits of the changes in terms of both, operational efficiency and mission focus.

Key among these were (in their own words):

- Better sustainability of income streams,
- Enhanced reach,
- Greater focus on capacity building with partners,
- A more child rights centric approach, and
- Investments in human resources and systems.

(vi) Development support and financial control support and resources

CRY disbursed Rs. 844 lakhs to child development initiatives across India—a decrease of 7% compared to the previous year. This disbursal enabled 2347 communities across 13 Indian states to work towards addressing the root causes that denied their children their rights to survival, development, protection and participation. By mobilising these communities CRY and its 174 project partners were able to directly provide 92,549 more children access to healthcare and education. 1053 of these communities today have 100% enrolment in education programmes. 437 villages are now completely child labour free and 494 government schools were reactivated in the fiscal year. These changes are clear indicate the efficiency and hard work which we can see.

Total income generated in the financial year 2002-03 stands at Rs. 2384 lakhs, a 12%, increase over last year. With the spread of face-to-face marketing to all regions, CRY was able to increase its donor base by a tremendous 59% to 82,409 donors. The introduction of face-to-face marketing allowed CRY to reach many more people at a much lower cost, thereby fulfilling its core mission of enabling more people to change the situation of underprivileged Indian children. With 70% of its income emanating from individual donors in India, CRY today is a true peoples' movement allowing people of varied ages, occupations and backgrounds to participate.

Implementation of new software and outsourcing of routine operations helped CRY focus on directly interacting with its donors to ensure a fruitful relationship.

Income from companies rose by 161% to Rs. 344 lakhs, 14% of total income. This was made possible through the acquisition of 146 new corporate partners across India and by strengthening relationships with existing partners.

CRY has witnessed inspiring examples of companies that believe in and demonstrate corporate social responsibility even during adverse economic times.

There is list of companies which recently help them in their projects—

- A grant of Rs. 78 Iakhs was sanctioned from ICICI for information technology needs that would enable the development of software that will in turn enhance productivity and effectiveness across all CRY functions.
- The year witnessed the third consecutive 'CRY Cadence Corporate Cricket Challenge'. *Cadence Design Systems* also launched the 'Spirit of Stars & Strikes' programme where Cadence employees the world over select one local organisation to support, and Cadence matches the funds raised. This programme contributed a commendable Rs. 40.5 lakhs to CRY in 2002-03.
- *Tata Chemicals* launched its Desh Ko Arpan programme on August 15, 2002. Under this programme 10 paise from the sale of every pack of Tata Salt sold that month was contributed towards the education of children across six CRY projects. The total amount contributed by TATA Chemicals was Rs. 33.14 lakhs.
- For the second year in succession, *Corporation Bank* contributed Rs. 5 for every savings bank account opened with it between August 12 and October 12, 2002. The amount raised through this unique partnership was Rs. 5.96 lakhs.
- *Flextronics Technologies* adopted an entire project in Chennai for a sum of Rs. 5.73 lakhs.
- CRY's inter-corporate quiz event FACT (Free A Child Today), conducted by Derek O'Brien went national for the first time thanks to the sponsorship from Maruti Suzuki and Digital Globalsoft. Numerous other organisations made contributions in kind including Blue Dart, Levi's Strauss, Pantaloons, BPL mobile, Pfizer Pharma, HDFC bank, DSP Merrill Lynch, Javed Habib's hair styling school, Sharda Exports.

(vii) Human Resources

CRY's HR department introduced a new competency-centered strategy. The framework for this was developed over the year and was launched in the organisation in July 2003.

A new grade and compensation structure was also implemented during the year post a thorough job and role analysis. They hope the move will help them to fill key vacancies at senior levels and make it feasible for talented individuals to join and stay in CRY.

(viii) CRY America Inc.

They introduce cry organisation in United States of America where they enroll them as CRY America Inc. It was registered as an independent not-for-profit organisation in November 2002. They constituted their Board of Directors and a volunteer Executive Committee and created financial reporting systems that ensure the high degree of accountability and transparency that CRY itself is known for.

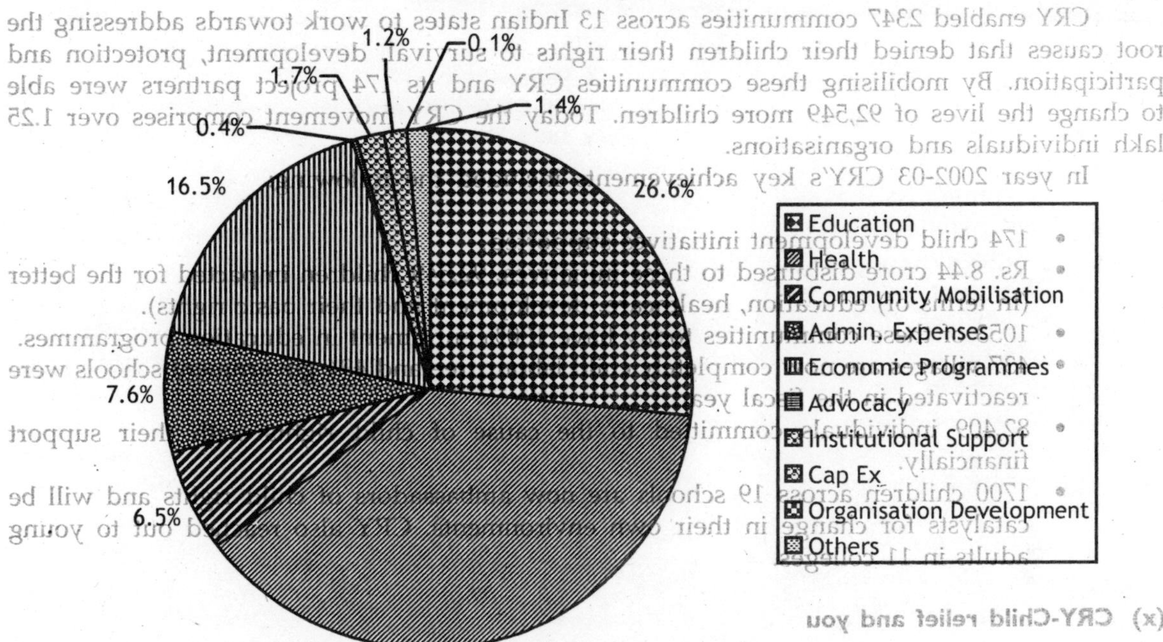
Where each Rupee went
1.2%
0.1%
1.7%
1.4%
0.4%
16.5%
26.6%
7.6%
6.5%
38.0%
Education
Health
Community Mobilisation
Admin. Expenses
Economic Programmes
Advocacy
Institutional Support
Cap Ex
Organisation Development
Others

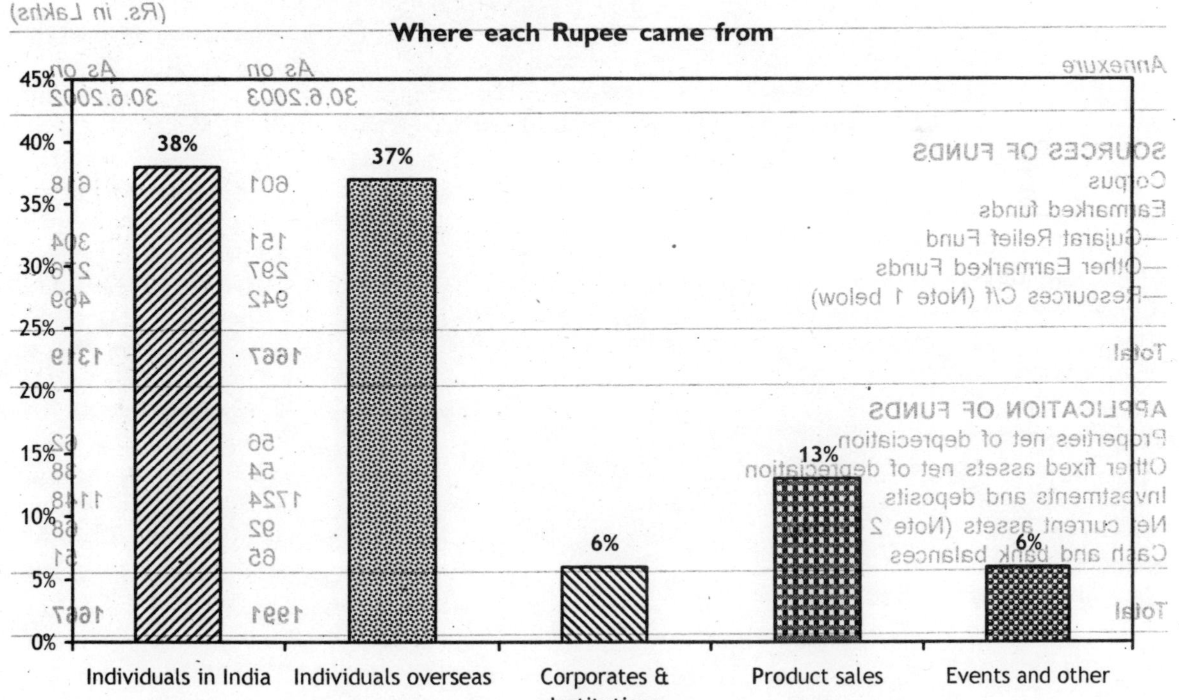
Where each Rupee came from
45%
40%
35%
30%
25%
20%
15%
10%
5%
0%
38%
37%
6%
13%
6%
Individuals in India
Individuals overseas
Corporates & Institutions
Product sales
Events and other

(ix) CRY Achievements

CRY enabled 2347 communities across 13 Indian states to work towards addressing the root causes that denied their children their rights to survival, development, protection and participation. By mobilising these communities CRY and its 174 project partners were able to change the lives of 92,549 more children. Today the CRY movement comprises over 1.25 lakh individuals and organisations.

In year 2002-03 CRY's key achievements included the following:

- 174 child development initiatives supported,
- Rs. 8.44 crore disbursed to these initiatives, 92,549 children impacted for the better (in terms of) education, healthcare, development and their basic rights).
- 1053 of these communities today have 100% enrolment in education programmes.
- 437 villages are now completely child labour free and 494 government schools were reactivated in the fiscal year.
- 82,409 individuals committed to the cause of child rights with their support financially.
- 1700 children across 19 schools are now ambassadors of child rights and will be catalysts for change in their own environments. CRY also reached out to young adults in 11 colleges.

(x) CRY-Child relief and you

Summary balance sheet as on 30th June, 2003

(Rs. in Lakhs)

Annexure	*As on 30.6.2003*	*As on 30.6.2002*
SOURCES OF FUNDS		
Corpus	601	618
Earmarked funds		
—Gujarat Relief Fund	151	304
—Other Earmarked Funds	297	276
—Resources C/f (Note 1 below)	942	469
Total	**1667**	**1319**
APPLICATION OF FUNDS		
Properties net of depreciation	56	62
Other fixed assets net of depreciation	54	38
Investments and deposits	1724	1148
Net current assets (Note 2 below)	92	68
Cash and bank balances	65	51
Total	**1991**	**1667**

(1) Represents resources net of surplus/(deficit) carried forward from the Income & Expenditure statement.

(2) Current assets—Rs. 171 lakhs, Current liabilities—Rs. 79 lakhs; Net current assets—Rs. 92 lakhs.

(xi) CRY—Child Relief and You

Summary—Income and expenditure account for the year ended 30th June 2003

(Rs. in Lakhs)

	Annexure	*For the period 1.07.2002 to 30.06.2003*	*For the period 1.07.2001 to 30.06.2002*	*Growth %*
INCOME				
Donations	II	2083	1727	21%
Sale of Products	III	165	315	–47%
Interest a others		136	94	44%
Total		2384	2136	12%
COST OF MOBILISING INCOME				
Generating Donations	II	711	447	59%
Manufacturing and Marketing Products	III	223	402	–44%
Total	934	849	10%	
NET RESOURCES				
Donations	II	1372	1280	7%
Sale of Products	III	–58	–87	–33%
Interest and others		136	94	44%
Resources available for deployment a Expenses	A	1450	1287	13%
ESTABLISHMENT AND OTHER EXPENSES				
Personnel	IV	26	26	–2%
General Administration	IV	46	33	40%
Depreciation		45	23	92%
Auditor's Fees and Reimbursement	IV	1	1	19%
Total Establishment Expenses	B	118	83	42%
Net resources available for deployment	A—B	1332	1204	11%

DEPLOYMENT OF FUNDS				
Child development initiatives	—	597	667	–10%
Awareness of child rights	VI	44	60	–26%
Capacity building for supported initiatives	VII	203	177	15%
Total		844	904	–7%
Resources/deficit c/f to Balance Sheet		488	300	

2. HELPAGE INDIA

HelpAge India is working for the cause and care of older persons, with the ultimate aim of empowering them to take decisions pertaining to their own lives.

From Welfare to Development

Over the years HelpAge India has changed its orientation from implementing welfare projects to those that focus on development. It now lays stress on income-generation and micro-credit projects that enable the participation of older persons in the mainstream of society.

HelpAge India is—

- A registered national level voluntary organisation.
- A secular, apolitical, non-profit and a non-governmental organisation.
- Registered under the Societies' Registration Act, 1860, in 1978.

Historical background

Formed in 1978 with active help from Mr. Cecil Jackson Cole, founder member of Help the Aged in United Kingdom.

Aims and objectives

- To foster the welfare of the aged in India especially the needy aged.
- To raise funds for projects which assist the elderly irrespective of cast or creed.
- To create in the younger generation and in society a social awareness about the problems of the elderly in India today.

Organisational structure

- Mr. R. Venkataraman and Mr. K.R. Narayanan, Former Presidents of India are the patrons of HelpAge India.
- It's Governing Body, comprising eminent persons from different walks of life, oversees the activities of the society.
- Mr. M.M. Sabharwal is the President and Mr. Mathew Cherian is the Chief Executive.
- The Chief Executive of HelpAge India looks after the forward planning and implementation of its policies and programmes with the support of functional Directorates at Head Office. HelpAge India has 33 regional and area offices located all over the country.

Advocacy

- HelpAge India maintains active liaison with both the Central and State Governments for advocating the cause of the elderly.
- HelpAge India is a member of the National Council of Older Persons in the Ministry of Social Justice and Empowerment.
- It is represented at the Working Committee of National Council.
- The organisation has also been represented on the Working Group for recommending Government thrusts and policies for the Eighth and Ninth Five Year Plans.
- It has successfully pressed for travel and tax concessions and other benefits for the elderly.

International connections

- HelpAge India is one of the founding members of HelpAge International, a high profile body having 51 member countries representing the cause of the elderly at the United Nations.
- It has received a special testimonial from the United Nations for "Dedicated service in support of the United Nations Programme on Ageing."

3. TERI—THE ENERGY AND RESOURCES INSTITUTE

A dynamic and flexible organisation with a global vision and a local focus, TERI was established in 1974.

While in the initial period the focus was mainly on documentation and information dissemination activities, research activities in the fields of energy, environment, and sustainable development were initiated towards the end of 1982. The genesis of these activities lay in TERI's firm belief that efficient utilization of energy, sustainable use of natural resources, large-scale adoption of renewable energy technologies, and reduction of all forms of waste would move the process of development towards the goal of sustainability.

A unique developing-country institution, TERI is deeply committed to every aspect of sustainable development. From providing environment-friendly solutions to rural energy problems to helping shape the development of the Indian oil and gas sector; from tackling global climate change issues across many continents to enhancing forest conservation efforts among local communities; from advancing solutions to growing urban transport and air pollution problems to promoting energy efficiency in the Indian industry, the emphasis has always been on finding innovative solutions to make the world a better place to live in. However, while TERI's vision is global, its roots are firmly entrenched in Indian soil. All activities in TERI move from formulating local- and national-level strategies to suggesting global solutions to critical energy and environment-related issues. It is with this purpose that TERI has established regional centres in Bangalore, Goa, Guwahati, and Mukteshwar, an office in Mumbai, and a presence in Japan, and Malaysia. It has set-up affiliate institutes: TERI-NA in Washington, DC, USA, and TERI-Europe in London, UK.

The Governing Council of TERI comprises eminent and distinguished individuals from a variety of fields.

TERI hosts the annual Delhi Sustainable Development Summit, which is swiftly gathering momentum as a major forum for the convergence of globally renowned leaders and thinkers dealing with the issue of sustainability.

With a staff strength of over 600, drawn from multidisciplinary and highly specialized fields, offices and regional centres equipped with state-of-the-art facilities, and a diverse range of activities, TERI is the largest developing-country institution working to move human society towards a sustainable future. TERI makes effective use of the latest developments in modern information technology in both its in-house and outreach activities.

TERI lays great emphasis on training, capacity building, and education. In 1999, it set-up the TERI School of Advanced Studies, recognized as a deemed university by the University Grants Commission, India. The TERI School is evolving as a research university, offering doctoral and master's programmes in bioresources, biotechnology, energy, environment, and regulatory and policy studies.

Having celebrated its silver jubilee in February 2000, TERI is now poised for future growth, driven by a global vision and outreach, with a philosophy that assigns primacy to enterprise in government, industry, and individual actions.

TERI
Darbari Seth Block, IHC Complex, Lodhi Road, New Delhi-110 003, India
Telephone +91 11 2468 2100, 2468, 2111
Fax +91 11 2468 2144, 2468 2145
E-mail mailbox©teri.res.in

4. DASTKAR: A SOCIETY FOR CRAFTS AND CRAFTSPEOPLE

A society for crafts and craftspeople Dastkar is a registered society that aims at improving the economic status of craftspeople, thereby promoting the survival of traditional crafts was founded in 1981 by six women, who had worked in the craft and development sector including Laila Tyabji, who is the current Chairperson.

Dastkar strongly believes in "craft" as a social, cultural and economic force that despite being marginalized due to urbanisation and industrialization, has enormous strength and potential and has a vital role to play within the economic mainstream of the country. The crux of its programme is to help craftspeople, especially women, to use their own traditional craft skills as a means of employment, income generation and economic self-sufficiency. Dastkar guides the process of developing a craft—from identifying the skill and creating awareness of its potential in both craftsperson and consumer, developing, designing, costing and then marketing the product, and finally suggesting the proper usages and investment of the income generated. The objective is to make the craftspeople self-reliant, independent of both the commercial middleman and organisations like Dastkar to market and sell contemporary products directly, and not to subsidise craft. Dastkar ensures that the end product is competitive—not just in its worthiness of purpose or the neediness of its produce, but in cost utility and aesthetic—a consumer does not buy out of compassion

The Dastkar cooperative shop, and the Dastkar exhibitions and Dastkari bazaars, who artisans sell their products directly to the customers, expose craftspeople to the march and given them a firsthand knowledge of customer tastes and trends. Recently, Dastkar acquired an export license, thus enabling it to provide an alternative as well as international market for the craftspeople.

As groups become self-sufficient, Dastkar directs its support to new groups and assists them in their growth. Presently, Dastkar is working in most of the states of India with over 100 groups of which at least 75% receive the full gamut of Dastkar services, and the rest benefit from its marketing activities. Crafts skills range from textile-based craft producer groups to terracotta. The product ranges developed include garments and accessories, home furnishings, toys, stationery and objects d'art.

Apart from the support services and craft development consultancies, Dastkar provides its own family of craft producer groups, it has increasingly been asked to provide evaluation and consultancy services to other government, non-government and international agencies. It has grown into a professional full-time development and alternative marketing organisation that works with groups all over the country. Its Delhi office of 17 travels all over India, and it has sister organisations in Andhra and Rajasthan.

Crafts and craftspeople have a vital role to play in contemporary India—not just as a part of its cultural and aesthetic past, but as part of its economic future. Dastkar is committed to help prepare the craftsperson, the craft product and the consumer for the future.

Elaben Bhatt, Founder of the SEWA, Self-Employed Women's Association said: "I see Dastkar as both an organisation and a movement. The organisation started the movement and gave many NGOs and craftspeople the confidence to make good crafts products and market them directly. It showed us the way and gave us direction. Today, there is consequently an all India movement of craft as a means to sustainable employment. It is not necessary for Dastkar to grow as large as the movement or to run the movement. At the same time without the organisation there would be no movement, and if there was no movement there would be little point in the organisation." This seems to sum up everything Dastkar feels about its growth and future development.

DASTKAR,
45-B, Shahpur Jat,
New Delhi-110049
Tel: +91-11-2649 5920/21, +91-11-649 4633, +91-11-649 1549
Email: dastkar@vsnl.net

5. PRIA

PRIA is a civil society organisation, that undertakes development initiatives to positively impact the lives of the poor, marginalised and excluded sections of society, by encouraging and enabling their participation in the processes of their governance. It strives for achievement of equity and justice, through a people centred approach, focusing on 'Citizens'—'their participation and inclusion', 'awareness and empowerment' and 'their democratic rights'.

PRIA recognises the value of people's knowledge, challenges traditional myths and concepts, raises awareness of people's rights and promotes experiential learning. It applies a multi-dimensional strategic approach to creating knowledge, training and capacity building of stakeholders, public education and policy advocacy and intervenes at various levels of the demand and supply segments, to reach out locally, nationally and globally.

Operating under two broad themes, 'Reforming Governing Institutions' and 'Civil

Society building', PRIA's people centered interventions aim at promoting active participation of the poor and marginalised in the effective utilisation of resources through local governance.

It engages itself in strengthening of Panchayati Raj Institutions and municipalities, promoting environmental and occupational health, facilitating a strong network of civil society organisations, promoting citizen leadership and in monitoring policies and programmes of bilateral, multilateral and government agencies, to achieve an agenda of 'Governance where People Matter'.

PRIA proactively involves and engages a range of stakeholders including academia, media, donors, civil society organisations, trade unions, private business and government agencies in its efforts and provides a platform for a multi-stakeholder development approach.

PRIA is an International Centre for Learning and Promotion of Participation and Democratic Governance.

6. ALL INDIA ASSOCIATION FOR MICRO-ENTERPRISE DEVELOPMENT (AIAMED)

AIAMED had beginnings in the South Asia Network (SAN) in 1994. It got registered as a Trust in 1997 to act as a support organisation and also as a network. Its mission is to strengthen non-governmental and other type of organisations involved in micro-finance and micro enterprise either fully or partially as its programme component. Apart from Capacity Building of these organisations, it is also involved in Institutional Strengthening of the sector. AIAMED though its work on networking, joint action, information sharing, training, study and research hopes to achieve its aims. The Board of Trustees and Board of Governors govern AIAMED.

AIAMED is a part of 'Micro-Credit Summit Campaign' to reach 100 million poor people by 2005.

Vision

AIAMED aims to make development finance a significant national strategy for enabling the poor to productive citizens and contribute with dignity in nation-building.

Mission

It's mission is to develop accountable and sustainable retail development finance organisations.

Strategy

AIAMED's strategy is to provide a platform for community development finance organisations to come together, share and experience similar vision of empowering the poor without handouts or subsidies. Our effort is to build effective coalitions and collective efficiency through networking joint action, capacity building and institutional strengthening study and a research documentation and sharing of information.

Core Values

AIAMED is guided by four core values:

1. Respect

Our respect for one another compels us to fully value and affirm the dignity and uniqueness of each client. This respect is also the foundation for our relationship with our clients'. communities and our relationship with others involved in our work—Donors, Creditors, Colleagues and Fellow members of the network.

2. Commitment to the cause of the poor

We focus our energy and efforts on our clients, their families and their communities. Their business needs and expectations determine the services we provide and their well being inspires what we do.

3. Integrity

We commit to integrating actively what we believe in what we do.

4. Stewardship

We are committed to being good stewards of our own resources and those of our clients, donors, creditors and colleagues by exercising a thoughtful and cost effective use of the time, skills and finances we have. Our efforts is to provide quality services and maximise the opportunities.

5. Reliability

Reliability and reducing the vulnerability of the poor.

Annexure VII

LIST OF EXAMPLES OF NON-PROFIT ORGANISATIONS (GLOBAL)

- AEGEE European Students Forum (Europe-wide student organisation)
- AmeriCorps
- AMORC (registered as non-profit educational organisation in USA charities and educational activities)
- Apache Software Foundation
- A.U.M.P. Church
- Better Business Bureau
- Bill and Melinda Gates Foundation
- BWARS—the Bees, Wasps and Ants Recording Society
- CompuMentor
- Council on Hemispheric Affairs
- Eurodoc
- Hong Kong Jockey Club
- Howard Hughes Medical Institute
- JINSA
- MacArthur Foundation
- Miss America
- Mothers Organised to Stop Environmental Sin
- Nature's Classroom
- Operation Lifesaver
- POACh
- Project Gutenbera
- Randolph Mountain Club
- SDF
- Shark Trust
- Solomon R. Guggenheim Foundation
- Toastmasters International
- Transnational Corporations Observatory
- US-based non-profit that supports literacy in rural India
- International Red Cross and Red Crescent Movement

List of Charities

- Orphan Helpers
- Charities Children

Multinationals

The following organisations have a significant presence in at least five countries:

- CARE
- Caritas
- Christian Children's Fund
- Habitat for Humanity
- Lawyers without Borders
- Medecins Sans Frontieres
- Oxam
- International Red Cross and Red Crescent Societies
- Society of Saint Vincent de Paul
- Toc H
- UNICEF
- Voluntary Services Overseas

Four global charities have offices in the Pacific Northwest of the USA:

- Mercy Corps
- Northwest Medical Teams International
- World Concern
- World Vision International

Australia

- Brotherhood of St Lawrence

Austria

- Licht ins Dunkel Nachbar in Not

Canada

- Big Brothers and Sisters of Canada
- Canadian National Institute of the Blind (CNIB)
- Children's Aid Society
- Children's Wish Foundation of Canada Engineers
- Without Borders (Canada)
- Kidney Foundation of Canada

Germany

- Brot fur die Welt

India

- Child Relief and You

- Pratham
- Sankara Nethralaya

Poland

- Great Orchestra of Christmas Charity (*Wielka Orkiestra Swiatecznej Pomocy*)
- Polish Humanitarian Organisation (*Poiska Akcja Humanitarna*)

United Kingdom

- Action Aid
- Barnardo's
- Cancer Research UK
- ChildLine
- Christian Aid
- Church of England Children's Fund
- Comic Relief
- Families Need Fathers
- Guide Dogs for the Blind
- The Haig Fund
- Haig Homes
- Help the Aged
- LEPRA
- Multiple Sclerosis Society
- NCH
- National Society for the Prevention of Cruelty to Children
- The National Trust
- Royal National Institution for the Blind
- Royal National Institution for the Deaf
- Royal Society for the Prevention of Cruelty to Animals
- Royal Society for the Protection of Birds
- Samaritans
- Save the Children Fund
- SCOPE
- Shark Trust
- Shelter
- War on Want

United States

- American Friends Service Committee
- American Society for the Prevention of Cruelty to Animals
- Christmas Seals
- Comic Relief
- Easter Seals
- Goodwill Industries

- Humane Society
- March of Dimes
- United Way
- Adamsmogeni foundation

I. PROFILE GREENPEACE

We shall elaborate under following headings:

1. About greenpeace
2. A history of greenpeace
3. Mission of greenpeace
4. Campaign overview
5. Working of greenpeace
6. Independent greenpeace
7. Greenpeace world-wide
8. Greenpeace victories
9. We need you
10. Conclusion

1. About greenpeace

Greenpeace exists because this fragile earth deserves a voice. It needs solutions. It needs change. It needs action.

Greenpeace is a non-profit organisation, with a presence in 40 countries across Europe, the Americas, Asia and the Pacific. To maintain its independence, Green peace does not accept donations from governments or corporations but relies on contributions from individual supporters and foundation grants. Therefore, Greenpeace seeks to:

- Protect biodiversity in all its forms;
- Prevent pollution and abuse of the earth's oceans, land, air and fresh water;
- End all nuclear threats;
- Promote peace, global disarmament and non-violence.

Greenpeace exists because the earth and all life on it deserve a clean and safe environment—now and in the future. As a global organisation, Greenpeace focuses on the most critical worldwide environmental issues such as:

- Oceans and ancient forests protection.
- Fossil fuel phase out and the promotion of renewable energies to stop climate change.
- Nuclear disarmament and an end to nuclear contamination.

2. The history of greenpeace

Greenpeace exists because this fragile earth deserves a voice. It needs solutions. It needs change. It needs action.

In 1971, motivated by their vision of a green and peaceful world, a small team of

Box I

Choose Positive Energy for Combating Climate Change

Greenpeace is committing to preventing dangerous climate change by reducing consumption of fossil fuels (oil, coil and gas) and ending the nuclear age. We champion a clean energy future, where all energy needs are met through clean and renewable energy. We promote the goals of energy saving, energy efficiency and clean energy provision. We fight for the phase out of potent industrial green-house gases. We investigate and expose the corporate powers and governments who stand in the way of international action to halt global warming and who drive continued dependence on dirty and dangerous sources of energy.

Protecting the Biodiversity of Oceans

Greenpeace is committed to defending the health of the world's oceans and the animals, plants and peoples that depend upon them. We investigate, confront and expose unsustainable industrial fishing and other destructive activities. We challenge governments to introduce and enforce laws to protect the marine environment and challenge industry to end its role in ocean destruction.

We support ecologically and socially responsible use of the oceans, including the rights of fishing communities to derive their livelihood from the sea.

We champion responsible scientific research to enhance understanding and appreciation of oceans and their ecosystems. We campaign for the establishment of large-scale marine reserves to conserve and restore ocean ecosystem and species.

activists set sail from Vancouver, Canada, in an old fishing boat. These activists, the founders of Greenpeace, believed a few individuals could make a difference.

Their mission was to "bear witness" to US underground nuclear testing at Amchitka, a tiny island off the West Coast of Alaska, which is one of the world's most earthquake-prone regions. Even though their old boat, the Phyllis Cormack, was intercepted before it got to Amchitka, the journey sparked a flurry of public interest.

The US still detonated the bomb, but the voice of reason had been heard. Nuclear testing on Amchitka ended that same year, and the island was later declared a bird sanctuary. Today, Greenpeace is an international organisation that priorities global environmental campaigns. Based in Amsterdam, the Netherlands, Greenpeace has 2.8 million supporters' worldwide and national as well as regional offices in 41 countries.

3. Mission

Greenpeace exists because this fragile earth deserves a voice. It needs solutions. It needs change. It needs action.

Greenpeace is an independent, campaigning organisation that uses non-violent, creative confrontation to expose global environmental problems, and force solutions for a green and peaceful future. Green peace's goal is to ensure the ability of the Earth to nurture life in all its diversity.

Greenpeace organises public campaigns for:

- The protection of oceans and ancient forests.
- The phase out of fossil fuels and the promotion of renewable energy to stop climate change.
- The elimination of toxic chemicals.
- The prevention of genetically modified organisms being released into nature.

4. Campaign Overview

Green peace has been active in India since 1994. We have been campaigning in India in the following areas:

(a) Toxics free future

The production, trade, uses, and release of many synthetic chemicals are now widely recognized as a global threat to human health and the environment.

Scientists estimate that all living species today carry at least 700 man-made chemical contaminants in their bodies. These chemicals are implicated in effects in living beings ranging from the gory to the subtle—from gross effects like cancers, deformed sex organs and hermaphrodites to hidden consequences such as falling sperm counts, aggressive behaviour and diminished intelligence.

The effluents in our rivers, toxic waste dumps in our fields, poisons in our groundwater, in the air we breathe, in the food we eat, these are all a result of short-sighted unsustainable practices being enforced upon the planet by corporations who want to control all our resources by playing god, abusing science for power and profit. Transnational corporations responsible for inventing, manufacturing and marketing these poisons have made huge profits at a massive cost to both the willing consumer and the unwilling victim, but they refuse to acknowledge or take responsibility for the liabilities arising out of their crimes against nature and humanity.

Greenpeace India is campaigning for Corporate Accountability, elimination of hazardous chemicals and to see that companies substitute them with safer alternatives. Greenpeace India is also concerned about the threat to India's bio-diversity from the new untested and dangerous Genetic Modification (GM) technology that these Corporations are pushing as the magic technology to replace their poisonous ones.

Greenpeace India is campaigning for a toxic-free, sustainable and peaceful future for all species on this planet.

(b) Say no to genetic engineering

Genetic Engineering techniques allow scientists to transfer genes from one organism to another, very often from one unrelated species, in order to create new organisms that have a desired characteristic. For instance resistance to pests, increased vitamin content, resistance to climatic conditions, etc.

Hence greenpeace now have a whole new range of new man-made species: tomatoes inserted with anti-freeze gene of a coldwater fish to enhance shelf life of the vegetable, soybeans that are resistant to herbicides, corn that throws up its own pesticides and so on. Disconcertingly, Genetic Engineering creates organisms that would never exist in our natural world. And we never know what repercussions this manipulating of the very essence of life—genetic material—would have.

Scientists, on the other hand, claim that if we don't embrace Genetically Modified

Organisms GMOs we "will be wittingly or unwittingly responsible for the looming calamities which may truly descend on us." In order to protect ourselves from this catastrophic technology, we must look at the results of prior experiments in GE.

Since India has not grown any GE food yet, the only experiences that we can learn from are international examples. One cannot help but wonder why an entire continent (Europe) will not feed its people GM food? The answer lies in the fact that people were furious when they were force fed genetically engineered corn in taco shells that contained a gene that was allergenic to human beings. They were not willing to accept the thought of pharmaceutical drugs being grown in plants, which could be unknowingly consumed!

But what most Indians would be more interested in, is to find out what's going on in our country? Have we any plans to introduce GM crops or are we taking a more precautionary approach?

The only GM crop in the Indian market today is the genetically modified cotton sold under Monsanto's brand name Bt Cotton. Although cotton is not technically a food crop, some communities use cotton seed oil for cooking and most often the seed cakes are used for animal feed—so growing Bt Cotton could have allowed the modified genes to enter our food chain—and any effects of this will probably manifest themselves generations down the line. Today agro-chemical companies and our government are conducting field trials of many more food crops.

Greenpeace is vehemently opposing the introduction of any of these. Our argument is simple. Science may show us the various possibilities as to what COULD be done. But wisdom and prudence is all about what SHOULD be done. How wise is it to proceed with dangerous, untested (indeed, untestable!) technology in our agriculture when a sizeable chunk of the scientific community has expressed its reservations? And how wise is it to march forth when we know that if mistakes are made, they are likely to be irreversible? And why do we have to walk this path when better alternatives based on a more appropriate vision for world agriculture is available for the taking?

(c) Other international campaigns include:

- Oceans
- Nuclear war
- Trade
- Forests

5. Working of Greenpeace

Greenpeace exists because this fragile earth deserves a voice. It needs solutions. It needs change. It needs action.

Greenpeace is an independent campaigning organisation, which uses non-violent creative confrontation to expose global environmental problems and to force solutions, which are essential to a green and peaceful future. Greenpeace's goal is to ensure the ability of the earth to nurture life in all its diversity. Greenpeace's core values are:

(i) Independence

We do not accept contributions from governments, corporations or political parties because it would compromise our core values.

(ii) Bearing witness

We follow the Quaker tradition of bearing witness. Philosophically and tactically, our peaceful protests work to raise awareness and bring public opinion to bear on decision-makers.

(iii) Non-violent direct action

We strongly believe that violence in any form is morally wrong and accomplishes nothing. While Greenpeace is best known for its non-violent direct actions, public protests are just one of many strategies we employ.

(iv) Research and science

Greenpeace uses scientific research to expose the risks of existing and emergent technologies. We use our laboratory in the University of Exeter, UK, to analyse soil, water and effluent samples. We present our findings in courts of law to ensure compliance with standards and justice for the wronged.

(v) Alternatives and solutions

Greenpeace, together with international experts, conducts scientific, economic and political research into the causes and effects of environmental pollution, in order to innovate alternatives and solutions that work.

(vi) Market forces and the powers-that-be

Our lobbyists, political and corporate campaigners regularly meet with governments and industry to ensure environmental considerations are factored into every level of decision-making.

We don't just react to government policy, we also try to anticipate it, and have been referred to as 'environmental watchdogs' because of our role in raising the alarm when a potentially dangerous situation is brewing.

(vii) Spreading the word

It isn't enough for us to know and act—we must guarantee that the world can bear witness too. We enlist the support of the mass media and our communications team to get the word out, guaranteeing our voice is heard around the world, in defence of people's Right to Know. We have conducted public hearings to make sure that knowledge is pooled and local people are empowered to exert pressure on the government and on businesses that directly impact their health and safety. Shareholders of businesses can also be allies, exerting pressure on their companies to act responsibly.

(viii) Working together

Our strategic partnerships with other non-government organisations (NGOs) allow us to reach new areas and communities. We encourage our volunteers—people from all walks of life—to get involved in our campaigns at every level. Cyber campaigns, peaceful protests, petitions to the government are all ways in which individuals can participate in making a difference.

6. Independent Greenpeace

Greenpeace does not solicit or accept funding from governments, corporations or political parties. Greenpeace neither seeks nor accepts donations that could compromise its independence, aims, objectives or integrity. Greenpeace relies on the voluntary donations of individual supporters, and on grant support from foundations.

Greenpeace is committed to the principles of non-violence, political independence and internationalism. In exposing threats to the environment and in working to find solutions, Greenpeace has no permanent allies or enemies.

Greenpeace has been campaigning against environmental degradation since 1971 when a small boat of volunteers and journalists sailed into Amchitka, an area north of Alaska where the US Government was conducting underground nuclear tests. This tradition of 'bearing witness' in a non-violent manner continues today. Greenpeace has played a pivotal role in, among other things, the adoption of:

- A ban on toxic waste exports to less developed countries.
- A moratorium on commercial whaling.
- A United Nations convention providing for better management of world fisheries.
- A Southern Ocean Whale Sanctuary.
- A 50-year moratorium on mineral exploitation in Antarctica.

7. Greenpeace Worldwide

Greenpeace has a unique presence around the world. Our strength lies in:

- Our commitment to truth and non-violence,
- Our determination to be funded only by voluntary donations of individual citizens. We have more than 2 and a half million members worldwide.
- And the international reach of our organisation.

8. Greenpeace Victories

Below are just some of the positive environmental changes that Greenpeace has directly helped to bring about since we began campaigning in 1971.

2000-2002

(i) 2002: Brazil declares a moratorium on export of Mahogany following revelations of the extent of illegal logging and timber trade. Greenpeace actions around the world help enforce the ban.

(ii) 2002: The European Union, followed by Japan, ratifies the Kyoto Protocol on climate change. Intensive Greenpeace lobbying must continue because, for the protocol to enter into force, 55 parties to the convention must ratify it.

(iii) 2002: Greenpeace helps defeat a major drive by pro-whaling nation Japan and its supporters to re-introduce commercial whaling through the International Whaling Commission.

(iv) 2001: Greenpeace turned 30 years old in September. The environmental group has grown from a small band of inspired volunteers to an international environmental organisation with offices in 30 countries. As always, Greenpeace thrives on committed activism and widespread, growing public support.

(v) 2001: After years of negotiations and pressure from Greenpeace, a global agreement for the elimination of a group of highly toxic and persistent man-made chemicals (Persistent Organic Pollutants or POPs), became a reality in May 2001 when a UN Treaty banning them is adopted.

(vi) 2001: A historic agreement with logging companies is reached on the conservation of Canada's remaining coastal rainforest and approved by the government of British Columbia. This follows years of campaigning by Greenpeace, most recently targeting the trade and investments of companies involved in logging the endangered Great Bear Rainforest.

(vii) 2001: Greenpeace lobbying, together with earlier expeditions to the Southern and Atlantic Oceans exposing flag of convenience (FOC or "pirate") vessels, are instrumental in the adoption of an "international plan of action" to combat illegal fishing in international waters.

(viii) 2000: An ever increasing and significant number of European retailers, food producers, and subsidiaries of multinational companies guaranteed to keep genetically engineered ingredients out of their products due to consumer pressure. Thanks to its consumer networks in 15 countries, Greenpeace tests products, collects information about food products and policies and exposes contamination cases.

(ix) 2000: Further to Greenpeace's April-May expedition exposing pirate fishing in the Atlantic, an import ban is adopted on all big eye tuna caught by FOC vessels in the Atlantic.

(x) 2000: Turkey's planned to build its first nuclear reactors at Akkuyu as part of a larger project to construct 10 reactors by the year 2020, is finally cancelled in July after eight years of campaigning by Greenpeace and others. The only remaining market for all major western nuclear companies is China.

1999

(a) 1999: Nine countries ban the use of harmful phthalates in polyvinyl chloride (PVC) toys for children under three and the EU introduces an "emergency" ban on soft PVC teething toys.

(b) 1999: Japan is ordered to stop "experimental" fishing of Southern Bluefin Tuna by the International Law of the Sea Tribunal.

1998

(i) 1998: The Environmental Protocol to the Antarctic Treaty comes into force.

(ii) 1998: A historic accord, the OSPAR Convention, bans the dumping of offshore installations at sea in the North-East Atlantic. The Convention also agrees on the phasing-out of radioactive and toxic discharges, as proposed by Greenpeace.

(iii) 1998: The oil company Shell finally agrees to bring its infamous offshore installation, the Brent Spar, to land for recycling. Greenpeace campaigned since 1995 to persuade the oil company not to dump disused installations in the ocean.

(iv) 1998: After 15 years of campaigning by Greenpeace, the EU finally agrees to phase out driftnet fishing by its fleets in EU and international waters by the end of 2001. France, Italy, the UK and Ireland, continued drift netting in the North-East Atlantic and Mediterranean after Japan, Taiwan and Korea stopped driftnet fishing on the high seas when the worldwide ban came into force at the end of 1992.

(v) 1998: Logging giant Macmillan Bloedel announces it will phase out clear-cut logging activities in British Columbia, Canada.

1997-1995

(a) 1997: After campaigning for urgent action to protect the climate since 1988 by Greenpeace and others, ministers from industrialized nations adopt the Kyoto Protocol agreeing to set legally-binding reduction targets on greenhouse gases.

(b) 1997: Greenpeace collects the UNEP Ozone Award for the development of Green freeze, a domestic refrigerator free of ozone depleting and significant global warming chemicals.

(c) 1996: The Comprehensive Nuclear Test Ban Treaty (CTBT) is adopted at the United Nations.

(d) 1995: Following a high profile action by Greenpeace, and public pressure, Shell UK reverses its decision to dump the Brent Spar oil platform in the Atlantic Ocean.

(e) 1995: Greenpeace actions to stop French nuclear testing receive wide international attention. Over seven million people sign petitions calling for a stop to testing. France, UK, US, Russia and China commit to sign the CTBT.

(f) 1995: Following a submission made with Greenpeace support, UNESCO designates Russia's Komi Forest as a World Heritage Site.

1994-1991

(i) 1994: After years of Greenpeace actions against whaling, the Antarctic whale sanctuary, proposed by France and supported by Greenpeace, is approved by the International Whaling Commission.

(ii) 1994: Greenpeace actions exposing toxic waste trade from Organisation for Economic Co-operation and Development (OECD) to non-OECD countries culminate in government negotiation of the Basel Convention banning this practice.

(iii) 1993: The London Dumping Convention permanently bans the dumping at sea of radioactive and industrial waste world-wide.

(iv) 1992: France cancels this year's nuclear tests at Moruroa Atoll, following the Rainbow Warrior visit to the test zone, and vows to halt altogether if other nuclear nations follow suit.

(v) 1992: Worldwide ban on high seas large-scale driftnets comes into force.

(vi) 1991: The 39 Antarctic Treaty signatories agree to a 50-year minimum prohibition of all mineral exploitation, in effect preserving the continent for peaceful, scientific purposes.

(vii) 1991: Major German publishers go chlorine-free after Greenpeace produces chlorine-free edition of Der Spiegel as part of campaign against chlorine-bleaching.

9. We need you

Greenpeace exists because this fragile earth deserves a voice. It needs solutions. It needs change. It needs action.

Green peace's goal is to ensure the ability of the earth to nurture life in all its diversity. To succeed, we need your help.

Greenpeace strives to save the planet on many fronts. We work to expose environmental scandals, stop the destruction of the planet and find viable solutions. And, thanks to our supporters, we are making a difference.

Greenpeace depends on your contributions. To ensure that we remain an independent voice for the planet, we don't accept corporate or government funds. We rely wholly on the small donations of millions of supporters like you, people who care about the world and want to share it with future generations, people who want to be part of the solution.

10. Conclusion

Green peace exists because this fragile earth deserves a voice. It needs solutions. It needs change. It needs action

In the end we would like to conclude that GREENPEACE INDIA has done a lot for the society and is also working independently and is not donations from the organisations but is taking donations from those who volunteer to give some thing for the nation and contribute for a good and prosperous nation.

4th June 2004: Or the eve of World Environment Day. Greenpeace India launched a consumer outreach activity to promote an eco-friendly, chemical-free lifestyle. Greenpeace campaigners bearing 6-foot high placards urged consumers to say not to toxics and suggested eco-friendly alternatives. Although industrial activity is by far the largest source of hazardous and toxic chemical pollution, Greenpeace is emphasizing how average urban consumers also contribute to pollution—directly and indirectly—through the products we choose, the chemicals we use and the energy we consume, and pointing out the long-term and long-range impacts of these demand-and-supply patterns. To coincide with the event, Greenpeace India also launched a web feature to help visitors replace toxic products in their food, homes and lifestyles—log on to www.greenpea-ceindia.org to see the full web feature.

References: www.greenpeaceindia.org; www.google.com

II. PROFILE OF POPULATION COUNCIL

The Population Council, an international, non-profit, non-governmental organisation, seeks to improve the well-being and reproductive health of current and future generations around the world and to help achieve a humane, equitable, and sustainable balance between people and resources.

Overview of Activities

Since 1952, the Population Council has been the premier international organisation conducting biomedical, public health, and social science research on population issues. The Council has been instrumental in the design of health products, service-delivery programmes, and public policies responsive to the needs of people living in the world's poorest countries.

Reflecting a commitment to excellence, objectivity, and policy relevance, Council research identifies promising, sustainable approaches to enhancing people's health and well-being. The widespread dissemination of its findings—and partnerships with nearly 200 governments, universities, and non-governmental organisations—ensure that Council researchers' work can and does make a positive difference in people's lives.

Policy-makers, programme managers, and others concerned with a wide array of population issues turn to the Council for evidence of what works in the real world to improve people's lives. The organisation's scientists and specialists around the world conduct research in a unique range of activities that include:

Biomedicine

Studying reproductive biology and immunology and developing and testing innovative products to allow people to enhance their health and expand their family planning choices.

Gender and Family Dynamics

Exploring how social, economic, and cultural factors such as education and gender roles affect individual well-being, earnings prospects, and ability to lead a healthy life.

HIV/AIDS

Identifying sustainable and cost-effective responses to the AIDS pandemic in the hardest-hit regions of the world.

Infants and Children

Investigating ways of improving the lives and health of infants and children.

Quality of Care

Improving quality of care in family planning and reproductive health programmes.

Reproductive Health

Investigating reproductive health and behaviour from biomedical, public health, and social science perspectives.

Social Science

Marshaling social science and demographic expertise toward a better understanding of population issues.

Strengthening Local Resources

Strengthening professional resources by providing training, technical assistance, fellowships, and awards to developing-country institutions and individuals.

Transitions to Adulthood

Understanding adolescents' lives and testing interventions to increase opportunities and reduce risks.

III. PROFILE OF ICA DOMUS TRUST: AN INTRODUCTION

Principles of Cooperation

- Voluntary and Open Membership

- Democratic Member Control
- Member Economic Participation
- Autonomy and Independence
- Education, Training and Information
- Co-operation Among Co-operatives
- Concern for Community.

"Co-operation is a very adaptable instrument and it is one economic method that applies in all circumstances."

Organisation

Karl Daniel Mouritz Bonow, was the President of the International Cooperative Alliance, Geneva. He was one of the pioneers in visualizing the essentiality for development of the cooperative movement as an instrument of socio-economic transformation and development of economy in the developing countries in general and for the upliftment of the weaker sections of the society in particular. In recognition of the valuable contribution made by Dr. Mauritz Bonow to the development of co-operative movements throughout the world and particularly in developing countries, the ICA Domus Trust (Dr. Bonow Memorial) was set-up on 1988 with its registered office in New Delhi, India.

Aims and Objectives

- To propagate co-operative principles and methods,
- To promote co-operatives,
- To safeguard the interests of co-operatives in all its forms,
- To assist the promotion of economic and social progress of farmers, workers and consumers through co-operative efforts,
- To work for the establishment of lasting peace and security through co-operation,
- To promote friendly and economic inter-co-operative relations,
- To convene and promote periodical co-operative conferences/meetings,
- To send experts/delegates to study and observe co-operative working and achievements,
- To bring out publications for the promotion of teachings and study in co-operation,
- To promote or carry out research studies relating to co-operatives and collect co-operative statistics,
- To formulate, assist and implement special programmes/projects for the involvement of youth and women in co-operatives and upliftment of the weaker sections of the community,
- To collaborate with co-operatives, United Nations, its specialized agencies, other voluntary and non-governmental international organisations which support the development of co-operatives,
- To disseminate the philosophy of co-operation,
- To offer scholarships for study of co-operatives,
- To provide material and guidance to educational institutions, co-operatives, and mass media regarding co-operatives,
- To work for the promotion of co-operative values in the society, and
- To do all such work necessary to achieve the objects of the Trusts.

Activities

1. ***Workshops on the Sensitization of DCHC officers on the Self-sustainability of Craft Clusters***

   - Sensitization of the participants on the issues governing self-sustainability of Craft Clusters
   - Mode of Community Empowerment and Women's participation in the development of Community-based Enterprises
   - Case studies on the participatory approach in democratic governance.

2. *Base Line Survey of Handicraft Clusters in Baster, Jodhpur, Leh (Ladakh), Puri and Sikkim*

   - Identification of the Benchmarks
   - Priority ranking of the economic activities
   - Problem identification
   - Development of intervention plans
   - Generation of awareness among the community members.

3. *Formalization of Cane and Bamboo Handicraft Clusters in Kerala, Assam, Meghalaya, Tripura, Manipur, Arunachal Pradesh & Nagaland under UNDP-GoI Collaboration Plan*

   - Rapid Rural Survey to identify the Benchmarks
   - Awareness on Community-based Enterprises
   - Democratic governance under professional guidance
   - Organisation of the informal groups into Co-operative Societies
   - Benchmark Survey through built-in evaluation mechanism.

4. *Workshop on the Integrated Development of Handicraft Clusters*

   - Situation Analysis
   - Need Assessment
   - Project Approach
   - Project Components for integrated development.
   - Financial Appraisal tools
   - Organisational design options in the light of enterprise specific requirements
   - Monitoring and Evaluation parameters for a built-in performance appraisal mechanism.

5. ***Exotic India Handicrafts Exhibition at Singapore in collaboration with the Handicrafts and Handloom Export Corporation of India Ltd. with the financial support of the Ministry of Textiles, Government of India from 24 to 26 August 2001 at Singapore Expo, Hall 6B, Singapore.***

"Co-operatives are more relevant today than they have ever been."

—Romano Prodi, President of the EU

Information Resource Centre

To maintain a library and information resource Centre—where all types of information on co-operatives and inter-related allied subjects in any form, duly processed and computerized is available under on roof. Any co-operator potential co-operator can avail the information through a network of information dissemination system.

Administration

The ICA Domus Trust has its office in New Delhi and governed by 5 trustees, comprising of the ICA President, ICA Vice-President for Asia and the Pacific, CA Director General, ICA Regional Director for Asia and the Pacific (Executive Trustee) and one representing the Indian co-operative movement.

IV. PROFILE OF INTERNATIONAL COOPERATIVE ALLIANCE EC-ICA DOMUS TRUST PROJECT ON POST EARTHQUAKE REHABILITATION OF HANDICRAFT ARTISANS IN KUTCH DISTRICT OF GUJARAT

ICA Domus Trust has been actively involved in the facelift operation of Indian handicrafts in collaboration with the office of the Office of Development Commission Handicraft, Ministry of Textile, Government of India. ICA-DT in collaboration with COHANDS, Artisans Bridge and BRIDGE as its partner agencies, has a very specific approach and emphasis upon organisation of Self Help Groups to evolve community action and initiation of thrift and credit activities with deprived women artisans for their empowerment. Thus it will provide the required technical support in orienting the target community/groups towards setting up their own self-reliant and user friendly Community-based Enterprises. This way the project will become the business arm of the poor and under-privileged artisans from the affected parts with the active support of European Commission and Government of India

Coverage and Targets

7050 Artisans
64 Villages

Project Activities

- Distribution of upgraded tool kits to artisans' family units.
- Organisation of artisans into Self Help Groups to evolve community action.
- Setting up common work centres at the village level and taluka (block) level.
- Initiation of thrift and credit activities with women members of the artisans' families for women empowerment.
- Workshops and training programmes on human resource development, skill upgradation, product development, market exploration and networking.
- Margin money support to avail institutional finance for working capital requirements.
- Installation of machinery and equipments for capacity enhancement quality control, cost efficiency and higher productivity and returns.
- Managerial subsidy to have better competitive strength to create market niche and serve target market segments.
- Institutionalization of self-help groups into co-operative societies with representative general body mechanism for institutional stability and long-term viability.

Craft-wise Sectors in Project

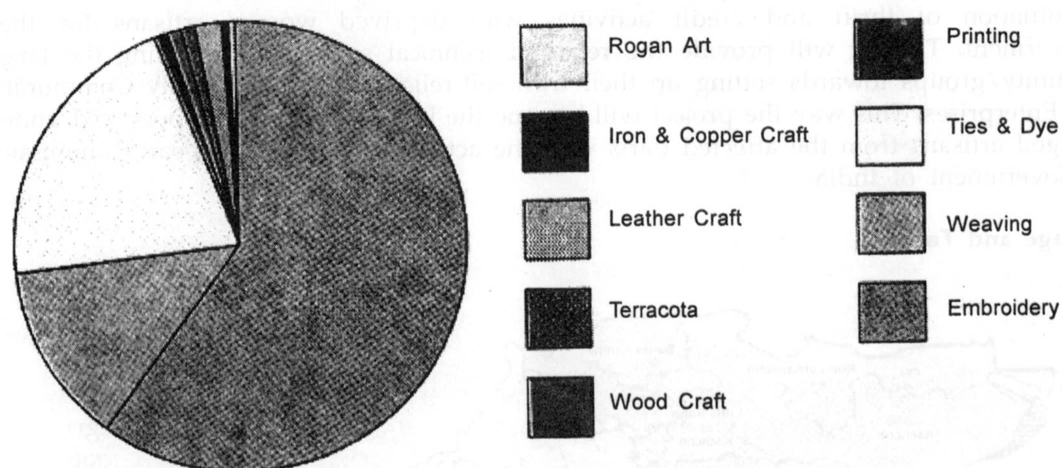

Project Objectives

- To regenerate capacity and capability of handicrafts artisans in the project area.
- To organise the groups of artisans in to self-reliant and user friendly Community Based Enterprises (CBEs) based on the philosophy and principles of self help and co-operation.
- To empower women artisans and non-artisans women members of the community through micro-credit operations and alternative income generation activities.

- To integrate artisans' community through bonds of solidarity establishment through women thrift and credit operation.
- To expand business operations through effective networking paradigm using Information Technology means.

For further information and co-operative publications, please contact or write to:

ICA Domus Trust
9, Aradhana Enclave (Ring Road),
Sector-13, R.K. Puram,
New Delhi - 110066
Tel: (91-11) 26888250
Fax: (91-11) 26888067
email: icaroap@vsnl.com

The **INTERNATIONAL COOPERATIVE ALLIANCE [ICA]** is an independent non-governmental association that unites, represents and serves the cooperatives worldwide. Founded in London on 18th August 1895 by the International Cooperative Congress, the ICA, the largest non-governmental organisation, is headquartered in Geneva. ICA is a member-based organisation with national and international cooperative organisations in 102 countries. ICA's five Offices in Africa (2), the Americas, Asia and Pacific, and Europe, together, serve more than 241 member organisations, including five international organisations, representing well over 760 million individual members around the world.

The ICA Asia & Pacific [ICA A & P], one of the five offices serves 54 national level organisations from 22 countries, and one international organisation [ACCU]. Main activities include: Coordination of cooperative development efforts within the Region and promotion of exchange and experiences; Project identification, formulation and evaluation; Promotion of establishment and development of national cooperative apex organisations; and Organisation of seminars, conferences and technical meetings on specific subjects including support for programmes aimed at the involvement of women and youth in cooperative activities.

The ICA enjoys Category-I Consultative Status with the United Nations Economic and Social Council [UN/ECOSOC] and has active working relations with UN and other international organisations.

The **INSTITUTE FOR THE DEVELOPMENT OF AGRICULTURAL COOPERATION IN ASIA [IDACA]** was established on July 8, 1963 by the Central Union of Agricultural Cooperatives of Japan [JA Zenchu], with funds raised from among agricultural cooperatives in Japan and with the support of the Government of Japan.

The Institute, established on the basis of the recommendations of the First Asian Agricultural Cooperative Conference held in Tokyo in April 1962, imparts training to overseas agricultural cooperators.

During the last 40 years, the IDACA has trained more than 4400 participants from 96 countries drawn from Agricultural Cooperative Movements and Governments from different countries of Asia, Latin America and Africa. It has active collaboration on technical assistance programmes with the ICA Asia & Pacific

The **INDIAN FARMERS' FERTILISER COOPERATIVE LIMITED [IFFCO]**, a member-organisation of the International Cooperative Alliance, was registered on November

3, 1967, under the Multi-State Cooperative Societies Act. The IFFCO is owned by more than 36,000 cooperative societies. It produces and sells more than 6 million tonnes of fertiliser every year. It has earned a pre-tax profit of 8070 million during the year 2002-3.

It operates its Fertiliser Marketing Development Institute [FMDI] besides several farmers' training centres and has established specialised professional Chairs in a number of universities and institutions of higher learning and research. It has been responsible for the creation of other organisations, e.g., Krishak Bharati Cooperative Limited [KRIBHCO], Cooperative Rural Development Trust [CORDET], Indian Farm Forestry Development Cooperative Limited [IFFDC], etc.

The **INSTITUTE OF RURAL MANAGEMENT, ANAND [IRMA]** was established in 1979 at Anand, Gujarat State, India. Beginning with providing management training and research support to the cooperatives in the dairy sector, its mission engages in teaching, training, research and consultancy. It conducts several well-structured, residential programmes—a two-year post-graduate programme in Rural Management [PRM], Certificate in Rural Management [CRM], and Fellow Programme in Rural Management [FPRM]—for training of young fresh graduates/post-graduates as well as in-service officers and managers of rural organisations, who are looking for a management career with a social purpose.

The IRMA has been able to develop a good working relationship with the ICA Regional Office on cooperative management leadership training and development activities.

The **DEWAN KOPERASI INDONESIA (DEKOPIN)**, was established in 1953, as the national apex of all types and sectors of cooperatives in Indonesia, which include, agriculture, fisheries, banking, workers' productive, multi-purpose, consumers, housing, insurance, dairy and service cooperatives. Its objectives are to strengthen competitiveness of cooperatives in the market economy through education and training to enrich professional management, business techniques, entrepreneurship development, provide suitable technologies, assisting cooperatives in funds mobilisation both internally and externally; to establish and develop education and training institutions for improving the operational viability and profitability of cooperatives; to increase the role of women in cooperatives, at all levels, members, board members and staff or personnel; to continuously assist member-cooperatives in legal matters, licensing, taxation, etc. and to establish a network of cooperative small and medium enterprises in Indonesia.

An Executive Board assisted by a board of supervision and board of advisors supervises the working of DEKOPIN. The Board of Directors consist of a Chairperson, four Vice-Chairpersons, a Treasurer and a Secretary General. The Board of Directors is responsible to the Annual General Meeting. The auxiliary operational bodies of DEKOPIN are: (1) LAPENKOP (The Cooperative Education and Training Development Institution); (2) JUK (The Centre for Cooperative Business Network Development); (3) BKWK (Women Cooperator Communication Committee; (4) BKPK (Youth Cooperator Communication Committee); and (5) BKPH (The Cooperative Legal Service and Counseling Committee).

The LAPENKOP (The Cooperative Education & Training Development Institution), Bandung, was established as Cooperative Member Education and Communication Project of the Dekopin and the Cooperative Centre Denmark (CCD) on September 1, 1993. It was named as Lapenkop in May 1995. It now functions as a training and development arm of the Dekopin. It has its presence in 22 provinces. The Institute has its own training facilities with a full compliment of well-qualified and experienced faculty members. Due to the decentralization of authority, government contribution to cooperative education and training activities has got considerably diluted. The government training institutions at the national and provincial levels have either been closed down or are being used for other purposes. The Lapenkop is the sole institution in the country which offers training and development programmes for cooperatives.

ICA-ROAP

Vision

International Co-operative Alliance

Regional Office for Asia and the Pacific

In this new millennium—and with nearly three-quarters of the world's population as potential co-operators—the ICA-ROAP plays a vital role in international co-operative development, presently serving over 520 million individual members from 53 national level member organisations in 21 countries and 1 international organisation.

Our Vision

We, the ICA in Asia and the Pacific believe in the ICA Co-operative Identity Statement (ICIS) as our guidepost to promote and enhance co-operative development in the region.

Mission

Our Mission

We, the ICA in Asia and the Pacific, shall strive to promote and strengthen the co-operative movement in the region.

Key Result Areas

- Co-operative Identity and Image;
- International Co-operative Presence;
- Co-operative Development;
  Networking; and
- Other cross-cutting issues like Gender, youth and environment.

Activities

Activities

- Co-ordinating co-operative development efforts within the region and facilitating exchange of experience;
- Project identification, formulation, preparation and evaluation;
- Organising Annual Co-op Think Tank Consortia;
- Convening Ministers' Conferences;
- Organising members' Regional Assembly and Specialised Committee meetings;

- Developing and facilitating human resource development, research and gender integration activities; and
- Co-ordinating other co-operative-related activities.

Membership and Sectors

Fifty-three national-level member organisations from 21 countries and one international organisation are being served by the ICA-ROAP Member countries in Asia-Pacific include: Australia, Bangladesh, China, India, Indonesia, Iran, Israel, Japan, Kazakhstan, Republic of Korea, Kuwait, Malaysia, Myanmar, Nepal, Pakistan, Palestine, The Philippines, Singapore, Sri Lanka, Thailand, Turkmenistan and Vietnam.

Specialised bodies have been created by ICA to address specific development and technical issues in key sectors. ICA-ROAP has 9 specialised committees and sub-committees, focusing on agriculture, banking/finance, consumer, fisheries, gender, health, housing, human resource development and research and university/college (youth). Committees for communications, energy, tourism and workers are co-ordinated by the Head Office.

Benefits

Membership Benefits

- Exposure to co-operative development in other countries;
- Network for inter-co-operative and international trade;
- Recognition by UN bodies (e.g. FAO, ILO, UNDP), with increased profile for funding and technological support;
- Increased knowledge about prospective development partners and projects;
- Strengthened interaction with governments and increased leverages for autonomous co-operative governance;
- Development, research and informational support from ICA specialised bodies;
- Representation at Regional Assembly, Executive Council, General Assembly and on ICA Board;
- Access to ICA training programmes, workshops, conferences;
- Access to ICA-ROAP Co-operative Resources; and
- Receipt of ICA-ROAP publications: Co-op Dialogue, Asia-Pacific Co-op News (both quarterly) and various others.

Partners

ICA-ROAP Partners

ICA-ROAP's development partners provide important project funding and support. Aside from ICA's own members, our development partners include, among others:

- Canadian Co-operative Association (CCA);
- Development International Desjardins (DID);
- Government of Japan—Ministry of Agriculture, Forestry and Fisheries;
- International Labour Organisation (ILO);
- JA-Zenchu/Institute for the Development of Agricultural Co-operation in Asia (IDACA);

- Japanese Consumers Co-operative Union (JCCU);
- Swedish Co-operative Centre (SCC);
- AGRITERRA—Netherlands;
- National Agricultural Co-operative Federation, Korea (NACF);
- All China Federation of Supply & Marketing Co-operatives (ACFSMC);
- Government of Kuwait—Ministry of Co-operatives;
- Union of Consumer Co-operative Societies, Kuwait; and
- Singapore National Co-operative Federation (SNCF).

Information

Co-operative Information Centre

The ICA-ROAP maintains the world's largest collection of co-operative literature. Over 30,000 books and publications on co-operatives and allied subjects (e.g. environment, gender, HRD, health, management) can be accessed from our Co-operative Information Centre (CIRC). CIRC is an invaluable resource for those interested in co-operative studies and research and the region's socio-economic development. Information regarding new cooperative publications as also the organisation can also be accessed from our website: http://www·icaroap.coop

For further information and publications, please contact:

9 Aradhana Enclave, Sector-13
R.K. Puram, New Delhi-110066, India
Tel: (91-11) 2688-8250
Fax: (91-11) 2688-8067/2688-8241
E-mail: icaroap@vsnl.com

Administration

Co-operatives throughout the region from grass-roots level up to national apex present their ideas, views and concerns forward at the Regional Assembly, ICA's highest policy-making body for the region. A Regional Assembly is co-ordinated by ICA-ROAP every second year.

A Standing Committee, comprising of elected delegates from member countries and the ICA Vice-President for Asia-Pacific, meets several times a year to advise on ICA-ROAP's overall policy and programmes and to review the results of ICA-ROAP's activities. Day-to-day functioning is carried out by the Regional Director and a team of professional staff.

Finances

The ICA is financed through member subscriptions, sponsorship of ICA activities and its own funds. We continue to seek and invite new partners, who understand and believe in the overall importance of international co-operative development work. If you or your organisation would like to share monetary or technological resources, please contact us directly.

"There are dramatic deprivations in the world in which we live—mass poverty and hunger, basic unsatisfied needs, violations of basic rights and liberty, contempt for the active role of women, increasingly serious threats to the environment and economic and social sustainability in our way of livin."

—*Amartya Sen*, Nobel Prize Winner for Economics

International Cooperative Alliance

The International Cooperative Alliance [ICA] is an independent worldwide international association of cooperative organisations of all types. Founded in London on 18th August 1895 by the International Cooperative Congress, the ICA has affiliates in 90 countries with 251 national and 4 international level organisations as members serving well over 800 million individual members worldwide.

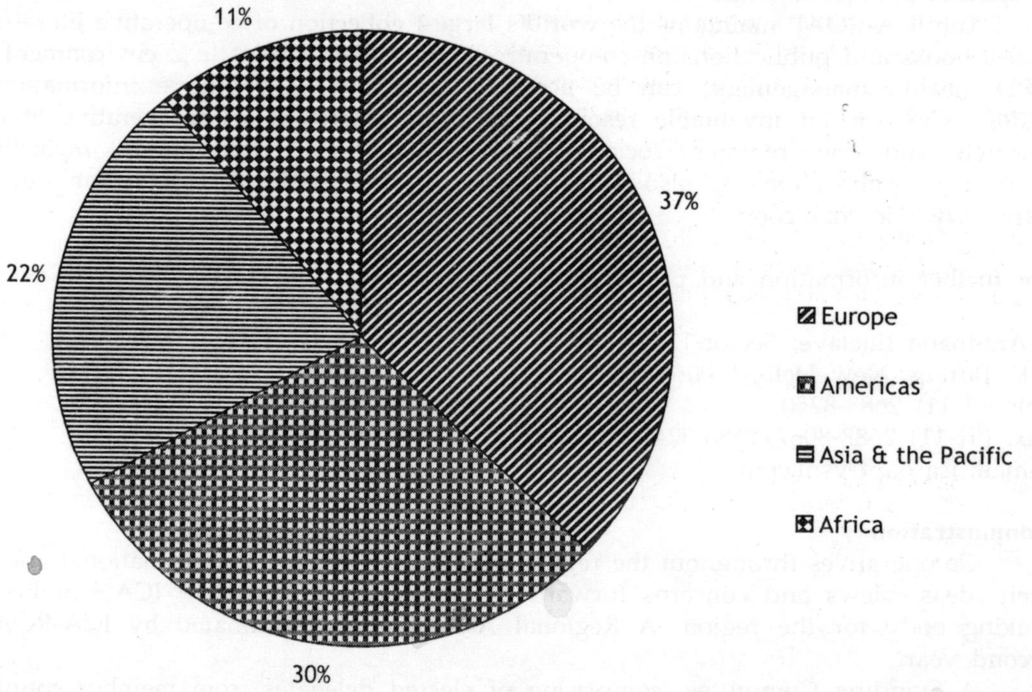

The ICA collaborates with several United Nations agencies, including the International Labour Organisation (ILO) and the Council for Trade and Development (UNCTAD). ICA enjoys Category-I Consultative Status within the United Nations Economic and Social Council (UN/ECOSOC).

"Co-operation, by definition, is an undertaking together and on equal terms—a choice bringing together business and solidarity and therefore, useful and effective in our present situation, as was also the case at the beginning of the last century. Often all this has been achieved contrary to the dominant economic culture and globalization processes, mainly characterized by a sort of "escape from responsibility".

—*Ivano Barberini*, ICA President at the Oslo General Assembly.

What are Co-operatives?

Co-operatives are a form of business enterprises, or community organisation, incorporated in service to its members and users, in order to meet their common economic, social or cultural needs and aspirations. Co-operatives are jointly-owned and democratically controlled by their members and users on the basis of one member, one vote.

Co-operatives use democrative, participatory, and transparent decision-making processes and organisational structures so that their members and users (i.e. owners, workers and consumers) may be directly responsible for benefitting themselves and the society in general.

Values

Values and Principles

Co-operatives are based on the value of self-help, mutual help, self-responsibility, democracy, equality, equity and solidarity. Co-operative members believe in the ethical values of honesty, openness, social responsibility, and caring for others. Guidelines by which co-operatives put their values into practice are:

- Voluntary and Open Membership
- Democratic Member Control
- Member Economic Participation
- Autonomy and Independence
- Education, Training and Information
- Co-operation among Co-operatives
- Concern for Community

"Cooperative enterprises provide the organisational means whereby a significant proportion of humanity is able to take into its own hands the tasks of creating productive employment, overcoming poverty and achieving social integration."

—*Kofi Annan*, UN Secretary-General.

INTERNATIONAL CO-OPERATIVE ALLIANCE

HEAD OFFICE

15 route des Morillons
CH-1218, Grand Saconnex
Geneva, Switzerland

Tel	(41) 22-929-8888
Fax	(41) 22-798-4122
E-mail	ica@ica.coop
Website	http://www.ica.coop

ICA REGIONAL OFFICES

The Americas (ICA-ROAM)
Apartado Postal 6648-1000
1000 San Jose, Costa Rica

Tel	(506) 231-4362, 231-5069
Fax	(506) 231-5842
E-mail	alianza@sol.racsa.co.cr I direccion@alianzaaci.or.cr
Website	http:/www.aciamericas.coop

East, Central and Southern Africa (ICA-ROECSA)
Kileleshwa, Off. Gichigu Road,
Nairobi, Kenya

Tel	(254-2) 560-865/565-771/43-060
Fax	(254-2) 560-865/565-771/43-204
E-mail	icamoshi@africaonline.co.ke

West Africa (ICA-ROWA)
Avenue Kwame N'krumah
01 BP 6461 Ouagadougou 01,
Burkina Faso

Tel	(226) 30 73 28
Fax	(226) 30 73 29
E-mail	acibrao@fasonet.bf

Europe (ICA-ROE)
15, route des Morillons
CH-1218, Grand Saconnex
Geneva, Switzerland

Tel	(41) 22-929-8831
Fax	(41) 22-798-4122
E-mail	http://www.ica.coop.europe

Asia and the Pacific (ICA-ROAP)
9, Aradhana Enclave, Sector-13, R.K. Puram,
New Delhi-110066, India

Tel	(91) 11-2688-8250
Fax	(91) 11-2688-8067/2688-8241
E-mail	icaroap@vsnl.com
Website	http://www.icaroap.coop

Business Office
510, Thomson Road,
#12-02 SLF Building, Singapore 298135

Tel	(65) 6358-2322
Fax	(65) 6358-2292
E-mail	jiroito@icaroap.org.sg

Annexure VIII

CHECK-LIST: TO REVIEW HEALTH OF NPOs

Introduction

The checklist below is meant to provide a quick overview of the health of organisational systems. It does not produce an organisational evaluation and will not let you know if your services are effective or efficient. It will, however, let you know if you have the systems in place that are necessary to operate effectively and efficiently.

Board of Directors

- The Board of Directors is elected by a membership that represents the community that the organisation serves.
- The Board of Directors is elected by a membership that represents the people who use or benefit from the programmes and services of the organisation.
- New Board members are given an information package on assuming their position that includes:
  - Board minutes from the previous two years
  - Financial statements from the previous two years
  - Annual and Auditor's Reports for the previous two years
  - A copy of the Constitution and By-Laws
  - An organisation chart
  - Summaries of all programme/services
  - Copies of any programme/service evaluations from the previous two years
  - A list of key staff and their positions
  - Brief biographies of all Board Members.
- New Board members are given an orientation to the organisation within their first month on the Board.
- Board job descriptions covering all Board positions are provided to all Board members.
- The Board meets at least quarterly.
- Written agendas are sent out before meetings.
- Minutes are sent out shortly after Board meetings.
- The Board sets annual goals for its own work.
- The Board evaluates its performance annually.
- The Board evaluates the C.E.O. annually.
- The Board has a process for handling emergencies between meetings.

Policy Management

- The organisation has a Values Statement that is reviewed regularly.
- The Mission Statement is reviewed by the Board at least every two years.
- The Constitution and By-Laws are reviewed by the Board at least every three years.
- In addition to the standard sections, the By-Laws have policies covering Board member conflict of interest, Board members who apply for jobs with the organisation, Board member absenteeism, and Board member liability.
- The Board sets annual goals for the organisation.
- The organisation has a Strategic Plan that is reviewed regularly.
- Every programme/service that the organisation provides has a set of measurable objectives/outcomes that are approved by the Board or its delegate committee.
- The Board controls signing authority.

Financial Management

- The organisation has a realistic annual budget and a plan for achieving it.
- Financial statements are presented to the Board at least quarterly.
- Financial statements provide comparative information for the previous year and for the current budget.
- The Board Treasurer is skilled at financial analysis.
- The organisation has unrestricted operating reserves to cover a minimum of three months' operating costs.
- The cost of fund raising does not exceed 25% of funds raised.
- At least 75% of all expenses are directed to the Charitable Objects of the organisation.
- The organisation has an annual independent audit.

Risk Management

- Limits are put on over-spending without Board approval.
- All staff/volunteers who are in regular contact with vulnerable people or who are in a position of authority over vulnerable people are screened by police.
- The organisation carries Directors, and Officers, liability insurance.
- The organisation carries a minimum of $2 million liability insurance.
- The organisation has, regularly educates its staff and volunteers on, and enforces policies on discrimination and harassment.
- The organisation has, and enforces policies on confidentiality where appropriate.
- The organisation has policies on the use of office equipment.
- The organisation makes all mandatory government filings and payments on time.
- Fund raising activities follow the ethical guidelines set out by the Canadian Society of Fund Raising Executives and/or the Canadian Centre for Philanthropy
- Independent contractors meet all the requirements of the Canada Revenue and Customs Agency for independent contractors.

Human Resources Management

- Staff are hired on a competitive basis through a formal process.
- The organisation has a written personnel policy.
- The personnel policy is provided to all staff.
- The organisation has a written volunteer policy.
- The volunteer policy is provided to all volunteers.
- Every staff person and volunteer has an up-do-date job description.
- Staff/volunteers are provided with a comprehensive orientation to the organisation within one week of arriving.
- Staff/volunteers are evaluated annually.
- Evaluations are growth-oriented.
- Staff/volunteers are provided with opportunities to upgrade their skills.
- Staff/volunteers are provided opportunities for promotion and/or change in assignment.
- The organisation recognizes staff and volunteer achievement.
- Administrative staff turnover is under 15% annually.
- Programme staff turnover is under 15% annually.

Programme/Service Delivery

- Programmes/services are delivered to meet identified needs.
- Goals that cover output and outcome are set for every programme/service.
- Individuals from all levels of the organisation participate in planning processes.
- Service users are involved in programme planning.
- Programmes are physically accessible.
- Programmes are culturally accessible.
- Programmes are linguistically accessible.
- Programmes are provided by staff and volunteers with appropriate training and expertise.
- Eligible human service users are not denied service because of an inability to pay.
- The organisation communicates regularly with its stakeholders.

Evaluation

- Every programme/service is evaluated against its output and outcome goals annually.
- Programme and administrative evaluations are compiled and published annually.
- The results of all evaluations are used in annual planning.
- Service users are involved in evaluations.

ANNEXURE IX

BLOOMING NGOs

They're thereafter every disaster, even if the difference between them and the government is down to 20 paise.

—*Samrat Choudhury*

On October 10, two days after a 7.6 magnitude earthquake added another 50,000 names to Kashmir's unending roster of untimely deaths, a group of NGOs met in Delhi to coordinate their relief efforts. The Indian Red Cross was sending 38,000 blankets, besides tents and kitchen sets. CARE was contributing a team of doctors, nurses and paramedics. Others came up with utensils and hygiene kits. Help was on its way.

Every disaster now sees a massive mobilisation of non-governmental organisations. They are often the first to provide succor in remote areas. Governments work with them. The help they provide saves lives. Yet the very growth of the sector has brought its share of problems.

Growing pains and connotations

Amit Sengupta is a member of the Delhi Science Forum and the World Social Forum. "I don't like the word NGO", he says. "How do you define NGO? The RSS and VHP are outside the government, so are the NGOs?" The term has acquired "certain connotations", says Sengupta, which is why many people in such organisations resent the label.

The "connotations" are easy enough to detect. An official of the Social Welfare Department in Srinagar notes that the last 15 years of militancy in Kashmir has seen the proliferation of two entities in the place: Netas and NGOs. "These NGOs are virtually money-making machines for their owners", he says.

"Setting up an NGO has become a profession for most people", says college teacher Mushtaq Ahmad. "A lot of money is coming for NGOs and accountability is just in name", he adds.

There's an NGO for every reason, every season, every incident and almost every locality in the Northeast as well. Several of these are known to be front organisations for militant groups. The Home Ministry blacklisted 824 NGOs in six states in the region in 2003. This followed a raid in Morigaon district in Assam where documents indicating links between ULFA and some NGOs was recovered.

NGOs are also used as cover by the invisible marketing arms of giant corporations, the World Bank, and US Federal funding agencies, says activist and author Vandana Shiva. These NGOs have an agenda, she says: shaping policies. "They do so by trying to bypass government structures while preaching accountability. It is a soft entry for those who have global reach". Such organisations do not empower people but instead increase their levels of dependency, says Shiva.

A question of credibility

The question of credibility is one that can afflict even the most credible of organisations. SEWA is an NGO that has won national and international acclaim for its work. The Gujarat-based organisation was running an earthquake rehabilitation project called 'Jeevika' which covered 40,000 quake-affected families in the state. Its project partners were the State Government, the Government of India and International Fund for Agricultural Development. SEWA pulled out of this and about 19 other projects on October 7 after the State government accused it of misappropriation and diversion of funds.

Juthika Banerjee, who resigned from her position as Project Director for the Jeevika project, says, "Expense statements and the physical status of the project work often do not tally". SEWA denies these charges and has accused the Modi Government of harassment.

"The relationship between the Non-profit Organisations (NPOs) and bureaucracy in India is a complex one, characterised by mutual suspicion and hostility", says former Planning Commission Secretary NC Saxena. Saxena co-authored a much-cited report on the topic with Ashok Thakur. According to this report, "While the NPOs regard bureaucracy as inherently insensitive, oppressive, inefficient, parasitic and corrupt, the image of NPOs among government officers is that of trouble-makers and wasters, and totally dependent on foreign funding. The fact that most NPO staff today, unlike their predecessors 20 years ago, no longer have an austere life-style and are well-paid professionals, opting for social work as a mainstream (and frequently globalised) career, adds to such an impression."

Saxena however holds that that civil society's involvement in policy advocacy brings many benefits. He also writes that, "In addition to grass-roots and delivery organisations there are many intermediary and specialised organisations that have been of immense utility in improving administration".

So who's bad?

Official estimates of the number of NGOs in the country currently stand between 1 and 1.2 million. Of these, roughly 5,000 have been blacklisted by the government. It is therefore not correct to conclude that the majority of NGOs are corrupt. However, there is no evidence that they are effective, either.

How many NGOs achieve the purposes so grandly stated in their Memorandums of Association? How many even really try? To whom are they accountable? No one in this country can accurately answer the first two questions simply because no one knows how many NGOs there are. The answer to the third question is that NGOs are accountable to their boards.

"That's the most important body to whom we are accountable", says CSE's Sunita Narain. She adds that the board meets twice a year. They also have to meet a lot of statutory compliances, she says, such as Income Tax, reports under the Societies Registration Act and the FCRA.

In her opinion, there are enough rules; the problem lies elsewhere."The government's entire way of funding today is based on a client-patron relationship. The attitude is to see whether a project can provide a job for some IAS officer's wife or daughter."

According to Saxena, "Weak monitoring mechanisms in government has prompted social climbers and manipulators (that includes defeated politicians and civil servants' wives) who use their extra-professional 'resources' to obtain grants from several Ministries/ Departments of Government and spend it fast, with no commitment to sustainable development or poverty alleviation. What used to be a sleepy office, the Registrar of Societies Office is now a prize posting for officials as they can extract rents from prospective NGOs for quick registration."

He adds that, "When Ministers find NGOs pocketing government funds they do not plug the loopholes but encourage their own supporters to join the loot."

This makes everyone part of the same corrupt system. The director of a human rights NGO says that the difference between NGOs and Government now is "about 20 paise". If a certain amount of money goes to the government, only 10 paise out of every rupee will reach the intended beneficiary, he says. If the same money goes to the NGO, about 30 paise reaches.

—With inputs from Brinda Sun in Delhi, Rashid Ahmed in Srinagar, Rahul Karmakar in Guwahati, G.C. Shekhar in Chennai and Rathin Das in Ahmedabad

ANNEXURE X

DISASTER MANAGEMENT

Floods

Floods in Mumbai, hurricanes Katrina and Rita, the devastating tsunami in South East Asia, and the recent earthquake in South Asia have caused over a hundred thousand deaths in countries across the world. Disasters such as these are occurring with greater frequency necessitating the need for a proper disaster management policy and strategy to deal effectively with them and minimise the damage caused.

Disasters are either natural, such as floods, droughts, cyclones, and earthquakes, or man made such as riots, conflicts, refugee situations, and others like fire, epidemics, industrial accidents, and environmental fallouts. Often, the difference between them is marginal. Globally, natural disasters account for nearly 80 per cent of all disaster-affected people.

The 15th World Conference on Disaster Management held in June 2005 brought together experts from across the globe in order to listen and learn, plan and prepare, educate and exchange views on the lessons to be learned from all disciplines of disaster and emergency management. Following the tsunami of December 26, 2004, a Ministerial Committee and Task Force were set-up by the Government of India and a National Disaster Management Centre was established to facilitate and co-ordinate emergency relief work.

What do I have to do?

Management of a disaster can be divided into the following tasks:

- Mitigation of the negative impact of disaster
- Immediate rescue and relief
- Rehabilitation
- Documentation and learning for the future

Thus, disaster management experts deal with housing, reconstruction and resettlement, economic livelihoods, health and psychosocial issues.

What should I study?

Anyone who has completed 10+2 is eligible to enrol for most of the Disaster Management courses which are designed to introduce students to the key concepts and practices of disaster management, to equip them to conduct thorough assessments of hazards, risks, vulnerability and capacity and to be able to critically evaluate and apply key elements of planning and management for the effective response to emergencies and disasters.

Some courses are designed in particular for professionals in the areas of emergency planning, risk assessment, community development, humanitarian aid, capacity building and associated professions to enhance their professional qualifications and gain an improved understanding of contemporary issues in disaster management.

What next?

Openings are mainly found in some government and non-government agencies. Large industrial establishments, particularly those in high-risk fields like chemicals, mining and petroleum have disaster management cells. The International Red Cross and some UN organisations like the World Bank and ADB also empanel trained professionals for working on humanitarian missions to handle major calamities and emergencies.

Disaster Management training is useful for NGOs, social work students or volunteer providing support and rehabilitation measures during disasters, home guard personnel, paramilitary organisations, civil defence personnel, scientists, meteorologists, and environmentalists. It is also useful for functionaries of rural development and primary health centres, services and relief workers.

Job prospects are expected to increase with the Government paying more attention to calamities.

INSTITUTES AT A GLANCE

Sikkim Manipal University of Health, Medical and Technological Sciences, Tadong, Gangtok, Sikkim (in association with the Indian Institute of Ecology and Environment).

Course: Master in Disaster Mitigation for graduates in any discipline.

PRT Institute of Post Graduate Environmental Education and Research, New Delhi, (in association with Institute of Open and Distance Education, Barkatullah Vishwavidyalaya, Bhopal).

Course: Master of Disaster Control (two-year) to graduates or working professionals through distance learning.

Indira Gandhi National Open University (IGNOU), New Delhi, (through distance education, in collaboration with Pune University).

Course: Disaster Management courses (six months to two years) after plus two/ equivalent.

National Civil Distance College, Nagpur (Maharastra).

Courses: Various courses in Civil Defence, and Disaster Relief Management.

The Centre for Disaster Management (CDM), Pune.

Course: CDM, in collaboration IGNOU, has launched a post-graduate Diploma course in Disaster Management in English, Hindi and Marathi.

All India Disaster Mitigation Institute, Ahmedabad, holds short courses on disaster management for specific needs.

School of Science and the Environment, Coventry University, UK.
Course: B.Sc. (Hons.) International Disaster Engineering and Management.

University of Birmingham, Edgbaston, Birmingham, UK.
Course: Undergraduate programme on Disaster Management and Sustainable Technology

George Washington University: Institute for Crisis, Disaster and Risk Management (ICDRM), George Washington University, Washington.
Course: Master of Science in Engineering Management and Systems Engineering with emphasis on Crisis, Emergency and Risk Management, and Graduate Certificates in Crisis and Emergency Management and Emergency Management and Public Health.

Source: *HT*, New Delhi.

Annexure XI

FIVE WAYS MANAGERS CAN USE SCENARIO PLANNING TO PREPARE FOR DISASTERS

The tallest building in New Orleans, 51 evacuated floors of very expensive office space, is known as 1 Shell Square, because Shell Oil has so many of its operations headquartered there. Shell is famous for popularizing the corporate use of a technique called scenario planning to anticipate dangerous occurrences—and now it has been forced out of its own building by just such an event.

Ironic? Not really. Like most big companies, Shell has a contingency plan for physical disasters which it implemented when Katrina hit, and no fancy scenarios were required to figure it all out. Far from being the kind of out-there event that scenario planning is designed to reveal, a major hurricane making land fall at New Orleans was the most predictable and predicted disaster in recent memory. You can't stop such an event; you can only deal with it, which Shell (like most companies affected) is managing to do.

The larger point is that while Katrina was a monster among storms, it was a pipsqueak in the realm of risk analysis. The most important thing for managers to realize about Katrina is this: If it gets you thinking more intensively about risk, that's great—but it is exactly the wrong kind of risk for you to focus on.

Understanding corporate risk has become a legitimate discipline in the past decade, with thousands of companies adopting "risk management" programmes and hundreds appointing chief risk officers. To the CEOs who've done those things: Bravo—you realize that risk is one of the most powerful factors driving your stock price, and you were probably stunned when you confronted the total amount of risk your company faces. What amazes me is how many companies still don't take full advantage of what risk management has taught us—specifically, *five lessons that every company could apply to better understand and control its risks.*

1. Turbocharge your imagination

The events that do the worst damage are the ones no one even conceived of 9/11. The idea that a passenger jet might crash into the World Trade Center had been thought of; it was a fairly obvious possibility, especially since a plane had once crashed into the Empire State Building. What no one imagined was the combination of large planes with nearly full fuel tanks plus the impact of the crashes jarring fireproofing from the girders, and how this could bring the towers down. In retrospect, it obviously could have been imagined. It just wasn't.

2. Build scenarios

Cold War military strategists originated planning, so by now the technique is well developed. Properly guided, it can help managers see important possible events they wouldn't otherwise have thought of—in Shell's case, famously, the Arab oil embargo of the 1970s. It's important to emphasize that no scenario told Shell's managers the embargo would happen; this is a strategic planning technique, nor Nostradamus.

To get into the scenario mindset, check the scenarios others have build, Shell publishes the outline of its annual exercise (www.shell.com/scenarios) and while it is intended to help a global energy company, it's widely applicable. The latest version foresees a world shaped by three large forces: a demand for efficiency and corporate performance as capitalism spread and capital markets become global, a demand for community as developing nations seek a more peaceful future, and a demand for security as the world seemingly becomes more dangerous.

Another recent set of deeply developed scenarios that will stimulate your mind comes from the National Intelligence Council (www.cia.gov/nic), picturing possible futures for 2020. Will globalization advance peacefully and prosperously with China and India becoming economic super-powers? Or will the U.S. continue to dominate the new global order? Or will spreading nuclear weapons lead to a world so secure it's Orwellian? Your company's future is no more than two steps removed from the answers to those questions.

3. Think in probabilities

If you can imagine an extent, you can try to assign a probability to it, if not in absolute terms—0.1%, 3%, 50%—then at least relative to other events. Sounds obvious.

4. Use the power of markets

You've heard of the remarkable success of predictive markets, where real people bet real money on the likelihood of specific events. Around for years, these markets attracted lots of acclaim after calling the squeaker 2004 presidential election. You can check them—In Trade.com is the best known—to see if they're offering contracts on events that might affect your business. For example, In Trade recently showed chances of private Social Security accounts being enacted by December 2006 at about 17%.

5. Create a culture that insists on facing reality

A tall order, admittedly. But much of the recent thinking on corporate risk assumes that in a volatile and fast-changing world, a great many events simply cannot be prepared for. Try though you may to imagine possible futures, you can never entirely succeed. The key then becomes responding quickly and effectively to the bolt from the blue, and the No. 1 impediment—incredible yet obvious—is failing to accept that the trouble has happened. Even in New Orleans, immediately after Katrina passed by, we saw TV images of people dancing in Bourbon Street; they thought everything would be okay.

A tendency to avoid reality, to minimize bad news, is embedded deep in corporate culture. But while most cultural change must start at the top, I believe this change can start anywhere. The penalty for not changing seems to be getting stiffer.

Take all these steps, and you'll be vastly better prepared for tomorrow than 95% of your competitors. But even if you take none of them right away, sit down in the next seven days, preferably with a few colleagues, and catalog as many risks for your business as you can think of—strategic, financial, operational, reputational, regulatory. You will never again think about your company's risks in the same way, and I guarantee that you'll feel forced to act. Make that response part of Katrina's legacy.

References

1. Managing the Non-profit Organisation: Principles and Practices, Peter F. Drucker (Paperback—August 1, 1992).
2. Forming and Managing a Non-profit Organisation in Canada (Self-Counsel Legal Series), Flora MacLeod (Paperback—May 1, 1995).
3. Managing the Non-profit Organisation, Peter F. Drucker (Paperback—October 31, 1995).
4. Managing Voluntary and Non-profit Organisations: Strategy and Structure, Richard J. Butler, David C. Wilson.
5. Managing for Impact in Non-profit Organisations, J. Hardy (Hader - June 1, 1984).
6. Managing the Budget in Non-profit Organisations, Jennifer Bean, Lascelles Hussey (Paperback—December 1, 2004).
7. Managing in the Voluntary Sector: A Handbook for Managers in Non-profit Organisations, Stephen P. Osborne (November 21, 1996).
8. Managing a Non-profit Organisation in the 21st Century, Thomas Wolf, A Fireside Book, Simon and Schuster, New York, NY 10020
9. Role of NGO in Developing Countries, Ravi Shambu Kumar Singh, Deep & Deep, New Delhi, 2003.
10. Strategic Management for Non-profit Organisation, Sharon M. Ostu, Oxford University Press, New York.
11. Development NGOs and Challenge, David Lewis and Tina Wallaz, Editors.
12. Magazine Women's Link, Social Action Trust, 10, Industrial Area, Lodhi Road, New Delhi.

Index